Ageing and Pension Reform Around the World

Ageing and Pension Reform Around the World

Evidence from Eleven Countries

Edited by

Giuliano Bonoli

Associate Professor of Social Policy, University of Fribourg, Switzerland

Toshimitsu Shinkawa

Professor of Political Science, Kyoto University, Japan

Edward Elgar
Cheltenham, UK • Northampton, MA, USA

Published by
Edward Elgar Publishing Limited
Glensanda House
Montpellier Parade
Cheltenham
Glos GL50 1UA
UK

Edward Elgar Publishing, Inc.
136 West Street
Suite 202
Northampton
Massachusetts 01060
USA

A catalogue record for this book
is available from the British Library

ISBN 1 84376 771 6 (cased)

Typeset by Cambrian Typesetters, Frimley, Surrey
Printed and bound in Great Britain by MPG Books Ltd, Bodmin, Cornwall

Contents

Figures

Tables

Contributors

Karen M. Anderson, University of Leiden, Netherlands

Daniel Béland, University of Calgary, Canada

Giuliano Bonoli, University of Fribourg, Switzerland

Maurizio Ferrera, University of Milan, Italy

Karl Hinrichs, University of Bremen, Germany

Matteo Jessoula, University of Pavia, Italy

Yeon Myung Kim, Chungang Univeristy, Korea

Kyo-seong Kim, Chungang University, Korea

Chen-Wei Lin, University of Hokkaido, Japan

Christelle Mandin, CEVIPOF, Paris, France

John Myles, University of Toronto, Canada

Bruno Palier, CEVIPOF, Paris, France

Toshimitsu Shinkawa, Kyoto University, Japan

Peter Taylor-Gooby, University of Kent at Canterbury, UK

R. Kent Weaver, Georgetown University, USA

Acknowledgements

This book is the result of a conference held at Sapporo, Japan in March 2003. Without the sponsorship of the Advanced Institute for Law and Politics at Hokkaido University, we could never have produced this volume. Our special thanks go to Jiro Yamaguchi and Taro Miyamoto, who kindly provided us with an opportunity to get together in Sapporo. We are also grateful to Satoshi Kurata, Mari Miura, Yukari Sawada, Shogo Takekawa and Koichi Usami for their inspiring comments on our papers. At the University of Fribourg, Switzerland, we are grateful to the Department of Social Work and Social Policy for support in the preparation of the manuscript and to Diane Baechler for her editorial work.

1. Population ageing and the logics of pension reform in Western Europe, East Asia and North America

Giuliano Bonoli and Toshimitsu Shinkawa

INTRODUCTION

Population ageing is a global phenomenon. According to currently available demographic projections virtually all countries in the world will see their population age structure get older over the next fives decades or so.[1] The process is occurring at different speeds in different world regions and starts from different levels, but is affecting every country. The potential impact of demographic change on the age structure and the size of populations is dramatic. According to UN projections, the median age of the population is expected to increase by eight years in Japan between 2000 and 2050, from 41 to 49 years. In Italy the median age is expected to reach 53 years in 2050, and the proportion of those aged over 65 will exceed 35 per cent. In addition to ageing, countries will also experience population decline. The EU as a whole is expected, between 2000 and 2050, to lose 10 per cent of its population. Italy, currently a country of 57 million, will in 2050 have a population of only 41 million. The population of Germany, currently 82 million, is projected to decline to 70 million by 2050.

These figures are impressive and the developments they point to will certainly influence several areas of social, political and economic life. They will also influence public policy, particularly those fields that are related to the population age structure of a country such as old age pensions. Growing proportions of older people means that younger generations will have to support a larger group of retirees. The financial effort required from working age people will increase correspondingly. These are just some of the well-known consequences of demographic ageing that are helping to shape pension debates. What is less clear is whether or not the demographic transition is affecting all countries in similar ways, whether it generates different pension politics in different countries and if pension systems are reacting similarly or differently to this common challenge.

The objective of the country studies contained in this book is to investigate these questions. The chapters use a common structure, which starts by examining the emergence of an ageing-related pension problem and follows the sequence of events through which most pension reform processes go. The studies cover Western European countries (France, Germany, Italy, Sweden, Switzerland and the United Kingdom), East Asian nations (Japan, South Korea and Taiwan) and North American states (Canada and the United States). The breadth of geographic coverage provides an almost global picture of the impact of ageing on pension reform, at least insofar as high income countries are concerned. The sample includes variation in relation to several important variables, such as the severity of the ageing problem, the stage reached in the demographic transition, the structure of the old age pension system, and the political system. This variation makes possible some degree of hypothesis testing in relation to the factors that shape pension politics in different contexts.

The main argument that we put forward in this chapter, is that it is a combination of the pattern of population ageing together with the institutional structure of pension systems that best explains variation in pension politics and policy-making. Demographic transitions are occurring at different paces and begin from different starting points, and as a result affect pension politics differently. In addition, their impact is most notably mediated by the institutional structure of pension systems, by the role that the state plays in the area and by instruments used to deliver old age income security. Taken together, these two variables explain a great deal of the observed variation in patterns of pension politics and policy-making.

This is not to say that other variables are unimportant, but they tend to emerge less as systematically related to policy change. Political institutions, for example, contribute to shaping the interactions between actors and can limit the options that are politically feasible and push reform in a given direction (Bonoli, 2000). The impact of political institutions, however, concerns more the kind of processes that are followed to adopt a pension reform. Of course, processes are related to content, but this link between the two does not emerge as systematic across countries. Countries where political institutions concentrate power with the executive are more likely to adopt unilateral reforms than those in which governments need broad consensus for their policies. But this tells us little about the actual policy measures that are likely to be adopted under different configurations of political institutions. The political orientation of the government in place is also a factor that can play a role in shaping reform. However, our analysis did not find any systematic effect in this respect. The political complexion of government is probably not unimportant, but does not seem to impact on the macro-decisions that concern the future of pension policy. Finally, the public policy literature has recently greatly focused on the role of ideas in shaping political decisions. In the case of pension reform an influential role in developing new ideas is certainly being played by international organisations such as the World Bank and the OECD. But it is difficult to isolate the importance of this factor in our study given that it probably affects all our countries in a similar way.

This chapter begins by looking at patterns of population ageing in the countries covered. It then moves on to the second independent variable of pension policy considered here: the institutional structure of pension systems. The following section tries to map out the different kinds of pension politics and policy-making that can be observed in combination with different patterns of demographic ageing and pension system structures. Finally, given the presence in our sample of three East Asian countries, we consider the relevance of approaches to social policy that highlight the existence of a distinctive welfare model for these countries.

GLOBAL PATTERNS OF POPULATION AGEING

Population ageing is a global process, but takes place at different speeds in different countries and is likely to reach different levels in different world regions. The pace of demographic change together with the current and predicted size of the older population are crucial variables insofar as the financial sustainability of pension systems is concerned, but, as will be argued below, also on the kind of politics that this problem generates. The actual and projected data presented in Table 1.1 show that it is possible to identify three types of demographic transitions, each of them corresponding to one of the world regions covered by this study. In Western Europe, ageing is taking place at a relatively moderate pace, but by 2040 the population older than 65 is expected to exceed 25 per cent of the total population in all countries. In North America, population ageing also takes place at a relatively moderate pace, and in the US it is unlikely to reach such extreme levels. Finally, East Asian countries are experiencing a much faster process of population ageing. It took France 117 years for its share of the 65+ age group to go from 7 to 14 per cent of its total population. In Japan the same development lasted only 24 years. Japan is also expected to face one of the worst population ageing problems over the next four decades, with about a third of its population expected to be over 65 years old in 2040. Other East Asian countries are also experiencing extremely rapid processes of demographic ageing, but given their lower starting point, the total proportion of older people is not going to reach worrying levels for a while. In 2040, however, Korea and to a lesser extent Taiwan, will have population age structures comparable to those of Western Europe.

The various contributions contained in this volume illustrate well the impact that different patterns of population ageing have on the politics of

Table 1.1   Proportion of the population aged 65 or over (%)

	1980	2000	2020	2040
France	14.0	16.2	20.1	25.1
Germany	15.5	16.0	21.6	30.7
Italy	13.4	18.2	23.7	33.1
Sweden	16.3	17.4	23.0	26.8
Switzerland	na	15.2	23.3	31.4
United Kingdom	14.9	16.0	20.0	25.6
Canada	na	12.5	18.7	26.8
United States	11.2	12.7	17.0	22.4
Japan	9.1	17.2	27.2	31.5
South Korea	3.8	6.7	13.0	24.6
Taiwan	4.4	8.6	13.2	19.9

Sources: OECD, 1988; World Bank, 2003; Republic of China, 2001.

pension reform. In Western Europe the key pressure is to secure financial sustainability in the long term. In order to do this, several reforms have been adopted in each of the countries covered, with the result of gradually reducing the size of the state's commitment to pension provision. North America, in contrast, thanks to a more tractable ageing problem, has not seen any major reform of public pension schemes. There is nonetheless an ongoing debate in the US on the assumed unsustainability of social security, which has not, to date, resulted in any major policy change.

The situation is more varied in East Asia. In this respect Japan is not so dissimilar from Western Europe, with the difference that there, ageing is occurring faster and the gradual approach that Western European countries seem to have taken may turn out to be insufficient. In contrast, ageing in Taiwan and South Korea has not yet reached worrying proportions as far as its impact on the financial sustainability of pensions is concerned. In the year 2000 these two countries had demographic structures that were comparable to those that were found in Western Europe in the 1950s. Older people are a fast growing group in society, but they are not numerous enough to constitute a problem for pension policy. This demographic situation is one that encourages expansion of old age insurance. Growing legions of older voters are likely to be sensitive to pension policy issues, and the fact that their number remains limited makes expansion in provision affordable. Ageing alone, however, does not explain the totality of pension policy in a country. There are also important institutional and political factors that contribute to shaping the decisions in this field of policy.

STARTING POINTS MATTER: INSTITUTIONAL VARIATION IN PENSION POLICY

Pension scholars, essentially on the basis of the observation of Western European pension systems, have developed a two-type classification of pensions, distinguishing between social insurance and multipillar systems.[2] The key dimensions of this distinction are the relative weights of the two main pillars of pension policy: the first pillar, generally a universal public pension scheme, and the second pillar, occupationally based or a private individual alternative to it.

Social insurance pension systems are based, predominantly, on one or more pension schemes of Bismarckian inspiration, that is, those that grant earnings-related benefits to former workers on a contributory basis. Typically, benefits depend on the payments made while in work. In addition, social insurance pension systems generally include a means-tested minimum pension, provided to those who reach the age of retirement without having paid contributions, or with a contribution record that is not sufficient to grant them a decent pension. Because of the earnings-related nature of public pension coverage in social insurance countries, private pension provision did not develop to any significant extent, at least until very recently (see below). The generosity and encompassing character of social insurance pension systems have crowded out private provision. To this 'world' of pension provision belong most continental European countries, for example, Germany, France, Italy and Sweden.

Multipillar pension systems are found in countries in which state pensions provide only flat-rate minimum benefits, sufficient to cover basic needs only. Typically, the objective of this sort of provision is not income maintenance in retirement, but the prevention of poverty among the older population. This limited role of the state in pension provision has left ample room for the development of private pensions, which have gradually been integrated into the pension systems of the relevant countries, generally on a compulsory or quasi-compulsory basis. Multipillar pension systems exist in the UK, the Netherlands, Denmark and in Switzerland, where the basic state pension is only moderately earnings-related.

This distinction is the result of developments in pension policy that took place in Western Europe over the 20th century, and which were in turn shaped by political, economic and institutional factors that are part of the history of that continent. As a result the distinction is not suitable for the classification of the non-European countries covered by this study. The only exception is

Table 1.2   Classification of pension systems on the basis of the relative weight of each pillar

		Second pillar	
		Voluntary and limited (coverage about 40–60% of workforce)	Compulsory and/or widespread (coverage around 80–90% of workforce)
First pillar	Non-existent	*Incomplete* Taiwan	
	Provides subsistence level benefits	*Bismarckian Lite* Canada US (*Japan*)	*Multipillar systems* Switzerland United Kingdom
	Provides full income replacement (at least 60% of earnings)	*Social insurance* France Germany Italy Sweden (pre-1990s) (*Korea*)	Sweden (post-1990s)

Korea, which in the late 1980s implemented a universal scheme of the social insurance kind, though this has been quickly retrenched. Three countries, the US, Canada and Japan, have pension systems that do not easily fit within the traditional classification. They have basic public pension schemes that provide earnings-related contributory benefits, but these are set at a considerably lower level than in the countries we have assigned to the social insurance category. For someone on an average wage, the replacement rate of the US social security pension is around 40 per cent: well below the German target replacement rate of 70 per cent. As in multipillar countries this modest level of provision is generally supplemented by a second pillar in the shape of an occupational/corporate or a personal pension. But this is neither compulsory nor widespread as a result of collective agreements, as is the case in the multipillar countries. Following Weaver (this volume), we call these systems 'Bismarckian Lite'.

Finally, Taiwan does not currently provide universal pension coverage. Some occupational groups, essentially the military and civilian government employees, enjoy a favourable treatment, but the bulk of the population is not in this situation. As a result, the impact of population ageing on pension politics is rather distinctive in Taiwan: as large cohorts of voters approach retirement age without adequate private provision, demographic change creates incentives for political entrepreneurs looking for credit claiming opportunities to support expansionist policies.

These distinctions are not only a useful tool to classify pension systems; they also tell us a great deal about the kind of problems faced in individual countries. In fact, the shape of a pension system is as powerful a determinant of the kind of pension problems a country has as the pattern of population ageing.

First, social insurance countries are facing the largest sustainability problems. The fact that in these countries the bulk of the intergenerational transfer is performed on a pay-as-you-go (PAYG) basis makes them extremely sensitive to demographic change. In addition, because social insurance pension schemes are controlled by governments,[3] elected officials are likely to be held accountable for any reduction in the level and extent of provision, thus providing a fertile terrain for electoral punishment. Under such conditions we are likely to observe restraint in retrenching pensions but also the use of blame avoidance strategies such as obfuscation, division or the adoption of side payments (Weaver, 1986; Pierson, 1994).

Bismarckian Lite countries, in contrast, are the least likely to experience big pension sustainability problems. The small size of their state pension means that a combination of additional finance and moderate austerity measures can ensure the financial viability of the schemes throughout the demographic transition. The exact balance of cuts and funding increases is going to be the result of political decisions, and can differ from country to country depending on the balance of power of the relevant actors. Voluntary occupational provision is also likely to be affected by population ageing. But because these forms of protection are not seen as the state's responsibility, cuts here are less likely to result in political backlash and electoral punishment against the government of the day. As a matter of fact, in the US, Canada and Japan, occupational pension schemes are being converted from defined benefits to defined contribution schemes at a rather fast pace. The result is that the burden of risk associated with population ageing and investment returns is going to be transferred from the employer to the employee. Of course, if Bismarckian Lite pension systems are less likely to suffer big financial viability problems as a result of population ageing, they are more exposed to the risk of providing insufficient coverage. The modest level of public pensions combined with lower occupational benefits (because of rising life expectancy and annuity prices) may result in more or less large cohorts reaching retirement age with insufficient coverage, being forced to defer retirement if labour market conditions allow them to do so, or ending up on means-tested pensions.

Multipillar systems are in a similar situation insofar as basic state pensions are concerned. As in Bismarckian Lite countries, the comparatively small size of the intergenerational transfer they perform is likely to make the financial sustainability of state pensions a tractable problem. Things are likely to be different, though, with regard to second pillar pensions. In multipillar systems these have been expanded to provide near-universal coverage as a result of political decisions taken in the 1970s. As a result, even though second pillar pensions are still provided by the private sector, the public has come to conceive them as rights, just as public pensions are perceived as rights. As a result, the adoption of austerity measures in the field of second pillar pensions is likely to be much more problematic from a political point of view in multipillar than in Bismarckian Lite systems. Developments in the UK and in Switzerland, where it seems clear that in many cases second pillar pensions are going to pay benefits falling short of people's expectation, confirm this view.

Finally, in countries with incomplete pension systems, such as Taiwan in our sample, the key policy problem is to provide universal pension coverage. Politics provides powerful incentives to do this, especially if there is a small but rapidly growing older population. Of course, financial issues are not going to be totally absent under such circumstances, but the small current size of the older population means that these are likely to be more tractable than in other countries.

Different starting points, combined with different patterns of population ageing, are not only important in shaping problems. They also affect the logic of pension policy.

THE DIFFERENT LOGICS OF PENSION REFORM

The different infrastructures of pension systems described above generate substantively different incentives for policy-makers and altogether different pension politics. Even the impact of a common social development, population ageing, as mediated by the existing institutional structures generates pressures that go in different directions. These are spelt out in this section.

Social Insurance Countries

Population ageing in social insurance countries generates the most controversial and intractable kind of pension problem. These systems in fact combine the strongest pressures for retrenchment with the strongest resistance against such moves. Pressures for retrenchment are due to a number of institutional features of social insurance systems. First, because the bulk of the intergenerational transfer is performed by PAYG basic schemes, pensions in these countries are extremely sensitive to variations in the relative proportions of the working and the retired population. From a strictly economic point of view, social insurance countries are those facing the biggest pension problem, and governments are under strong pressure to secure the financial sustainability in the medium/long term. Second, pressure is reinforced by the fact that it is relatively easy to predict the evolution of the finances of PAYG schemes. Even though the functioning of funded pension schemes may also be affected by population ageing, the link is less clear than in the case of social insurance systems. The fact that government actuaries and statistical agencies are able to pinpoint a moment in the future at which basic pension schemes become bankrupt is obviously a factor of pressure on governments to act and contain or reduce expenditure. The image of a demographic time bomb works well for these schemes. The third factor of pressure for retrenchment is the link between pension policy and employment. Social insurance pension schemes are essentially financed by employer–employee contributions (payroll taxes) and have a direct impact on labour costs and as a result on employment creation. The weakness of the German employment performance in the 1990s and 2000s has been largely blamed on excessive labour costs, which are in turn due, among other things, to some of the world's highest pension contribution rates (Hinrichs, this volume).

The current context of economic globalisation reinforces these pressures. International investors dislike large budget deficits, which are associated with high pension expenditure. High pension contribution rates discourage inflows of foreign direct investments. In addition, Eurozone countries have to respect the convergence criteria laid down in the Maastricht Treaty, which do not allow deficits in excess of 3 per cent of GDP, though at the time of writing it is not clear how strongly this rule will be enforced. But there are also internal pressures. The financial services sector in countries like France, Germany or Sweden, has long campaigned for the introduction of a funded pension sector, which, as shown by British, Swiss or Dutch examples is a lucrative business for financial institutions. More in general, employers, worried about the direct link between pension expenditures, pension contributions and labour costs, tend to support pension cuts. Overall it seems that countries that have developed a social insurance pension scheme display all the characteristics that are conducive to strong pressures for pension retrenchment.

At the same time, the institutional structure of social insurance pension systems makes them the most resistant to change. First, workers, especially those approaching retirement age, have little else to rely upon in order to finance their retirement. Funded schemes are underdeveloped and in order to accumulate sufficient funds to compensate for possible cuts in the generosity of the basic pensions, workers would need to start contributing to funded pensions relatively early on, say in their 30s or early 40s. Attempts at cutting pensions for older workers are thus likely to generate massive public opposition. Second, even assuming that cuts concern only younger workers who have the possibility of building up a sufficient capital to provide for their retirement, social insurance pension systems are confronted with the so-called double payment issue: those younger workers who begin to save for their own retirement would still need to contribute heavily to the generous social insurance pension scheme, which would otherwise be unable to provide benefits to the currently retired population (Pierson, 1997). Finally, social insurance pension systems have generally been instituted in their present form in the post-World War II years, and are widely regarded as a social contract between the state and the citizen. Even though in most social insurance countries the management of pensions is delegated to the social partners (employers and employees' organisations), governments are widely regarded as responsible for what goes on in the field of pensions. Pension retrenchment tends as a result to be seen as unilaterally reneging on that contract (Myles and Pierson, 2001). This can result in anti-government feelings that can materialise in terms of mass protest and/or electoral punishment.[4] In France, pensions are seen as a deferred wage, and pension cuts are as a result perceived as a fundamentally unjust act (Palier, 2002).

This situation of strong contrasting pressures leaves little room for manoeuvre for governments. They cannot resist the pressures to retrench, as this would have disastrous economic (and subsequently political) consequences. At the same time, if they retrench they expose themselves to the risk of electoral punishment. In this context, the strategy adopted by seemingly all social insurance countries is a combination of blame avoidance techniques, procrastination and incremental change. Blame avoidance techniques have been largely documented in the literature (Weaver, 1986; Pierson and Weaver, 1993; Pierson, 1994), and consists mostly in the obfuscation of retrenchment through changing complicated formulas, the effect of which are unclear for most voters. A second strategy that has clearly been used in social insurance countries is that of delaying the effect of reform. This has been most notably the case of Italy, where the reform adopted in 1995 does not fully come into force until 2030. Most current workers are either not affected by the changes or are concerned only marginally. In the Italian case delaying the effect of the reform has proved an effective strategy to avoid mass protest and electoral punishment (Ferrera and Jessoula, this volume).

Moving to East Asia, with a universal pension providing a target replacement rate of 60 per cent, Korea can be considered as a borderline member of the social insurance family. However, it differs from its older siblings in one important respect: the considerably shorter time lag between the setting up of the scheme and the emergence of a pension financing problem, as a result of which retrenchment has proven politically more feasible than in Western Europe. Korea completed its pension system with the establishment of the National Pension Scheme in 1988, which, at the time, was designed to provide 70 per cent earnings replacement. Only a decade after, as it became clear that population ageing was going to impact on the financial viability of the new scheme, the replacement rate was reduced to 60 per cent. This happened as a result of lengthy political negotiations between various arms of government, and after more radical retrenchment options had been discarded. What helped Korean legislators, was the youth of the scheme and the fact that the new pensions had not become as entrenched in political and social life as they are in Western Europe. In fact, because the scheme had not reached maturity by the time of the reform, no one will ever receive the full original benefit based on the 70 per cent replacement rate. In addition, it is quite likely that further retrenchment will come sooner or later due to the unsolved question of fiscal sustainability and extremely rapid population ageing that recently attracted public attention. Retrenchment is also facilitated in Korea by the fact that the mandatory retirement allowance is universal and more important than pension as a financial source of the retired (Kim and Kim, this volume).

In social insurance countries the politics of pension reform is characterised by policy-seeking and blame avoidance. Governments, under tight national and international economic constraints, need to find ways to contain future pension expenditure with minimal political costs. Korea is exceptional because the youth of the scheme created scope for radical and visible retrenchment, and as a result retrenchment was carried out visibly. However, in that case too, the electoral value of pension promises played an important role in moderating the size of retrenchment.

Multipillar Countries

The politics of pension reform in multipillar countries is likely to take a different shape. The intergenerational transfer in these systems is performed by a combination of PAYG and funded instruments, so that the impact of ageing on pension policy is different depending on the instrument, or pillar, that is being considered (Bonoli, 2003). Multipillar pension systems contain a PAYG financed basic pension, which is exposed to the same ageing-related problems seen in relation to social insurance schemes: demographic change means a deterioration of the beneficiaries/contributors ratio, with the consequence that in order to preserve a financially balanced system, contributions need to be increased or benefits reduced (or a combination of the two measures).

The difference, and it is a significant one, is that the magnitude of the problem is considerably smaller in multipillar systems than it is in social insurance ones. The basic pensions of Switzerland or Britain account for less than 7 per cent of GDP, whereas the social insurance pensions that exist in France, Germany or Italy cost these countries more than 10 per cent of GDP. The gap between these two worlds of pension provision is likely to get even bigger in the future. According to projections, the four social insurance countries included in this study (France, Germany, Italy and Sweden) will spend in 2050 on average 16.9 per cent of their national income on public pensions. The same figure for three multipillar countries is a much lower 9 per cent (average of Denmark, the Netherlands and the UK. No data available for Switzerland) (Roseveare et al., 1996).

The politics of the basic pension in multipillar systems are thus unlikely to differ from those of social insurance pension reforms, except in the magnitude of controversy. Governments and other political actors who are sensitive to ageing-related economic pressures will try to impose cost-containment measures on actors representing current and future beneficiaries and with substantial problems in building support for their case. As a result, policy-making will be driven by a policy-seeking logic and framed in an overall blame-avoidance setting, with large use made of the well-known strategies of obfuscation, side payments and so forth.

The situation is likely to be rather different in relation to second pillar pensions. These are generally fully funded instruments, often employer- or branch-based, that are less sensitive to demographic change. It would nonetheless be incorrect to claim that population ageing will not affect the viability of these pension schemes. Conventional wisdom has it that fully-funded pension schemes are not likely to be affected by the process of ageing. Unlike pay-as-you-go pensions these schemes do not perform intergenerational transfers, and as a result changes in the relative size of generations are irrelevant to the financial viability of schemes. Over the last few years, however, it has become clear that although less vulnerable to the direct impact of population ageing, funded pensions may still be affected by it. This could happen as a result of the impact that longer life expectancy has on annuity prices and as a result of the impact that demographic change may have on financial markets.

Pension funds allow members to accumulate capital, which, depending on national regulations, can or must be converted into an annuity. The size of the annuity will depend, among other things, on the life expectancy of the relevant cohort at the time conversion takes place. Rising life expectancy at age 60 or 65, means smaller annuities for the same capital. In Western Europe, life expectancy at the age of 65 has increased from around 15 years in 1950 to 18–19 years in 2000, and is expected to increase further over the next decades. According to actuarial calculations, a rise in life expectancy of four years increases the price of annuities by 18 per cent (Merrill Lynch, 2000). As a matter of fact, over the last few years, as a result of rising life expectancy (and falling interest rates), the UK has seen an increase in the price of annuities.

A less well-known, but potentially more serious development concerns the impact that population ageing may have on financial markets in which pension funds play an important role. Traditionally, and for the next two to three decades, pension funds have been a major source of savings for market economies. Because they were developed essentially after World War II, they have not yet started paying out pensions on a large scale. In aggregate, across OECD countries, a majority of pension funds members are contributors and only a minority receive a pension. This situation, however, will not last indefinitely. As the large cohorts of baby-boomers, born between 1945 and 1965 reach the age of retirement between 2010 and 2030, the aggregate number of retirees will exceed that of contributors. As a result, in order to meet their obligations, pension funds may be forced to sell off some of their assets. If this happens on a large scale, it may drive down the price of assets and result in lower than expected returns on the invested capital and consequently lower than expected pensions.

In sum, funded pensions in multipillar systems may also come under pressure as a result of demographic ageing, but the extent to which this essentially financial pressure is translated into a political risk depends on the degree of state involvement in the regulation of occupational pensions. Unlike social insurance systems, governments are not directly responsible for setting the level of pension benefits. Depending on the rules in place, the level of someone's pension will depend among other things on stock market performance, on the skills of the fund manager and on luck. Lower than expected private pensions, as a result, are in principle less likely to result in electoral punishment against the government of the day than cuts in social insurance pensions (Myles and Pierson, 2001). However, in countries where occupational pensions are mandatory or quasi-mandatory, or in countries where the government has taken a proactive role in encouraging workers to buy private pensions, and this is the case in all the countries classified under the multipillar label in this study, voters may still feel that the government does bear some responsibility for lower-than-expected benefits. Governments as a result cannot consider themselves as totally protected against the risk of electoral punishment.

Second pillar pensions, however, also generate a different kind of politics. Multipillar systems are characterised by a very large degree of private pension coverage, but nowhere does it reach 100 per cent. There are various reasons for this, having to do essentially with the presence in contemporary labour markets of a proportion of unstable, low wage, intermittent employees that are technically difficult to insure. Most multipillar countries have taken steps in recent years towards reducing the numbers of those who are excluded from private pension coverage, be it by making second pillar pensions mandatory (Switzerland, see Bonoli, this volume) or by encouraging mid–low income workers to take out private pensions described as suitable to their needs (UK, see Taylor-Gooby, this volume), but there is still scope for improvement, also because the career profiles that are generally excluded from occupational pension coverage are on the increase. Workers who are not well covered by existing arrangements are increasing in numbers and constitute, at least potentially, an electorally interesting constituency. As a result we can expect political entrepreneurs to be responsive to their needs and bring them into the pension policy arena, where they compete for attention with other pension issues such as adapting to population ageing. The co-presence of these two pressures on pension policy may provide a much appreciated opportunity for political exchange between political actors that worry about the long-term financial sustainability of pension arrangement and those who care about the inclusion of atypical workers in a decent pension settlement. The logic of policy-making here is one of political exchange, combining blame avoidance techniques in relation to cost-containment measures with credit claiming with regard to targeted expansion of coverage.

The complex pattern of pension reform in multipillar systems reflects the co-presence of different schemes that generate different politics. However, if the analysis is broken down to the level of individual instruments, it becomes possible to recognise the same sort of mechanisms that shape pension politics everywhere: blame avoidance techniques in relation to retrenchment, and credit claiming with regard to expansion. The two can be combined in single reforms, with the result of strengthening their political acceptability.

Bismarckian Lite

The paradigmatic case of a 'Bismarckian Lite' pension system is certainly the US. The earnings replacement rate of the Old Age Security Insurance (OASI) is set at 40 per cent for an average wage. OASI plays a crucial role for low income individuals who rely almost exclusively on its modest benefits (approximately 90 per cent of their incomes come from Social Security). More fortunate people instead gain their incomes almost equally from social security, private pensions, investments and employment (Employee Benefit Research Institute, 1997, p. 62). Today some 50 per cent of the workforce is covered by an occupational pension, but recent tax code revisions have promoted a shift from defined benefit to defined contribution schemes, thereby alleviating financial burdens of firms and reinforcing employees' responsibility to invest and manage their own registered accounts.

The Canadian pension system does not fit into the Bismarckian Lite category as well as its US counterpart, but still exhibits its critical features. Canada deviates from the Bismarckian Lite model in that it has a tax-financed first tier composed of a flat-rate Old Age Security pension (OAS) and an income-tested Guaranteed Income Supplement (GIS). On top of that, however, Canada has an earnings-related contributory tier called the Canada/Quebec Pension Plan (C/QPP). Altogether, OAS, GIS and C/QPPs provide a modest replacement rate of 45 per cent of earnings for someone on the average wage. C/QPP plays the biggest role as it replaces alone some 25 per cent of earnings. The claw-back introduced in OAS in the late 1980s reduced its value by 15 per cent for each dollar of individual income above a threshold. In Canada, private pension plans cover slightly over 40 per cent of the paid workforce. The number of defined contribution plans is larger than that of defined benefit ones, but the majority of employees who have access to occupational pensions belong to defined benefit plans (Béland and Myles, this volume; Pearse, 2003).

Japan can also be considered a member of the Bismarckian Lite family, even though its slightly more generous basic pension puts it on the borderline of this category. Japan's public pension, like the Canadian one, has two tiers, a flat-rate and an earnings-related occupationally divided tier. Both are contributory, but a third of the first-tier expenditures and the administrative costs of the second tier come from general government revenues. Considering that continuous improvements in benefit standards entitled a private sector employee to receive 68 per cent of the average monthly salary after 32 contri-bution years in the mid-1980s, Japan may not seem to be appropriately classi-fied under the Bismarckian Lite group. But the period of deviance from the Bismarckian Lite model did not last long. After repeated retrenchment since the mid-1980s, the current replacement rate is set at 59 per cent of the average monthly salary, and is, according to the current plan of the 2004 reform, to be lowered down to 50 per cent. Retirement payments and enterprise pension schemes are of importance. More than 90 per cent of companies provide some form of retirement allowance, but only slightly over 50 per cent offer proper pension schemes. Differences in benefit standards are essentially related to firm size and generate a dual structure in the provision of occupational pensions. Today occupational pensions do not cover the majority of retired households. These are limited to those who have enjoyed regular employment in relatively large companies. It is this dual structure that in the end persuaded us to classify Japan together with the US and Canada rather than with Western European social insurance countries.

The politics of pension reform in Bismarckian Lite systems shares features found in both social insurance and multipillar pension systems, but is distinc-tive with regard to the absence of an explicit state commitment to guarantee-ing high levels of income replacement for middle-class workers. This is important, because the financial implications of that commitment, which is made in both social insurance and multipillar pension systems, are substantial and are a major source of the sustainability problems that these systems are facing.

The basic pension in Bismarckian Lite system does face sustainability problems, but these, because of the smaller size of the scheme, are not compar-able to those that are afflicting social insurance countries. In Japan, however, given the speed and extent of the demographic problem, the sustainability of the largest basic pension scheme (the Employee Pension Insurance, EPI) is likely to be put under serious pressure over the next two decades or so. According to the newly released population projection in 2002, the EPI equilibrium contribution rate will probably exceed 21.6 per cent, a level that in the 1999 reform was assumed to be the maximum possible rate. The equilibrium contribution rate is now expected to peak at 26.2 per cent in 2036. The situation, however, is less dramatic in the US, where population ageing will be considerably easier to manage. The US Federal Old Age and Survivors Insurance Trust Fund is expected, on the basis of current legislation being applied consistently throughout the projection period, to exhaust its assets by the year 2041 (Weaver, this volume). It is a situation that in the US is widely regarded as problematic, but that is incomparably more favourable than the one found in social insurance countries, which unlike the US have not built up a reserve fund. The fact that the comparatively smaller pension problem in the US is nonetheless attracting a good deal of political attention is due also to the extremely long time period taken into consideration (by law) in pension expenditure projections. While Americans look 75 years ahead, Europeans tend to rely on projections for the next 15 sometimes 20 years and Canadians look at the year 2030 as the time horizon for their pension expenditure projections. If the US did the same, there would probably be far less debate on the long-term sustainability of pensions in that country.

The picture of basic pension reform in the Bismarckian Lite group is characterised by big variations, but there is more similarity within this group of countries if we turn to developments in occupational pensions. These are not mandatory, but, given the rather modest level of state pensions, are widespread among middle-class employees. Population ageing, as seen above, is affecting the financial viability of these schemes in a number of ways, the most visible of which is by extending the number of years during which pensions must be paid. Longer life expectancy, as a result, translates into higher pension expenditures for funds that provide annuities. In the past, increases in life expectancy have been rather easy to predict, so that this development should not constitute a major problem for pension planners, however, its impact has been compounded by the crisis of international stock markets of the early 2000s and by concerns for the future possible impact of population ageing on asset prices. These developments have been interpreted in terms of additional risks imposed upon pension providers, who have as a result increasingly opted for less committing forms of provision.

As a result, both the US and Japan are seeing a shift away from defined benefit to defined contribution occupational pensions. In the US, this has taken the shape of an expansion in individual defined contribution schemes (the so-called 401(k) plans) and a 'policy drift' among occupational pension providers away from defined benefit and towards defined contribution schemes (Hacker,

2002). In Japan, the transformation of a defined benefit scheme into a defined contribution one is strictly regulated, but this does not prevent policy drift from taking place. Since 2002 employers can close down a defined benefit pension and reopen it as a defined contributions scheme. Preliminary evidence suggests that the new rule will result in a shift away from defined benefit schemes, not unlike the one seen in the US. Canada is on the same track. It is quite common for employers to shift their Registered Pension Plans from defined benefit to defined contribution schemes. What sometimes prevents them from doing this is the resistance opposed by strong labour unions, but these are rare in Canada.

The politics of pensions in Bismarckian Lite systems has two specific features. First, keeping demographics constant, basic pensions face less dramatic sustainability problems than in social insurance systems. Second, the absence of a clear state commitment to secure earning replacement benefits to the middle classes makes occupational pensions less politicised than in social insurance and multipillar countries. Developments like the 'policy drift' from defined benefit to defined contribution schemes do not generate major political controversy, because the state is not held responsible for it. This of course does not mean that the policy drift will not result in sizeable pension losses for middle-class employees. On the contrary, the shift to defined contribution coupled with expected increases in life expectancy and possibly lower returns to capital makes the prospect of lower pensions likely. However, the primary result of the shift is not so much a reduction in benefits, but a transfer of the burden of risk from the employer to the employee.

Incomplete Pension Systems

Taiwan is the only country covered by this study that does not have a universal, fully-fledged pension system. The absence of pension provision at the beginning of the demographic transition generates yet another kind of pension politics. First, concerns for financial sustainability do not receive any significant attention in the public domain. This is due to the fact that the existing pension system is rudimentary, and therefore has made smaller commitments than most of its counterparts, but also to the fact that sustainability issues are obscured by the interest that so many actors and individuals have in the setting up of a comprehensive pension system.

Taiwan's population is relatively young, but it is ageing rather quickly. In addition, the cohorts that are approaching retirement age are going to increase in their size over the next few years. This demographic situation creates a particularly fertile ground for the development of expansionist pension policies. The financial cost of a new pension scheme is limited, at least in its initial period of operation, but the political rewards are likely to be substantial. It is thus not surprising that the last few years have seen major competition among political parties and individual politicians in making proposals for the expansion of pension provision.

The debate has been influenced by the limited extent of provision that exists at the moment, in particular the rather generous tax-financed, non-contributory allowance paid to retired military personnel. In fact, in Taiwan, the military, essentially of Mainland Chinese descent, enjoy by far the best treatment as far as pensions are concerned, and in the political debate the pension issue became framed in terms of extending this favourable treatment to other social groups, such as the farmers. As a result, the standard pension policy options of contributory social insurance or the extension of occupational pension coverage were de facto pushed out from the political agenda as the pension debate gathered momentum in the late 1990s. The Democratic Progressive Party, which gained power in 2000, had promised to introduce a non-contributory, tax-financed universal retirement allowance, but was later forced to shelve its plans because of worsening economic and budget conditions. The failure to introduce a comprehensive pension scheme in Taiwan can be largely explained with reference to the over-generous character of the plan, itself influenced by the cleavage in retirement between the military and the rest of the population. The kind of political dynamics seen in the late 1990s around the pension issue, however, suggest that the introduction of a universal pension scheme remains a likely development (Lin, this volume).

The developments that have taken place in Taiwan in the late 1990s are reminiscent of pension politics in Western Europe in the 1950s and in the 1960s. In fact, if the first stages of pension policy-making in the old continent were in most cases characterised by conflict and confrontation, the extension of old age income security programmes that took place in the post-war years was much more driven by political competition. Countries where pension provision had remained modest, essentially those that belong to the multi-pillar group discussed above and Sweden saw a succession of proposals originating from different political actors on how to give the middle classes a better and a more secure deal in pension provision (on Sweden, see Anderson, this volume). The similarities between current Taiwanese pension politics and developments that occurred in Western Europe some 40 years ago is striking.

PENSION POLITICS ACROSS WORLD REGIONS

The above discussion of pension politics suggests that the sort of political confrontation that takes place in this field is shaped by the interplay between patterns of demographic ageing and existing institutional structure. Once we have taken these two factors into account, there seems to be relatively little variance left to explain. What is particularly striking is the absence of clear similarities in pension politics within world regions. Had we defined three groups of countries based on their geographical position (Western Europe, East Asia and North America) we would probably be in a situation where intra-group differences are just as big as inter-group variations. The politics of pensions seems to cut across cultural factors that differ among countries.

This finding is particularly striking in relation to East Asia. Even though this volume contains studies on three East Asian countries, Japan, Korea and Taiwan, we have not found evidence of a distinct East Asian welfare model. This may be due to our exclusive focus on pensions, which prevents us from seeing aspects of the welfare state in which cultural variables play a more important role. Overall, however, it has been hard to find common features among the three East Asian countries that distinguish them from Western experiences. Japan, Korea and Taiwan face different problems and challenges, reflecting different stages of demographic, economic and political development. Democratisation in Korea and Taiwan precipitated political competition for credit claiming, which made the introduction of a nationwide pension programme a central issue in the political agenda. Korea succeeded in 1988 and quickly moved toward retrenchment, entering in the 1990s, while Taiwan is at a stalemate, waiting for another chance to open a policy window. Compared with these two cases, Japan experienced democratisation and political competition for pension expansion a number of decades earlier and has been engaged in retrenchment since the mid-1980s.

Perhaps one distinguishing feature of East Asian pension policy is the fact that developments in pension policy take place in a shorter period of time, a few decades or less, compared with the long history of Western pension systems, which for most countries spans over nearly a century. This is particularly true in the case of the Korean experience. Korea turned to retrenchment soon after the introduction of the new National Pension Scheme in 1988, way before full benefits would start in 2008. The prompt turnaround was due to the fiscal vulnerability of the new programme, which had essentially been shaped by political considerations. The projection that pooled reserves will dry out in a few decades made policy-makers, welfare experts and relevant societal actors anxious over sustainability of the new scheme. The recently released population projections that predict extremely rapid population ageing due to a sharp decline of the fertility rate is likely to precipitate further the process of pension retrenchment in Korea. Gradual and slow as it may be, compared to Korea, Japan went through a similar pattern. Financially unsound programmes were created as a result of political competition and their sustainability was in question when the rapid economic growth was over and evidence of population ageing became available.

If the timing of pension policy developments is distinctive in East Asia, not much else is. Like for Western democracies, institutional constraints and political mechanisms are of importance in understanding pension developments and retrenchment. Assumptions of path dependency and veto points (or players) especially help to understand why and how policy changes. The bottom line here is that patterns of pension expansion and retrenchment in Japan, Korea and Taiwan, can be perfectly well analysed with tools developed by Western welfare state research. We do not need special tools nor to develop an East Asian model of social policy in order to study pension policy in Japan, Korea or Taiwan.

This has broader implications for comparative welfare state research and its extension to East Asian countries. Our view is that approaches claiming the distinctiveness of East Asia can fall into a trap of cultural reductionism or impressionistic specification of universal phenomena. The first umbrella with which to cover East Asian nations was Confucianism (Jones, 1993). Leaving aside the plausibility of assuming common Confucian values in East Asian countries, it is not clear how best we can explain actual social welfare developments with such socially shared values. No one would dare to assert that all North American and European countries belong to a single category due to their shared Christian values, because the importance of intermediate variables between social values and actual policy developments (power configurations, institutional settings and historical contexts) are taken for granted. Why not in East Asian nations?

When Confucianism is modified as 'popular Confucianism' (Jones, 1993, p. 202), a different problem occurs. Considering that only a small number of people understand exactly what Confucian teachings are, at least in Japan, such a modification makes sense, but, on the other hand, it blurs the difference between Confucian values and Western traditional values. Group-oriented postures as seen with respect to hierarchy, duty, compliance, consensus, order, harmony and so on are not unique in Confucian societies but common in any traditional society. In this case, the concept of 'Confucian welfare state' means nothing more than a reference to pre-modern East Asia. If East Asian nations still belonged to the pre-modern era, however, they certainly would have no welfare states and accordingly we would have no reason to discuss a variant of the welfare state in East Asia. It is of little help to distinguish Confucian beliefs and values from the language of Confucianism, or Confucian rhetoric, and assert that the latter helps form specific 'political discourses which reflect and rationalize certain basic developmental motives and political forces' (White and Goodman, 1998, p. 16; see also Goodman and Peng, 1996, p. 195), because Confucian rhetoric has no power to legitimise a certain course of policy development and mobilise popular support unless Confucian beliefs and values are deeply rooted in society.

Recent attempts to present an East Asian model of the welfare state as the fourth type in addition to Esping-Andersen's three types escape the trap of static orientalism by employing the concept of productivism or the developmental state. It is argued that social policy in East Asian nations is subordinated to economic policy or used as a means of economic development and nation-building (White and Goodman, 1998, p. 15; Gough, 2000, p. 5; Holliday, 2000). Such arguments sound plausible, but fail to distinguish East Asian welfare states from their European counterparts, as welfare states everywhere help improve productivity and contribute to economic growth by facilitating social cohesion and peaceful class relationships. In that sense, all welfare states are productivist or work-centred. By confirming centrality of work-centredness in the 'three worlds of welfare capitalism', Goodin characterises the liberal welfare state as 'work, not welfare', the corporatist one as 'welfare through work', and the social democratic one as 'welfare and work' (Goodin, 2001, pp. 13–14). Keeping in mind that Esping-Andersen's typology was produced only after studies of individual Western welfare states were accumulated, we should deepen our understanding of concrete social policy development in East Asia before attempting to create a comprehensive welfare state model of East Asia.

CONCLUSION

Our analysis suggests that the main factors shaping pension reform across countries are patterns of demographic change and pensions systems' institutional structures. The way in which these two variables interact determines the kind of politics that is likely to surround pension reform, and, subsequently, the direction taken by policy change. This finding underscores the political salience of pension policy issues in contemporary democracies, where the majority of those who turn out to vote are or are about to become pensioners. The various institutional and demographic effects highlighted in this chapter, in fact, influence political decision-making by affecting patterns of political competition in the electoral and in the policy-making arenas. When demographic change and pension system design put strong pressure on governments to maintain the financial viability of pension schemes, these are likely to operate according to a policy-seeking logic. Politicians need to take painful decisions in order to contain future increases in pension expenditure and are likely to do this by resorting to blame avoidance techniques. In contrast, when the context of pension policy contains incentives for politicians to adopt an expansionist stance, their attitude will be dominated by a vote-seeking logic, and they are likely to make use of credit claiming techniques. In some cases, such as in multipillar pension systems, these two logics can combine to generate particularly complex form of pension politics.

In contrast, other factors that, especially in consideration of the diversity of countries contained in our sample, could have been expected to play an important role, do not seem to impact on pension politics and policy to any significant extent. This is the case in particular of cultural factors, seen here as virtually irrelevant in shaping pension politics. Values such as respect for older generations or emphasis of financial prudence may and probably do differ across our sample of countries, but their significance insofar as the politics of pension is concerned seems limited to the point of not being visible.

NOTES

1. For comments on an earlier version of this chapter, we would like to thank Karen Anderson, Daniel Béland, Yeon Myung Kim and Peter Taylor-Gooby.
2. Terminologies found in the literature include social insurance vs. multipillar systems (Bonoli, 2003); Bismarckian vs. Beveridgean (Bonoli, 2000; Myles and Quadagno, 1997); mature systems vs. latecomers (Myles and Pierson, 2001; Haverland, 2001); social insurance vs. latecomers (Hinrichs, 2001; Palier, 2003).
3. Although in some countries (France, Germany) social insurance schemes are formally run jointly by representatives of labour and employers, all important decisions concerning, for instance, eligibility and benefit levels of contributions are taken by governments of parliaments.
4. Italian and French political leaders have learned the difficult lesson of how strongly pension retrenchment was resisted in their countries. In Italy, in 1994 a general strike orchestrated by the unions against pension reform plans resulted in the fall of the right-of-centre government headed by Silvio Berlusconi (Ferrera and Jessoula, this volume). In France, the Juppé reform of public sector pensions was successfully fought by the unions and arguably led to an electoral defeat of the centre-right coalition (Mandin and Palier, this volume).

REFERENCES

Bonoli, G. (2000), *The Politics of Pension Reform. Institution and Policy Change in Western Europe*, Cambridge, UK: Cambridge University Press.

Bonoli, G. (2003), 'Two worlds of pension reform in Western Europe', *Comparative Politics*, **35**(4), 399–416.

Employee Benefit Research Institute (EBRI) (1997), *Databook on Employee Benefits*.

Goodin, R.E. (2001), 'Work and welfare: Towards a post-productivist welfare regime', *British Journal of Political Science*, **31**, 13–39.

Goodman, R. and Peng, I. (1996), 'The East Asian welfare states', in G. Esping-Andersen (ed.), *Welfare States in Transition*, London: Sage, 192–224.

Gough, I. (2000), 'Welfare regimes in East Asia and Europe: Comparisons and lessons', a paper presented at: 'Towards the New Social Policy Agenda in East Asia', conference, (http://www.bath.ac.uk/ifipa/GSP/).

Hacker, J. (2002), *The Divided Welfare State*, Cambridge, UK: Cambridge University Press.

Haverland, M. (2001), 'Another Dutch miracle? Explaining Dutch and German pension trajectories', *Journal of European Social Policy*, **11**(4), 308–323.

Hinrichs, K. (2001), 'Elephants on the move. Patterns of public pension reform in OECD countries', in S. Leibfried (ed.), *Welfare State Futures*, Cambridge, UK: Cambridge University Press, 77–102.

Holliday, I. (2000), 'Productivist welfare capitalism: Social policy in East Asia', *Political Studies*, **48**(4), 706–723.

Jones, C. (1993), 'The Pacific challenge: Confucian welfare states', in C. Jones (ed.), *New Perspectives on the Welfare State in Europe*, London: Routledge, 198–217.

Merrill Lynch (2000), *Demographics and the Funded Pension System*, Merrill Lynch & Co.

Myles, J. and Pierson, P. (2001), 'The political economy of pension reform', in P. Pierson (ed.), *The New Politics of the Welfare State*, Oxford: Oxford University Press, 305–333.

Myles, J. and Quadagno, J. (1997), 'Recent trends in public pension reform: A comparative view', in K. Banting and R. Boadway (eds), *Reform of Retirement Income Policy. International and Canadian Perspectives*, Kingston (Ontario): Queen's University, School of Policy Studies, 247–272.

OECD (1988), *Ageing Populations: The Social Policy Implications*, Paris.

Palier, B. (2002), *Gouverner la Sécurité Sociale*, Paris: Presses Universitaires de France.

Palier, B. (2003), *La Réforme des Retraites. Travailler Plus?*, Paris: Presses Universitaires de France.

Pearse, J. (2003), *Overview of the Canadian Private Pension System*, Ottawa: Department of Finance Canada.

Pierson, P. (1994), *Dismantling the Welfare State. Reagan, Thatcher and the Politics of Retrenchment*, Cambridge, UK: Cambridge University Press.

Pierson, P. (1997), 'The politics of pension reform', in K. Banting and R. Boadway (eds), *Reform of Retirement Income Policy. International and Canadian Perspectives*, Kingston (Ontario): Queen's University, School of Policy Studies, 273–294.

Pierson, P. and Weaver, K. (1993), 'Imposing losses in pension policy', in K. Weaver and B. Rockmann (eds), *Do Institutions Matter? Government Capabilities in the United States and Abroad*, Washington, DC: The Brookings Institution, 110–150.

Republic of China (2001), *Social Indicators*, Taipei.

Roseveare, P., Leibfritz, W., Fore, D. and Wurzel, E. (1996), *Ageing Populations, Pension Systems and Government Budgets: Simulation for 20 OECD Countries*, Paris: OECD, Economic Department Working Papers, No. 168.

Weaver, K. (1986), 'The politics of blame avoidance', *Journal of Public Policy*, **6**(4), 371–398.

White, G. and Goodman R. (1998), 'Welfare orientalism and the search for an East Asian welfare model', in R. Goodman, G. White and H. Kwon (eds), *The East Asian Welfare Model*, London: Routledge, 3–24.

World Bank (2003), *World Development Indicators*, CD-ROM, Washington, DC: World Bank.

2. Reconfiguring Italian pensions: From policy stalemate to comprehensive reforms[1]

Maurizio Ferrera and Matteo Jessoula

1. INTRODUCTION

Italy experienced an early start in the field of pensions, introducing in 1919 a compulsory funded scheme for all the employees whose earnings were under a certain threshold.

The system was built according to the Bismarckian model, along occupational lines. The subsequent evolution of the Italian pension system was similar to that of many Bismarckian countries, and followed two major directions: 1) coverage extension to protect all categories of workers (farmers 1957; artisans 1959; dealers-shopkeepers 1966); 2) introduction of a basic means-tested scheme aimed at preventing poverty in old age (1969). Moreover, in 1969 the original funded system was eventually replaced by a fully PAYG one. The same year was crucial for the level of old age pensions, as Law 153/69 modified the earnings-relating method of benefits calculation introduced one year before (Law 238/68), making it more generous (80 per cent of earnings after 40 years of insurance).

The result of such expansive interventions was a high increase of pension expenditure relative to GDP – which passed from 4.5 per cent in 1960, to 6.8 per cent in 1970 and 10.8 per cent in 1980 (Ministero del Tesoro, 1981) – and huge unbalances in the accounts of INPS[2] and other autonomous funds.

In fact, the shift from a funded system to a PAYG one, the expansion of coverage and the increase in the generosity of benefits took place in many well-developed nations during the post-war period, yet in Italy pension policy assumed peculiar traits.

The Italian political system that emerged from the ashes of World War II has often been described (until the early 1990s) as a consociational and scarcely legitimized system, presenting a weak government, a turbulent parliament – *locus* of both harsh confrontations and 'hidden', wide-ranging *quid pro quo* agreements – and a fragmented and polarized party system (Sartori,

1982). Against such background, and supported by a fast economic growth that provided considerable fiscal dividends, the fragmentation of political demand (many interest groups exerting micro-corporatist pressures) coupled with the fragmentation of political offer (many parties) led to a 'distributive sliding' of welfare policy (Ferrera, 1998). In other words social policies, originally crafted as redistributive measures, turned their nature into distributive policies, offering concentrated benefits to selected social groups while dispersing and obfuscating their costs. Such policies represented the main instruments in the hands of politicians to attract voters' support in a context where the diminished importance of 'class politics' loosened the ties between parties and interest groups. In Italy this was also made possible by the early and undisciplined conversion of policy-makers to deficit spending that shifted the burden of welfare state financing on public debt – and on future generations (Ferrera and Gualmini, 2004). This was in line with the polarization of the Italian political system, where social policies turned out to be one of the most powerful ways to enhance the legitimacy of the system.

Due to the occupational design of the pension system, old age (and disability) policies emerged as the typical currency of such political exchanges. The (expansive) reforms were rarely preceded by serious forecasts on their impacts, and virtually no pension expenditure projection was carried out till the end of the 1970s. A clear example of such developments is represented by the introduction of very favourable 'seniority pensions', especially for public sector employees (1956), that were allowed to retire after only 20 years regardless of age (so-called 'baby pensions'). Seniority pensions were also introduced for private sector employees and self-employed workers (1965), permitting them to retire after 35 years, even prior to reaching the pensionable age. The result was a bizarre system, generous, costly and extremely fragmented along occupational lines – with many different schemes for the various categories, each with peculiar regulations about eligibility conditions, contributions and benefits.

This expansion also conditioned the development of the whole Italian social protection system, orienting it towards the overprotection of old age. Expenditure for pensions increased constantly in the last 30 years, representing almost two-thirds of overall social expenditure in the mid-1990s.

In the following section the emergence of the pension problem in Italy will be illustrated, also providing a brief account of the main reasons that prevented any change in the field of pensions during the 1980s. Section 3 sketches an analytic framework to examine the Italian shift from stalemate to pension reforms during the 1990s, then provides a detailed description of both the reform process and its content. Finally, section 4 will focus on the future evolution of the Italian pension system, highlighting the positive and negative effects of the implemented reforms.

2. THE 1980s: CRISIS AND STALEMATE

In the early 1980s, the Italian pension system was basically made up of a single, public and highly fragmented pillar, articulated in a labyrinth of schemes with different regulations. Five major schemes constituted the bulk of the pension system: the first scheme covered public sector workers, the second protected private sector employees, and three schemes provided coverage to the self-employed, farmers, artisans and dealers-shopkeepers respectively (see below Table 2.1).

However, alongside the public pension pillars another peculiar scheme existed, which could be considered a 'quasi second pillar pension'. The TFR (*trattamento di fine rapporto*) was, and still is, a severance pay that firms must compulsorily grant to their employees when either they retire or leave the company for any other reason. It is financed through payroll taxes (6.91 per cent of gross wages) and operates as a defined benefits scheme for private sector employees.[3] In fact it is basically a 'deferred wage' for all private employees, providing modest but guaranteed returns: every year 6.91 per cent of annual earnings are accumulated and are credited with an interest rate of 1.5 per cent plus 75 per cent of the inflation rate. As contributions are only *virtually* accumulated, the TFR represents an important (and relatively cheap) source of financing for companies. The TFR is not portable and is always paid out in cash (usually as a lump sum). In the case of a lay-off, it also functions as an unemployment subsidy in disguise.

The modification of economic and demographic patterns, which affected the PAYG pension systems of many well-developed countries, had a tremendous impact on the Italian pension system that already presented deep internal imbalances. In 1981 the Treasury Ministry set up a commission that provided the first comprehensive evaluation of the pension system since the 1960s. The commission's report (Ministero del Tesoro, 1981) contained also one of the first projections of pension expenditure. Two different periods were considered (1980–85 and 1980–2000) with two diverse scenarios: the situation was critical in both scenarios for both periods. Pension expenditure was projected to rise to 11.7 per cent of GDP in 1985 in the best case scenario and to 12.4 per cent in the worst, and so would transfers from public budget from 4.2 per cent to 6.1 per cent of GDP. Thus, pension expenditure would be around 18–19 per cent of GDP in 2000.

The commission proposed some reform measures, which mainly aimed at restoring the financial viability of the system by harmonizing the regulations for the different regimes. Such proposals addressed the pension problem in the wider framework characterized by the overprotection of old age within the social protection system and, from a financial and economic point of view, a high deficit, which was to rise from 8.6 per cent (1980) to 11.1 per cent (1990) of GDP, and a large public debt, 58.1 per cent of GDP in 1980, then exploding to over 100 per cent of GDP during the 1980s.

However, the Italian political system seemed not to be ready to embark on a pension reform process. The Italian political system was still marked by high fragmentation and strong polarization of the party system, and weak governments usually relying on wide coalitions. During the 1980s five parties participated in the diverse governmental coalitions with an average of 3.7 parties per coalition, so that the coalitions were 'colourful' and heterogeneous, usually spanning from the centre-right to the centre-left of the political spectrum, around the pivotal Christian Democratic Party. Such coalitions also displayed deep internal conflicts – especially between the increasingly influential Socialist Party and the Christian Democrats – which affected government stability and often led the latter into harsh confrontations with parliament. Therefore, governments remained in power only 300 days on average, consequently meeting formidable obstacles on their way to comprehensive pension reforms.

After the first alarming reports, the subsequent lack of consensus on the relevance of the pension problem also played a role in the never-ending postponement of reforms (Franco and Marino, 2001). However, since 1978 almost every Minister of Labour and Welfare proposed reform projects that always faced the same destiny: they were abandoned because of a change of government. Most of the proposals shared some objectives like harmonizing the regulations for the different schemes in terms of contribution rates, benefit formulas and retirement age. Some of them were more innovative, envisaging a new configuration of the system based on different pillars.

At the end of the 1980s more than ten years had passed since the debate on pensions had first appeared in the political arena and still no significant change had occurred. The shift from the distributive policies typical of the expansionary period – mostly actions of 'credit claiming' – to the subtractive ones requested by the modified external and internal environment, proved to be difficult, almost impossible, in Italy. Though the relation between power concentration ('majoritarianism') and the chances to pass a pension reform is far from being straightforward (Pierson, 1994), in Italy the government had too little autonomy from the supporting coalition, and was therefore too often involved in struggles with the parliament, to commit itself to a delicate exercise of 'blame avoidance' and carefully control it in the various stages of a pension reform.

On the contrary, the last government supported by the five-party coalition (*pentapartito*[4]) of the 'First Republic' passed a reform act that followed the old policy pattern of the 'golden age': in spite of population ageing, rising unemployment, huge public debt and increasing deficit, the generous earnings-related system was extended to the self-employed workers, without increasing the low contribution rates they were required to pay. This represented another expansionary change, introduced without forecasting its impact on public expenditure, which deeply worsened the financial situation of the schemes affected by the reform (Franco, 2002).

In the early 1990s, however, Italy was on the edge of a new era, where the inefficiencies and the vices of its pension system were no more tolerable because of the joint impact of both external and internal factors.

3. THE RECONFIGURATION OF THE ITALIAN PENSION SYSTEM THROUGH NEGOTIATED PACTS

3.1. Institutions and Learning

Reforming pensions is a delicate and risky operation for governments that have to modify extensive institutional arrangements defended by dense networks of interest groups emerged around social protection (pension) programmes (Pierson, 1994). The importance of the institutional configuration of the pension system for the process and the content of reform, has been highlighted by some recent neo-institutionalist studies, together with the strategies pursued by governments in order to successfully reform public pensions. Among these, a seemingly indispensable condition for success consists in obtaining the consensus of either opposition parties or social actors (Schludi, 2001), above all the unions, through a negotiation process (Myles and Quadagno, 1997; Pierson, 1997; Bonoli, 2000; Hinrichs, 2000; Myles and Pierson, 2001). Then, other specific elements can facilitate the approval of reform proposals: the introduction of long phase-in periods and mechanisms for automatic adjustment (reduction) of pension benefits (Pierson, 1994; Pierson, 1997); the possibility for policy-makers to play different groups against each other in order to justify the adoption of some policy solutions. Moreover the new institutionalism has pointed to the relevance that formal political institutions have for successful reforms (Bonoli, 2000; Taylor-Gooby, 2002). This digression is useful because Italian pension policy during the 1990s has proved to be a case in which all the elements described above operated; allowing two major pension reforms, and a further adjustment some years later, that significantly recast the Italian pension system.

However, such deep reconfiguration cannot be explained without introducing further elements. The point is that the factors highlighted by the neo-institutionalist analysis operated in a very peculiar environment, characterized by the multifaceted crisis that affected the Italian economic, financial, political and social protection systems at the beginning of the 1990s. More precisely, the reforms were the result of a complex learning process, prompted by a sudden change of the actor constellation in the early 1990s, in the wake of both internal and external developments. External pressures coming from the run towards EMU and financial markets generated relevant learning processes among domestic societal and political actors, operating through the typical form of 'operational conditioning'. Domestic dynamics, like the profound reconfiguration of the political and institutional arenas of the early 1990s, facilitated these processes that largely altered actors' preferences and the overall stake of the game. Indeed, in the diverse stages of the reform process actors – especially the unions – realized that the failure to reform could no longer mean maintaining the distributive status quo, but implied instead suffering unexpected and unavoidable losses.[5] Learning processes and collective 'puzzling' helped to overcome the long-lasting stalemate in the pension field as well as the dynamics of 'powering' and the political exchanges noted above.

3.2. The Amato Government: Emergency Management and (Partially) Negotiated Pension Reform

In the early 1990s the economic performance showed some fluctuations, including a significant recovery in 1994 (+2.2 per cent) and 1995 (+3 per cent), but the financial situation was dramatic with public debt rising to 104.5 per cent on GDP in 1990 – and further rising to 108.4 per cent in 1991 and 117.3 per cent in 1992 – and the public deficit at 11.1 per cent of GDP in 1990 and 10.5 per cent in 1991. The situation was even worse in the light of the European convergence criteria, laid down in Maastricht in 1992, which prescribed the target of 60 per cent for the debt/GDP ratio and 3 per cent for the deficit/GDP one.

But Italy also suffered from a deep political and institutional crisis, whose first signs appeared in spring 1992 when the big '*Tangentopoli*' (Bribesville) scandal broke out. A widespread system of corruption involving top politicians and businesspeople was unveiled, soon leading to a deep crisis for the traditional parties that had dominated the political stage for over 40 years.

As noted some years later by the Prime Minister that led the government after those elections – the socialist Giuliano Amato – in such a situation he clearly perceived that the country needed firm guidance to ensure that the economic, financial and political-institutional challenges, together with those brought in by the Mafia, which killed two well-known magistrates in the spring of 1992, could not sweep the whole democratic system away (Cazzola, 1995). Amato then constituted a mostly 'technocratic' cabinet – supported by a four-party coalition (DC, PSI, PLI and PSDI) – and then embarked on the so-called process of *risanamento*, that is, restoring-to-health public finance. Central in this process, for the specific character of the Italian welfare state,

Table 2.1 Main features of the Italian pension system at the beginning of the 1990s

	Eligibility conditions for pensions		Contribution rate	Benefit calculation	
	Old age retirement age	Seniority contribution period		Assessed earnings	Formula[a]
Private sector	55 women 60 men	35 women 35 men	26.22% of which: 18.93% employers 7.29% employees	Last 5 years	$N/40*80\%$
Public sector					
Central government	65 women 65 men	20 (15) women 20 men	7% employees	Last month	$N/40*94.4\%$
Local government	60 women 60 men	20 women 25 men	7% employees	Last month	$N/40*100\%$
Self-employed	60 women 65 men	35 women 35 men	12%	Last 10 years	$N/40*100\%$

Note: [a] N years of contribution.

Source: Elaboration by the author.

was the reform of the pension system, then consuming about two-thirds of social expenditure.

Moreover, in 1991 a new consensus on the alarming trend of pension expenditure had emerged based on the projections of both INPS and the General Accounting Office. These estimates showed the gloomy future for the scheme for private sector employees, but the situation was not better in the schemes for public sector employees and the self-employed. Expenditure for public pensions had reached 12.8 per cent of GDP in 1992 (Ministero del Welfare, 2000) and the projections were even more dramatic: 23.4 per cent of GDP in 2040 according to the General Accounting Office.

Thus, the issues that had to be addressed were the same as those addressed since the early 1980s and could be roughly grouped in three categories: 1) stabilizing pension expenditure and achieving financial sustainability; 2) harmonizing regulations to increase intra-generational fairness between the different occupational categories, that is public/private sector employees and employees/self-employed workers; 3) clearly separating contributory benefits (*previdenza*) from social assistance (*assistenza*), the latter to be financed by general revenues.

The government followed a twofold strategy: reducing public expenditure in the short term through emergency measures, while nominating a commission to design an organic reform of the system. For their part, the unions protested against the short-term measures included in the budget law for 1992, but proved their willingness to negotiate on the draft bill for a comprehensive pension reform. However, during summer, external pressures strengthened: Italy sharply devalued its national currency, and this led to the exit from the EMS, thus putting pressure on the government to recover credibility *vis-à-vis* financial markets and also via a more incisive pension reform. Yet the government did not abandon the dialogue with the social actors, even more relevant in a climate of stricter austerity, and absolutely necessary in a situation in which the channel of inter-parties negotiation was unavailable, because of the discredit into which the major parties had fallen (Natali, 2001). Some temporary measures concerning pensions were introduced in the huge budget law for 1993, thus provoking some harsh protests by the unions, which organized several strikes and demonstrations in September and October mobilizing thousands of people and workers. Nevertheless, the reform process was not blocked and, although with some stop-and-go, the tripartite informal negotiation between the government, the unions and the employers association (*Confindustria*) went on till the adoption of the bill empowering the government to revise pensions (October 1992 – Law 421/92).

Law 421/92 allowed the government to issue two legislative decrees aimed at moving the Italian pension system towards a multipillar configuration: the first decree (D. Lgs. 503/92) concerned the revision of the first public pillar, while the second (D. Lgs. 124/93) would establish a regulatory framework for supplementary occupational and private pensions.

The plan to reform the public pillar was informed by two basic principles: 1) stabilizing pension expenditure and 2) harmonizing the different regulations for private and public employees. The two goals were often pursued together. In this perspective the first intervention modified the pension formula of the earnings-related system by lengthening the period to assess the *reference earnings* from the last five years (private employees) or last month (public employees) to 10 years for those workers with at least 15 years of contributions – and the whole career for the new entrants in the labour market. Likewise, the modification of *retirement age* was directed to both (partially) harmonizing the rules and reducing the number of future pensions: the retirement age for private sector employees was raised from 55 to 60 for women and from 60 to 65 for men (public sector: 65 for both men and women). Finally, in the field of *seniority pensions* the eligibility conditions were tightened, putting an end to the anomaly represented by the so-called 'baby pensions' in the public sector: the minimum contributory period to be entitled to seniority pensions was equalized at 35 years for public and private employees (see Table 2.1). In spite of these important changes, the gradualist character of the reform stands out if we consider that extremely long phase-in periods were introduced for all of these measures (INPS, 1993; Cazzola, 1995; Artoni and Zanardi, 1997) – the price to pay to obtain the acquiescence of the unions.

However, these were not the only measures adopted in 1992. Another important change, which was expected to generate a great part of the projected savings, affected not only future pensions but also the benefits of current retirees: the previous, generous *indexation mechanism* that linked benefits to both prices and wages was replaced by a new index adjusting pensions to *prices* only. Finally, in both schemes for employees and self-employed the *minimum contributory period* to be entitled to an old age benefit was raised from 15 to 20 years, and the possibility of *cumulating* pensions and wages was limited.

The Amato reform also created a legal framework for the development of *supplementary pension pillars*. Two kinds of pension funds were envisaged: 'open' and 'closed' pension funds. The main difference consists in the relevant role played by employees' and employers' representatives in the 'closed', mainly occupational, pension funds, which are thought to constitute the second pillar of the system. Due to the scarcity of resources – for both the high contribution rates in the first pillar and the constraints on the public budget – the possibility of using the TFR to finance pension funds was introduced, together with tax incentives. For those workers entering the labour market after 1993 the TFR must be compulsorily transferred to a pension fund, if they decide to subscribe a supplementary pension plan. Pension funds for employees can only follow the defined contributions principle. The tax model is the ETT,[6] which anyway avoids any 'double taxation' through some specific regulations.

The (projected) results of the Amato reform were relevant in terms of both harmonization and cost containment, but limited because of the introduction of transition periods and 'key' exemptions. Rules regarding pension formulas and seniority pensions had been harmonized between the schemes for private and public employees and the most striking anomalies (for example baby pensions) were being phased out. Projections also showed that expenditure for pensions would be contained also with a sharp decrease of future liabilities (Franco, 2002). Moreover, the changes brought into the pension formula were to enhance fairness, reducing (or even eliminating in the case of the new entrants) the favourable treatment that the former system provided to those workers with the less 'flat' careers; similarly, the lengthened minimum contributory period for old age pensions would improve the equity of the system at the individual level because of the stricter link between benefits and contributions.

On a negative note the issue of the (comparatively) short minimum contributory period – 35 years – to get an entitlement to seniority pensions and the persistent different regulations between the schemes for public and private sector employees and the self-employed had not been tackled.

3.3. From Berlusconi to Prodi: Different Bargains, Different Outcomes

After the Amato reform of 1992 a comprehensive report was released by INPS (1993) analysing the main schemes of the Italian pension system. It showed that if the first retrenchment interventions adopted one year before had improved the overall condition of the system, some aspects required further action. More precisely, the projections smoothed the worries around the scheme for private sector employees, where the impact of the reform was evident. The schemes that displayed much more alarming perspectives were actually those for self-employed workers, that is, artisans, dealers-shopkeepers and farmers. These programmes had always shown a structural deficit and the situation had dramatically worsened after the 1990 reform (INPS, 1993).

Therefore, the debate around pensions remained lively: welfare and pension reform became crucial issues in the electoral campaign for the 1994 elections (Natali, 2001). The general election, the first fought with the new mainly majoritarian electoral system introduced in 1993, saw a partial restructuring of the party system and the formation of a new centre-right majority that supported the first truly 'political' government[7] after two 'technocratic' cabinets (led by Amato and Ciampi). Silvio Berlusconi was appointed Prime Minister. Determined to continue the austerity policy inaugurated by his predecessors, Berlusconi chose Lamberto Dini as Treasury Minister and

Clemente Mastella as Minister of Labour and Welfare. The latter soon started to work on a new pension reform, setting up a commission, which included some experts appointed by the social actors.

Though committed to negotiation with the unions and Confindustria, the government led by Berlusconi did not speak with a single voice in the debate on pensions, threatening the unions with radical interventions and privatization of the Italian social security system (Natali, 2001). Although this behaviour made the unions suspicious, a very loose kind of negotiation between the government, the unions and Confindustria went on during summer and the early autumn. A bill empowering the government to reform pensions was eventually submitted at the end of September. The proposal aimed at: 1) strongly discouraging early retirement through seniority pensions by lowering the benefit by 3 per cent per year below the legal retirement age; 2) reducing the accrual factor from 2 per cent to 1.75 per cent per contribution year for all those workers with at least 15 years of contribution, who had been less affected by the 1992 reform; 3) replacing the existing indexation to prices with a new indexation mechanism linking pensions to projected inflation rate only.

These three measures, praised by the employers' association, were enough to provoke massive protests by the unions: on 14 October thousands of workers went on a general strike, on 12 November one million people crowded Rome for one of the largest demonstrations in a decade and a general strike was threatened for December.

In the meantime, the parliamentary majority was flaking off and at the beginning of December the government beat a retreat. The agreement signed on 1 December 1994 between the government and the unions retained only few and mostly temporary measures, like the suspension of the right to retire with seniority pensions in 1995. The agreement also allowed the government to keep in the budget law (Law 724/94) the acceleration of the transition period (introduced by the Amato reform) to raise the retirement age, also stating that before June 1995 an organic and structural reform had to be adopted or else the contribution rate would be increased by decree.

On 22 December Silvio Berlusconi resigned, concluding his first political experience with a defeat in the field of pensions. As noted above, the commitment to concertation leading to a substantial consensus among political and social actors, especially between the government and the unions, seems to be a fundamental prerequisite for successful pension reform. The cabinet led by Berlusconi, obliged to deal with different preferences within its heterogeneous majority, and within the government itself (some differences emerged between the rigorous approach of the Treasury Minister and the Minister of Labour and Welfare), did not fully commit itself in the negotiation with the unions. On the contrary the government, backed by Confindustria pressuring for a structural intervention (Natali, 2001), decided to attack just on the most sensitive issues for workers and their representatives: that is, seniority pensions, the level of benefits for the older workers (by changing the accrual rate) and pensions of the current retirees (via the indexation mechanism).[8]

In brief, the governmental plan failed because it aimed at achieving financial sustainability and expenditure cuts without providing any (compensatory) measures in a direction that might please the unions.

After Berlusconi's resignation no new elections were held and President Scalfaro worked to form a new government, which was led by the former Treasury Minister Lamberto Dini and was supported by a centre-left coalition.[9] The cabinet had an evident 'technocratic' character and it was thought necessary for it to remain in power for a limited period in order to adopt some extremely urgent measures, clearly expressed in its programme. In fact, if on the one hand the economic situation was improving (GDP growth was at 2.2 per cent in 1994 and deficit had decreased to 7.1 per cent of GDP), on the other hand public debt reached the level of 125 per cent of GDP and the political unrest of 1994 had provoked a sharp decline in the value of the national currency, requiring some firm interventions (Ferrera and Gualmini, 2004). Against this background the reform of pensions, as stated in the agreement of December 1994, was central in the governmental plan.

The government soon proved its willingness to start a process of concertation with the social partners in the pension field, paying particular attention to the unions' requests. For their part, the latter seemed to be convinced that a further pension reform had to be prepared, and they supported the idea of rewriting the 'social pact' by preparing a proposal to reform the pension system (Cazzola, 1995; Lapadula and Patriarca, 1995; Natali, 2001).

The Minister of Labour and Welfare committed himself to a more institutionalized and smooth dialogue and negotiation with the unions than in previous years. The concertation focused on three major issues: institutional and financial separation of social insurance and social assistance, modification of the pension formula and revision of seniority pensions. On 8 May a formal agreement was signed by the government and the unions, which later verified acceptance by the workers through a referendum that approved the reform draft. On the other hand, Confindustria refused to sign the pact, lamenting its too prudent approach to the issue of seniority pensions. Despite this defection, the bill did not find insurmountable obstacles in parliament, so that at the beginning of August Law 335/95 was passed.

The Dini reform operated a substantial reconfiguration of the Italian pension system along the lines of financial sustainability and cost containment, intra-generational fairness, modernization and flexibilization. The main intervention was the modification of the pension formula with the shift from an earnings-related system to a *contribution-related* one for private and public sector employees and the self-employed. As suggested below, this shift per se

could not be so relevant without the introduction of some less visible mechanisms for benefits adjustment. In the new system pensions not only reflect the
length of contributory period (as in the previous system) but also the amount
of contributions actually paid. Moreover, the pension level depends on the age
of retirement, economic trends and demographic dynamics. Nonetheless, the
system remains PAYG and benefits are calculated as follows: the contributions
paid by the workers are 'virtually' accumulated in a personal account and
indexed to mean GDP growth over the last five years. At the moment of retirement, this amount is converted into a pension through a *conversion coefficient*
that varies in relation to the age of the worker: the reform in fact introduced a
flexible retirement age – between 57 and 65 – with the maximum benefit
obtained when retiring at 65. It is also important to stress that such conversion
coefficients must be compulsorily revised every ten years to take into account
the changes occurred in both economic and demographic factors. The flexible
retirement age represents an element of modernization of the system together
with the *reduction to five years of the minimum contributory* period to be entitled to old age pension.

However, to prevent the opposition by the unions, the reform largely
protected the so-called 'acquired rights' of the older workers by introducing a
long transition period. In fact, the contributions-related system fully applies to
the new entrants in the labour market only, while the reform differently affects
the other workers according to the length of the contribution period already
matured in 1995. For those with at least 18 years of contribution, the old
earnings-related system (as reformed by Amato) remains in force. For those
with less than 18 years the new system applies *pro rata*: that is, for working
years before 1995 pension will be calculated with the old rules, while the
contributions-related method will apply to working years beyond 1995.
During retirement pensions will be indexed to prices only.

A similar protection of the 'acquired rights' was granted when the new
regulation of *seniority pensions* was laid down: the eligibility condition was
tightened by lengthening the minimum contributory period from 35 to 40
years. This measure de facto phases out seniority pensions, though with a long
transition period. In 2008, workers will be thus allowed to retire either at the
age of 57 with at least 35 years of paid contributions or (at any age) after 40
years spent in a regular job.

Other interventions of the Dini reform concerned: the introduction of
credits for periods of both child rearing and care activities; the creation of a
new scheme for workers hired with the new 'atypical' contracts; the increase
of the contribution rate for the self-employed; specific rules for those
employed in particularly hard jobs; the abolition of both the so-called
pensione sociale and the supplement for lower pensions, replaced by a new
means-tested benefit (*assegno sociale*) for all the citizens over 65 years

without other incomes; the creation of a permanent body responsible for monitoring pension expenditure.

The introduction of the contribution-related system harmonized the regulations of the schemes for private and public sector employees and the self-employed – all of them subject to the new system in the future. When the latter is fully operative, the regulations of retirement age and seniority pensions will also be the same in the different schemes. Coupled with the new rules for seniority pensions, the reformed system should also induce workers to retire later because of the links between retirement age and pension amount (via the conversion coefficients) (Lapadula and Patriarca, 1995). Besides, it should reduce contribution evasion as benefits closely reflect the contributions actually paid.

Finally, the government revised the 1993 regulation for supplementary pensions, providing more generous tax incentives to develop a second pension pillar. Contributions to pension funds were made deductible up to 2 per cent of the annual income (or 1291 euros).

The Dini reform has deeply modified the Italian pension system, which now rests on sounder financial bases, also by reducing fragmentation and intra-generational unfairness. This seemed to be the factor that played the crucial role in the negotiations between the government and the unions. Differently from Berlusconi, Dini and his Labour Minister greatly considered the requests of workers' organizations, carefully delivering a final proposal that allowed a successful political exchange with the unions on this basis: substantial savings – especially in the long run – in exchange for the protection of benefits of older workers and pensioners, and greater equity within the system via the elimination of the privileges for the self-employed.[10]

As we will show below, on the grounds of intergenerational equity, a 'generational break' was created by the introduction of the contribution-related system and the long transition period, thus overburdening younger generations with most of the costs of reforming pensions and restoring-to-health of public finance (see Table 2.2).

After the 1996 election, won by a centre-left coalition, a new government led by Romano Prodi was appointed, relying on the parliamentary support of the coalition formed by the Olive Tree (*Ulivo*) and Rifondazione Comunista.

The new government set up a commission (*Commissione Onofri*), charged with the task of carrying out a detailed evaluation of existing social and labour market policies and formulating some policy proposals. In the field of pensions it suggested: 1) quickly implementing all the measures introduced by the Dini reform; 2) unifying the different regimes; 3) fully applying the contribution-related system, removing the existing exemptions; 4) introducing mechanisms for automatic revisions of the conversion coefficients; 5) accelerating both the harmonization of transition periods for private employees and public employees and the establishment of supplementary pension funds for the latter. A heated debate arose around such proposals within the government itself, that had to confront the opposition of Rifondazione Comunista to the most important recommendation of the Onofri plan, that is, a much faster phasing in of the new pension formula introduced in 1995. In the end, this particular proposal was withdrawn, however, in spite of such conflicts, some measures were approved. These measures aimed at tightening the conditions for seniority pensions, harmonizing those (looser) for public sector employees with those for private sector employees. Moreover, a one-year freeze of the indexation was introduced, the combination of pensions and income from work was in part restored, and basic pensions were raised.

4.   LIGHTS AND SHADOWS AFTER A DECADE OF STEPWISE REFORMS

As stressed by the Italian report (Ministero del Welfare, 2002) prepared for the process named 'Supporting national strategies for safe and sustainable pensions through an integrated approach',[11] and recently confirmed by the Joint Report of the Commission and the Council of the European Union, the:

> three major reforms during the 1990s took on the challenge of securing financially sustainable pensions and radically transformed the Italian pension system . . . [Such efforts] have started to stabilise public pension expenditure and will control the future spending dynamics. The move towards a notional defined-contribution pension scheme represents a thorough modernisation of the first pillar, which is of critical importance also for its financial sustainability. (European Commission and Council 2003, p. 134)

In particular, the reforms prevented the collapse of the system by acting on different fronts: 1) financial sustainability and cost containment; 2) normative fragmentation; 3) move towards a multipillar configuration with the development of supplementary pension funds.

On the first front, it must be stressed that the targets set in 1995 for the ensuing five years have been reached, as reported by the Brambilla Commission in 2001 (Ministero del Welfare, 2001). On a positive note, the projections of pension expenditure for the medium–long-term are much more reassuring than ten years ago, with a projected increase of roughly two points, up to a peak of 16 per cent (from 13.8 per cent in 2001) of overall pension expenditure as a percentage of GDP in about 30 years (Figure 2.1). Pension expenditure is then likely to decrease thanks to the impact of the new system (fully operative only after 2035) and the expected change in the demographic situation (Ministero del Welfare, 2002).

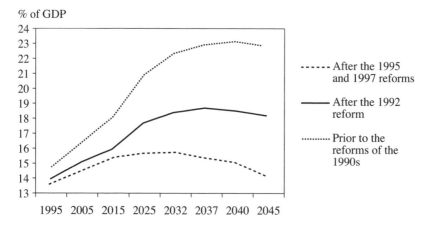

% of GDP

Source: Ministero del Tesoro (1998).

Figure 2.1   Pension expenditure projections: 1995–2045

These figures are even more meaningful if we consider that the projected economic dependency ratio[12] is really worrying in the Italian case, given that it is expected to grow from 48.8 per cent in 2000 to 64.5 per cent in 2020, 79.9 per cent in 2030 and 97.8 per cent in 2040 (Ministero del Welfare, 2002).

Such results will also be made possible by two crucial mechanisms operating in the new contributions-related system, which automatically link the value of future benefits to economic and demographic dynamics. These are: the revaluation of paid contributions according to the mean GDP growth rate of the last five years and the compulsory revision of the conversion coefficients every 10 years.

Consequently, as can be seen in the following table, the reduction of the gross replacement rate provided by public pensions is substantial for the current 'standard retiring' worker, that is, who leaves the labour market at the age of 60 with 35 years of contribution: in the period 2010–30 the replacement rate diminishes by 17.5 points.[13]

Also in terms of the total replacement rate a significant decline is to be expected as the figures reported by the government (Table 2.2) are somewhat misleading. In fact, the figures for supplementary private pensions are calculated assuming a contribution rate of 9.25 per cent (of gross wages) constituted by the whole TFR (6.91 per cent) plus further contributions paid by employers and employees. Such values gradually incorporate the full TFR. Therefore, for a fair comparison the latter should be fully added to the figures shown for the year 2000.

Table 2.2   Projected gross replacement rates for a private sector employee who retires at 60 with 35 years of contributions: 2000–2050 (%)

	2000	2010	2020	2030	2040	2050
Compulsory public pensions	67.3	67.1	56.0	49.6	48.5	48.1
Supplementary occupational pensions	0	4.7	9.4	14.5	16.7	16.7
Total	67.3	71.8	65.4	64.1	65.2	64.8

Source: Ministero del Welfare (2002, p. 11).

As for the second front, the harmonization between the different schemes, we have already noted that the Dini reform was quite incisive, putting an end to the privileged treatment of the self-employed, though with a transition period. This stands out considering the reduction of the replacement rate for this category, which is expected to diminish by 34 points in 20 years (2010–30). In a similar vein, the revisions operated by the Amato and Prodi reforms in the field of seniority pensions for public sector employees eliminated some unjustified favourable regulations and the most striking anomalies (entitlement with only 20 years of contribution and very long periods to phase out seniority pensions after 1995). Besides, both the Amato and the Dini reforms abolished the favourable treatment provided by the previous earnings-related system to those workers with sharp wage increases towards the end of their career.

On the third front, the stepwise processes of system reconfiguration (L. 124/93; Law 335/95 and recently D. Lgs. 47/2000) have created a legal framework to foster the development of supplementary pensions (see below).

In addition to these achievements, one should also point out a number of shortcomings in the reforms adopted in the 1990s. Due to the long period of transition for the implementation of several changes, it seems appropriate to distinguish the problems affecting the system in the short–medium term from those forecast for the long run, that is, the condition of steady state, in which the new contributions-related system will be fully operative (around 2035).

As for the financial sustainability, in the short term the slow phase-in does not help to contain the increase of the equilibrium contribution rates in the schemes for artisans and dealers, while the situation is relatively better in the scheme for private sector employees, though the level of the equilibrium contribution rate is already quite high. This would probably lead to more generous transfers from public budget, as there seems not to be so much room to further raise the actual level of contributions.

In the meantime, the old system, still in force for the older workers, continues to provide only weak incentives to keep on working when the minimum condition for seniority pensions is met. Moreover, the coexistence of diverse regulations for different cohorts will create sharp intergenerational iniquities in the medium term, especially for those employed in the public sector (Fornero and Castellino, 2001).

For the long run, critics usually focused on the possibility of amplifying the variation of conversion coefficients in relation to the different retirement ages in order to discourage early retirement. Alternatively, the bracket of retirement (57–65 years old) could be modified, raising the minimum age to 60 or 62 (Franco, 2002). Moreover, the combination of pensions and wages should be made easier, also taking into account the new logic incorporated in the contributions-related system. This measure has already been included in a draft bill on pension reform prepared by the current Berlusconi government (see Figure 2.2). These three proposals aim at reducing early retirement and raising the actual retirement age in a country that has one of the lowest employment rates for people over 55 in the EU. However, the reforms of the 1990s seem to have produced some positive effects, as the downward trend of the average age of retirement has been stopped and, recently, inverted.

Finally, let us briefly address the issue of supplementary pensions that is crucial in the context of the retrenchment in the public pillar. Since 1993 different legal provisions tried to foster the take-off of the pension funds sector. In spite of this, most studies maintain that the transition to a multipillar pension system still appears like a far prospect in Italy. This is partially true, but a careful investigation of the sector and some recent developments encourage a slightly different view. First of all, it must be remembered that after the first intervention in 1993, the landscape of supplementary pensions remained 'frozen', the first 'closed' pension fund being established only in 1998; since then, the number of pension funds has rapidly grown. In 1998, four 'closed' (occupational) and 46 'open' pension funds have been set up, while in 2003 these figures have grown to 37 and 93 respectively (COVIP, 2003). Members have also grown in the last years up to over 1 000 000, although the take-up rate remains modest, 15.4 per cent of potential beneficiaries[14] at the end of 2001, rising to 34.7 per cent if we exclude those (recently authorized) funds that are still in a very initial phase. Moreover some positive notes come from the average level of contributions paid to supplementary pension funds, 9.25 per cent of gross wage for those entered in the labour market after 1993, and from the performances of some particularly successful funds (COVIP, 2002).

On a negative note, critical points are still represented by the low participation rate among young workers – a serious problem if we consider the projected reduction of the replacement rate of public benefits – and the de facto exclusion (until 2001) of public sector employees from the possibility of joining a pension fund.

The main factors behind the slow take-off of second and third pillar pensions seem to be: 1) the scarce resources available to finance the system, because of the already high contribution rates for public schemes and the constraints on public budget; 2) the limited tax incentives provided by the law – at least till 2000, when the threshold to deduct contributions was raised to 12 per cent of income, or 5165 euros.

On the other hand, the existence of the TFR opens up some possibilities to overcome the first kind of problem; in fact, in 2001, the current government proposed the compulsory transfer of the TFR to pension funds for the new entrants in the labour market (see below). This measure could generate completely different prospects for supplementary pensions in Italy, by making available between 12 and 13 billion euros per year (Ministero del Welfare, 2002). However, the issue is controversial as the trade unions strongly opposed such possibility: in fact, the workers transferring the TFR to pension funds would lose the guaranteed return of the former in favour of the uncertain return of the latter.

As already indicated, in December 2001 the Berlusconi government asked the Parliament for a delegation of powers to pass a new pension reform, suggesting some adjustments to the existing regulations for both the pension pillars. Particularly the government aimed at: 1) fostering the development of second and third pillars; 2) gradually raising the retirement age.

After a first revision of the draft proposal, the delegation law was submitted to Parliament in the context of the financial law for 2004. The government proposed a two-step reform process. During the first phase (until 2007), the main measure would be a set of incentives to encourage later retirement, even if the entitlement to a seniority pension has been matured based on the transition rules set out by the Dini and Prodi reforms. The second phase would rest on 'structural' changes: a higher age of retirement for old age pensions and tighter conditions to be entitled to seniority pensions. Moreover the government proposed a reduction (3–5 per cent) of social security contributions for newly hired workers – without prejudice to future benefits and – to foster the development of supplementary pillars – the compulsory transfer of the TFR to pension funds. In the projections of the Treasury, the savings estimated from this reform could amount to approximately 1 per cent of GDP per year, thus substantially lowering the spending curve in the critical years between 2010 and 2040.

The government's new plan has encountered harsh opposition by all trade unions. A general strike in October 2003 brought millions of protesters to the streets. The government responded by saying that the specific content of the reform could be changed (even after Parliament's approval of the delegation bill) through negotiation, as long as its structural effects on spending trends are maintained.

Expert comments on the reform plan have been mixed. Criticisms focus in particular on: 1) the sudden character of change in 2008 (as opposed to a softer

---

- Period 2004–2007: incentives for private employees who decide to retire later than the lower age limit (now 57): 100 per cent of due social security contributions are paid directly to the workers.
- From 2008. Minimum requirement for seniority pensions in both the earning related system and the contributions-related one: 35 years of contribution and 60 years of age (raising to 35 and 61 in 2010) or 40 years of contribution.
- Requirement for an old age pension in the contributions-related system: 5 years of contribution and 65 (for men) years of age (60 for women).
- Extra contributions (ca. 7 per cent) now paid for the TFR will be transferred to supplementary pension funds unless workers formally disagree.
- Gradual elimination of the non-cumulability between pension and earnings for work.
- Further incentives to supplementary pension funds.
- Extra-contribution (4%) for those pensions over 516 daily euros.

Figure 2.2   The delegation law on pensions: main provisions

phasing in period); 2) the proposed reduction of contributions – which is seen as a violation of the whole logic of the Dini reform; 3) the absence of a guaranteed minimum return in the case of compulsory transfer of the TFR to a pension fund.

Between February and May 2004 the government was induced to further modify the delegation law because of the persistent harsh opposition by the unions and the emerging different positions within its own parliamentary majority. The compulsory transfer of the TFR to pension funds and the reduction of social security contributions were withdrawn, conditions to be entitled to seniority pensions were relaxed with respect to the former proposal.

On July 28 the new version of the reform – as summarized in Figure 2.2 below – was finally approved by the Senate, following the approval by the *Camera dei Deputati* at the end of May; in both cases the government had to rely on a vote of confidence (*voto di fiducia*) to secure the adoption of the delegation bill.[15]

5.   CONCLUSIONS

Whatever the future of the Italian pension system will be, some lessons can be drawn from the events of the last decade. After more than ten years of debate on the crisis of the pension system, three reforms[16] have altered its main traits, stabilizing pension expenditure and harmonizing the different schemes. Despite the risk of being blamed for such unpopular measures, the governments led by Amato and Dini have implemented two major reforms, carefully committing themselves to a process of concertation with the social actors. In Italy the reform path has been facilitated by a dynamic of rapid politico-institutional change, linked to the transition from the First to the Second Republic. The external constraints posed by the Maastricht process played in its turn a major role in pushing all actors in a reformist direction (Ferrera and Gualmini, 2000; Radaelli, 2002). But the reforms were essentially made possible by the close interaction between the government and the trade unions: an interaction resting on both policy learning and political exchange dynamics (Baccaro, 2002; Culpepper, 2002; Ferrera and Gualmini, 2003).

In the past pension, benefits were usually generous and secure, while in the future they will probably be significantly reduced and their actual amount will depend on several (uncertain) factors. This is even more true if we keep in mind that the Italian pension system will combine a first public pillar, providing contributions-related benefits linked to demographic and economic dynamics, with a second (and third) defined contributions private pillar. As recently noted by a well-known Italian expert, Elsa Fornero (2002), in such a system there will be no guarantee for the actual amount of pensions.

From another point of view, the likely compression of pension benefits operated by the new contributions-related system seems to leave some room for the possibility that Italy will move, though in the long run, towards the group of the so-called 'Latecomers' countries – as suggested by Hinrichs (2002) with reference to Germany and Sweden – especially if some recently formulated proposals, including provisions like partial opting out (Fornero and Castellino 2001), will be actually legislated.

NOTES

1. This chapter is the result of a joint effort. Matteo Jessoula has written parts 2, 3 and 4 while the introduction and conclusion sections have been written by Maurizio Ferrera.
2. INPS is the major public institution for pensions.
3. Public sector employees had a similar and more generous scheme.
4. Socialist Party, Social Democratic Party, Christian Democratic Party, Republican Party and Liberal Party.
5. For a full illustration of this argument, see Ferrera and Gualmini (2004).
6. Contributions Exemption, returns Taxation, benefits Taxation.
7. The coalition was formed by the newborn Berlusconi's party called Forza Italia, the renovated former neo-fascist party Alleanza Nazionale, the Lega Nord and some smaller centre parties.
8. It is worth noting that in the mid-1990s retirees represented the majority of members of the major workers' organization (CGIL).

9. PDS, Popular Party, Lega Nord and some smaller centre parties constituted the coalition.
10. See Natali (2001) for a detailed analysis of the political exchanges in the Italian pension reforms during the 1990s.
11. Such process, aimed at applying the so-called 'open method of coordination' in the field of pensions, was launched by the European Commission in summer 2001.
12. Ratio between the population of 65 and over and the employed people aged 15–64.
13. Those workers retiring at 65 with 40 years of contributions would face a slightly better situation – due to the incentives to postpone retirement incorporated in the new contributions-related system – with a reduction of the gross replacement rate by 12.7 points in the period 2010–40.
14. Potential beneficiaries are all the employees that can join a 'closed' pension fund because such a fund has been actually established for their category.
15. The vote of confidence regulation binds the government to resign in the case of defeat, thus putting pressure on the parliamentary majority to approve the bill.
16. The legislative *iter* of the recent Berlusconi reform still has to be completed with the drafting of the legislative decree.

REFERENCES

Artoni, R. and Zanardi, A. (1997), 'The evolution of the Italian pension system', in MIRE, *Comparing Social Welfare Systems in Southern Europe*, Florence Conference, vol. 3, Paris, 243–266.

Baccaro, L. (2002), 'Negotiating the Italian pension reform with the unions: Lessons for corporatist theory', *Industrial and Labor Relations Review*, **55**(3), 413–431.

Bonoli, G. (2000), *The Politics of Pension Reform*, Cambridge, UK: Cambridge University Press.

Cazzola, G. (1995), *Le Nuove Pensioni degli Italiani*, Bologna: Il Mulino.

COVIP (2002), *Relazione Anno 2001*, Web site: www.covip.it.

COVIP (2003), *La Previdenza Complementare: Principali Aspetti Quantitativi*, Web site: www.covip.it.

Culpepper, P.D. (2002), 'Powering, puzzling, and "pacting": The informational logic of negotiated reforms', *Journal of European Public Policy*, **9**(5), 774–790.

European Commission and Council (2003), *Joint Report on Adequate and Sustainable Pensions*, Brussels.

Ferrera, M. (1998), *Le Trappole del Welfare*, Bologna: Il Mulino.

Ferrera, M. and Gualmini, E. (2000), 'Italy: Rescue from without?', in F. Scharpf and V. Schmidt (eds), *Welfare and Work in the Open Economy*, vol. 2, Oxford: Oxford University Press, 351–398.

Ferrera, M. and Gualmini, E. (2004), *Rescue by Europe? Social and Labour Market Reforms from Maastricht to Berlusconi*, Amsterdam: Amsterdam University Press.

Fornero, E. (2002), *Il transferimento del Tfr alla previdenza complementare: rischi e possibili garanzie*, summary of the contribution to the conference promoted by Generali Assicurazioni, Rome, 11 October 2002.

Fornero, E. and Castellino, O. (2001), *La Riforma del Sistema Previdenziale Italiano*, Bologna: Il Mulino.

Franco, D. (2002), 'Italy: A never-ending pension reform', in M. Feldstein and H. Siebert (eds), *Social Security Pension Reform in Europe*, Chicago, US and London, UK: The University of Chicago Press, 211–261.

Franco, D. and Marino, M. (2001), 'The role of forecasts in social security policy', Paper presented at the conference 'New Frontiers of Economic Policy 2001. Pensions: A Real Check-up?', 20 September, Rome: Ministero dell'Economia e delle Finanze (Ministry of Economics and Finance).

Hinrichs, K. (2000), 'Elephants on the move: Patterns of public pension reform in OECD countries', *European Review*, **8**(3), 353–378.

Hinrichs, K. (2002), 'Basic security plus private employment-related pensions: Do Australia, Denmark, the Netherlands and Switzerland show the way for public pension in European social insurance countries?', Paper prepared for the Second Cost A15 Conference, 'Welfare Reforms for the 21st Century', Oslo, 5–6 April 2002.

INPS (1993), *Le Pensioni Domani: Primo Rapporto sulla Previdenza in Italia*, Bologna: Il Mulino.

Lapadula, B. and Patriarca, S.(1995), *La Rivoluzione delle Pensioni*, Rome: Ediesse.

Ministero del Tesoro (1981), *La Spesa Previdenziale e i Suoi Effetti sulla Finanza Pubblica*, Rome: Istituto Poligrafico e Zecca dello Stato (Italian Government Printing Office and Mint).

Ministero del Tesoro (1998), *Convergenze dell'Italia Verso l'UEM*, Rome.

Ministero del Welfare (2000), *Gli Andamenti Finanziari del Sistema Pensionistico Obbligatorio*, Rome.

Ministero del Welfare (2001), *Verifica del Sistema Previdenziale ai Sensi della Legge 335/95 e Successivi Provvedimenti, nell'Ottica della Competitività, dello Sviluppo e dell'Equità*, Web site: www.welfare.gov.it.

Ministero del Welfare (2002), *Report on National Strategies for Future Pension Systems*, Web site: http://www.welfare.gov.it.

Myles, J. and Pierson, P. (2001), 'The comparative political economy of pension reform', in P. Pierson (ed.), *The New Politics of the Welfare State*, Oxford: Oxford University Press, 305–333.

Myles, J. and Quadagno, J. (1997), 'Recent trends in public pension reform: A comparative view', in K.G. Banting and R. Boadway (eds), *Reform of Retirement Income Policy: International and Canadian Perspectives*, Kingston: Queen's University Press, 247–272.

Natali, D. (2001), *La Ridefinizione del Welfare State Contemporaneo: La Riforma delle Pensioni in Francia e in Italia*, Ph.D. dissertation, EUI – Florence.

Pierson, P. (1994), *Dismantling the Welfare State?: Reagan, Thatcher and the Politics of Retrenchment*, Cambridge, MA: Cambridge University Press.

Pierson, P. (1997), 'The politics of pension reform', in K.G. Banting and R. Boadway (eds), *Reform of Retirement Income Policy: International and Canadian Perspectives*, Kingston: Queen's University Press, 273–294.

Radaelli, C.M. (2002), 'The Italian state and the euro: institutions, discourse and policy regimes', in K. Dyson, *The European State and the Euro*, Oxford: Oxford University Press, 212–237.

Sartori, G. (1982), *Teoria dei Partiti e Caso Italiano*, Milan: SugarCo.

Schludi, M. (2001), 'The politics of pension in European social insurance countries', MPIfG Discussion Paper 01/11.

Taylor-Gooby, P. (2002), 'The silver age of welfare state: Perspectives on resilience', *Journal of Social Policy*, **31**(4), 597–621.

3. New century – new paradigm: Pension reforms in Germany

Karl Hinrichs

1. INTRODUCTION

After a series of changes enacted between 1989 and 2001, at the end of 2003, the Red-Green government in Germany got involved in another enterprise of reforming pensions. Apart from closing a short-term deficit of the public pension scheme, the main rationale for the latest reform initiative is again *demographic aging*. It results from both below-replacement fertility and ever greater life expectancy and concerns those welfare programs disproportionately utilized by the elderly. This includes health and long-term care services, but most heavily affected are old age pension schemes. The combination of an ever more elderly-biased age structure and a shrinking population of what presently is defined as employable age poses severe problems for a welfare state that, in its expenditure orientation, is elderly-biased anyway, not the least since public pensions regularly represent the largest single item of total social spending (Lynch, 2001; Esping-Andersen and Sarasa, 2002).

Germany is among those Western countries where fertility has been very low since about the mid-1960s. This will – according to the median variant of the latest official projections – lead to a shrinking population size: from presently 82.4 million to 75.1 million in 2050. Due to increasing longevity, a smaller population size goes along with a rising share of elderly. The percentage of elders (60+) already exceeds that of the young generation (below age 20) since the 1990s, and more than one-third of the population will be 60 years of age and older in 2030 (34.4 percent) and thereafter (2050: 36.7 percent – Statistisches Bundesamt, 2003, p. 42). It is obvious that compelling an ever smaller working age population[1] to finance pension benefits for a growing percentage of the population for an ever longer period of their lives constitutes a serious political challenge. It adds to the other strains that mature welfare states are facing: lower growth rates as post-industrialism progresses, structural changes in the labour market (decline of the 'standard employment relationship'), more diversity in private (family) households and, finally, *globalization*. Paul Pierson (2001) has questioned whether globalization indeed represents an *autonomous* cause of pressure on welfare states and a major threat to their central features. Notwithstanding the validity of this argument, globalization reinforces the pressure on political actors in the welfare state to tackle the aging problem through pension reforms, and it becomes effective in the reform discourse in at least three ways.

First, globalization not only means a rapidly growing volume, intensity and speed of cross-border transactions regarding goods, services (financial) and capital investments, but also of *information*. Epistemic communities are part of an increasingly transnational exchange of information. Their role in the political discourse on potential responses to demographic aging and the future of (public) pensions has increased, and it is further fuelled by interference of supranational organizations (like the World Bank, the International Monetary Fund or the OECD). This is so because the interest in 'successful' or 'innovative' pension reforms abroad and to adopt seemingly 'best practices' has grown. The *open method of coordination*, applied by the European Commission in the area of old age pensions, is another attempt to put that interest into practice when national pension systems and reform strategies in EU member states become exposed to some kind of competition.

Second, recent pension reforms in developed nations regularly imply a larger role of (mostly private) funded schemes and thus, for the time being, more savings have to be invested most profitably. In view of largely liberalized (deregulated) financial markets, pension funds and other institutional investors have become global actors when they operate worldwide and on a still growing scale. These multinational corporations and/or corresponding interest associations are attempting to gain a stake in national discourses on pension reform and to influence the direction of the reform process with regard to state regulation of their activities and the potential volume of their business.

The third relationship between globalization and population aging with regard to pension reform is particularly relevant for Germany as *the* 'social insurance state' par excellence: in no other OECD country do contributions to social insurance schemes make up such a large share of GDP as in Germany, namely, 18.6 percent in 2001, which is about 43 percent of total public revenues (Bach et al., 2002, p. 662; see also below, Table 3.1, col. 2). High proportional taxes on employing labor (up to an earnings ceiling) are presumed to have two effects. 1) In particular, jobs yielding low productivity are endangered, to be substituted by capital, and in the labor-intensive service sector the creation of corresponding jobs is impeded. That problem will be aggravated when, due to population aging, contribution rates to the public pension scheme as well as to statutory sickness funds and long-term care insurance have to be raised. Fewer jobs for low-skilled workers would shrink the contributory base, increase outlays (unemployment benefits) and, thus propel a vicious cycle. 2) Since social insurance contributions are partly shifted forward into labor costs, a country like Germany is prone to lose out on 'locational competition', that is, to be no place of profitable investment and production anymore. In a globalized economy high total wage costs may not only scare off investors of capital, but also employees due to the tax wedge: it could cause a 'brain drain' of domestic workers with a high earnings potential and, vice versa, make Germany a comparatively less attractive place for potential immigrants. The influx of preferably young and well-educated migrants is a most important option to *moderate* the effects of demographic aging. Framing the aging issue in the globalization context thus urgently calls for pension reforms containing the combined contribution rate to the social insurance schemes as a 'no alternative' policy.

A major obstacle to coping with this seemingly irrefutable demand is that of all welfare state programs a pension scheme organized as social insurance turns out to be the one most resistant to change. According to Titmuss (1976, p. 60), 'contributory "rights" and privileges, spanning perhaps fifty years, become sacrosanct'. This is so because entitlements are 'earned' through prior contributions and are regarded as 'quasi-property rights'. Moreover, the opportunities of workers to adjust to policy changes decline to zero as they approach retirement age. The metaphor of the 'generational compact' is thus a conceptual arrangement meant to bridge the temporal cleavage between the stages of a complete adult life, ranging from first covered employment to the last pension benefit paid. Maintaining *confidence* in the scheme's continuity and stability is thus an essential requirement. Additionally, the generational compact signifies a self-reproducing cooperative solution for income redistribution: based upon serial reciprocity it ties together the elderly, being interested in fair as well as sufficient pensions, and contributing members of the working age generation who want to see their parents and, after all, themselves well provided with public pensions. Therefore, these schemes regularly enjoy high esteem and support among citizens of all ages, adding up to a *broad constituency*. Living up to current and future beneficiaries' expectations of reliable income security nonetheless poses a difficult challenge for public policy. In order to overcome *inertia* as an institutional feature of pension schemes, reform considerations of policy-makers in this area of social policy are typically shaped by a very long time frame, stretching well beyond one parliamentary period. It entails a specific pension *politics*, among others, regularly resulting in attempts to spread the consequences of adjustments into the future. Generous phasing-in or phasing-out clauses avoid immediate hardships, but timely responses to imminent problems are essential.

Germany started early to meet the challenge of an aging population and passed the Pension Reform Act 1992 (hereafter: PRA92) in 1989. Due to this foresighted change the assessment prevailed among all relevant political actors that no substantial legislative change had to be considered much before the year 2010. Actually, already when the PRA92 was coming into effect a changed interpretation of the scheme's financial viability in the short and long run began to spread. It became the starting point of further so-called 'structural' reforms, which, however, remained within the realm of *parametric* changes, but led the way to a *paradigmatic* shift in 2001.

The reform process until the 2001 legislation is dealt with in section 2, which, in order to show the subsequent paradigm shift more clearly, begins with a short review of the pension reform of 1957. Section 3 describes the emergence and elements of an old age security system that, with regard to goals, principles, actor constellations and possibilities for further development, substantially differs from the traditional one-pillar approach. Thereafter it is analyzed *how* such a path-departing turn towards a multipillar pension system came about, and special attention is given to policy-*makers'* strategies vis-à-vis the perceptions of policy-*takers* since issues like institutional trust (reliable income security) and the legitimacy of the pension system were most important. Besides looking into the political and socio-economic constellations, facilitating or even demanding a break in continuity, in section 4, the most recent reform attempts are described and evaluated as well. Starting from the German case, the concluding section discusses the ' "frozen" welfare state landscape' argument (Esping-Andersen, 1996, p. 24).

2.   PUBLIC PENSION POLICY IN GERMANY, 1989–97

2.1.   The Starting Point

Until 1957, central traits of the German public pension scheme,[2] which are assumed to be generically 'Bismarckian' – particularly the equivalence principle and status maintenance – were merely embryonic. Although benefits were linked to preceding contribution payments right from the beginning, elements of basic security, representing remnants of Bismarck's original plan of a tax-financed flat-rate pension, still played a role after World War II. Nevertheless, benefits emanating from this static scheme were low and, conceptually being part of a 'multipillar approach' (as would be today's terminology), meant to simply *contribute* to other sources securing livelihood in old age, like private provision, family support, reduced earnings from continued work or (selective) occupational pensions. Despite an incremental expansion of the scheme since 1889 and several ad hoc benefit increases after 1951, in 1956 the *average* pension amounted to no more than 25 percent of net earnings for blue-collar workers so that, for almost all low-skilled, being old was synonymous with being poor. White-collar workers who attained an average

Table 3.1 Social expenditure and public pension financing in Germany

Year	Social expenditure in percent of GDP	Combined contribution rate to social insurance schemes	Public pension expenditure in percent of GDP	Net standard pension in 1995 euro/in % of real net average earnings	Contribution rate to the public pension scheme (earnings ceiling in % of gross average earnings)
	(1)	(2)	(3)	(4)	(5)
1957		21.6			14.0 (178.5)
1960	21.1	22.4	6.4		14.0 (167.2)
1970	25.1	26.5	7.7		17.0 (161.9)
1975	31.6	30.5	9.8		18.0 (154.1)
1980	30.6	32.4	9.6		18.0 (170.9)
1985	30.0	35.1	9.5		19.0 (183.6)
1990	27.8	35.8	8.8		18.7 (180.2)
1991	28.4	36.7	8.9		17.7 (175.6)
1995	31.2	39.3	10.3		18.6 (184.7)
1996	32.1	40.8	10.5		19.2 (185.8)
1997	31.6	41.8	10.5		20.3 (188.7)
1998	31.5	42.1	10.6		20.3 (190.5)
1999	31.9	41.2	10.6		19.5 (190.6)
2000	31.9	41.0	10.7		19.3 (190.2)
2001	32.1	40.8	10.9		19.1 (190.9)
2002		41.3			19.1 (189.4)
2003		42.1			19.5 (209.4)

Net standard pension in 1995 euro (column 4):
5 517/66.8 ; 8 398/65.0 ; 9 995/66.8 ; 11 527/71.1 ; 11 171/72.4 ; 11 849/68.0 ; 11 902/67.8 ; 11 822/69.9 ; 11 733/70.1 ; 11 594/71.0 ; 11 552/70.1 ; 11 619/69.9 ; 11 537/69.1 ; 11 375/67.7 ; 11 440/68.4

Sources: (1) BMAS 2002, pp. 19 and 22 [figures not comparable to OECD calculations; figures 1991 and after relate to united Germany]; (2) VDR 2003, p. 243; (3) BMAS 2002, pp. 35 and 38; (4) VDR 2003, p. 240 [for the definition of 'standard pension' see n. 4; all figures relate to West Germany]; (5) VDR 2003, pp. 239 and 245 [1992 and after: contribution assessment ceiling valid in West Germany].

51

replacement ratio of about 40 percent were somewhat better off (Alber, 1989, p. 183; Döring, 2000).

The pension reform of 1957 had an *immediate* impact on the economic well-being of current retirees when the benefit formula and the post-retirement adjustment of benefits were made *dynamic* (Hinrichs, 1998). Taking into account individual, lifetime earnings in relation to average earnings of all insured (thereby granting credits for military service, spells of unemployment and education) when calculating the pension amount and annually upgrading it according to *gross* wage growth, helped the retirees to participate in economic progress. The benefit increase of almost 70 percent in spring of 1957 transformed public pensions as a floor of retirement income into an actual wage replacement that went up to a higher ratio subsequently (see Table 3.1, col. 4). Although basic security elements were abolished completely, the number and rate of elderly people being dependent on (additional) social assistance payments declined.

Providing (future) pensioners with a stake in the 'economic miracle' substantially contributed to the support for the new *economic order* ('social market economy'). At the same time, the reform helped to further consolidate the legitimacy of the restored *democratic system* as it effectively demonstrated its ability to deliver 'social security'. Albeit the 1957 legislation established the pattern of consensual pension policy (lasting until the 1990s; see below) when it eventually passed parliament with the votes of both Christian Democrats and Social Democrats, competitive party politics was central: the Social Democrats came forward with a reform bill first and pushed the government to present a more generous proposal than it originally planned. However, only the incumbent Christian Democrats were given credit for this most popular post-war social policy reform when, for the first and only time, they attained an absolute majority in parliament after the federal elections in September 1957.

Assessments differ as to whether features of institutional continuity prevailed in the 1957 reform (Conrad, 1998) or whether it factually meant a *path shift* (Döring, 2000). Supporting the latter position, Mätzke (2002) argues that a conversion had happened that manifested itself as a 'conservative innovation'. Within this combination *conservative* relates primarily to 'organizational form', that is, preserving occupationally segregated schemes with still no universal coverage or the continuing role of social partners in the schemes' administration. *Innovation* mainly concerns 'institutional form' and refers to the goal shift that occurred on the benefit side of the scheme when this institution was assigned a new mission, namely to provide *wage replacement* according to the equivalence principle at a level that maintains pre-retirement living standards after a full occupational career *and* all through retirement. Hence, not earlier than 1957 the old age income system attained its specific shape that is usually associated with Germany as the prototype of a conservative welfare state regime.

Moreover, the 1957 reform meant the birth of the *one-pillar approach* in Germany because a *net* replacement ratio hovering around 70 percent even for employees with earnings up to about 1.7 to 1.9 times the average[3] (see Table 3.1, columns 4 and 5) reduced the need to strive after further income for an extended and from now on virtually work-free period of life. Whereas elderly people's resource mix during the late 19th century and beyond most often signaled straitened circumstances, after 1957 a more varied public/private mix of retirement income, almost regularly, became an indicator of affluence: due to the relatively high level of public benefits, occupational pension coverage remained low. Like additional private provision for old age (financial assets or home equity) of some significance it was largely confined to the more prosperous parts of the work force. Despite much rhetoric about the 'three-pillar model', due to the 'crowding-out' effect of quite generous public pensions still about 80 percent of total retirement income stems from unfunded public sources (when the civil servants' pensions are included – Deutscher Bundestag, 2002, pp. 317–321).

2.2. Containing the Future Rise of the Contribution Rate: General and Selective Retrenchments

Increasing outlays and declining contribution revenues out of actual earnings beleaguered all social insurance schemes in Germany after the sudden death of full employment in 1974. In the public pension scheme, additionally burdened with the costly consequences of the expansion concluded in 1972, this pressure implied a series of discretionary interventions into the indexing formula so that instead of steady gross wage adjustments a *factual* net wage development of pensions occurred after 1977. Moreover, the contribution rate was increased several times. Apart from dutiful protests from the respective opposition parties, these 'first-order changes' (Hall, 1993) were largely undisputed due to the 'grand coalition of path dependants' (Conrad, 1998, p. 112) that had been established in 1957. It was a policy network with a shared belief system regarding the techniques and principles of social insurance, and it included the social policy experts of both *Volksparteien* (People's parties – CDU/CSU and SPD), representatives of the social partners, the administrators of the public pension scheme as well as the academic advisers. Thanks to its interpretative hegemony, that policy network was able to fend off attacks on the prevailing policy paradigm and to successfully push through reforms *within* the system as against system shifts (for example, moving towards capital funding or a tax-financed basic pension scheme). Commitment to now consolidated institutional features meant a preference for technical solutions that, after a joint learning process, usually resulted in compromises acceptable for all actors involved.[4]

Therefore, the preparation of the PRA92 was a highly depoliticized and deparlamentarized course of events. There was almost no controversy on the implications of demographic aging and the need for timely action when, at that time, the equally non-acceptable alternatives either were to exempt retirees from any benefit cuts, and then gradually have to increase the contribution rate from about 18.7 to 36.4 percent by 2030, or to cut benefit levels by half while maintaining a stable contribution rate. The final reform bill was a compromise between the government parties (CDU/CSU and Liberal Party) and the Social Democrats, and both social partners had agreed to it as well. The cumulative effect of the altogether incremental reform elements should reduce the increase of the expected contribution rate by almost 10 percentage points (Schmähl, 1993; Sozialbeirat, 1998, p. 242).

The difference to the pre-reform projections mainly stemmed from the three changes mentioned first in Figure 3.1, that is, an increased and in future constant share of federal subsidies, introducing permanent deductions if pensions are claimed before age 65, and the shift to net wage adjustment. The central idea of the new indexing formula was the 'fixed relative position' (Myles, 2002, p. 141, referring to Musgrave), that is, to ensure a *stable target replacement ratio of 70 percent* and to make pensioners participating in demographically (or otherwise) induced alterations of social insurance contributions and income tax codes that would change employees' *net wages*.

When the PRA92 that passed the legislative bodies in November 1989 became effective in 1992, the 'unification boom' was almost over in West Germany and employment in East Germany was still in steep decline. As a result of the deteriorating labor market situation the number of elderly unemployed who claimed an early retirement pension (starting at age 60) nearly exploded. The concomitant rise in social spending and the increased contribution rates to the social insurance schemes can be read off from Table 3.1 (columns 2 and 5). This development contributed to another round of retrenchments of the public pension scheme being included in an omnibus bill enacted in 1996 (WBG – see Figure 3.1 for the main elements). The WBG enhanced the effects of the PRA92 when it accelerated the phasing-out of early retirement options without permanent benefit deductions and further reduced various non-contributory entitlements. The Social Democrats and the unions vehemently opposed these changes (and further elements of the omnibus bill, for example, waiting days for sickness benefits). The passing of the WBG in parliament and the subsequent preparations for another major reform (PRA99) by the Christian Liberal government marked the end of the traditional 'pension consensus' between the two large parties (and also created less unanimity

Pension Reform Act 1992 (PRA92) – legislated: 1989; effective: 1992 + subsequently
- Benefit adjustment according to preceding year's net wage development
- Federal subsidies increased to 20% of the scheme's annual expenditure (permanently)
- All provisions to retire before age 65 without benefit reduction phased out in 2012 (exception: seriously handicapped workers); permanent deduction: 0.3% per month
- Credits for periods of schooling and tertiary education reduced: from max 13 yrs to 7 yrs at max 75% of average wages
- Four instead of 5 first yrs of covered employment revalued at 90% of average wages
- Child-care credits for births after 1991 increased from 1 to 3 yrs at 75% of average wage)

Growth and Employment Promotion Act 1996 (WBG) – legislated: 1996; effective: 1997 + subsequently
- Phasing out of first benefit receipt without permanent deduction before age 65 accelerated (completion: December 2004 instead of December 2012)
- Credits for periods of schooling and tertiary education after age 17 reduced: from max 7 yrs to 3 yrs
- Three instead of 4 first yrs of covered employment revalued at max 75% of average wages formerly: 90%)
- No credits for periods of unemployment and sickness if no benefits from respective social insurance scheme; credits reduced for recipients of unemployment assistance

Pension Reform Act 1999 (PRA99) – legislated: 1997; effectiveness *scheduled* for 1999 and subsequently
- Retirement age for seriously handicapped persons lifted from 60 to 63 yrs (benefits deducted if claimed between 60 and 63 yrs of age)
- Benefit calculation of disability pensions changed to the disadvantage of claimant and requirements for claiming disability pensions as such strengthened
- Increase of life expectancy at age 65 taken into account when calculating initial benefit and adjusting current pensions ('demographic factor')
- Credits from simultaneous covered employment can be added to child-care credits whose value increased from 75 to 100% of average wages

Pension Reform Act 2001 (PRA2001) – legislated: 2001; effective 2002 and later
- Benefit adjustment formula incorporates changes of the contribution rate to public pension scheme and to certified private pensions (effect: decreasing replacement ratio)
- Survivors' pensions: more comprehensive income test; supplements for children in household
- Revaluation of low earnings for parents when child is between 3 and 10 yrs or additional credits if non-employed while raising 2 or more children below age 10
- Special, tax-financed means-tested basic security scheme for old age and disability pensioners without reverting to children's income support
- Tax-subsidized contribution to certified supplementary provisions (starting in 2002, gradually increasing to 4% of maximally covered earnings in 2008): Riester-Rente
- Political action triggered if foreseeable that contribution rate will exceed 20% before 2020 or 22% before 2030 or target replacement ratio falls below 67%

Figure 3.1   Central elements of pension reform acts legislated in Germany between 1989 and 2001

among the social partners) – although there was no principled dissent on all changes included in the reform bill enacted in 1997.

For example, higher federal subsidies, financed out of an increased VAT rate (already beginning in April 1998) and meant to cover non-contributory components of the benefit package more completely, were not contested as was a further improvement of child-care credits (see below). However, the two most momentous reform elements of PRA99 were, at the same time, the most controversial ones. 1) In order to push through a higher *actual* retirement age, individual efforts to evade permanent benefit deductions by resorting to *disability pensions* were made unattractive, and access to them was rendered more difficult. 2) The core piece of the PRA99 was the 'demographic factor' by which, beginning in 1999, the hidden expansion of the scheme due to decreasing mortality rates at higher ages should be halted when lower benefits were stretched over a prolonged period of retirement. Further life expectancy at age 65 was integrated into the formula that determines the *initial benefit level* as well as the *annual adjustment*. Rising longevity assumed, the demographic factor would gradually lower the *net* standard pension level from nearly 70 to 64 percent (but not below).

Contrary to the expectations that after implementing the PRA99 no further adjustments would be necessary until about 2010, the legislation of the WBG and PRA99 already in 1996 and 1997 and the end of the pension consensus between the CDU/CSU and the SPD accompanying their passage demonstrate a changed, but not yet universally shared interpretation of aging and globalization issues. When the PRA99 was read in the Bundestag, the spokesperson of the Liberal Party, Gisela Babel, expressed the difference to the 1989 situation most clearly: 'At that time no discontent with a contribution rate to the pension scheme of 26 percent or 28 percent was discernible. That was flatly considered acceptable then. Today we do not consider it acceptable anymore' (Deutscher Bundestag, 1997).

Including the effects of the PRA99, now a contribution rate of 23.5 percent in 2030 was estimated. It was substantially lower than the 36.4 percent that had been projected *before* the PRA92 became law (Sozialbeirat, 1998, p. 242). Although the reforms enacted between 1989 and 1997 were clearly parametric, the moderation of the expected rise of the contribution rate by about 13 percentage points will inevitably leave grave traces in the future structure of benefits and the actual level of pensions – even if the lower figure is partly due to more funding out of general (and partly earmarked) revenues and to savings from making early retirement more costly for pensioners. The scheduled decrease of the target replacement ratio (from 70 to 64 percent), a widely used indicator of benefit generosity, only partly displays the most serious consequences on the level and overall distribution of benefits. The cumulative effect is much larger and not immediately visible. It mainly stems from a strengthened insurance principle (PROGNOS, 1999). The full impact hinges upon future pensioners' improved or diminished chances to realize a standard employment career and thus to earn sufficient credits for attaining the (lower) target replacement ratio. If ongoing changes in the labor market indeed diminish these chances it is most important for the individual pensioner whether those developments are compensated for by corresponding adaptations of the entitlement rules or are aggravated when exactly those provisions aiming at social adequacy of benefits are removed.

For these reasons it is clear that stabilizing the contribution rate *and* status maintenance increasingly become contradictory goals. Although the latter goal had not been officially abandoned by the Christian Liberal government and thus the basic model of 1957 remained unchanged (Döring, 2000, p. 180), it is obvious that after this series of reforms, in future, fewer employees can expect a factual wage replacement well above the social assistance level. This is exactly what the term 'creeping disentitlement' (van Kersbergen, 2000, pp. 28–9) means when several incremental adjustments are evaluated according to their cumulative impact – namely, a *tacit system shift* in the long run (Hinrichs and Kangas, 2003). To the majority of insured a number of single changes were intangible, and in particular the combined impact for oneself remained obscure. Therefore, these non-transparent adjustments failed to produce the effect the government had hoped for: in future, lower pensions were not regarded as 'more secure', and lost confidence in the reliability of the public pension scheme could not be regained. Additionally – and not least as a result of a transnational discourse diffusion – a new interpretative frame emerged when social insurances were no longer regarded as a solution to workers' typical risks, but rather as a central *problem* for international competitiveness and employment growth. It linked to amplified fears of indeed unprecedented population aging and, for the first time, notions of *intergenerational equity* emerged as an imperative. As a result of the failure to re-establish confidence and of changes in the cognitive map of political actors, at the end of the 1990s the German pension system arrived at a critical juncture when a learning process was triggered, which finally led (in 2001) to a 'path dynamics' that initially implies almost no outcome change, but becomes irreversible and thus is tantamount to a paradigm shift.

3. FROM PUBLIC PENSION REFORM TO RETIREMENT INCOME POLICY: THE 'RIESTER-RENTE' OF 2001

During the 1998 election campaign the Social Democrats created difficulties for themselves when they announced the revocation of the 'demographic factor', which had been denounced as a 'pension cut' before. After coming into office these difficulties were enlarged when the Red-Green government actually kept that promise.[5] In addition, the government became under time pressure because it merely *suspended* this element of the PRA99 as well as the massive retrenchments affecting future disability pensioners until end of the year 2000.

The first draft of reform proposals was presented in June 1999, and it was not earlier than May 2001 when the Bundesrat passed final pieces of the reform package (hereafter: PRA2001). This lengthy process was due to numerous and sometimes very detailed changes in response to objections from various actors as well as to attempts to revive the inter-party pension consensus that had lasted until the mid-1990s.[6] Parallel to the reform project PRA2001 the government enacted several changes concerning the public pension scheme: it introduced a gradually increasing energy tax (*Ökosteuer*). The revenues are earmarked as a supplementary federal grant to the public pension scheme in order to further cover non-contributory benefits and to facilitate a lower contribution rate. Furthermore, pension credits on behalf of recipients of unemployment assistance were reduced. Instead of wage indexing, pensions were arbitrarily adjusted according to consumer prices only in 2000, and in 2001 a moderated version (compared with the PRA99 provisions) of disability pension reform went into effect. Three innovations included in the PRA2001 (see Figure 3.1) justify speaking of a *paradigmatic change* (see also Michaelis and Thiede, 2000) towards a retirement income policy that has happened and that supersedes the institutionally confined public pension policy:

1. Hitherto, like in many other pay-as-you-go, defined benefit public pension schemes, in Germany the contribution rate functioned as the dependent variable of all parameter changes affecting revenues and expenditures, for example, it was increased when the available funds fell below a certain contingency reserve. In future, this practice will be reversed because *upper limits* were fixed: the contribution rate *must not* exceed 20 percent until 2020 and 22 percent until 2030. In order to realize this transition to a 'revenue-oriented expenditure policy', apart from funding a higher share out of general taxation, only savings on the benefit side remain an option. A new benefit (adjustment) formula comprising a complicated 'brake mechanism' and that replaced the suspended demographic factor was expected to deliver most of the required savings (Schmähl, 2003). It should lead to roughly the same result in the long run, namely a standard replacement ratio of 64 percent although, due to a redefinition of net wage, the factual decline appears to be less large: the officially projected figure for 2030 is about 67 percent. In case higher contribution rates than those mentioned before *or* a replacement ratio

lower than 67 percent come into reach, it is stipulated that the government has to take 'appropriate' action. The expectation to actually live up to *both* targets was based on overly optimistic assumptions (about declining unemployment, demographic development etc.), and very soon it became foreseeable that if a conflict arises such a trade-off would be decided in favor of containing the contribution rate at the expense of the pension level (see section 4.2).

2. Among the 18 traditional OECD member countries, so far, only Germany has had no special minimum protection scheme for the elderly. Persons without sufficient insurance claims were referred to the general social assistance scheme. At the beginning of this decade only about 1.3 percent of retirement age people received those means-tested benefits. The new basic security scheme for old age and disability pensioners is still means-tested, but the legal obligation of adult children to support their elderly parents has been virtually lifted since 2003. The official justification for introducing this scheme was to increase the take-up rate, and that will indeed be the immediate consequence. In its explanation to the reform bill the government also admitted that changing (un-)employment careers may lead to more pensioners receiving benefits lower than the social assistance level (Bundesregierung, 2000, p. 43). Therefore, the major role of this 'social assistance *de luxe*' for the elderly will make 'new risks' in the labor market and the consequences of *past* and *future* pension retrenchments socially more bearable when there is an increasing number of newly retired persons whose insurance entitlements prove to be insufficient.

3. The core element of the PRA2001 is an incentive for a new type of *voluntary* private pension savings, which is named after the then Minister of Social Affairs, Walter Riester (Riester-Rente). Although officially called *supplementary* provision for old age, this component of future retirement income is in fact meant to *compensate* for the declining target replacement ratio and to ensure income security: after the various measures taken in order to contain the contribution rate have created a 'social protection gap' it is now 'filled by private provision' (Bonoli et al., 2000, p. 46). When institutionalizing private pensions, the Red-Green government has not only made up for the 'forgotten' compensation in the PRA99 of its predecessor. Moreover, the extension towards *retirement income policy* has irrevocably converted the German pension system into a multipillar approach again after it had been tantamount to *public pension policy* and a one-pillar approach since 1957 (see section 2.1). The Riester-Rente started in 2002. Contributions to certified savings plans, gradually increasing to 4 percent of gross earnings in 2008, benefit from direct subsidies or tax privileges with a bias in favor of families raising children and high-income earners.

Different from the public pension scheme employers do not financially participate in the Riester-Rente so that their compulsory contribution payments will be limited to 11 percent of covered wages at maximum. Sparing employers from joint financing may be regarded as a further innovation. For the trade unions and the traditional Left it was of high symbolic value although economically it is irrelevant because employers' social security contributions always added to total wage costs, and increases were considered in subsequent wage bargaining. In any case, for those employees who voluntarily engage in supplementary provision their total contribution rate is higher than before. It is the inevitable consequence if one moves from a complete PAYG system to partial capital funding and represents the well-known 'double payment problem' that goes along with it. Therefore, the shift away from the one-pillar approach will proceed very slowly. If employees save for the Riester-Rente as recommended and these savings were to yield a constant interest rate of 4 percent, according to government estimations (Deutscher Bundestag, 2001, p. 7), the personal pension accrual would amount to no more than 10.5 percent of the combined pension benefits for a worker retiring in 2030. While the 1957 pension reform within the PAYG framework immediately produced a large improvement (see section 2.1), as a result of asymmetrical reversibility when turning to partial capital funding, the full effect of this element of PRA2001 only evolves gradually.

So far, employees have not embraced the Riester-Rente enthusiastically. After 18 months the take-up rate has remained low (about 12 percent – BMGS 2003; Dünn and Fasshauer, 2003). One has to take into account, however, that there is also the option to benefit from corresponding tax privileges when it is provided as an occupational pension. Converting parts of the salary (up to 4 percent right from the start in 2001) into savings to single employer plans or those set up by industry-wide collective agreements can be advantageous due to cost efficiency, and the individual employee has not to invest much in 'financial literacy'. Understandably, occupational pension coverage has mushroomed since 2001 (April 2001: 29 percent; March 2003: 57 percent – BMGS 2003) whereas it was comparatively low before and even on the decline for about 25 years. Moreover, outside the public sector, almost nowhere had occupational pensions been an element of collective bargaining until 2001. Within the new architecture of the German pension system, occupational pensions will change their character: up to now they were first of all an instrument of firms' human resource policy in order to recruit, motivate and tie personnel and thus *supplemented* (sufficient) first-pillar pensions. This function (and employers' financial responsibility) will fade in importance against a new role, namely to become a genuine element of social policy, providing status maintenance for a substantially larger share of employees when public pension benefits alone no longer perform that role.

Whether employees take out savings contracts for the Riester-Rente on their own or convert a part of their earnings into occupational pension plans, in any case, on a *voluntary* basis the take-up rate will remain incomplete. This will, in addition to the fact that these defined contribution type pensions contain no redistributive elements, lead to enlarged economic inequality in old age because only employees who can afford to forego present consumption will additionally provide for retirement, and only those who actually do may take advantage of the tax privileges in addition to their own savings efforts (or when they divert savings correspondingly). Thus, mainly employees with medium and high wages will benefit from the transition towards the multipillar approach (Bulmahn, 2003; Schmähl 2003). Another criticism relates to the legitimacy of contribution payments: compared with tax payments, social insurance contributions are usually less resisted because they 'earn' benefits that in most cases exceed the social assistance level by a considerable margin. If selective curtailments and the declining replacement ratio result in public pensions below or close to what one would receive as means-tested basic security anyway, from the individual perspective, contributions to the public pension scheme were paid for virtually nothing in return. Schmähl (2003), who is particularly concerned about the delegitimation of the contributory scheme, therefore favors an index-linked increase in retirement age (that entitles to full benefits) instead of lowering benefits (see Schmähl and Viebrok, 2000).

When considering the PRA2001 as a clear paradigm shift three conclusions may be highlighted. First, its central parts cannot be simply interpreted in categories of 'more' or 'less'. Rather, the term 'recalibration' (Pierson, 2001, pp. 425–426) is appropriate. The new goals assigned to the different components of old age security and the new components itself (the certified savings plans entitling to subsidies or tax privileges as well as the means-tested basic security scheme) will lead to a substantially changed public/private mix of retirement income – albeit not to an identical composition across income classes.

Second, the transition towards retirement income policy cannot be simply treated as equivalent to (partial) *privatization* or less state responsibility. Fiscal expenditure increases due to subsidies covering non-contributory benefit components within the public pension scheme.[7] Furthermore, a growing number of the elderly will claim benefits from the means-tested basic security scheme, and tax expenditures to induce voluntary savings efforts for the Riester-Rente are on the increase. At the same time efforts to (re-)regulate the non-public components of the income mix (personal pensions, occupational pensions) have to be intensified since they are no longer supplementing actually sufficient public benefits, but rather compensate for exactly the loss of their status-maintaining function.

Finally, the institutional dynamics has brought new actors, themes, conflicts and modes of conflict resolution into play, which, as yet, have not fully consolidated (Hinrichs, 2000b; Nullmeier, 2001). For example, in the *new politics* of retirement income policy those actors who occupied a more or less marginal position so far have gained a stake, as there are the various branches of the financial service industry offering the certified defined contribution schemes, the Ministry of Finance, which is involved with considerably more tax money than before, authorities regulating the emerging 'welfare market' and its products, organizations protecting consumers' interests, and the social partners in a new role as they enter collective agreements on occupational pensions. Moreover, it is foreseeable that after the interpretative hegemony of the 'old' pension policy network, rallying behind the pay-as-you-go public pension scheme and its established principles, has gone, the new retirement income policy will take place in different, partly parallel arenas with possibly more conflictuous relationships among each other and within.

4.   AFTER THE PARADIGM SHIFT

4.1.   How Could it Happen?

Bridging long time spans is a central feature of all pension systems (see section 1). An *immediate* and *substantial* reduction of public pension expenditures is thus most unlikely. Changes of pension programs aiming at such a goal usually comprise 'grandfather clauses' or provisions that cut back on entitlements are phased in. Consequently, the pension reforms enacted between 1989 and 1997 *largely* spared current pensioners and employees close to retirement age – not the least because they represent a significant group within the electorate. The PRA2001 factually implied no curtailments over and above the PRA99, but merely lower increments that are perceived differently from direct cuts (although present and future pensioners' benefits are partly decoupled from net wage development during their retirement). Moreover, by introducing the Riester-Rente the government went beyond a *synchronous* redistribution between covered employees and pensioners and the consequences arising from their shifting numerical ratio. Thereby, it enabled current employees to take an intertemporal perspective, that is, to pursue an 'investment strategy' that demands to (additionally) sacrifice consumption now for not being worse off later (than the present generation of pensioners) when a declining replacement ratio of public pensions is offset by a parallel increase of the Riester-Rente (see also Jacobs, 2002).

   In order to understand why it was mainly the Social Democrats who realized this investment strategy one has to recall the problem they faced after returning to office: successful social policy institutions perform a socializing

function when by way of their lasting and well-known operation they create
their own basis of support – a *culture of solidarity* as a fundament (Hinrichs,
2002). These formative effects largely preclude positive answers to questions
of how *could* or *should* it be different and foster expectations of stability and
continuity. Today, the existence of the public pension scheme for more than
100 years no longer generates confidence automatically, and the working of
the generational compact in the past is no guarantee for the continuance of
rules and levels in future. Official assertions that there is no reason to be afraid
of the challenges lying ahead contrast with questions by the (younger) insured
how it will go on.[8] After recurrent policy adjustments and still uncertain
prospects regarding security in old age, at the end of the 1990s, one was not
simply 'running out of options', as Lamping and Rüb (2001, p. 16) argue, but
rather, public pension policy had lost its *credibility* and the institution as such
had used up *plausibility*. Parametric reforms of the public pension scheme
have not come to an end yet and will continue in order to attain defined upper
limits of the contribution rate (see section 4.2). However, merely confining
oneself to again turning those well-known 'adjustment screws' and afterwards
declaring 'less' as more 'secure' would have been absolutely pointless for
restoring confidence. On the contrary, it had again betrayed expectations of
reliability. The situation in Germany was similar to that in Sweden where only
a fundamental reform was suitable for reconstituting credibility (Scherman,
1999, pp. 44–47). Instead of asking higher contributions to a *collective* security scheme from the insured, they were given the opportunity to put subsidized savings into pension plans that offer true *property rights* and *freedom of
choice*. Moreover, the government pointed out that public pensions plus
Riester-Rente were going to amount to a *higher* retirement income level than
at present (Deutscher Bundestag, 2001, p. 7). In this way a strategy of blame
avoidance was combined with the one of 'credit claiming' (Weaver, 1986;
Pierson, 1994, pp. 13–26).[9]

Opting for *individualistic* solutions to securing a sufficient level of
pensions in view of *individualization* as a societal 'mega-trend' clearly
matched the credo of a modernized ('New') Social Democracy that places
self-responsibility and efficiency on an equal footing with (intergenerational)
solidarity and social justice (see for example, Clasen, 2002). From numerous
similar quotations from leading Social Democrats in Germany only one may
suffice to prove the frame shift that occurred. Gabriele Behler (1999, p. 85), a
former Minister in North Rhine-Westphalia, asked the population to say
farewell to the desire for a welfare state that in a paternalistic way takes away
individual responsibility for providing against risks.

The attempt to gain *reputation* by making up for the 'forgotten' compensation of the preceding government and pushing the transition to the multipillar
approach nonetheless implied that the Social Democrats (much more than

their coalition partner, the Green Party) got involved in a very risky enterprise. This was so because several criteria for a smooth implementation of loss-imposing changes were not met and which any government should bring home to the public in a discursive manner in order to ensure acquiescence and to minimize the threat of electoral retribution (Hinrichs, 2000b; Schmidt, 2002). 1) The immediate impact of the reform package was indeed *small*, but fore-seeably growing over time. In addition, there were the phasing-in effects of all reforms prior to the PRA2001. 2) When the PRA99 was at stake the Social Democrats had outright denied its *necessity*, but proclaimed own reform plans as indispensable after the federal elections of 1998. 3) It remained contested whether the overall burdens of the PRA2001 were distributed in a *socially fair* manner and therefore satisfied established values of social policy. 4) Much emphasis was put on convincing the public that the reform meant a *coherent redesign* of the pension system in response to well-known challenges, ensuring sustainability *and* sufficient retirement income. However, the corresponding attempts have not proved very successful (Bulmahn 2003; Leinert 2003). 5) In any case, the PRA2001 was not broadly *consented* among the relevant political actors so that no blame diffusion occurred.

In view of the credibility problem and own ambitions to modernization ('strengthening self-responsibility'), the government – and that was much more the Federal Chancellery than the Ministry of Social Affairs that had been most decisive in the process of all former reforms – proved extremely capable of learning when it integrated initially vague reform conceptions and a conflicting paradigm. Although one should always be cautious towards conspiracy theories, one can hardly avoid conceding that the financial services industry (assisted by economists advocating pension funding and who had not conquered a voice in the pension policy arena until the 1990s) has successfully contributed to the destruction of confidence in the public pension scheme and, moreover, exerted substantial influence on the reform discourse. Following Peter Hall (1993, p. 290), it shows the power of interest groups to change interpretative frames. Inasmuch as the social (re-)construction of a *policy* problem and the responses it suggests was successful, the established policy network lost ground and was no longer capable of unassailably defining the problem and a solution that would match traditional goals of public pension policy.[10]

The Left among the Social Democrats ('traditionalists') could hardly be convinced to abandon the quasi-monopoly of the public pension scheme and, likewise, the trade unions only reluctantly accepted the PRA2001. Eventually, they were appeased by the stipulation that the replacement ratio must not fall below the 67 percent level (see above). The special (tax) privilege of occupational pensions also accommodated their interests since it benefits the unions' core membership and opened up an attractive terrain for collective agreements on pension funds (and for participating in their administration then). Finally, it is hard to prove whether there was a tacit deal, trading compliance with the PRA2001 for an extension of works councils' rights that was firmly demanded by the trade unions and actually legislated later in 2001.

Until the end of the parliamentary process the government attempted to win over the Christian Democrats for a consensus. In principle, the party supported the system shift, but continuously caviled at the concrete form. Eventually, it shied away from thwarting the Riester-Rente in the Bundesrat, which had to agree on this element of the PRA2001. Utilizing their majority in the Bundesrat would have meant that the CDU/CSU had denied future pensioners the chances to attain a higher retirement income. Despite considerable concessions to the CDU/CSU (particularly on family-related benefits) it refused an overall compromise with the government. One reason may be lasting disgruntlement about the SPD's successful strategy to blame the Kohl government for the pension cuts during the 1998 election campaign. More important was that the Christian Democrats were very much on the defensive after a financial scandal (about 'soft money' and other unlawful deeds) was uncovered in November 1999. In such a situation it was hardly opportune to simply give away a potentially mobilizing theme for the next election campaign by striking an agreement with the political opponent. Thus, the government learned that in order to reach a compromise it needed a strong negotiating party on the other side of the table.

Paradigm shift in a policy area does not imply that basic programmatic structures are completely thrown out. Central elements of the German pension scheme, like employment-relatedness or contribution financing, have been maintained ever since 1889 as it is also true for countries that realized an alternative starting point (based on citizenship) for their pension system. Nor is it required that, in order to claim a paradigm shift, all political actors involved have already adopted the new interpretative frame in full. Finally, such a claim may be made even if the impact of the corresponding policy changes has not yet fully materialized. Substantiating the path departure as being irreversible would suffice, and such further drifting away from the one-pillar approach will be shown next.

4.2. How Will It Go On?

Contrary to expectations in 2001, the contribution rate had to be increased to 19.5 percent in 2003, and a rise to 20.4 percent already in 2004 would have been inevitable without emergency measures. Such development was caused by a declining employment level and was partly self-inflicted due to reduced fictitious contributions on behalf of unemployment assistance recipients and revenue losses as a growing number of workers converted parts of their earnings into occupational pension plans (see also Schmähl, 2003). Moreover, the long-run targets fixed in the PRA2001 are in jeopardy as well: projections included in the report of the so-called Rürup-Kommission (Kommission, 2003, p. 101) arrive at a rate of 21.5 percent in 2020 and of 24.2 percent in 2030. They are based on less optimistic assumptions than the government employed in its calculations when the PRA2001 was prepared. The commission's central proposals to nonetheless achieve the 20/22 percent target are 1) gradually increasing the age at which 'full benefits' can be claimed from 65 to 67 (starting in 2011) and 2) including a 'sustainability factor' in the benefit (adjustment) formula. By this factor the changing *worker/pensioner ratio* will determine the replacement rate of newly and already retired persons (whereas the demographic factor of the PRA99 took into account further life expectancy at age 65). A variable factor will adjust the weight of this standardized dependency ratio so that sustainability is ensured, that is, the 20/22 percent target is always met.

In view of the unpleasant prospects in the short as well as long run, the government disregarded the doctrine to reform the pension system only occasionally. In 2003 it came forward with two reform packages and a third one that will translate the Constitutional Court's demand for equal tax treatment of all retirement income recipients. The emergency package that will ensure a contribution rate at the 2003 level has already passed parliament. It includes a suspension of benefit adjustment in 2004, and the pension scheme as the 'quasi-employer' will no longer pay half of the contributions to the long-term care insurance, so that pensioners have to bear the full rate (1.7 percent). Beside this understandably unpopular benefit cut there will be a further (temporary) reduction of the scheme's contingency reserve and some minor changes.

In its second reform package the government has adopted all proposals of the Rürup-Kommission with the only exception that the decision on whether to raise retirement age will be postponed until 2008 when the labor market situation might have improved. Moreover, the reform bill provides for a complete abolition of non-contributory pension credits for periods spent in school or university education (and which had been reduced to a maximum of three years already).

In 2002, the Constitutional Court has again (see note 9) proved to be a powerful veto player in German pension politics when it ruled the unequal treatment of civil servants (whose pensions are fully taxable) and beneficiaries of the public pension scheme unconstitutional. Hitherto, white- and blue-collar workers pay contributions largely out of post-tax income, and the accruing benefit is regularly tax-free if the retiree has no substantial income (like occupational pensions) in addition. Beside provisions that will simplify the Riester-Rente, but not making it mandatory, the third reform package aims at realizing the 'EET principle', that is, up to a certain limit contributions to public as well as private pension plans are *exempted* from taxation as are the funds' earnings, but benefits paid are liable to income *taxation*. Due to the tax revenue losses it implies (and which can only be recouped later) such a transition has to occur gradually and therefore will last from 2005 until 2040.

The government argues that the increasing tax relief will enlarge the scope for additional pension savings (but obviously most for employees with higher earnings). Those savings become all the more necessary since the sustainability factor will aggravate the decrease of the benefit level. While the Riester-Rente more or less filled the 'social protection gap' that had arisen (see above), it is created again when the *gross* replacement ratio[11] for the standard pensioner declines from, currently, 48 to 40 percent in 2030 (Kommission, 2003, p. 107), that is, by one-sixth (if he or she does not earn extra pension credits by working beyond age 65). It has been estimated (Schnabel 2003, p. 13) that an average employee who is going to retire in 2030 *should* have started already in 2000 to save 7 percent of his or her income in order to end up with the same disposable income as present cohorts of pensioners. These figures point to a problem of savings incentives for voluntary (tax-privileged) pension plans (Disney, 2000): if the emerging income security gap appears to be small no such savings are deemed necessary. In contrast, if the gap is large individual efforts are likewise discouraged because, in view of one's disposable income, it seems hopeless (or no longer worthwhile) to strive for adequate retirement income. In view of the standard replacement ratio having further declined (below the minimum level stipulated in the PRA2001 will be abolished), even the Council of Economic Advisers, ideologically most committed to market liberalism, is concerned about incalculable public pensions and the legitimacy of the contributory scheme (Sachverständigenrat, 2003, sections 346, 348 and 353).

Have these reform plans caused conflicts among relevant political actors? Obviously, there is less resistance than when the PRA2001 was at stake because the dominance of political parties has been strengthened, particularly as against organized labor. The Christian Democrats have appointed their own commission chaired by the former Federal President Roman Herzog (Christlich Demokratische Union Deutschlands, 2003). Its proposals *largely* overlap with the government's plan and also include an identical sustainability factor (BMGS, 2003). It remains to be seen whether there will be a return to an inter-party pension consensus this time. However, apart from the largely 'technical' taxation package, the government is not dependent on approval by the Bundesrat. The trade unions that had forced the government to moderate the PRA2001 are in a weak position after the Metal Union, the usual spearhead, has lost a labor dispute on working hours reduction in East Germany in May 2003 and, moreover, the trade unions were unable to massively mobilize against *Agenda 2010*, a comprehensive program for a far-reaching overhaul of the German welfare state and of which the current pension reform is an element. Likewise, the Left among the Social Democrats fought in vain against *Agenda 2010*. At an extra-party congress convened at their initiative in June 2003 they were clearly defeated. Therefore, in early 2004 it seems most likely that the second and third package of the current reform will pass without major changes whereas it is hardly foreseeable how the electorate will respond to the retrenchments that are not confined to pensions, but affect other areas of social policy as well.

5. CONCLUSION: PENSIONS STILL FROZEN?

In comparative welfare state research, explaining obvious institutional resilience against varied pressures and path-dependent development as the dominant pattern, have become central topics. Since Pierson's (1994) seminal work institutionalist approaches prevail, not the least, because quantitative methods are hardly capable of proving or disproving notions of a ' "frozen" welfare state landscape' argument (Esping-Andersen, 1996, p. 24). Predominantly, case studies on single welfare states or cross-country comparisons of certain programs are useful to show whether there are changes 'beyond incrementalism' (Wiesenthal, 2003) and, if so, why. In view of major reforms that occurred at accelerating speed during the 1990s and when welfare states became increasingly 'defrosted' (Palier, 2000), discontent with deterministic notions of almost static institutions has engendered concepts of large, path-breaking changes or 'path creation' and how they came about (Crouch and Farrell, 2002). Starting from the premise that 'history matters', institutionalist approaches are not necessarily tied to a strict path-dependence theorem although they can more easily explain immobility and inertia than fundamental policy changes. If the latter are not a priori denied, 'critical junctures' are important when during periods of reorientation different routes are conceivable and the course for future development is set.

At the end of the 1990s, Germany's public pension policy had reached such a critical juncture. Despite the difficulties of defining and, subsequently, measuring whether a policy change is incremental or paradigmatic, particularly in the pension area (Hinrichs, 2000a; Hinrichs and Kangas, 2003), clearly a change of the latter type happened in 2001 and that will be reinforced in 2004. It has been demonstrated that a once 'coherent policy paradigm' (Hall, 1993, p. 290) concentrating on truly earnings-replacing public pensions has been shaken and was replaced with a multipillar approach. The current reform legislation will further enforce this transition as the 'hard budget line', following that the shift towards a 'fixed contribution rate' principle has maintained absolute priority. It supersedes the alternative of a 'fixed relative position' (Myles, 2002, pp. 140–145), the core of the PRA92, when the financial consequences of aging should be shared between pensioners (constant ratio of net earnings), the insured (somewhat higher contributions) and the state (increased subsidies out of general revenues).

Nevertheless, it is remarkable that the paradigmatic shift from public pension policy towards retirement income policy occurred within a short period of time and concerned a policy domain prototypical for path-dependent development (Pierson, 1994; Haverland, 2001). Theoretically assumed 'lock-in effects' of a mature pay-as-you-go scheme obviously dissolve with accelerating speed and contradict notions of a most immovable object. It is furthermore astonishing that the break with institutional inheritance happened in a country that is characterized by lacking power concentration and numerous veto players. Finally, one would hardly expect it to be the Social Democratic party that departed from an established welfare state consensus and the routine of incremental adjustments as a technology of preserving social policy institutions, and instead realizing an almost bottomless decline of benefit levels and pushing self-responsibility as a dogma.

NOTES

1. Whatever extreme assumptions about an increased participation rate of women and higher net migration are made, the potential labor force in Germany will definitely start to decline after 2010. According to the most realistic scenario, between 2010 and 2040 it is going to decrease from 40.5 to 29.9 million persons – about 25 percent (Fuchs and Thon, 1999).
2. Nowadays, the 'public pension scheme' compulsorily covers all white-collar and blue-collar workers above a certain earnings threshold and, additionally, the artisans (other self-employed may join voluntarily). Civil servants (nearly 6 percent of all employed persons) are provided for through a uniform, tax-financed program without own contributions. Farmers are included in a special scheme, and the professionals (doctors, lawyers etc.) have to join nonpublic pension funds.
3. The 'target' or 'standard replacement ratio' is defined as net benefit level for a fictitious pensioner after spending 45 years in covered employment and constantly receiving an average wage as percentage of former net earnings.
4. It almost looks as if Peter Hall (1993, p. 291) has had in mind the German public pension scheme when he argued that '(policy) paradigms are most likely to be found in fields where policymaking involves some highly technical issues and a body of specialized knowledge pertaining to them (and) . . . are likely to have greatest impact in institutional settings where policy is superintended by experts or by administrators with long tenures in office'.
5. The influence of the pension and health care issue on the election result cannot be ascertained exactly. However, exit polls show that the SPD gained disproportionately among voters of retirement age (60 years and older) or approaching retirement (between 45 and 59 years of age), which in turn are the age groups where the decline for the CDU/CSU was largest. In particular, elderly women, traditionally its most loyal followers, turned away from the CDU/CSU. Moreover, there is a further indicator demonstrating the salience of the pension issue at the 1998 federal elections: compared with other themes it ranked high among the electorate, and the Social Democrats were believed capable of 'securing pensions' much more frequently than the Christian Democrats (Emmert et al., 2001).

6. Lamping and Rüb (2001, pp. 20–21) accurately speak of 'experimental lawmaking' to characterize the way the government pushed ahead the reform process. For a chronology of the course of events see Dünn and Fasshauer, 2001.
7. Nowadays about 33 percent of scheme's expenditure stem from tax revenues (Sachverständigenrat, 2003, pp. 216–17).
8. The long-standing Minister of Social Affairs, Norbert Blüm (1982 to 1998), again and again maintained that public pensions are secure (*'Die Rente ist sicher!'*). Increasingly, the public cynically interpreted this message as a joke.
9. The only benefit improvements included in the PRA2001 again concerns persons who raised children (see Figure 3.1). That development started in 1986 and, subsequently, it was strongly pushed by several rulings of the Federal Constitutional Court demanding to compensate families raising (or having raised) children for the positive externalities they produce. Due to its far-reaching rights to actually stipulate concrete legislative action, the Court has become a major actor in this policy domain when it comes to family-related benefits like child-care credits. By another judgement in 2002 regarding the taxation of (public) pension benefits the Court has again obliged the legislator to take action (see section 4.2).
10. An indicator of the approaching change of course was that Walter Riester, Deputy President of the Metal Union and renowned as a modernizer, was appointed Minister of Social Affairs instead of Rudolf Dreßler, a dyed-in-the-wool protagonist of the social insurance approach and experienced social policy spokesperson of the Social Democrats in the Bundestag. The intention of the government to execute the transition towards retirement income policy also became obvious when in 2000 the long-standing Chairperson of the Advisory Council (Sozialbeirat), Winfried Schmähl, was not reappointed, but rather replaced with the more 'flexible' multi-purpose advisor Bert Rürup, also a Professor of Public Finance.
11. Due to the change in taxing pension benefits, net figures (see note 3) can no more be applied.

REFERENCES

Alber, Jens (1989), *Der Sozialstaat in der Bundesrepublik 1950–1983*, Frankfurt and New York: Campus.
Bach, Stefan, Bernhard Seidel and Dieter Teichmann (2002), 'Entwicklung der Steuersysteme im internationalen Vergleich', *DIW-Wochenbericht*, **69**, 657–668.
Behler, Gabriele (1999), 'Für eine neue Sozialstaatlichkeit. Individuelle und gesellschaftliche Verantwortung zusammenführen', in Ulrich von Alemann, Rolf G. Heinze and Ulrich Wehrhöfer (eds), *Bürgergesellschaft und Gemeinwohl*, Opladen: Leske + Budrich, 83–92.
BMAS (2002) (Bundesministerium für Arbeit und Sozialordnung) (ed.), *Materialband zum Sozialbudget 2001*, Bonn: BMAS.
BMGS (2003) (Bundesministerium für Gesundheit und Soziale Sicherung), *Informationen zur Weiterentwicklung der Rentenreform des Jahres 2001 und zur Stabilisierung des Beitragssatzes in der Gesetzlichen Rentenversicherung*, Berlin: BMGS.
Bonoli, Giuliano, Vic George and Peter Taylor-Gooby (2000), *European Welfare Futures: Towards a Theory of Retrenchment*, Cambridge: Polity Press.
Bulmahn, Thomas (2003), 'Zur Entwicklung der privaten Altersvorsorge. Vorsorgebereitschaft, Vorsorgeniveau und erwartete Absicherung im Alter', *Kölner Zeitschrift für Soziologie und Sozialpsychologie*, **55**, 29–54.
Bundesregierung (2000), *Entwurf eines Gesetzes zur Reform der gesetzlichen Rentenversicherung und zur Förderung eines kapitalgedeckten Alters vorsorge vermögens (Altersvermögensgesetz – AVmG)*, Berlin: Deutscher Bundestag, Drucksache 14/4595.

Christlich Demokratische Union Deutschlands (2003), *Bericht der Kommission 'Soziale Sicherheit' zur Reform der sozialen Sicherungssysteme*, Berlin: CDU.

Clasen, Jochen (2002), 'Modern social democracy and European welfare state reform', *Social Policy and Society*, **1**, 67–76.

Conrad, Christoph (1998), 'Alterssicherung', in Hans Günter Hockerts (ed.), *Drei Wege deutscher Sozialstaatlichkeit*, Munich: Oldenbourg, 101–116.

Crouch, Colin and Henry Farrell (2002), *Breaking the Path of Institutional Development? Alternatives to the New Determinism*, Max-Planck-Institut für Gesellschaftsforschung, MPIfG Discussion Paper 02/5, Cologne.

Deutscher Bundestag (1997), *Plenarprotokoll 13/185 vom 27. Juni 1997*, Bonn.

Deutscher Bundestag (2001), *Beschlussempfehlung des Ausschusses für Arbeit und Sozialordnung (11. Ausschuss)* [zu Drucksachen 14/4595 und 14/5068], Berlin: Deutscher Bundestag, Drucksache 14/5146.

Deutscher Bundestag (2002), *Schlussbericht der Enquête-Kommission 'Demographischer Wandel – Herausforderungen unserer älter werdenden Gesellschaft an den Einzelnen und die Politik'*, Berlin: Referat Öffentlichkeitsarbeit, Reihe 'Zur Sache' 3/2002.

Disney, Richard (2000), 'Declining public pensions in an era of demographic ageing: Will private provision fill the gap?', *European Economic Review*, **44**, 957–973.

Döring, Diether (2000), 'Grundlinien der langfristigen Systementwicklung der gesetzlichen Rentenversicherung', in Stefan Fisch and Ulrike Haerendel (eds), *Geschichte und Gegenwart der Rentenversicherung in Deutschland*, Berlin: Duncker & Humblot, 169–187.

Dünn, Sylvia and Stephan Fasshauer (2001), 'Die Rentenreform 2000/2001 – Ein Rückblick', *Deutsche Rentenversicherung*, **56**, 266–275.

Dünn, Sylvia and Stephan Fasshauer (2003), 'Ein Jahr Riesterrente – eine Übersicht aus Sicht der gesetzlichen Rentenversicherung', *Deutsche Rentenversicherung*, **58**, 1–12.

Emmert, Thomas, Matthias Jung and Dieter Roth (2001), 'Das Ende einer Ära – Die Bundestagswahl vom 27 September 1998', in Hans-Dieter Klingemann and Max Kaase (eds), *Wahlen und Wähler. Analysen aus Anlass der Bundestagswahl 1998*, Wiesbaden: Westdeutscher Verlag, 17–56.

Esping-Andersen, Gøsta (1996), 'After the Golden Age? Welfare state dilemmas in a global economy', in Gøsta Esping-Andersen (ed.), *Welfare States in Transition: National Adaptations in Global Economies*, London: Sage, 1–31.

Esping-Andersen, Gøsta and Sebastian Sarasa (2002), 'The generational conflict reconsidered', *Journal of European Social Policy*, **12**, 5–21.

Fuchs, Johann and Manfred Thon (1999), *Nach 2010 sinkt das Angebot an Arbeitskräften*, Nuremberg: Institut für Arbeitsmarkt und Berufsforschung, IABKurzbericht, Nr. 4 (v. 20.05.1999).

Hall, Peter A. (1993), 'Policy paradigms, social learning, and the state', *Comparative Politics*, **25**, 275–296.

Haverland, Markus (2001) 'Another Dutch miracle? Explaining Dutch and German pension trajectories', *Journal of European Social Policy*, **11**, 308–323.

Hinrichs, Karl (1998), *Reforming the Public Pension Scheme in Germany: The End of the Traditional Consensus?*, Bremen: Universität Bremen, Zentrum für Sozialpolitik, ZeS-Arbeitspapier Nr. 11/98.

Hinrichs, Karl (2000a), 'Elephants on the move: Patterns of public pension reform in OECD countries', *European Review*, **8**, 353–378.

Hinrichs, Karl (2000b), 'Auf dem Weg zur Alterssicherungspolitik – Reformperspektiven in der gesetzlichen Rentenversicherung', in Stephan Leibfried and Uwe Wagschal (eds), *Der deutsche Sozialstaat*, Frankfurt and New York: Campus, 276–305.

Hinrichs, Karl (2002), 'Health care policy in the German social insurance state: From solidarity to privatization?', *The Review of Policy Research*, **19** (3), 108–140.

Hinrichs, Karl and Olli Kangas (2003), 'When is a change big enough to be a system shift? Small system-shifting changes in German and Finnish pension policies', *Social Policy & Administration*, **37**, 573–591.

Jacobs, Alan M. (2002), 'Making tradeoffs over time: Retrenchment, investment, and the reform of pension systems', Paper prepared for delivery at the 2002 Annual Meeting of the American Political Science Association, Boston, 29 August–1 September 2002, Cambridge, MA (mimeo).

Kommission Nachhaltigkeit in der Finanzierung der Sozialen Sicherungssysteme (2003), *Bericht der Kommission*, Berlin: Bundesministerium für Gesundheit und Soziale Sicherung.

Lamping, Wolfram and Friedbert W. Rüb (2001), *From the Conservative Welfare State to 'Something Uncertain Else': German Pension Politics in Comparative Perspective*, Hannover: University of Hannover, Centre for Social and Public Policy, Discussion Paper No. 12.

Leinert, Johannes (2003), *Altersvorsorge 2003: Wer hat sie, wer will sie? Private und betriebliche Altersvorsorge der 30- bis 50-Jährigen in Deutschland*, Vorsorgestudien 18, Gütersloh: Bertelsmann Stiftung.

Lynch, Julia (2001), 'The age-orientation of social policy regimes in OECD countries', *Journal of Social Policy*, **30**, 411–436.

Mätzke, Margitta (2002), 'Conservative innovation: The development of Germany's social insurance system in the decade after WWII', Paper prepared for delivery at the 2002 Annual Meeting of the American Political Science Association, Boston, 29 August–1 September 2002, Evanston, IL (mimeo).

Michaelis, K. and R. Thiede (2000), 'Reform der gesetzlichen Rentenversicherung: Zwischen Kontinuität and Paradigmenwechsel, Die Angestellten Versicherung, **42** (12), 1–11.

Myles, John (2002), 'A new social contract for the elderly?', in Gøsta Esping-Andersen, Duncan Gallie, Anton Hemerijck and John Myles, *Why We Need a New Welfare State*, Oxford: Oxford University Press, 130–172.

Nullmeier, Frank (2001), 'Sozialpolitik als marktregulative Politik', *Zeitschrift für Sozialreform*, **47**, 645–667.

Palier, Bruno (2000), ' "Defrosting" the French Welfare State', *West European Politics*, **23** (2), 113–136.

Pierson, Paul (1994), *Dismantling the Welfare State? Reagan, Thatcher and the Politics of Retrenchment*, Cambridge: Cambridge University Press.

Pierson, Paul (2001), 'Coping with permanent austerity: Welfare state restructuring in affluent democracies', in Paul Pierson (ed.), *The New Politics of the Welfare State*, Oxford: Oxford University Press, 410–456.

PROGNOS (1999), *Versorgungslücken in der Alterssicherung: Privater Vorsorgebedarf für den Schutz im Alter, bei Erwerbsminderung und im Hinterbliebenenfall*, Gutachten im Auftrag des Gesamtverbandes der Deutschen Versicherungswirtschaft e.V., Basel: PROGNOS AG.

Sachverständigenrat zur Begutachtung der gesamtwirtschaftlichen Entwicklung (2003), *Staatsfinanzen konsolidieren – Steuersystem reformieren. Jahresgutachten 2003/04*, Stuttgart: Metzler-Poeschel.

Scherman, Karl Gustaf (1999), *The Swedish Pension Reform*, International Labour Office, Social Security Department, Issues in Social Protection, Discussion Paper No. 7, Geneva: ILO.

Schmähl, Winfried (1993), 'The "1992 Reform" of public pensions in Germany: Main elements and some effects', *Journal of European Social Policy*, **3**, 39–51.

Schmähl, Winfried (2003), 'Wem nutzt die Rentenreform? – Offene und versteckte Verteilungseffekte des Umstiegs zu mehr privater Altersvorsorge', *Die Angestelltenversicherung*, **50**, 349–363.

Schmähl, Winfried and Holger Viebrok (2000), 'Adjusting pay-as-you-go financed pension schemes to increasing life expectancy', *Schmollers Jahrbuch*, **120**, 41–61.

Schmidt, Vivien A. (2002), 'Does discourse matter in the politics of welfare state adjustment?', *Comparative Political Studies*, **35**, 168–193.

Schnabel, Reinhold (2003), *Die neue Rentenreform: Die Nettorenten sinken*, Cologne: Deutsches Institut für Altersvorsorge.

Sozialbeirat (1998), 'Gutachten des Sozialbeirats', in Bundesregierung, *Rentenversicherungsbericht 1998*, Bonn: Deutscher Bundestag, Drucksache 13/11290, 239–251.

Statistisches Bundesamt (ed.) (2003), *Bevölkerung Deutschlands bis 2050. 10. koordinierte Bevölkerungsvorausberechnung*, Wiesbaden: Presseexemplar.

Titmuss, Richard M. (1976), 'Pension systems and population change', in Richard M. Titmuss, *Essays on 'The Welfare State'*, 3rd edn, London: George Allen & Unwin Ltd., 56–74.

van Kersbergen, Kees (2000), 'The declining resistance of welfare states to change?', in Stein Kuhnle (ed.), *The Survival of the European Welfare State*, London and New York: Routledge, 19–36.

VDR (2003) (Verband Deutscher Rentenversicherungsträger) (ed.), *Rentenversicherung in Zeitreihen. Ausgabe 2003*, DRV-Schriften 22, Frankfurt am Main: Verband Deutscher Rentenversicherungsträger.

Weaver, R. Kent (1986), 'The politics of blame avoidance', *Journal of Public Policy*, **6**, 371–398.

Wiesenthal, Helmut (2003), 'Beyond incrementalism – Sozialpolitische Basisinnovationen im Lichte der politiktheoretischen Skepsis', in Renate Mayntz and Wolfgang Streeck (eds), *Die Reformierbarkeit der Demokratie*, Frankfurt and New York: Campus, 31–70.

4. The politics of pension reform in France: The end of exceptionalism?

Christelle Mandin and Bruno Palier

INTRODUCTION

For long, France appeared as the extreme example of a country where welfare reforms, and especially pension reforms, seemed almost impossible. In spite of the fact that demographic trends were known since the mid-1980s, one had to wait until 1993 to see a first (partial) reform. The failed attempt of the Juppé reform to complete the process in 1995 is well known, as is the fact of millions of people demonstrating against this reform and blocking France for almost one month in order to (successfully) prevent its implementation. One had to wait another seven years before a new reform was attempted and achieved.

One should refer to the framework of the French pension system to understand why it was so hard to change. The French pension system is typical of continental welfare states, which are qualified as conservative and corporatist by Esping-Andersen (1990). This system is primarily funded by social contributions paid by employers and employees and is managed by administrative boards composed of their representatives. Partly due to their role within the system, trade unions may be considered as strong veto players (Tsebelis, 1995) in the process of reform, as they appear to represent the French population's attachment to its pension system. Indeed, French people contribute during their working life to obtain a generous pension, which represents on average 70 percent of their previous earnings, and are strongly attached to pensions that they consider as a 'deferred wage'. Generous benefits, management by the social partners and not by the state, corporatist fragmentation of the system, all these characteristics explain the difficulty of reforming the French pension system, although the financial consequences of population aging and the financing of the future pensions could justify a structural reform.

However, a comprehensive overview of recent trends in the politics of pension in France shows that things are now rapidly changing, and leading France along the same way as other major European countries. In ten years, two main reforms have been adopted: in 1993 and in 2003. In parallel, a gradual development of pension funds has been organized. Pension funds have become more and more accepted by French citizens and by traditional actors in the pension area, and in practice more opportunities are offered to the French population for complementing their future pension with savings and funded schemes. Finally, even more recently, the French traditional use of early retirement is being reversed, and more and more policies aimed at increasing the employment rate of the 'senior' are implemented.

On the whole, pension reforms in France are thus increasingly following the line defined at the European level, controlling public pension expenditure, developing funded schemes and implementing active aging policies. In this chapter, we will start with the presentation of the French pension system. Its features are crucial in order to understand the specific French politics of pension. Second, we will analyze how retrenchment policies have progressively and chaotically developed from 1993 to 2003, in a succession of procrastination, reports, debate, demonstration, negotiation and reforms. Third, we will show how a consensus on the development of pension funds in France has occurred and is starting to lead to the development of complementary funded schemes. Finally, we will refer to the most recent (and still limited) attempt to develop active aging in France.

THE FRENCH PENSION SYSTEM

The French social security plan of 1945 defined the structure of the current pension system. The plan created a basic pension scheme, called the 'general regime' (*le régime général*), covering private sector employees, with the aim of expanding coverage to the whole population in the following years. While the first goal of the social security plan was to implement the Beveridgian principles of unity and universality, the founders had to cope with the existing institutions. Indeed, different pension schemes were founded before World War II but were very fragmented and did not cover the whole population. The law of 1930 asserted the compulsory character of social insurance but the choice of the insurance organization remained free. Most of the workers were covered by employers' institutions and the state created a specific regime for its employees. The French plan of 1945 has been obliged to keep part of this legacy, and appeared to be an institutional compromise, which meant to achieve the universality principles of Beveridge with Bismarckian insurance means (Palier, 2002). The French pension system clearly reflects the logic of insurance, with the centrality of the principle of work: social security benefits are provided to 'workers and their families', benefits are related to wages and financed through contributions paid by employees and employers. The representatives of workers and employers are in charge of the management of the system that is supposed to be relatively independent from the state (especially in the case of complementary pension schemes). The French pension system is almost exclusively based on compulsory social insurance, which operates on a pay-as-you-go basis. This choice can also be explained for historical reasons, because the previous pension system, created in the 19th century, was based on capital-funded arrangements and had undergone financial difficulties in the 1920s, in the 1930s and during World War II due to monetary and financial crises. In 1945, the pay-as-you-go method appeared as a more secure way of financing pensions.

Despite the will of unity of the system, the founders also had to face the opposition of different social and occupational groups (public sector employees, farmers, self-employed etc.), who wanted to preserve the advantages of their own systems founded before 1945, and called for autonomous schemes. Consequently, in spite of a movement towards greater harmonization between pension schemes in the 1970s, there are still more than 100 different schemes for the first pillar of the French pension system, and thousands for the second pillar. Today, almost all the French population is covered, but this generalization has been achieved through juxtaposition and addition of particular occupational schemes. Besides the general regime, which covers two-thirds of the working population, there are numerous autonomous regimes, which cover civil servants and employees (EDG-GDF (electricity and gas), RATP (Paris metro), and SNCF (national railways), and specific occupational groups (self-employed, farmers and farm workers etc.).

The French pension system in *le régime général* is composed of two main tiers: the first tier concerns the legally mandatory base pension regimes that propose a basic benefit level (a maximum of 50 percent of a reference wage, calculated over the 25 best years for those covered by the general regime). The second tier is made up of complementary pension systems, which also operate on a PAYG basis. Two main schemes provide complementary benefits for the private sector employees: AGIRC for managers and ARRCO for employees. Other complementary pension regimes are organized by economic sectors (agriculture, commerce, industry etc.) as well as by job type. While the general regime is based on defined benefits, the complementary regimes are based on defined contributions. Employees receive points in return for contributions. The social partners regularly decide the value of these points on the basis of economic and demographic conditions; the number of points acquired during the working life and the value of one point at retirement determines the final pension.

The French pension system also includes other arrangements that play only a marginal role. For those who did not pay sufficient contributions, there is an old age assistance system (the 'old age minimum': *minimum vieillesse*), which was created in 1956. This scheme provides benefits that are not related to work but to residence and guarantees minimum income benefits to all French residents aged 65 and over. The old age minimum answered a great need, when introduced, it covered 60 percent of the retired population. Today, the assistance system plays a marginal role, and the number of beneficiaries is regularly decreasing: 1.2 million people are receiving this benefit, as compared to 2.9 million in 1970 (Sterdyniak et al., 1999).

In the 1970s and the 1980s, a period that has been described as a 'golden age of pensions', the expansion of the pension system took the form of a progressive improvement of the generosity of benefits. The 'Boulin law' in 1971 extended the required contribution period entitling to a full rate pension (from 120 to 150 three-month periods), but also seated the calculation of the reference wage on the best ten years of wage (instead of the last ten years) and raised the full rate pension from 40 to 50 percent of the reference wage. The law of 1973 did away with the minimum contribution period of 15 years and took into account inactive periods for the calculation of the pension benefits. The progression of pension benefits has also been increased by the favorable indexation of pension entitlements. Until the early 1980s, the annual adjustment of pension benefit levels was based on gross wage growth, generally the most generous indexation method.

FROM THE BALLADUR TO THE FILLON REFORM

In the 1980s, pensions became an important challenge in France. A series of reports denounced the evolution of the demographic ratio and proposed plans of reforms.[1] The projections showed that if the goal was to preserve a balanced pension system in 2025, it was necessary either to increase contributions by 170 percent or reduce benefits by 50 percent (Ruellan, 1993). The reports also underlined the necessity to change the calculation formula in order to preserve the financial sustainability of the pension system. They proposed the following options: to increase the required period of contributions to obtain the right to a full pension; to change the reference wages for the calculation of the pension amount; or to change the mode of indexation.[2]

All these reports were similar concerning the demographic diagnostic and the solutions. However, no reform was adopted during the 1980s and early 1990s, in spite of the fact that the general regime was constantly showing a deficit and projections were especially pessimistic. Faced with these difficulties, but fearing unpopularity and trade unions' opposition to reforms, successive governments preferred to postpone the implementation of the reforms proposed in the different reports and reproduced the traditional recipes that entail less political risk: increasing social contribution instead of cutting benefits. Between 1985 and 1991, the employee's contribution to the old age insurance funds increased from 4.7 to 6.55 percent of earnings.

The Balladur Reform

In March 1993, a political window of opportunity opened up the pension debate. After the legislative elections, which gave a strong majority to the center-right coalition UDF-RPR in a context where the situation of social security seemed catastrophic, the Balladur government adopted a reform that implemented the propositions of the past reports. This had become possible thanks to concessions of the government to the trade unions. Between April and June 1993 the government met the social partners and explained its project. The government tried to obtain the support of CFDT[3] and the neutrality of other trade unions (Bonoli, 1997). The reform proposed to reduce benefits but was limited to the private sector's employees (*régime général*) and didn't concern the civil servants (*régimes spéciaux*), although their pension schemes were more generous (but where the trade unions were more present and the employees better prepared to resist).

The 1993 reform changed the calculation formula and the indexation method of pensions. Since this reform, the level of pension has been calculated with reference to the wages of the best 25 years (before it was the best ten years). To receive a full pension (50 percent of the reference wage under the ceiling of the social security equal to 2352 euros in January 2002), employees need to have contributed for 40 years, instead of 37.5 years before the reform. The measure has been gradually carried out and the process will be achieved in 2004. Furthermore, the indexation of pensions is officially not based on gross wages any more but on consumer price inflation. This proposition was adopted in 1993 for five years, but has been extended by the Jospin government. This reform stressed the link between contributions and benefits, like other reforms introduced in Bismarckian pension systems, and will result in a reduction in the replacement rate of pensions under the general regime (from 50 percent to 33 percent of the reference salary by 2020, according to Babeau, 1997).

In order to convince trade unions and to reach a consensus, the government proposed another reform, which separated the expenses that can be associated with social insurance (contributory benefits) and those linked to social assistance. A *Fonds de Solidarité Vieillesse* (FSV – old age mutual aid fund) was created in order to finance non-contributory benefits for retirees who had made insufficient contributions to the system during their working lives (*minimum vieillesse*, means-tested benefits). The FSV is financed by a 1.3 percent increase in the rate of CSG (*Contribution Sociale Généralisée*, a new tax created in 1990). These benefits no longer represented a financial liability for the social insurance budget. The creation of the FSV was a response to one of the main demands of trade unions, who argued that the state should pay for the non-contributory benefits, and not old age insurance funds. Although the change of the calculation formula was accepted only by CNPF (main employers' organization at that time), CFDT and CFTC,[4] the creation of the FSV was supported by all the confederations, except CGT[5] (Bonoli, 1997). After this negotiation, the government carried out this reform, announced in August 1993, during the holiday period. Only CGT and FO[6] officially protested against this reform, without organizing any demonstration of employees.

The social partners also adjusted the system of the obligatory supplementary pensions (AGIRC and ARCCO) in 1993 and 1994, using a classical method: they raised the level of the social contributions and diminished the rate of replacement by indexing the indexation of pensions on inflation and no more on gross wages. In 1996, the employers' organization refused to increase the contribution rate further, and a new agreement was adopted to diminish the replacement rate by about 25 percent.[7] This last agreement also meant a sharp decrease in the level of complementary pension of the people working in the private sector. So far, the public sector remained untouched.

The Juppé Plan

As he tried to extend the reform to the public sector employees, Alain Juppé was not as cautious as Edouard Balladur, which may explain the failure of his 1995 reform initiative. The reform elaborated by Edouard Balladur and Simone Veil concerned only the private sector's pension schemes, and was not extended to the the public sector's employees (SNCF, RATP, EDF-GDF, etc.), where the rate of unionization is highest and where pensions are most generous. In a plan presented on 15 November 1995, Alain Juppé announced the reform of these specific regimes. He wished to extend the rules for calculating pensions from the private systems to the public ones, and especially to increase the contribution period for a full pension from 37.5 to 40 years. Alain Juppé thought he had enough political support from the right-wing majority: the presidency, parliament and the senate were all dominated by the right-wing majority and the next elections were programmed three years later. Because he feared that negotiations with the social partners would water down the reform, he chose to prepare his social security reform in secret. Reactions of the trade unions came quickly. On 23 November, the public sector's employees decided to go on strike (SNCF, RATP etc.). Massive strikes developed until 22 December 1995, and this social protest became one of the biggest that France had ever seen in recent years.

Given the extent of the strikes, which were also focused on a plan to restructure SNCF, the government withdrew its pension reform plan. The formula for public pensions remained unchanged: public sector employees still had to contribute 37.5 years to be entitled to a full pension and the amount is calculated win reference to earnings during the last six months of the career. Public pension schemes continued to provide 75 percent of the salary.

In comparison, some projections showed that the basic private employees' pension scheme would in 20 years guarantee only 33 percent of the last wages, compared with 50 percent today. With the extension to 40 years of the period of contribution, many employees would have to work after 60, which seems unrealistic given current labor market trends. The reform therefore will most likely result in lower pensions (Babeau, 1997). Less pessimistic, the Conseil d'Orientation des Retraites, created in 2000 in order to consult the social partners and to prepare the next reform, declared in its report of December 2001 that the rate of replacement will decline from 78 percent today to 64 percent in 2040 (COR, 2002).

The Wait-and-See Policy of Jospin

Between 1997 and 2002, the Jospin government did not take any political risk in the field of pensions. Lionel Jospin learnt from Alain Juppé's failure and did not attempt any major pension reform but rather prepared the ground for the future pension reform. He also took a few measures in order to preserve the future of the PAYG system and prepared a reform on funded pensions schemes.

In 1999, the Prime Minister asked the Commissariat au Plan to consider possible reforms of pensions. The Charpin Report[8] was presented to the Prime Minister on 29 April 1999. It proposed the same kind of analysis as the one included in the reports published in the early 1990s. It showed that the proportion of older people in the population will increase dramatically after 2006, when the baby boom generation retires. If actual trends continue (low fertility, low immigration, longer life expectancy), one French person in three will be older than 60 in 2040; the dependency ratio (population of retirees/active population) would go from four retirees to ten working people to seven retirees for ten workers. Without reform, the viability of PAYG pension schemes will be in jeopardy by 2010. The report proposed to reform the private sector pension scheme again, by further extending the contribution period needed to obtain a full pension to 42.5 years. It also proposed to align the future of public employees (and associates) with those of the private sector. Nevertheless, this report did not generate a consensus amongst all key players. While CFDT approved the report, and CNPF went further, calling for the years of contribution to be increased to 45, the other trade unions were opposed to these orientations.

Another series of reports were published in the following months, with much contrasted opinions, contrary to the relative consensus of experts in the late 1980s. For example, a report by the Copernic Foundation[9] was published several months after the Charpin Report and criticized the idea of a demographic shock threatening the pension system (Khalfa and Chanu, 1999).

According to the Charpin Report, the problem was that expenditure would increase from 12 percent of GDP in 2000 to 16 percent in 2040. Nevertheless, the level of pensions doubled in the last 50 years without any difficulty. The Copernic Foundation also contested the view that any increase in pension contributions was impossible, because they could be partly financed by future productivity gains, and because increased contributions could save the PAYG pension system. This report underlined that the aging of the population also implied a decrease in the number of children and young people, and maybe the unemployed, and hence the reduction of the corresponding social spending. It would be possible to use these future savings to finance the pensions without diminishing their generosity.

Faced with these opposed positions, the Prime Minister preferred to ask for further expertise, rather than close the discussion. In September 1999, Dominique Taddéi published a study entitled *Retraites Choisies et Progressives* for the Conseil d'Analyse Économique,[10] which underlined the contradiction between raising the period of contributions required to be entitled to a full pension and the early retirement's practices. Effective retirement age in France is not 60 years but 57.5 years, and people enter late into the labor market. In these conditions, extending the contribution length means the incapacity for many to work the number of years required to get a full pension. Dominique Taddéi suggested introducing a progressive transition from full activity to retirement, with a combination of revenue from employment with retirement income, and the possibility of retiring '*à la carte*' (on a voluntary basis).

A few months later, René Teulade[11] wrote a report for the Conseil Économique et Social. This report reflected the point of view of the Council (composed of trade unionists, employers and representatives of the civil society), stressed the uncertainty of demographic projections in a perspective of 40 years, and was restricted to a perspective of five years. The report also criticized the proposal to increase the contribution length in a context of high unemployment and of low activity rates among workers over 50. Unlike the Charpin Report, this report proposed raising the level of pensions by changing the way of indexation for private employees' pensions again, and by taking more account of periods outside formal employment when calculating pension rights (unemployment, training, education, children etc.). The report did not agree with aligning the period of contribution of the special regimes of the public sector to the general regime, and recommended changing the period of contribution required to obtain a full pension in the private sector employees' schemes back from 40 years to 37.5 years. To guarantee the financial sustainability of PAYG pensions, the report suggested increasing the reserve fund (*fonds de réserve*) and the state's role in the financing of the non-contributory related pension rights. The Teulade Report like the Taddéi Report favored an economic approach rather than a demographic and a financial one, highlighting that the real solution was linked to economic growth and to the rise of the employment rate amongst older workers.

The question of pensions created an important debate, which worried the French people about their future pension. Opinion surveys multiplied in 1999. The opinion polls underlined that the French people seemed to be convinced that the PAYG pension system would not be able to guarantee sufficient pensions in the future. So, the necessity of a new reform seemed to be accepted. Seventy-two percent of 952 people interviewed by IFOP for the newspaper *Notre Temps* in April 1999 thought that it was urgent to reform the pension system (Bonoli and Palier, 2000). Nevertheless, Lionel Jospin preferred to wait until after the elections in 2002 before reaching any major decision.

However, in order to show his intention to consolidate – and not to question – the PAYG principle, the Jospin government created a reserve fund under the *loi de financement de la sécurité sociale* (voted in 1998) and implemented in 1999 with a first donation of 304 million euros. The reserve fund was supposed to be supplemented with future surpluses of the social insurance schemes, half of all earnings from social deductions paid on inheritance income and with any exceptional revenue (it was planned that income generated by the sale of the third generation of the mobile phone licenses (UTMS) would be given to this fund, but funds raised were less than expected). The reserve fund is in fact increased irregularly through governmental decisions. The initial objective was to attain 150 billion euros in 2020. Today, however, the rhythm of the donations seems to be insufficient to attain this objective. According to the projections made in the frame of the *projet de loi de financement de la sécurité sociale* for 2003, the reserve would pass from 7.1 billion euros in 2001 to 13 billion euros in 2002 and 17 billion euros in 2003.

In March 2003, during a press conference, Lionel Jospin announced he wanted to reform the specific regimes of the public sector. He proposed guaranteeing the pensions of the civil servants through a 'pact' that would contain the following features: the progressive lengthening of the period of contribution to 40 years, and in compensation some specific measures that would better take into account the difficulty of certain work, and the integration of the bonuses in the calculation of the pensions. These announcements were immediately followed by the mobilization of the public sector's trade unions, which blocked the project of the reform.

In order to reach a consensus, Lionel Jospin also announced the creation of a Pension Steering Committee (Conseil d'Orientation des Retraites, COR), created in April 2000, composed of experts and trade union representatives. However, MEDEF, the new employers' organization, refused to participate in these meetings. The COR organized in April 2001 a conference around the theme 'Age and Work' and published its first report in autumn 2001 (COR, 2001). Its goal was to reconcile the objective of increasing the length of the period of contribution and the increase in the total employment rate.

However, Lionel Jospin did not find a common ground for a compromise that would allow him to undertake a reform. Employers were also confronted with the mobilization of trade unions, when they tried to impose an extension of the length of contribution required for a full supplementary pension. In the frame of the negotiation on a new social constitution, MEDEF tried to change the rules for calculating supplementary pensions for the AGIRC and ARRCO schemes. The employers' organization wished to impose an extension of the period of contribution to 45 years. In order to impose its point of view, MEDEF asked its members to stop paying part of their contributions to complementary pension schemes. However, these positions, which were seen as blackmail, caused a virulent opposition of the trade unions. On 25 January 2001, more than 300 000 people went on strike against MEDEF. MEDEF negotiated an agreement with CFDT, CGT and CFTC, that froze contribution rates to AGIRC and ARRCO until 31 December 2002, and brought the two complementary regimes more into line with each other. The agreement also envisioned a global reform of pension schemes, including all the schemes, public and private.

The Fillon Reform

During the electoral campaign leading to the presidential elections of 2002, Lionel Jospin, like Jacques Chirac, announced a reform of the pension system. Jacques Chirac was re-elected and appointed Jean-Pierre Raffarin as Prime Minister, who had pension reform on his agenda. Jean-Pierre Raffarin was very cautious in order to avoid political failure such as the one experienced by Alain Juppé but also took some initiatives in order to avoid being accused as Lionel Jospin had been, of procrastinating and postponing reform indefinitely. During the first eight months of his term (from June to December 2002), the ministers in charge of pension reform, François Fillon (Social Affairs) and Jean-Paul Delevoye (Civil Servants Ministry) tried to create a project to respond to the known problems (an increase of four points of GDP if nothing was done, according to the projections of the COR), but also tried to avoid too big a social movement. The main objective of the reform was rapidly presented: to bring the public sector into line with the private sector.

At the beginning of January, trade unions launched a joint call for reform, following the CGT, showing that they were prepared to reform the pension system, but trying to impose their conditions (especially to maintain the generosity of pensions). From January to April 2003, the two ministers met with all the concerned actors, political parties, experts, trade unions and employers' organizations. In the media, there was speculation on whether the government would launch some negotiations on the pension reform or if it would only listen to the different actors without negotiating the content of the reform.

Although they met with the social partners several times, it was only on 18 April 2003 that the government presented its plan. The government announced that public sector employees would have to contribute for 40 years for a full pension like those in the private sector. Furthermore, this period of contribution will be increased for everybody to 41 years in 2008 and to almost 42 years in 2020. It was also announced that the indexation of pensions will be based on prices for all retirees (for civil servants pensions were indexed on wages). A new system of incentives for people to retire as late as possible was also created: a bonus *(surcote)* will be attributed to people retiring after the legal age and a sanction *(décote)* in case of retirement before this age and in case of missing years of contributions. However, there were no clear measures announced in order to finance all the projected deficit of the pension system.

These propositions attracted the opposition of all the trade unions, who responded through the organization of several days of strike: 1 May, 6 May and 13 May 2003. Before the negotiations, planned for after 13 May, trade unions tried to show their force and the government observed the degree of mobilization. The strength of the mobilization of 13 May (especially by the teachers, who were also concerned by a reform of their working conditions) surprised the government and also the trade unions (social partners estimated that some two million people participated in the social movement, which corresponds to the highest level of mobilization reached in 1995). FO confirmed its desire to be opposed to the reform; CGT, which at the beginning wished to participate in this reform in order to show a change (it refused to sign any reform for several decades) revised its strategy. CFDT affirmed its position, especially a will to allow retirement before the age of 60 for people who started to work at a very young age, and the increase of very low pensions.

Despite the demands of the trade unions, there were no real negotiations on these measures before the night of 14 May. During this night, CFDT and CGC obtained several concessions and decided to sign the agreement. The government announced that it would guarantee a replacement rate of 85 percent for someone on the minimum wage (the average rate of replacement in France in 2003 was 74 percent). It announced that the workers who will have worked for more than 40 years before the age of 60, and who began to work between 14 and 16, will be able to retire at 58. It also announced the creation of a supplementary scheme for the civil servant, in order to include bonuses received during his or her career in the calculation of pension. It also announced an increase of 0.2 percent in the social contributions after 2006 in order to finance retirement before 60, and counted on the decrease of unemployment in order to finance the deficit of the pension systems. In fact, these measures would only cover one-third of expected future deficits.

FO, CGT, UNSA and FSU refused to sign the agreement and called for another strike. Between May and June 2003, there were numerous strikes in the public sector, the railways, the metro and the schools. The government did not change its position concerning the pension reform but withdrew its project for the teachers (decentralization, reform of the universities). The social movement gradually stopped, especially because the teachers did not want to penalize the students in a period of exams.

Parliament adopted the pension bill on 24 July 2003. It implemented the broad orientations announced by François Fillon and was accepted by CFDT and CGC. CFTC obtained from parliament an improvement in contribution credits for carers in the civil servants' scheme. Although it did not really argue this point with the trade unions during the discussions in the spring, the government announced more clearly in front of the parliament the introduction of the new voluntary pre-funded individual pensions for the private sector's employees (PERP: Plan d'Epargne Retraite Populaire) and an improvement in the saving schemes created by the socialist Laurent Fabius so that they became real individual pensions.

On the whole, the main recipe for preserving the future of PAYG pensions includes an extension of the period of contribution necessary for a full pension, which means either an increase in the effective age of retirement or a decrease in the amount of pensions. As the actual trend is not towards an increase in the time spent at work, one can expect a gradual reduction in the level of public PAYG pensions. This leaves room for the development of voluntary supplementary pension-funded schemes. The development of saving schemes for old age is one of the most recent and new trends in France, although it is a general trend in industrialized countries.

TOWARD A MIXED SYSTEM

Although even in recent years funded pensions schemes seemed to be excluded from the French pension system, things changed fast in 2003. Numerous developments show the emergence of funded provision: the Thomas law (repealed), the bill on savings schemes for old age, the creation of PEIR. It reflects the agreement of the majority of the actors to develop a pillar financed by capitalization and the development of private savings.

An Ambiguous Agreement Concerning Pension Savings

Although funded provision seemed to be taboo for many actors of social protection in the 1970s (especially trade unions and left-wing parties), increasingly, political and union representatives seem today ready to introduce a funded element into the French pension system. They agree to a development of pension funds as long as it will help to complement PAYG pensions (and not replace them). This is nevertheless an important change, in comparison with debates that opposed the PAYG camp to supporters of funded provision. There is nowadays a consensus about the general framing of these discussions: the debate concerns more the implementation than the principle itself. There is also an agreement on the terminology of 'pension savings funds' (*épargne retraite*), which replaces the term 'pension funds', as too polemic and associated with big US or British private pre-funded pension funds.

However, each of the actors at stake has a different reason for supporting the development of funded schemes. Banks and insurance companies as well as MEDEF promote the advantages of capital-funded supplementary pension schemes. Insurance companies wished to develop pension funds several years ago in order to develop their own market. One of the spokespeople of pension funds lobbies, Denis Kessler, became the Chairman of Fédération Française des Assurances (FFA), and formerly number two in MEDEF, and promoted the advantages of developing pension funds, in order to develop French and European financial markets and therefore the capacities to finance firms and to develop investment.

The right-wing political parties also agreed to the development of pension funds for the same economic reasons, to which they added a 'sovereignty' argument. Since 14 July 1999, Jacques Chirac criticized the Jospin government and defended the introduction of pension funds. Beyond the interests of businesses, he claimed that there was the national interest of France at stake, faced with the power of foreign investments (US and British pension funds): 'We have to make a system of pension funds . . . so that the pensioners and the French workers regain the property of their company.'[12] As he was re-elected in April 2002, and could enjoy the support of a strong right-wing majority, Jacques Chirac could decide to implement this project.

The members of the Socialist party as well as the trade unions' representatives are also becoming less reticent about the introduction of pension funds, but they tend to justify this evolution by anti-US arguments rather than on the basis of economic arguments. They underline the necessity of developing French pension funds to reinforce the power of French companies faced with the international competition. Nicole Notat, at the time Chairperson of CFDT, repeated the argument: 'European and French employees should ask themselves if they want to continue to let American pension funds have the monopoly of intervention in the capital of French and European enterprises.'[13]

A second argument comes from the Left: some saving schemes for old age managed by trade unions would become a way to reinforce their power of negotiation in industrial relations and would justify the implementation of pension funds in France. In a report by Michel Sapin for the Socialist Party on savings schemes and the rights of workers (2000), this argument is refined: 'For us, it is a way for the opinion of workers to penetrate the firm that is different to the "pension fund shareholder" method or those of management'. For some on the Left and for some trade unionists, pension savings funds, managed collectively by workers, constitute a way to strengthen their control and decision-making power in the firm, thereby justifying the establishment of pension funds in France.

Today, a majority of the protagonists and a majority of French people (two-thirds of them in the opinion polls) think that the future of pensions will be a combination of PAYG pensions and pre-funded supplementary schemes. In 2003, FO and the Communist Party are still extremely opposed to this plan. CGT is opposed to this project too, but its position is less extreme. Other main trade unions, CFDT, CFTC and CFE-CGC agreed, but under the condition that they would take part in the management of these pension savings funds.

This idea also seems to have the support of most French people. Between November 1996 and December 1999, numerous surveys showed that a major-ity of those questioned (between 43 percent and 80 percent, nearly two-thirds on average) favored the creation of a pension savings regime that comple-mented PAYG pensions (Bonoli and Palier, 2000).

The Development of Private Saving Schemes

Beyond the debate, some elements show that France is progressively develop-ing these saving schemes for old age. Some supplementary pension plans are provided by big firms and often established though collective branch agree-ments or at firm level. These schemes are totally or partially funded. These include PREFON, established in 1967 for state employees, FONPEL estab-lished in 1993 for locally elected councilors. In the mid-1990s, these plans tended to develop, parallel to the French debate on pension reform about the extension of capital-funded schemes. Since 1994, tax deductions have been available for savings schemes that are for pensions or general provident purposes. Additional supplementary pensions, called *chapeaux* (hats), have been created since the mid-1990s by large corporations and are run as funded pension schemes. Nevertheless, these schemes remain relatively marginal, concerning state employees and liberal professionals, and are not available for employees covered by the *regime général*, who represent two-thirds of the French population.

A first attempt, to generalize the access to savings schemes for old age, was made by the Juppé government in the mid-1990s, which proposed to imple-ment a capital-funded supplementary scheme, in order to maintain the replace-ment rate that had been reduced by the 1993 reform. In 1997, the Thomas law, supported by Juppé, introduced non-obligatory private savings schemes for old age for the private sector's employees. A law, adopted 25 March 1997, launched this new system of pension savings funds for 14.5 million employees. These schemes were to be financed by employees and occasionally by employers and were to be encouraged through fiscal and contribution incentives. This law could only be applied after the publication of decrees that would define the conditions of implementation. These decrees should have been published in June 1997. However, the dissolution of the parliament and the arrival of a new majority have disrupted the process. The new Prime Minister, Lionel Jospin, was opposed to this law, because he was afraid that it would menace the PAYG pension schemes. Indeed, the money given by employers to the funded scheme would be partly exempted from social contributions, so that employers could propose to pay a part of the wages in the form of contribution to the pension funds and therefore reduce the amount of money given to the public system financed by social contributions. The Jospin government blocked the decrees in 1997 and repealed the bill in 2001.

However, although the Jospin government repealed the Thomas law, it also contributed to preparing the future of these funded pensions schemes. Laurent Fabius, Minister of Economy and Finance, introduced new *plans partenariaux d'épargne salariale volontaire* (partnership voluntary wage-earners' saving plans (PPESV)). These plans offer the possibility to employees to save money in the long run (ten years and more if it is permitted by the collective agreement). These savings are exempted from taxes and may eventually be topped up by employers. The accumulated savings will be paid back as annuities or as a lump sum.

The Raffarin government decided to transform these plans into a *plan partenarial d'épargne salariale volontaire pour la retraite* (partnership voluntary wage-earners' retirement plan (PERCO)), which is clearly oriented towards pension savings. Although the PPESV was limited to ten years, the savings of the PERCO will be blocked until the retirement. Furthermore, even if this topic was not central in the debate around the Fillon reform, the government has also implemented individual savings accounts for retirement (Plan d'Épargne Individual pour la Retraite, PERP). The PERP is elaborated like an insurance product, managed in the financial market by an insurance company, and is placed under the control of a committee, which is composed of the individuals who are saving for their retirement. This committee will have the administrative statute of an association. Its role is to receive the individual savings and to distribute after the retirement a rent. The government also foresees some fiscal deductions, whose amount will be fixed by the *loi des finances* of 2004.

Before this acceleration of governmental policy towards funded pension provision, French people had already become aware of the likely reduction in PAYG pensions and the share of their savings allocated to old age increased during the 1990s. The savings rate in pension products grew steadily throughout the 1990s even though purchasing power did not change. In 1999, nearly one household in two saved for its retirement. Strictly defined pension savings (the institutional forms of which are poorly developed, as we have seen) are used by 20 percent of households aged between 40 and 50. In the case of non-salaried workers, the rate rises to 31 percent. It is nearly 24 percent for agricultural workers and commercial artisans and nearly 20 percent of managers (INSEE, 1999, p. 294). For want of proper pension funds, life insurance is the substitute most used by households to prepare for retirement. This product provides a reasonably good return to capital (the return was 5.4 percent in 1999) and benefits from tax exemptions. Investment in life insurance plans has steadily increased through the 1990s: 'In 1997, life insurance represented 18 percent of total investment, compared with less than 5 percent ten years earlier' (INSEE, 2001, p. 147).

Savings are developing independently from government's incentives because individuals anticipate that PAYG pensions will fall. The main question today is whether the future funded pension system, which will receive contributions from the state and employers, will be compulsory or optional. It does not concern the development of private pension savings, which is already well underway in French households. In this, France is merely following the same path as other developed countries. Another general trend, aimed at increasing the employment rate of the older worker, is also touching France.

TO WORK LONGER?

Another trend is appearing in France: the development of policies that intend to raise the employment rates of older workers and to delay the age of retirement. These policies are more and more necessary insofar as the Fillon reform lengthens the period of contribution to obtain a full pension.

Early retirement policies, which had been the main instrument in the fight against unemployment during the 1980s, are now questioned. Several measures have recently been adopted in order to reduce the early withdrawal from work. For example, a new system of early retirement (Cessation Anticipée d'Activité pour Certains Travailleurs Salariés, CATS) was introduced in February 2000. This scheme has been created with the aim of restricting the access to early retirement to workers who had difficult working conditions only; like 15 successive years of shift work or production-line service, or more than 200 night shifts a year over 15 years, or if they are disabled. The creation of the scheme reflects the political aim, not to completely remove early retirement schemes but nevertheless to restrict and target early exit. This system is implemented by sector and company-level agreements, and makes workers eligible for a full or partial early retirement pension from the age of 55, for a maximum of five years. The introduction of this new scheme reveals the desire of the governments to restrict the access to early retirement. In the long run, it may replace most of the other pathways towards early retirement, which in 2003 concerned about 550 000 persons.

In the same way, the government decided to restrict access to the Special National Employment Fund program (*Allocation Spéciale du Fonds National pour l'Emploi*), and the contribution paid by firms was raised in February 2001, increasing the direct cost of the early exit scheme. Another scheme, the Job Substitution Allowance Scheme (ARPE, *Allocation de Remplacement pour l'Emploi*), is no more accessible since 1 January 2003. This measure was financed by the unemployment insurance scheme, and gave the possibility to a worker to retire at 55 and to receive 65 percent of his or her primary wage until 60, if he or she had worked during 40 years, and if his or her departure was compensated by the creation of a job for another worker.

In the public sector, the *Congé de Fin d'Activité* (CFA), which was accessible to every person older than 56, who worked at least for 40 years, was closed at the end of 2002. François Fillon announced the progressive closing of most of the early retirement schemes, which are presented as a 'waste' for France. The inherent difficulty of this policy change is that restricting early exit schemes does not mean that older workers will remain in the labor market. Indeed, while there is a slight reduction in total early exit schemes, it has been largely offset by the increase of DRE (*Dispense de Recherche d'Emploi*), the exemption from seeking a job for the unemployed, a category that now represents 70 percent of all inactive workers of 55 and over (Jolivet, 2002). In relation to this problem, some specific measures are planned in order to reintegrate people older than 55 in the labor market, especially thanks to the PARE (Plan d'Aide au Retour à l'Emploi).

That's why the Pension Steering Committee argued that one of the most important strategies in dealing with the pension problem is to let people 'work until the legal age of retirement'. It proposes to develop a specific employment policy for people over 50, which, as in Finland or Denmark, is based on information campaigns, a program of lifelong learning, the restriction of early retirement schemes, and the introduction of gradual retirement on a voluntary basis, know in France as *retraites à la carte*. In order to attain this objective, it is also necessary to modify overall working conditions so that people are willing to work longer (today, generally speaking, workers tend to retire as early as possible). Finally perceptions of the employers must also be changed, so that they accept keeping older workers who have more experience but are also more costly than the younger ones (COR, 2002; Guillemard, 2002).

In the end, the extent to which pensioners will be paid full pensions will depend on the success of the policies aimed at extending the duration of the working life. This is a necessary condition so that the increase in the contribution period needed to get a full pension would not result in a diminution of pension levels. However, although it has made much of the lengthening of the working life, the Raffarin government has not really mentioned what policies will be launched to increase the effective age of retirement. The only possible measure mentioned is a threat of contribution increases for employers who do not keep the older workers in their enterprises. Consequently, the increase of the employment rates among older workers is likely to become a main objective of employment policy in the next few years.

CONCLUSION

After a century marked by the expansion, the French pension system has entered a new era in the last 15 years. The policies launched since the mid-1980s were essentially aimed at limiting public expenditure on pensions. These reforms have been adopted in order to face the population aging challenge, and especially the increase in life expectancy. The likely reduction in the replacement rate provided by PAYG pensions will induce the development of private funded pensions. This shift to private pensions allows the government to transfer the consequences of the demographic shock onto the private sphere. The current stake is no more the choice between funded and PAYG financing. The principle of a combination of both systems seems to have been accepted, first because it is encouraged by the government and other actors at stake, second because the individuals spontaneously begin to save for their retirement.

As a result, the main policy objective during the next decade is likely to be the regulation of these funds. If the pensions-funded schemes develop without any specific regulation, the logic of the market could produce undesirable social outcomes as is the case in Great Britain (see Taylor-Gooby, this volume). There would be higher contributions for women, because of their longer life expectancy, administrative costs proportionally more important for the low wages, and the individuals will have to face the insecurity of the ups and downs of stock markets. The uncontrolled development of funded provision will mean increasing inequalities and more difficulties especially for those on precarious jobs. Those for whom access to savings schemes for old age is most problematic, part-time workers, low-wage earners, and people who have some irregular careers (especially women) are likely to be the main losers of the recent reforms.

NOTES

1. Tabah, L. (1986), *Vieillir Solidaires*, Rapport du Commissariat Général du Plan, Paris, La Documentation française; Schopflin, P. (1987), *Evaluation et Sauvegarde de l'Assurance Vieillesse*, Ministère des Affaires sociales; Teulade, R. (1989), *Rapport de la Commission Protection Sociale*, Paris: La Documentation française; *L'Avenir des Retraites*, 1990, Rapport de l'INSEE; *Livre Blanc sur les Retraites. Garantir l'Équité des Retraites de Demain*, 1991, Rapport du Commissariat Général du Plan, Rapport de la Mission Retraites, 1991, Mission Cottave; Bruhnes, B. (1992), *Rapport sur les Retraites*.
2. These ideas are proposed in the *Livre Blanc sur les Retraites. Garantir l'Équité des Retraites de Demain* of 1991, which synthesizes most of the previous reports.
3. Confédération Française du Travail, the most reformist of the various French trade union federations.
4. Small Christian trade union federation.
5. Communist trade union.
6. Force Ouvrière, trade union that was the main partner of employers in the 1970s and 1980s, and which became more and more confrontational in the 1990s.
7. Antoine Math, 'Réforme des retraites et revenus des personnes âgées: un aperçu comparatif', Working paper, IRES, No. 02.04, 2002.
8. *L'Avenir de nos Retraites, Rapport au Premier Ministre* (1999), Paris: La Documentation française.
9. Foundation created in October 1998, composed of academic teachers opposed to neo-liberalism and of unionists who were opposed to the Juppé plan.
10. Group of economists close to the Prime Minister.
11. *L'avenir des Systèmes de Retraite*, Paris: Conseil Économique et Social, Direction des journaux officiels.
12. Speech of the French President 14 July 1999.
13. *Libération*, 14 September 1999, p. 15.

REFERENCES

Babeau, A. (1997), 'Problèmes posés par l'introduction des fonds de pension en France', in MIRE (1997), *Comparer les Systèmes de Protection Sociale en Europe du Sud*, volume III: Rencontres de Florence, Paris: MIRE, 293–306.

Bonoli, G. (1997), 'Pension politics in France: Patterns of co-operation and conflict in two recent reforms', *West European Politics*, **20** (4), 160–181.

Bonoli, G. and Palier, B. (2000), 'From the cradle to . . . where? Current pension policy trends in Western Europe', *Yearbook of European Administrative History*, **12**.

Conseil d'Orientation des Retraites (COR) (2001), *Age et Travail, un Axe de Réflexion Essentiel pour l'Avenir des Retraites*, Paris: La Documentation française.

Conseil d'orientation des retraites (COR) (2002), *Retraites: Renouveler le Contrat Social Entre les Générations, Orientations et Débat*, Paris: La Documentation française.

Esping-Andersen, G. (1990), *The Three Worlds of Welfare Capitalism*, Cambridge, UK: Polity Press.

Guillemard Anne-Marie (2002), 'L'Europe continentale face à la retraite anticipée – barrières institutionnelles et innovations en matière de réforme', in *Revue Française de Sociologie*, April–June, 333–369.

INSEE (1999), *Données Sociales, la Société Francaise*, Paris: La Documentation française.

INSEE (2001), *Revenus et Patrimoine des Ménages* (47), 147.

Jolivet, A. (2002), 'Active strategies for older workers in France', in M. Jepsen, D. Foden and M. Hutsebaut (eds), *Active Strategies for Older Workers*, Brussels: ETUI, 245–275.

Khalfa, P. and Chanu, P.-Y. (eds) (1999), *Les Retraites au Péril du Libéralisme*, Paris: Syllepse.

Palier, B. (2002), *Gouverner la Sécurité Sociale, les Réformes du Système Français de Protection Sociale Depuis 1945*, Paris: PUF.

Ruellan, R. (1993), 'Retraites: L'impossible réforme est-elle achevée ?', *Droit Social*, (12), 911–929.

Sterdyniak, H., G. Dupont and A. Dantec (1999), 'Les retraites en France: Que faire?', *Revue de l'OFCE* (68).

Tsebelis, G. (1995), 'Decision making in political systems: Veto players in presidentialism, parliamentarism, multicameralism and multipartism', *British Journal of Political Science*, **25** (3), 289–325.

5. Pension reform in Sweden: Radical reform in a mature pension system

Karen M. Anderson[1]

INTRODUCTION

The public pension system has long been considered one of the crown jewels of Swedish social democracy. After a protracted political conflict, the Swedish Social Democrats (SAP) adopted the so-called 'ATP' reform in 1957 that added a public earnings-related tier to the existing flat-rate basic pension. The conflict over pensions pitted employers against unions, Social Democrats against the bourgeois parties, and prompted the break-up of the Social Democratic-Agrarian Party coalition government. Voters went to the polls twice in two years over the pension issue; once for new elections in 1958 and once for an advisory referendum (1957) on the new pension system. The Social Democrats finally prevailed in parliament, adopting the ATP legislation by a razor-thin majority made possible by the abstention of a Liberal MP.

The victory of the Social Democrats in the struggle over public pensions ushered in a long period of expansion and consolidation. By the early 1990s, the pension system was the largest single welfare state program in terms of spending; what is more, the ATP system also generated relatively large publicly controlled pension funds (AP Funds). In 1992, these funds stood at SEK 512 billion, or 35 percent of GDP (Proposition 1993/94: 250).

By the early 1990s, welfare state reform in general and pension reform in particular reached the top of the political agenda again, but instead of open conflict, behind the scenes cooperation across the political spectrum marked the reform process. Since the early 1990s, policy-makers have adopted a series of reforms designed to correct program weaknesses in the welfare state and to improve its financial sustainability. Pension reform has been a centerpiece of this process of welfare state modernization, and the results are arguably among the most far-reaching in the OECD. By adopting a radical pension reform, Swedish political actors have succeeded in refashioning the part of the welfare state that should be most immune to change because of the political risks associated with retrenchment (Pierson, 1994, 1998, 2001; Weaver and Pierson, 1993).

The 1994/98 pension reform is a radical overhaul of the existing system. A new pension-tested 'guarantee pension' replaces the flat-rate basic pension, and two defined contribution (DC) schemes replace the old earnings-related ATP pension. The new 'income pension' is a 'notional defined contribution' (NDC) system that provides the bulk of retirement income, while the new 'premium pension' is a funded individual account administered by a state agency.

This chapter investigates the politics of pension reform in Sweden during the 1990s. The analysis begins with a discussion of the pension policy environment prior to the adoption of major reform in 1994/98. I describe the structure of pension policy prior to reform, discuss the emergence of the pension problem in the 1980s and the development of a serious pension reform debate in the early 1990s. The chapter then analyses the political processes that led to major reform as well as the effects of the revamped pension system. Two questions animate the analysis. First, why did political parties and interest groups cooperate in a radical reform that involved tangible losses for important groups of voters? Second, what were the political conditions that facilitated reform? To answer these questions, the analysis relies on three sets of explanatory variables: political institutions, organized interests and policy legacies.

PENSION POLICY PRIOR TO THE 1994/98 REFORM

In 1990, the public pension system consisted of two tiers: the flat-rate basic pension (*folkpension*) and the national supplementary pension (ATP). Both tiers operated as pay-as-you-go (PAYG) systems financed by earmarked employer contributions. The basic pension contribution (7.45 percent of payroll) financed 85 percent of benefits (the state paid the rest), while the ATP contribution (13.5 percent of payroll) financed both current benefits and the accumulation of savings in the AP funds. For retirees with insufficient ATP pension rights, the basic pension system provided a flat-rate and means-tested supplements while the ATP system provided income-related pensions calculated according to 'defined benefit' principles. A full ATP pension paid 60 percent of average income for the best 15 years of at least 30 years of labor market participation, up to the benefit ceiling. Combined with the basic pension, the replacement rate was 65 percent of average wages. Both the basic pension and the ATP pensions were indexed to inflation every year.

THE EMERGENCE OF THE PENSION PROBLEM

Demographic and economic pressures began to constrain pension policy earlier in Sweden than in many other West European countries. In 1990, 18 percent of the population were already aged 65 or older, making Sweden one of the world's oldest societies (Ackerby, 1992, p. 27). Like many other countries, Sweden will also experience a rapid increase in its elderly population beginning in 2010 as baby boomers begin to retire. According to recent estimates, the ratio of workers will fall from 100 workers for every 30 pensioners in 2000 to 100 workers for every 41 pensioners in 2025 (Ministry of Health and Social Affairs, 2002, p. 9).

Besides these demographic pressures, the rapid deterioration of the Swedish economy in the early 1990s dramatically altered the political and economic foundations of the pension system. Between 1990 and 1993, Sweden went from budget surplus to recording a deficit of 12.3 percent of GDP. During the same period, open unemployment increased dramatically, from 1.7 percent to 8.2 percent, with another 4–5 percent of workers engaged in public training and employment programs. Economic output decreased for three years in a row, Sweden was forced to devalue its currency, and a series of bank failures plagued the financial sector. The recession undermined two preconditions of the Swedish welfare model – full employment and stable growth – and prompted massive reductions in public spending (Huber and Stephens, 1998; Pontusson, 1992). As economic growth stalled and unemployment skyrocketed, the pension system faced the twin shocks of shrinking tax revenues and increasing expenditures because of the growing number of retired persons.

The economic crisis exposed the instability of the pension system and pushed pension reform to the top of the political agenda. The design of the earnings-related ATP system assumed a stable annual economic growth rate of 3–4 percent and full employment in order to keep contribution rates stable (Palmer, 2002, pp. 186–187). Even before the recession hit, in 1982, ATP contributions had ceased to cover expenditures, and the gap increased in the early 1990s because of the economic crisis. Between 1982 and 1992, AP Fund strength (the number of years the AP Funds can finance benefits) declined from 7.4 years to 5.1 years (Proposition 1993/94 no. 250, p. 16; Riksförsäkringsverket, 1994). Revenue shortfalls in the basic pension system also exacerbated central budget deficits as the state absorbed higher proportions of program financing. Table 5.1 shows how different levels of real GDP growth affect the level of pension contributions required to finance existing pension rights. With the economy in free fall in the early 1990s, dramatic increases in contribution rates seemed increasingly likely.

Another growing problem was the design of the ATP benefit ceiling, which was indexed to prices rather than real wage growth so that over time, the relative level of the ceiling decreased relative to the development of real wages. This meant that many wage earners, including blue-collar workers had income above the ceiling for which they earned no benefits. If this development

Table 5.1   *Projected pension expenditure as percentage of payroll*

Year	Yearly real GDP growth		
	0%	1%	2%
1995	26.5	24.7	23.3
2015	43.7	32.7	25.1
2025	48.1	33.1	23.3

Note: Does not include AP funds.

Source: Ståhlberg 1993, p. 85.

continued, the ATP system would be transformed (unintentionally) into a flat-rate basic pension for many workers. This threatened the legitimacy of the ATP system and led to pressure to increase occupational pensions to fill the gap (Ståhlberg, 1993; Anderson, 1998; 2001).

Finally, the ATP system had unintended distributional consequences. Because benefits were based on the best 15 of 30 years of earnings, benefits flowed disproportionately to workers with higher education and steeply rising earnings over a relatively short period (that is, 15 years). In contrast, blue-collar workers with many years of slowly rising earnings benefited less than in a system based on lifetime earnings (Ståhlberg, 1993; Palmer, 2002).[2]

EMERGENCE OF THE PENSION REFORM DEBATE

Reform of the public pension system had been studied since the mid-1980s, but until the recession of 1989–93 there was little political support for major change. In 1984, the SAP government appointed an Official Commission of Inquiry to investigate pension reform. In the early 1980s, the ATP system was approaching maturity, so the Pension Commission was charged with studying the effects of the system and pinpointing areas needing reform. In 1990, the Pension Commission presented its final report, and it was circulated for comment in 1991 (SOU 1990: 76).

After five years of deliberations, the Pension Commission could not agree on significant proposals for reform despite widespread agreement about the need for adjustments in light of demographic and economic developments. The final report did, however, identify several serious weaknesses in the pension system and urged major reform. The final report argued that public confidence in the pension system was threatened by the weak link between contributions and benefits. Because of the relationship between the ATP system and the basic pension and means-tested benefits available to low-income pensioners, a person with a basic pension and no ATP points received a pension equal to the ATP pension of an industrial worker. In this sense, the earnings-related principle was seriously weakened. Moreover, these unintended consequences meant that the pension system was no longer performing its intended function: the earnings-related aspect of the pension system was meaningless for many groups of wage earners. More ominously, ATP contributions ceased to cover current expenditures in 1984. Since then, income from the AP Funds covered the shortfall.

The final report laid out several possible avenues for reform, including strengthening the link between contributions and benefits and combining the means-tested benefits and the basic pension into a higher basic pension. There was also some discussion of raising the number of 'best' years used to calculate benefits from 15 to 20, as well as increasing the number of minimum qualifying years and decreasing the level of benefits. However, the white-collar union federation TCO (Tjänstemännens Centralorganisation, or Central Organization of Salaried Employees) opposed any departure from the best 15 of 30 years benefit formula since this would disadvantage their core membership.

The commission also identified the indexing mechanism as a weakness and discussed the possibility of linking the index to economic growth rather than to inflation. When the report was circulated for comment many of the groups responding considered the proposed changes to be inadequate and voiced their desire for substantial reform. Most of the organizations commenting on the report voiced their support for a more actuarial ATP system, except as noted, the TCO. Only the pensioners' groups opposed any change in benefit indexing.

Although there was little agreement on specific changes, the 1990 report was a turning point. The commission report was an in-depth investigation of the pension system that was crucially important in pinpointing weaknesses in the pension system and in advancing the policy debate about pension reform. Still, in 1990 the political mood was not urgent, and politicians felt no particular need to rush into pension reform.

THE PROCESS OF REFORM

The electoral hegemony of the SAP (Swedish Social Democrats) has heavily influenced the design of the pension system. The SAP has governed Sweden from 1933 to 1976 (sometimes in coalition with the Farmers' Party); from 1982 to 1991; and from 1994 to the present. Political necessity led the non-socialist parties to accept the basic features of the pension system, despite their opposition to the 1959 ATP reform. Since the constitutional reform in 1969, Swedish electoral rules have tended to produce minority governments. The SAP has chosen to form minority governments and rely on the support of other parties, while bourgeois governments have typically formed multiparty governments consisting of three or four parties. In September 1991, a four-party bourgeois coalition led by the Conservative Prime Minister, Carl Bildt, took office after the 'earthquake' election of 1991. The Social Democrats' inability to prevent the impending recession resulted in one of the party's worst election results since the 1930s.

One of the first steps taken by the Bildt government (November 1991) was to appoint a working group comprised of representatives from the parliamentary parties to investigate pension reform. Bo Könberg (Liberal Party), the Minister of Health and Social Affairs, chaired the working group, which was directed to make proposals aimed at making pensions more responsive to the general state of the economy, strengthening the link between contributions and benefits, and encouraging an increase in long-term savings. The parties, including the opposition SAP, agreed that the broadest possible unity was desirable.

The process of negotiating pension reform was atypical by Swedish standards. Rather than trying to negotiate reform in an Official Commission of Inquiry, the non-socialist government appointed a working group composed of representatives from the five main parliamentary parties, including the SAP, to formulate reform legislation. The non-socialist government was composed of the Conservatives, Liberals, Christian Democrats and Center Party. The Conservatives dominated the government, but the Minister of Social Affairs came from the Liberal Party. Despite the change in government, the SAP was the largest party in parliament, with 38 percent of the seats. Unlike the Pension Commission of the 1980s, only representatives of the political parties served in the working group. Interest groups, including the unions, were not directly represented. TCO, SACO and LO unions were still consulted and their views were well known, especially to the SAP, but they could not directly influence the content of the reform.

The pension working group issued their first report in August 1992 (Ds 1992: 89). The report predicted that the ATP system would collapse in 20 to 30 years if low economic growth continued, necessitating dramatic increases in contribution rates. With tax rates among the highest in the OECD, payroll tax increases were hardly a politically feasible option. In addition, the working group argued that the gradual erosion of the earnings-related aspect of the system was a serious threat to ATP's legitimacy. To deal with these problems, the working group recommended strengthening the link between benefits and contributions in the ATP system by replacing the 15–30 rule with a benefit formula based on lifetime earnings. The report also proposed that pensions be indexed to developments in real wages instead of to inflation in order to stop the gradual erosion of ATP benefits. Finally, even though the working group included four non-socialist parties, it specifically rejected any type of reform that would transform the current system into a private premium reserve system because of the double payment problem involved (Ds 1992: 89, p. 52).

Several of the changes proposed in the 1992 report have been suggested elsewhere. Jan Bröms, chief economist for the Swedish Federation of Professional Employees (Sveriges Akademikers Centralorganisation, SACO), argued for an obligatory system based on actual work performance in a debate book published in 1990 (Bröms, 1990). In its annual survey of the Swedish economy in 1991, the Institute for Economic Studies (Konjunkturrådet) painted a picture of the ATP system 'in crisis' and argued for a more actuarial system, in particular through the abolition of the 15–30 rule (Söderström,1991). In the analysis of pensions conducted as part of the 1992 Medium Term Survey of the Swedish economy, Stefan Ackerby advocated a tighter link between contributions and benefits, the stimulation of savings, and an index based on economic growth rather than the CPI (Ackerby, 1992). Economist Assar Lindbeck also pleaded for a shift to a more actuarial system based on defined contributions rather than defined benefits (Lindbeck, 1992). The Economic Commission appointed in 1993 by the Bildt government to propose changes in Swedish institutions also argued for similar provisions (SOU 1993: 16). In sum, even before the working group issued its final report, the basic problems in the pension system had been identified, and the broad principles for pension reform had been made public.

Nevertheless, agreement on the final proposals for pension reform was difficult. The final report was due in the summer of 1993, but was delayed until January 1994 because of lingering disagreements. The issue of whether to introduce a premium reserve into the ATP system and whether contributions should be paid on incomes above the earnings ceiling were the two biggest problems. The issue of contributions above the income ceiling resulted in tough last minute negotiations. In particular, the Liberals and Conservatives opposed the payment of contributions above the ceiling, arguing that because contributions paid above the income ceiling did not earn pension credits, they amounted to a pure tax and should be abolished. With equal vigor, the SAP asserted that the system must retain its redistributive character, and they pressed for keeping contributions above the ceiling. In January 1994 a compromise appeared imminent when the group agreed that half of the ATP contribution would be paid on incomes above the ceiling. As a concession, the SAP agreed that this would be called a 'tax' rather than a contribution, and the revenue from it would go to the state budget rather than to the ATP system. As Bo Könberg put it, 'the most important thing is to get the Social Democrats to agree. Then the proposal rests on a foundation that corresponds to 85 to 95 percent of the Parliament and the Swedish population' (*Svenska Dagbladet*, 12 January 1994).

On 24 January 1994, the working group presented its final report (SOU 1994: 20), and it echoed many of the problems identified in earlier studies. The report cited the rising cost of pensions and low economic growth as the major reasons for reform and noted that there was widespread doubt that the pension system could remain solvent as the number of retired persons increases. The working group also linked the pension system to the structural problems of the Swedish economy such as low savings rate and a high tax burden. Without fundamental reform, major problems would occur when the generation born during the 1940s begins to retire in 2010. Revamping the system to make it more responsive to economic developments would also increase public confidence in the pension system.

The working group based its proposals on those published in 1992. Briefly, the reform blueprint proposed to replace the basic pension and the ATP pension with a modified PAYG system based on defined contribution principles. ATP benefits would be based on lifetime earnings rather than the best 15 years of 30, pension contributions would be evenly split between employers and employees, and pension contributions above the income ceiling would be reduced by one half. Benefits would also be linked to the rate of real economic growth, taking both inflation and wage growth into account, thereby improving the financial stability of the system. Military service, higher education and child rearing were made eligible for pension credits, financed by general revenues. The new earnings-related system would also include mandatory individual funded accounts to supplement PAYG benefits, and spouses would be able to share pension rights. Finally, the old basic pension and pension supplement would be replaced by a higher guaranteed pension indexed to inflation. Details of the final agreement are discussed below.

The final proposal reflects the nature of compromise among five parties. The Christian Democrats and Center Party wanted shared pension rights for spouses, the SAP wanted to retain the obligatory system with high replacement rates, while the Liberals and Conservatives wanted a more explicit link between contributions and benefits, the elimination of contributions above the ceiling, and the premium reserve. All of the political parties advocated the introduction of real wage indexing. Although the influence of the SAP in the reform process has been substantial, they have acquiesced in three main areas: contributions above the ATP ceiling, shared pension rights and the premium reserve system. The switch to visible individual contributions was also a concession by the SAP.

When the details of the final report were made public in early February, they immediately attracted criticism. The leader of TCO, Björn Rosengren, attacked the proposal publicly, charging that the switch to the lifetime earnings principle was unfriendly to women who take time off to care for children (*Dagens Nyheter*, 27 January 1994). In addition, Rosengren complained that pension credits for higher education were too low and would disadvantage white-collar workers. In April 1994, TCO announced that it was prepared to join forces with LO and SACO to fell the proposal (*Dagens Nyheter*, 25 April 1994), but this move failed. LO disapproved of several parts of the reform, but was less critical than TCO. In contrast to the unions, business groups were more or less satisfied. The Employers' Organization (SAF) applauded the proposal, saying that it would send a positive signal to the rest of the world, it would strengthen the krona, increase savings and increase work incentives (*Dagens Nyheter*, 22 February 1994).

Economists also criticized the reform proposal, arguing that it was not fully financed. Whereas the proposal largely solved the problem of future demographic shocks, it still did not respond adequately to current financing problems. In addition, the new system required the state to pay the pension contributions for education, care of small children, and military service, requiring additional state outlays. The working group proposed to use AP Funds to cover these transition problems. Given that the pension system (guarantee and ATP pensions) was calculated to cost significantly more than the level of revenues from payroll contributions (*Dagens Nyheter*, 19 February 1994), the pressure on the AP Funds would be substantial. In the meantime, assets would accumulate in the new premium reserve, and it would eventually replace the AP Funds as a source of savings and investment capital. Although this aspect of the reform would not affect the level of benefits, it was a major victory for the bourgeois parties.

The SAP rank and file was also slow to embrace the reform proposal. The party conducted an internal comment process in March, and two-thirds of all responses advised that the reform should be postponed until after the election in September (*Svenska Dagbladet*, 8 April 1994). The SAP executive committee resisted this pressure and agreed that the Riksdag should make a decision on the principles for the reform but also remove certain issues from the decision for further investigation. In particular, the SAP wanted more deliberation about the change in contributions and the administration of the new premium reserve system (*Dagens Nyheter*, 9 April 1994). The decision to proceed with legislation met with massive criticism in the media and in the comment statements. The pressure on the SAP to wait has been intense, especially from their youth organization and women's organizations (*Svenska Dagbladet*, 8 April 1994).

The final report was circulated for official comment in March and April, and the comment period was short by typical standards. In their official comments, the SAF and the Federation of Swedish Industries (Industriförbundet, IF) again voiced their cautious support, but also argued for a lower pension level and a larger premium reserve. LO, TCO and SACO opposed the swap of employer contributions for individual contributions. LO in particular voiced doubts that the employers would raise wages to compensate for the fee swap. SAF and IF fanned the flames of this disagreement when they issued a joint statement declaring that it was not the intention of the working group that workers would be fully compensated for the change in financing. SAF accused the unions of using their opposition to the fee swap as a back door method to get SAF to agree to centralized wage bargaining. SAF agreed to the fee swap in principle, but would not promise anything. In particular, SAF pointed out that because of economic conditions or tax policies, there might not be room for wage increases equal to the decrease in employer contributions (*Svenska Dagbladet*, 9 February 1994). In response, Bo Könberg accused SAF of playing a high stakes game that could endanger the reform agreement (*Dagens Nyheter*, 4 February 1994).

Clearly, the parties backing the agreement did their utmost to preserve the compromise and prevent pension reform from becoming an election issue. Having eliminated all veto points prior to formal approval by the Riksdag, the last thing the working group wanted was a potential veto point in the form of electoral punishment (see Immergut 1992). Moreover, sealing the agreement in the spring would ensure that blame would be divided between five political parties. To the extent that pension reform was discussed in the September election campaign, it would be difficult for voters to punish a specific party for agreeing to pension reform.

Several changes were made in response to the comments and these found their way into the legislation presented to the Riksdag. The most important change concerned the fee swap. Instead of phasing in the fee swap, the bill stated that this would occur immediately. This change would minimize the risk that employers failed to compensate wage earners fully for the reduction in employer contributions. Instead of 1995, the new system would go into effect in 1996 so that there would be more time to negotiate the unresolved issues. This change would not affect the introduction of payroll taxes in 1995 or the other provisions of the reform. The bill also left unresolved the issue of which economic adjustment index to use.

The Riksdag approved the basic contours of the pension reform in June 1994 and appointed an implementation group to work out remaining details for a more precise proposal in 1995. The items left unresolved were whether the new guarantee pension would be reduced for those who have collectively agreed upon pensions, the swap in contributions, the economic adjustment index, and pension rights for students (*Riksdag och Departement* 22, 1994).

Since the adoption of principles for the new system in 1994, subsequent decisions have delayed implementation several times. However, the new financing rules of the pension system took effect in January 1995, including the 1 percent individual pension contribution and the construction of the premium reserve system. Events in late 1995 further delayed full implementation. SAP Prime Minister Ingvar Carlsson announced he would step down in early 1996, and this led to several months of speculation about who would replace him. In any event, the change in leadership would require a special Social Democratic party congress during which the pension reform could easily have become a major issue. The four bourgeois parties agreed to wait until after the SAP congress, but issued stern warnings in the media about a possible SAP defection. In January, motions from the SAP rank and file began to flood into party headquarters. A total of 320 motions demanded that the pension reform be shelved and the previous system re-introduced (*Svenska Dagbladet*, 9 January 1996).

The toughest resistance came from grass roots pressure in both LO and the Social Democratic Party. LO congresses in this period were deluged with motions critical of the pension reform proposal. Patterns within the Social Democratic Party were similar (Palme and Wennemo, 1998, pp. 22–23). In the fall of 1996, the SAP conducted its *third* intraparty consultation procedure in response to continued criticism from rank and file members (earlier consultations were held in 1993 and 1994). During this process, the party leadership was criticized for providing inadequate information to members about why the pension system required reform in the first place, for the closed nature of the process, and for not communicating what the party had 'won' in terms of concessions from the bourgeois parties (Lundberg, 2002, p. 43). Given that the reformed pension system would provide better benefits to many LO members than under the ATP system, it is surprising that this message was so poorly communicated.

Despite this pressure, fears of fracturing the party in the general election campaign and of damaging the party's ability to make deals with the bourgeois parties helped the Social Democrats to forge a compromise with dissidents at their 1997 party congress and stick to the multiparty agreement with some modifications. The SAP accepted a somewhat larger premium reserve (2.5 percent instead of 2 percent) in return for weakening the earlier accord's commitment to move to parity employer–employee financing of pensions. In addition, SAP leaders rejected pressure from LO and many in the party to make the premium reserve voluntary, while the bourgeois parties agreed to the introduction of a publicly administered fund to compete with private funds for individual accounts, as well as a provision that those who do not choose a fund will have their money invested in a publicly-managed fund (Anderson and Weaver, 2003).

As criticism swelled, the Conservative Party member of the working group stated that an SAP defection would be a 'disaster (*olycka*) for Sweden' and that the Conservatives would never make a cross-party agreement with the SAP again (*Svenska Dagbladet*, 10 January 1996). The SAP leadership managed to resist the pressure from below, and the pension reform survived the scrutiny of the congress. In its budget bill presented in September 1996, the SAP proposed a one-year delay in the implementation of the eligibility rules of the new system, to 1 January 1999. The first pensions paid according to the new rules would also be moved up one year, to 2001 (Proposition 1996/97:1). The motivation for this second delay was the need to adapt the social insurance administrative apparatus to the new eligibility rules. Beginning in 1998, wage earners contribute one half of program financing. This was accomplished by transferring the individual contributions to sickness insurance to the ATP system.

THE NEW PENSION SYSTEM

By early 1999, nearly all aspects of the reform had been implemented, and in 2002, the revamped pension system paid its first benefits. The reform is remarkable not only in terms of programmatic innovation, but also because the new system rests on a clear set of principles not present in the old system. One of the overarching objectives of the pension reform is to separate 'social insurance' (collective provision for risk) from 'social policy' (objectives not based on shared risk), both in terms of program structure and financing. A second goal is to ensure the financial sustainability of the system by introducing several mechanisms for automatic financial stabilization. The following section discusses the main characteristics of the reform along three dimensions: benefits, financing and administration.[3]

Benefits

A notional defined contribution pension based on lifetime earnings
One of the most radical changes in the new pension system is the switch from a relatively generous defined benefit formula (a full pension was based on the best 15 years of 30 years of employment) to a notional defined contribution scheme based on lifetime earnings. This means that even though the new income pension system is not funded, the scheme emulates a funded defined contribution scheme by estimating an internal rate of return for accumulated pension contributions. This change increases the insurance character of the pension system significantly. Additionally, the old basic pension has been abolished and integrated into the new income pension. The new system counts all contributions, and the monthly benefit is calculated based on (gender neutral) life expectancy at the time that the person begins receiving benefits. The income pension is financed entirely by a 16 percent payroll tax split evenly between employers and employees (see below).

The notional defined contribution principle means that there will be no redistribution between age groups and/or between individuals. Each age cohort is supposed to receive a total payout from the income pension equal to its contributions plus a return on those contributions, while each individual within a specific cohort will receive a share of the total 'pie' available to their cohort that is equivalent to their share of total contributions for the cohort.

A new pension guarantee

As noted, the new 'guarantee pension' receivable at age 65, provides minimum income support for workers with low lifetime earnings from both the old pension supplement and the universal *folkpension*. Unlike the old basic pension, the guarantee pension is financed entirely by general government revenues, but unlike the income pension, the guarantee pension is indexed to prices. This new pension will provide a higher pension for some low-income pensioners than the old *folkpension*/pension supplement combination, making the reform package more politically palatable. Another novelty is that the guarantee pension is income-tested against the new income pension and the premium pension, but not against other sources of income, dramatically simplifying administration and eliminating the need for a stigmatizing recertification process. For immigrants, the guarantee pension is pro-rated based on the number of years that they have lived in Sweden as adults. A complex system of income-tested housing supplements is also available to seniors.

The premium reserve

In addition to the income pension, the new system contains what Swedes call a 'premium reserve': of the total 18.5 percent in pension contributions, 2.5 percent will be placed in an individual investment fund based on the defined contribution principle. To minimize administrative costs, pension contributions and fund choices are centrally managed by a government agency, and individuals have a wide range of fund choices. Social organizations, notably LO, were offered the opportunity to partner with fund companies in offering fund choices. All fund balances will be annuitized at the time of retirement. In addition, an existing quasi-mandatory supplementary pension that covers blue-collar workers was also converted into a defined contribution plan (Palmer 2002, p. 181).

Flexible retirement age

Another major change is the introduction of a flexible retirement age. The new system allows individuals to begin receiving retirement benefits at any age beginning at 61, with no upper limit. Moreover, they can begin by receiving 25, 50, 75 or 100 percent of their full pension entitlement, weakening the need for a separate partial pension program.[4] Early retirement results in lower benefits, but older workers can always increase their pension amount by working longer, even after they have begun to draw a pension. Thus their incentives to remain in work are strengthened. However, given the interaction between the income pension and the income tested guarantee pension (described above), increased work may not always increase pension benefits, especially for those with very low pension rights (Regeringskansliet, 2002, p. 19). No new claims under the old separate system of partial pensions were allowed after 2000.

Financing

Parity financing
Another major feature of the reform is that pension contributions will be divided between employers and employees. The switch to employee payroll taxes is intended to increase public awareness of the costs of retirement. Previously, employers paid the pension payroll tax, and it was not reported on wage earners' paychecks. Originally this was supposed to be an even division between the two, but currently employers pay about 60 percent of the total. In fact, however, employee payroll taxes were increased only slightly: most of the employee contribution was generated by taking an existing employee contribution for sickness insurance, relabeling it as a pension contribution, and having employers take over responsibility for sickness insurance contributions. The employee pension contribution has nevertheless been extremely unpopular, and the current Social Democratic government has improved the tax deductibility of the individual contribution.

Stable contributions
Because total anticipated payouts for each age cohort are automatically adjusted to correspond to a cohort's contributions (and returns attributed to those contributions), payroll tax rates should not increase over time, even if life expectancy rises or the economy performs poorly. A contribution rate of 18.5 percent of qualifying income can thus continue indefinitely. In addition, the wage base for pension contributions will rise with average wage growth rather than prices, so it will not erode as a share of wages as in the past. The automatic balancing mechanism will also ensure that there is an annual adjustment of benefits (downward) if contributions are insufficient to cover liabilities.

Smaller buffer funds
Like the old system, the new pension system will operate largely on a pay-as-you-go rather than on a funded basis. Current contributions are used largely to pay current retirees. Thus it avoids the double payment problem encountered with trying to move to advanced funding. As in the current system, however,

'buffer' funds will help to even out demographic peaks and valleys. However, the size and function of the buffer funds in the new system is much different. The old AP Funds functioned not only as a buffer but they also earned investment income and provided investment capital for public housing. The new buffer funds are less ambitious and smaller in size. One reason for the decline in fund assets is that transfers from the AP Funds to the central government budget have been used to finance the extra costs for the central government in the new system. Over time, the assets in the premium reserve will exceed those in the AP Funds. This is a major shift in the structure of collective capital formation.

Full funding
The new system also eliminates unfunded liabilities. In the old system, pension points earned for periods of non-employment (military service, unemployment, etc.) were not financed by contributions from the state or other social insurance bodies. In the new system, part of the effort to separate social insurance and social policy is accomplished by introducing full financing of all pension liabilities. Pension points will be earned for military service, child rearing and education, as well as time spent in disability and receiving unemployment and sickness benefits. But instead of simply imputing the credits as in the past, the Swedish government will actually make contributions to the new pension system (both the income pension tier and the individual account tier described below) at the time that those credits are earned. In other words, the pension contribution base has been broadened, although it is the general government budget that is the source of those contributions. In the year 2000, 83 percent of all pension rights earned were from contributions based on employment income, while 11 percent came as transfers from other social insurance funds (for example, for unemployment) and 6 percent for disability pensioners, those in national services, students in higher education, and childrearing (Settergren, 2002, p. 42).

Automatic financial stabilization
The income pension scheme also includes a mechanism designed to ensure that future benefit obligations in the system do not exceed resources if there are increases in life expectancy or the economy performs poorly. Under the new income pension, these developments would cause annual benefit adjustments in retirement annuities, which normally follow changes in the consumer price index, to be uprated at a lower rate until anticipated total payouts and resources are brought back into balance.[5] Thus the new NDC, like true defined contribution individual account systems, transfers substantial risks of increased longevity and lower than anticipated economic growth from the state to individuals in different age cohorts. Politically, having this mechanism

in place means that politicians will not have to make difficult decisions to cut benefits; those cuts will occur automatically.

Administration

Increased transparency

The pension system is also designed to be transparent in that individuals receive an annual statement about the size of their projected pensions from both the pay-as-you-go income pension and individual account (premium pension) tiers, as well as the guarantee pension, where applicable. Predicted benefits are given under several different economic scenarios regarding retirement age and overall performance of the Swedish economy. Thus workers are provided with increased information about their future pensions, but also face increased uncertainty because their pensions depend on economic and demographic developments over which they have no control.

Removing survivor and disability benefits from the pension system

Under the new pension system, financing of survivor benefits is transferred from the contribution-financed pension system to a separate payroll tax. Moreover, consistent with the orientation of the Swedish system to increasing labor force participation, the system is being transformed from long-term survivor benefits to a temporary 'adjustment pension'. Similarly, responsibility for financing disability benefits has been transferred to sickness insurance. Thus the pension contribution is more purely dedicated to old age pensions than in the past.

A long transition

The transition to the new system will take 15 years. Workers born in 1937 and earlier will have their pension right determined entirely in the old system, and those born in 1954 and earlier will be entirely in the new system. In the intermediate group, an increasing share of pension rights will be determined under the new system. Thus current and soon-to-be retirees are protected from cutbacks entirely, and those most heavily affected are almost two decades from retirement.

THE POLITICAL AFTERMATH

Both the bourgeois coalition government and the SAP immediately claimed credit for pension reform and each side declared its satisfaction with the results of the working group as well as the importance of the fact that there is broad parliamentary agreement about the proposal. The SAP also emphasized their view that the new pension system was acceptable from a redistributive point of view. Representatives for the bourgeois parties emphasized the significance of the fact that wage earners would now have better opportunities to plan for retirement (*Svenska Dagbladet*, 25 January 1994). In essence, the bourgeois government and the SAP had very different interpretations of the pension agreement. Prime Minister Carl Bildt (Conservative) said that the pension proposal 'meant a historical departure from a system that no longer functions and that the foundation had now been laid for a new and stable pension system in Sweden'. At the same time, the SAP's representatives saw the agreement as a way to 'modernize and maintain the system for a long time to come . . . it means that one of the biggest and most important social reforms of our time will continue to play a decisive role for people's security and welfare' (*Svenska Dagbladet*, 25 January 1994). Thus far, the pension reform package has proven to be politically durable, with one major exception. As noted above, the new 7 percent payroll tax contribution for pensions has proven to be extremely unpopular, despite the fact that much of it was simply a reshuffle of existing payroll taxes. In 2002, the SAP government legislated an income tax credit to compensate wage earners for the individual contribution.

EFFECTS OF THE REFORM

The pension reform is an extremely complex set of new rules, and sorting out the effects on future retirees is difficult. There is no doubt, however, that the new system is a major departure from existing pension policy. In particular, the switch from defined benefits to defined contributions in the ATP system is a radical change, and this will mean that the new system will have much less potential for 'decommodification' than the old system. Of course current pensioners, the group most likely to mobilize against a reform, were left virtually untouched. Moreover, the long phase-in period means that many others will be only partially affected. A study conducted by the National Insurance Board (Riksförsäkringsverket) estimated that two-thirds of those studied would be losers in the new system, mainly TCO members and women.[6] The biggest losers are those who work 20 to 40 years before retirement. The biggest winners are those who work less than 20 years and receive the new higher guaranteed pension. In order to receive the same pension benefits under the new system as in the old, one must work at least 40 years. Still, this group, about 80 percent of the population, loses about 7–8 percent in pension value because of the new index rules. Women with little or no education fare the best, while women with higher education and fewer working years lose the most, about 17 percent. These calculations are based on a yearly economic growth rate of 1.5 percent. At higher rates of growth, pensions go up. Still, under the new system, at a yearly growth rate of 1.5 percent, pensions would be 12 percent lower. Only if growth is 2 percent will pensions remain about the same. In sum, the effects of the reform differ widely among social groups, but the overall impact is that of less redistribution.

These losses must be considered in the context of the 'improvements' introduced by the reform. First, the new pension system is much more resistant to economic and demographic shocks so its long-term stability is vastly enhanced. Second, the new indexing rules will stop the erosion in the value of ATP pensions. The old index rules meant that more and more workers earned income above the pension qualification ceiling, for which they accumulated no pension rights. This trend threatened to transform the ATP system into a bigger basic pension (Ståhlberg, 1993), thereby significantly reducing the legitimacy of the pension system's goal of earnings replacement. Third, the new system corrects the unintended redistribution from lower income groups to higher income groups because of the best 15 years of 30 benefit rule.

Overall, the short-term impact of the general state budget is negative: Sweden's Finance Ministry estimated that in 1999, the pension reform would drain an additional 46 billion kronor from the general state budget, while increasing flows to the AP 'buffer funds' by 41 billion kronor. The financial aspects of the pension reform provided an unexpected opportunity for Sweden to improve its ability to meet the EMU convergence criteria in two ways, however. First, the assets accumulating in the premium reserve after 1995 could be recorded as public savings for accounting purposes. Second, huge transfers of 245 billion kronor were made between 1999 and 2001 from the AP Funds to government in recognition of the increased role that the state budget would play in the future pension system. These transfers reduced public debt significantly.

EXPLAINING OUTCOMES

How do political institutions, policy legacies, and the structure of organized interests explain the dynamics of the Swedish pension reform? Two aspects of pension policy design are crucial for explaining the Swedish success story. First, the accumulation of substantial pension reserves in the AP Funds lessened the time pressure on political actors to find a solution to the pension system's financing problems (reserves were sufficient to finance ATP benefits for at least five years) and the AP Funds could be used to finance the transition to the new system, thereby obviating any 'double payment' problems. Transfers from the AP Funds to the central government covered the costs of increased budget expenditures for the guarantee pension and the pension contributions for the unemployed, those in military service etc. The AP Funds also allowed reformers to introduce the premium pension without increasing contributions beyond the old system's level of 18.5 percent of qualifying income. This was possible only because the state assumed the 'social policy' elements of the new system without incurring extra net costs. As noted, most of the state's additional costs have been financed by transfers from the AP Funds. Most pension systems do not present political actors with the degree of financial latitude enjoyed by Swedish reformers.

Second, the pre-reform pension benefit formula in Sweden provided an opening to pursue a strategy of 'rationalizing redistribution' (Myles and Pierson, 2001). In Sweden, the benefit earning index (best 15 years of 30) provided the opportunity to reduce advantages that white-collar workers enjoyed at the expense of blue-collar workers. By making benefits more equal to contributions, politicians could also claim that the system was fairer. This self-legitimating strategy made it difficult for opponents of the reform to make their case.

Several other aspects of program structure help to explain the dynamics of reform. First, the ATP system was nearly mature and private pensions are relatively insignificant, so a radical departure from the system was politically impossible. However, significant losses have been imposed on future beneficiaries with the switch to the lifetime earnings principle and changes in indexing. Second, the complexity of the system created opportunities to compensate those negatively affected by the new lifetime earnings principle. For example, the introduction of pension rights for education and child rearing was a compensatory method for minimizing opposition. More important, the technical complexity of the pension reform was so great that many, if not most, citizens were unable to follow all of the political discussions concerning reform. The media's attempts to identify winners and losers in the reformed system only added to the confusion. Thus many of the more technical aspects of the proposed reform, such as the introduction of a life expectancy index, and the replacement of the current inflation index with the economic adjustment index were shielded from criticism.

As the retrenchment literature suggests, organized interests with a stake in existing programs are often formidable opponents to change. In Sweden, trade unions were the most important interest group representing the interests of current and future pensioners, and given that the reform involved tangible losses for some groups, why did the unions tacitly support pension reform, and how did their influence contribute to the content of the reform? First, Swedish union structure, especially the high level of union density and the membership heterogeneity in terms of age and gender, provided incentives for the unions to pursue an encompassing interest strategy, although there were important differences between the white- and blue-collar unions. The blue-collar unions accepted the introduction of private savings accounts within the public system, parity financing, and a tighter link between contributions and benefits in return for a revamped pension system capable of resisting financial and demographic shocks. In addition, some blue-collar union members stood to benefit from the introduction of the lifetime earnings benefit formula.

The Social Democratic Party also had similar reasons for supporting reform, although the process was especially tricky. Coming on the heels of cuts in other social insurance programs, the pension reform could have been explosive. The pressure from LO and the rank and file to preserve the system has been strong. The ATP is, after all, the heart of SAP reform politics. As noted, the 1959 ATP reform marked the shift from flat-rate benefits to the income replacement principle in social insurance programs. It was this decisive shift that sealed the alliance between the LO and TCO in favor of a vastly expanded state role in pension provision (Esping-Andersen, 1985; 1990). Although the SAP had to compromise on details, the party clearly preferred a revamped pension system more than it preferred the status quo. There was expert consensus about the weaknesses of the existing system, and there were credible predictions that the existing system was headed for collapse.

CONCLUSION

The 1994/98 pension reform in Sweden is remarkable in two ways. First, the pension reform is among the most far-reaching in the OECD. Swedish political actors have succeeded in refashioning the part of the welfare state that should be the most difficult to change because of the political risks associated with policy changes that involve retrenchment. Second, a broad multiparty coalition supports the pension reform. Although the major political parties disagree on some details, they have largely put these differences aside in favor of a series of broad compromises. The Social Democratic Party (SAP) was a crucial player in this coalition.

One of the most interesting aspects of the Swedish reform is that it 'takes the politics out of pensions'. If the notional defined contribution system and the automatic balancing mechanism function as intended, politicians no longer need to make significant legislative decisions about the level of pension rights and benefits. The new pension law prescribes detailed formulae for calculating pension rights and adjusting benefits each year, and these formulae are designed to automatically adjust pensions to changes in economic output, the level of employment, wage growth, inflation, life expectancy and other risks. This means that much of the (considerable) risk of financial market volatility, poor performance of the Swedish economy, and increases in life expectancy has been shifted from the state (and ultimately taxpayers) to successive cohorts of retirees. It remains to be seen how durable this aspect of the reform will be.

NOTES

1. This chapter draws heavily on Karen M. Anderson and R. Kent Weaver (2003), 'Pension politics in Sweden: Fundamental reforms in a policy cartel', unpublished manuscript.
2. The best 15 of 30 years benefit formula was intended to benefit white-collar workers and thereby attract their support for the ATP reform. However, the architects of the ATP system did not intend the degree of redistribution from blue-collar to white-collar workers that eventually occurred.
3. For overviews of the new pension system in English, see Ministry of Health and Social Affairs, 1998; Palmer, 2002; and Sundén, 2000.
4. Legislation enacted in 2001 ended mandatory retirement prior to age 67 (Palmer, 2002, p. 195).
5. For details see Palmer, 2002, pp. 176–177; Sundén, 2000, p. 9 and Settergren, 2002.
6. SOU 1994:21, *Reformerat pensionssystem. Kostnader och individeffekter. Bilaga A.*

REFERENCES

Ackerby, S. (1992), *Pensionsfrågan. Bilaga 12 till Långtidsutredningen 1992.*
Anderson, K.M. (1998), *The Welfare State in the Global Economy: The Politics of Social Insurance Retrenchment in Sweden*, PhD dissertation: University of Washington.
Anderson, K.M. (2001), 'The politics of retrenchment in a social democratic welfare state. Reform of Swedish pensions and unemployment insurance', *Comparative Political Studies*, **34**(9), 1063–1091.
Anderson, K.M. and R.K. Weaver (2003), *Pension Politics in Sweden: Fundamental Reforms in a Policy Cartel*, Unpublished manuscript.
Bröms, J. (1990), *Ur askan av ATP [Out of the Ashes of ATP]*, Stockholm: SACO.
Dagens Nyheter, various issues.
Ds 1992:89, *Ett reformerat pensionssystem-Bakgrund, principer och skiss*, En promemoria av Pensionsarbetsgruppen.
Esping-Andersen, G. (1985), *Politics Against Markets. The Social Democratic Road to Power*, Princeton: Princeton University Press.
Esping-Andersen, G. (1990), *The Three Worlds of Welfare Capitalism*, Princeton: Princeton University Press.
Huber, E. and J.D. Stephens (1998), 'Internationalization and the social democratic model. Crisis and future prospects', *Comparative Political Studies*, **31**, 353–397.
Immergut, E.M. (1992), *Health Politics*, Cambridge, UK: Cambridge University Press.
Lindbeck, A. (1992), *Klarar vi pensionerna? [Can we Reform Pensions?]*, Stockholm: SNS Förlag.
Lundberg, U. (2002), 'Socialdemokratin och 1990-talets pensionsreform', in J. Palme (ed.), *Hur blev den stora reformen möjlig? Politiken bakom den svenska pensionsreformen*, Stockholm: Pensionsforum.
Ministry of Health and Social Affairs (1998), *The Pension Reform: Final Report*, Stockholm: The Ministry of Social Affairs.

Ministry of Health and Social Affairs (2002), *National Strategy Report on the Future of Pension Systems.*

Myles, J. and P. Pierson (2001), 'The comparative political economy of pension reform', in P. Pierson (ed.), *The New Politics of the Welfare State*, Oxford: Oxford University Press.

Palmer, E. (2002), 'Swedish pension reform: How did it evolve, and what does it mean for the future?', in M. Feldstein and H. Siebert (eds), *Social Security Pension Reform in Europe*, Chicago and London: University of Chicago Press.

Palme, J. and I. Wennemo (1998), *Swedish Social Security in the 1990s: Reform and Retrenchment*, Stockholm: Ministry of Social Affairs.

Pierson, P. (1994), *Dismantling the Welfare State*, Cambridge, UK: Cambridge University Press.

Pierson, P. (1998), 'Irresistible forces, immovable objects: Post-industrial welfare states confront permanent austerity', *Journal of European Public Policy*, **5**(4) 539–560.

Pierson, P. (2001), 'Coping with permanent austerity: Welfare state restructuring in affluent democracies', in P. Pierson (ed.), *The New Politics of the Welfare State*, Oxford: Oxford University Press.

Pontusson, J. (1992), 'At the end of the third road: Swedish social democracy in crisis', *Politics and Society*, **20**, 305–332.

Proposition 1993/94: 250.

Proposition 1996/97: 1.

Regeringskansliet (2002), *National Strategy Report on the Future of Pension Systems*, 19.

Riksdag och Departement, 1994, issue no. 22.

Riksförsäkringsverket (National Insurance Board), *Social Insurance Statistics. Facts*, Stockholm: Riksförsäkringsverket, various years.

Settergren, O. (2002), *Pensionssystemets årsredivisning 2001*, Stockholm: Riksförsäkringsverket.

Söderström, H.T. (ed.) (1991), *Sverige vid vändpunkten. Konjunkturrådets rapport 1991* [*Sweden at the Turning Point. SNS Economic Policy Group Report 1991*], Stockholm: SNS Förlag.

Ståhlberg, A.C. (1993), *Våra pensionssystem*, Stockholm: SNS Förlag.

Statens Offentliga Utredningar [Official Commission of Inquiry] (1990), *Allmän pension*, report no. 76.

Statens Offentliga Utredningar [Official Commission of Inquiry] (1993), *Nya villkor för ekonomi och politik*, report no. 16.

Statens Offentliga Utredningar [Official Commission of Inquiry] (1994), *Reformerat pensionssystem*, report no. 20.

Statens Offentliga Utredningar [Official Commission of Inquiry] (1994), *Reformerat pensionssystem, Kostnader och individeffekter, Bilaga A*, report no. 21.

Sundén, A. (2000), *How Will Sweden's New Pension System Work?*, Chestnut Hill, MA: Boston College Center for Retirement Research Issue Brief No. 3, March 2000.

Svenska Dagbladet, various issues.

Weaver, R.K. and P. Pierson (eds), (1993) 'Imposing losses in pension policy', in *Do Institutions Matter? Government Capabilities in the US and Abroad*, Washington, DC: Brookings Institution.

6. UK pension reform: A test case for a liberal welfare state?

Peter Taylor-Gooby

BACKGROUND: THE UK POLICY CONTEXT

The UK combines a majoritarian polity with a liberal welfare system. State pensions have always been relatively weak compared with those elsewhere in Europe. The self-consciously right-wing Conservative government of Mrs Thatcher undertook a radical expansion of private pensions in the 1980s, seeking to extend them from the dominant form of provision for higher-income people to the dominant form for the whole population. This involved cut-backs in state pensions and deregulation of the private sector in accordance with a general philosophy of 'rolling back the state'. The New Labour government from 1997 onwards retained the themes of constrained state spending and reliance on competitive markets, but sought to redirect the liberal system towards welfare goals by expanding specific services, most notably the National Health Service, providing targeted benefits for poorer groups and regulating the private sector more strictly. This approach was legitimated as consonant with social democratic citizenship ideals through an ideology of equality of opportunity presented as a 'third way'. In pensions, the government has expanded means-tested provision as a pensioner 'tax credit', but is finding difficulties in designing a regulation regime that both delivers secure affordable pensions and is acceptable to the private sector.

UK experience offers an interesting test case of whether it is feasible to combine welfare and market liberalism. The case is particularly valuable, since the UK contains the most centralised system of government authority in Europe, currently administered by a reforming centre-left party with an exceptionally strong electoral mandate and an exceptionally weak opposition. The New Labour government is also committed to ensuring that the country enhances its international competitiveness and retains a highly flexible labour market. The case study shows how a liberal government that wishes to provide retirement benefits for its citizens is driven to combine tax-financed means-tested welfare for the poor with private provision for the better off. However, commitment to market competitiveness compels governments to constrain the means-tested sector (to keep taxes low and maintain incentives for private provision), so that it is necessary to introduce additional subsidised contributory pensions for those who cannot afford adequate private market pensions. Unless government is prepared to countenance substantial tax increases, such benefits are likely to remain at a level close to that available via the means-test. In addition, commitment to successful private provision, particularly in a country with a highly developed financial sector, precludes government from imposing strict regulation of private pensions. This leads to problems in ensuring the security of benefits for middle and higher income people, especially when demographic pressures are anticipated and economic growth is uncertain.

The UK is unusual among welfare states in its commitment to non-state welfare. The 'liberal test case' may offer useful insights; elsewhere, since the pension programmes of the EU, OECD and World Bank promote the expansion of private provision, and since reforms in the major European welfare states establish private supplementary pillars, which may eventually grow to the size and independence of that in the UK.

KEY FEATURES OF UK PENSIONS

The relatively lower involvement of the UK government in pension provision compared with other European countries is indicated by the Government Actuary's estimate that the unfunded liabilities generated by pay-as-you-go state pensions are only 24 per cent of GDP in the UK, as against 60 per cent for Italy, 102 per cent for France and 150 per cent for Sweden (Daykin, 1998). Similarly, ESSPROS data shows that by 1996, the UK spent 48 per cent of per capita GDP on each person above retirement age, compared with 62 per cent in Italy, 70 per cent in France, 64 per cent for Germany and 98 per cent for Sweden (EC, 2000a, Chart 31). Data from the UK Family Expenditure Survey shows that occupational and private pensions and investments have been long-standing sources of a substantial proportion of UK pensioners' incomes (Table 6.1). The proportion has increased from 27 per cent in 1979 to 43 per cent by 2000, while the contribution of state pensions has declined slightly from 60 to 67 per cent.

Pensioner incomes are markedly unequal. Table 6.2 shows that the richest fifth of pensioner couples have incomes five times those of the poorest fifth, while among single pensioners the ratio is four to one. Private pensions and investments make up the biggest component in income for the top fifth (two-thirds for couples, just over half for single pensioners) while for the poorer group, private sources are much less important and about 90 per cent of income comes from state pensions. Pension inequality has increased over

Table 6.1   Components of pensioners' household incomes, 1979–2000 (%)

	1979	1990–91	1999–2000
State pensions	60	50	52
Occupational pensions	16	22	26
Investments (inc. private pensions)	11	20	14
Earnings	11	7	8

Note: 1979 and 1990–91, UK data; 1999–2000, GB only.

Source: Calculated from ONS (2002) Table 5.4.

Table 6.2   Source of pensioners' incomes – lowest and highest quintiles and pounds, 1999/2000

	Lowest fifth	Top fifth
Pensioner couples		
State pensions	85	19
Non-state pensions	9	40
Investment income	5	26
Earnings	1	19
Other income	0	1
Gross income	£147	£746
Single pensioners		
State pensions	90	38
Non-state pensions	5	33
Investment income	5	19
Earnings	0	9
Other income	0	1
Gross income	£82	£338

Source: DSS Pensioners' Income Series 1999–2000.

time. Median retirement income is now just over half average earnings, having risen from about two-fifths in 1971. However, the median income of the top 20 per cent of pensioners, who are much more likely to have access to non-state pensions and investments, has gone up by 80 per cent in real terms since 1979 whereas that of the bottom 20 per cent has only increased by 34 per cent (Mayhew, 2001, p. 12). Not surprisingly, poorer pensioner households tend to be more reliant on state benefits. One indication of this is the fact that single person pensioner households, who tend to be older, receive 63 per cent of their income from state pensions, whereas two person pensioner households receive only 38 per cent (ONS, 2001).

The outcome is that UK pensioners are at greater risk of poverty than pensioners in most European countries. Thus, analysis of the 1994–96 European Community Household Panel Survey shows that, for the UK, the risk of a person over 65 having had an income below 60 per cent of the median for the whole three years was 48 per cent greater than that for the general population. In Italy the risk was 33 per cent lower, in France only 4 per cent higher, in Spain 1 per cent higher, and in Germany 4 per cent lower. For the EU 12 the risk is 14 per cent higher (EC, 2000b). The UK system spends a greater proportion on means-tested support for the poorest pensioners – about a tenth of state pension spending, as against 3 per cent in France, 2 per cent in Germany and virtually nothing in Denmark (Mayhew, 2001, p. 11).

THE POST-WAR PENSION SETTLEMENT AND THE FIRST WAVE OF REFORMS

The original 1948 pension scheme, based on the Beveridge Report, was a simple flat-rate, 'pay-as-you-go' scheme: flat-rate contributions, flat-rate benefits, with payments financed by contributions. Older people with inadequate contributions records were 'blanketed in', financed through general taxation. Means-tested National Assistance provided a safety net for the poorest. By 1960, the Basic State Pension was equivalent to around 15 per cent of average earnings. The private pensions industry expanded, largely providing occupational pension schemes for white-collar workers.

During the early 1970s, the growing recognition that the Basic State Pension left many pensioners on, or below, subsistence-level income (highlighted forcefully in an influential academic report: Abel-Smith and Townsend, 1965), the penalties suffered by 'early leavers' in occupational pension schemes, and the unwillingness of governments to make occupational pensions compulsory for all employers led to a pension reform debate in which Labour governments pursued proposals for a state second-tier contributory pension and Conservative governments for extending the private sector. In 1975, Labour passed a Social Security Act to provide a state second-tier pension, designed in such a way that good opportunities for the private market remained. The new State Earnings Related Pension Scheme (SERPS) provided a compulsory second-tier pension based on earnings-related National Insurance contributions. Employees contributing to an occupational pension scheme, which guaranteed a pension at least equivalent to SERPS, were permitted to 'opt out', and paid a reduced National Insurance rate. The scheme provided an additional pension equivalent to some 25 per cent of earnings, based on an employee's best 20 years of earnings. Meanwhile, the basic pension was to be increased in line with earnings or prices (whichever rose fastest), in order to reduce the need for means-tested supplementation for low-income workers.

The result of this settlement was that, by the beginning of the 1980s, some 60 per cent of workers could anticipate receiving their main source of income in retirement from state pensions and about 40 per cent from private, occupational or personal provision (DSS, 2000, ch. 2). The market for the private sector remained and would expand as more higher-income workers pursued a private third-tier option instead of or in addition to SERPS, as economic growth enabled them to do so. Employers were reconciled to the scheme since it was they, not individual workers, who decided who was to be included in occupational and SERPS pensions. They could thus provide private occupational pensions to attract key workers, without being forced to include those on lower incomes. Occupational pensions remained within a weak regulation regime so that, for example, employers (with actuarial approval) could invest a pension fund in their own business or decide to reduce their contributions.

PENSION PROBLEMS AS IDENTIFIED IN THE 1980S

The 1979 Thatcher government sought to expand private provision. The justification for reform was demographic. Population ageing (it was argued) would increase the cost of the 1975 settlement to an unsustainable level: 'we shall put a halt to the enormous growth in pension expenditure in the next century which the continuation of SERPS in its present form would have entailed' (DHSS, 1985a, p. 45). The Government Actuary's department estimated in 1986 that the total contribution rate necessary to fund the schemes would rise from 14.5 per cent in 1990 to 18.5 per cent by 2030 with a subsequent fall to 15 per cent by 2050, assuming that pensions continued to be indexed to prices. A later report in 1990, based on assumptions about more rapid increases in the retired population, put the rates by 2030 and 2050 between 3 and 4 per cent higher (Government Actuary, 1990). Such contributions are high by comparison with UK experience but do not exceed private sector or continental rates. A number of writers point out that UK demographic forecasts were actually more favourable than those experienced during the post-war expansion of the demographic system and did not obviously require major cut-backs in pension commitments (Disney, 1996). The Government Actuary estimates do not allow for the likely increase in the proportion of women in employment.

The Conservative Fowler pension review, described by the Secretary of State as 'a thorough review of the largest single element of social security provision in this country' (House of Commons statement, 2 April 1984), was set up in November 1983 and extended by a Housing Benefit Review and by reviews of Supplementary Benefit (assistance) and provision for children and young people in 1984. The pensions review team consisted of seven ministers and five senior figures from the pension industry.

The review recommended compulsory contributory occupational or portable private pensions, minimum contribution to be 4 per cent of income, split equally, 3 per cent of it rebated from National Insurance contributions. These would be Defined Contribution (DC) schemes, the resulting pension depending on the state of the annuity market at the time of retirement. SERPS would be phased out over time, the Basic State Pension would be continued, but not uprated and women and men should have equal rights (DHSS, 1985b, pp. 7–9).

This implies a radical transition to a liberal market system following the market ideology of the Thatcher government. The state would withdraw (as inflation whittled away at the value of the Basic State Pension and SERPS disappeared) to the role of pensioner provider for the poor. Unless workers could pay contributions at substantially over the minimum level, benefits were likely to be low, and all the risks associated with market fluctuations were borne by the pensioner rather than the provider.

THE SECOND WAVE OF REFORM

The most interesting feature of the resulting debate was the opposition of business and private interests to the wholesale extension of private pensions. The trajectory of reform illustrates the difficulties that even a committed right-wing government experiences in directing private providers to follow its plans and the difficulties it faces in regulating private actors, once it decides to use them to deliver its policies.

The Secretary of State (Norman Fowler) records: 'I had against me almost the whole of the pension industry . . . even more ominous both the CBI and the influential Engineering Employers' Federation had moved against me' (Fowler, 1991, p. 222). The pensions industry (most importantly the National Association of Pension Funds) opposed the changes because they wanted a secure market for occupational pensions and were concerned that small compulsory personal pensions with a 4 per cent minimum contribution would not be viable either for providers or for workers on low incomes, especially if they had interrupted contribution records. The contributions would not finance management costs, a seller's commission and profits, and provide a pension. The CBI and the employers' groups were concerned about the compulsory nature of the scheme and the implications for employers in terms of contributions (House of

Commons Library, 1995; see Pierson, 1994, p. 61). In this they were reinforced by the Treasury. The Chancellor (Nigel Lawson) opposed the compulsory second-tier pension on the grounds that it would increase commitments
to tax relief on contributions and would impose a burden on public and
private sector employers (Timmins, 1996, p. 403). Fowler regarded the
Treasury opposition as crucial. The CBI did not wish to defend SERPS in the
longer term but were concerned about a rapid transition and about compulsion (CBI, 1984, p. 7). The Institute of Directors, conversely, disapproved of
the scheme because it did not go far enough, and proposed the additional
privatisation of the basic National Insurance pension (House of Commons
Library, 1995).

The compromise scheme embodied in the 1986 Social Security Act diluted
the reforms and satisfied opposition by allowing SERPS to continue in a
reduced form. The target rate for SERPS was cut from 25 to 20 per cent of
relevant earnings, the pension was to be based on revalued lifetime earnings
rather than the 20 best years and surviving spouses' pensions were cut to half
of the deceased contributor's pension. These changes would halve the cost of
SERPS by the early years of the next century, so that only those unable to
gain access to private pensions would use it. At the same time personal
pensions were introduced on an optional basis, but with a Treasury subven-
tion of 2 per cent of National Insurance contribution for those who switched
before 1994. This made the scheme so attractive that by 1993 nearly 5 million
rather than the half million originally estimated had moved to personal
pensions and the cost to the Treasury in tax relief exceeded £2 billion, against
an original estimate of £500 million. An advertising scheme for the new
pension settlement (budgeted at £2 million) was deemed unnecessary. The
problem of mis-selling (whereby individuals for whom the shift was clearly
inappropriate since they would be unable to accumulate a satisfactory funded
pension before retirement were persuaded to switch by salespeople who were
keen to gain commissions) also arose. The government, however, needed the
private sector to promote private pensions and found regulation of their activities difficult.

The new legislation led to a rapid change in pension provision. However,
many personal pensions are likely to be relatively small and will thus simply
lift people on Basic State Pensions above the means-test level, so that the
scheme effectively offers a private substitute for state assistance.

Table 6.3 shows the rapid expansion of personal pensions, the fact that individuals may cease to contribute after taking them out or may hold more than
one pension and the relatively small proportion giving fully index-linked
pensions. The new pension settlement is outlined in Table 6.4.

Conservative reforms in the 1980s established the new portable personal
pensions (intended to supplant SERPS, which was drastically cut back) and

Table 6.3   The growth of personal pensions

	Individuals contributing (millions)	Policies in force (thousands)	% giving index-linked pensions
1973	–	0.6	–
1979	–	1.6	–
1989	4.2	11.6	45
1994	5.6	18.9	50

Source: Glennerster and Hills, 1998, Table 7.13.

Table 6.4   The UK pension system, 1979–2000

First-tier	PAYG basic state pension (indexed to prices only 1980–88, then de-indexed)
Second-tier state	PAYG SERPS (from 1979; in decline from 1988)
Second-tier Private	Funded occupation or funded portable personal (from 1988)
Assistance	Means-tested IS pension

simplified the regulatory regime for private and occupational pensions. At the end of the 1980s some 40 per cent of workers were entitled to SERPS second-tier pensions and 55 per cent to private, occupational or personal provision, so that about 15 per cent would be likely to have their basic pension supplemented by assistance (Agulnik, 1999, p. 59; DSS, 2000, ch. 2). By 1999, the proportion in SERPS had shrunk to about 20 per cent, 29 per cent were in personal pension schemes and 30 per cent in occupational schemes (House of Lords, 1999). Personal schemes initially grew rapidly, but then stabilised as concerns developed. Over 90 per cent of those on incomes of about £20 000 as against 40 per cent of those on £7000 were in private or occupational schemes (Agulnik, 1999, p. 60). Most of those entitled only to first-tier pensions would also receive some means-tested support.

THE EMERGENCE OF FRESH PROBLEMS: REGULATION AND THE MIS-SELLING SCANDAL

The new scheme involved a sharp expansion of reliance on private pensions. It had little impact on the living standards on the poorest pensioners who remained reliant on state pensions, supplemented by means-tested support. In the UK government system, a party in power with a strong parliamentary majority can afford to ignore minorities who are not in a position to influence election results. Thus problems with the new pensions only emerged gradually and took time to find their way onto the political agenda, becoming significant as a continuing conflict within the Conservative Party over membership of the euro, challenges to the leadership and a series of prominent corruption scandals weakened the government in the mid-1990s.

The two main parties positions offered contrary policies in the 1992 election campaign. Labour proposed restoring SERPS, uprating basic pensions and cutting back subsidies for the private sector. The Conservatives offered further incentives to choose private pensions. The latter won with a much reduced majority (21 seats) and from this stage Labour abandoned the idea that state pensions could in the future provide a central element in second-tier provision for the mass of the population, along with much of its state-centred programme.

Within the Conservative Party, the main conflict was between right- and left-wing groups in the party. The experience of the UK's ejection from the ERM in 1992 strengthened demands for tighter fiscal polices. These led to the 'Portillo reviews' of public spending designed to identify areas 'where better targeting can be achieved or from which the state can withdraw altogether' (Hansard, 8 February 1993, col. 683). The reviews constitute a proactive Treasury intervention in other policy areas, in contrast with the former reactive annual Public Expenditure Review system (Deakin and Parry, 1997). They presage the 1997 Labour government's 'Comprehensive Spending Review' and form part of the process whereby direct Treasury control of a widening range of aspects of social policy was introduced. The reviews led to the introduction of the Job Seeker's Allowance, the cuts in Invalidity Benefit (which were estimated to reduce the numbers entitled to claim by about 240 000 – Glennerster, 1997, p. 262), the justification of the final decision to equalise pension ages at the age of 65 rather than earlier (to be phased in by 2020), the abolition of a Guaranteed Minimum Pension requirement for portable pensions and the ending of SERPS indexation in the 1995 Pensions Act and of the arrangement whereby Income Support would pay mortgage interest but not capital repayments in 1996. The 1995 Act tightens the rules governing the calculation of earnings on which the SERPS pension is based. The net effect is to reduce projected SERPS spending by about 25 per cent by 2020 and by nearly half by 2040.

Despite opposition from the Conservative left, led by the Chancellor, Kenneth Clarke, the privatisation of pensions continued. The right-wing 'No Turning Back' group of Conservative MPs published proposals for the abolition of SERPS and the reduction of state pensions to provide a very basic means-tested minimum (Timmins, 1996, p. 513), echoed by John Biffen, First Secretary to the Treasury. The Bill to retrench SERPS was in fact defeated in the House of Lords on the issue of pension splitting after divorce, but the clauses were reinstated by the government. The Social Security Secretary, Peter Lilley, proposed that the state's role be limited to 'basic pension plus' – whereby the government provided the basic National Insurance pension and subsidised contributions to private sector schemes to continue the trajectory of privatisation in the run-up to the 1997 election, and the free market Adam Smith Institute launched proposals for the transfer of social security funds to stock market investments as the basis for a complete privatisation. These approaches fitted that advocated by the NAPF in a paper published in April 1995, which recommended that state involvement should be confined to those on low incomes and proposals by both the Institute of Directors and NAPF to privatise the second-tier of pensions in commentary on the election manifestos.

The regulation of the private pension industry also became a prominent issue in the early 1990s, brought to a head by revelations that a leading newspaper owner, Robert Maxwell, had misappropriated occupational pension funds to shore up unsuccessful businesses in 1991. However, regulation did not enter the policy agenda until it was combined with allegations of mis-selling against the industry after the 1992 election.

The scandals surrounding the mis-selling of personal pensions to individuals encouraged to opt out of SERPS when it was not in their interests to do so, emerged in the early 1990s. The influence of the industry weakened response. This problem is estimated by a government inquiry to affect nearly 1 million people, mainly older workers who were sold personal pensions by agents eager for commissions, although their contributions would have insufficient time to generate an adequate fund (Waine, 1995, esp. pp. 326–327; Goode, 1994). The Goode committee recommended stronger controls over private and occupational pensions and arrangements for the compensation of those who suffered as a result of mismanagement of funds. NAPF, the CBI, the TUC and the Securities and Investments Board endorsed these.

The CBI mounted a strong campaign, which succeeded in securing the crucial recommendations that employers would be in a majority on pension boards and that the employer should be able to make the key decisions on the nature of the pension scheme, despite opposition from the TUC. Goode recommended that employees should form a third of members and that employers should be in a position to decide benefit levels and conditions. This was embodied in the 1994 Act. In addition, concern was expressed by employees' representatives, the TUC and also by the Institute of Actuaries about the dilution of requirements for minimal solvency to a minimal 'level of funding' in the stipulations for the schemes, which effectively reduced the margin funds would be required to allow for changes in market conditions. The CBI lobbied successfully for the dilution of the minimum solvency requirement and for limitations to the ban on schemes investing their funds in the employers' company.

After an attack on pension commission agents by NAPF in 1984, the supervisory body, Lautro, launched a series of enquiries into companies and demanded that they compensate those who had lost money as a result of bad advice. The TUC had identified the power of employers as a major issue in occupational and personal pensions from the Maxwell scandal in 1991 (for example, *Annual Report*, 1993, p. 60) but did not start to campaign on the issue of mis-selling until much later (the first reference to active campaigning in the *Annual Report* is in 1996, p. 70). Some companies were fined for their unethical practices from the end of 1996 onwards, although it was not until 1998 that action was taken against the Prudential, the largest company and the one most prominent in mis-selling.

THE RE-MAKING OF LABOUR POLICY

Meanwhile, the Labour Party had substantially remade its policies in order to broaden its appeal outside its traditional (and shrinking) working class constituency, in response to the experience of successive election defeats. The party abandoned commitment to nationalisation, redistributive taxation and a strong provider welfare state and developed a programme that stressed instead the role of government as an enabling institution, ensuring that the UK retained a dynamic market-based economy, a flexible labour force and a strong competitive position in the world market. Social policy was intended to provide security for the poor through targeted benefits and programmes for the most deprived areas, but opportunities for the rest of the population, with a heavy commitment to education spending and a more active labour market policy, and a vigorous private sector.

This overall policy shift was reflected in the new approach to pensions. Although some figures, such as Tony Lynes (an advisor to the 1970s Wilson government), and Barbara Castle (the minister in that government responsible for the SERPS legislation), continued to advocate the restoration of SERPS, the main current of thinking in the party moved against the scheme. This was aided by the influential report of the party's Commission on Social Justice (1994). The report rejected the increase of the basic pension as too expensive and proposed a minimum pension guarantee, combining the basic pension and means-tested support (1994, p. 9). A universal second pension would supplement this, based on SERPS or a vaguely-described National Savings Pensions Plan. Occupational and personal second-tier private pensions would continue, under improved regulation. By the time of the election, party policy was moving towards a combination of the means-tested guarantee for lower income pensioners and second-tier regulated private or state second pensions for others – a substantial shift towards liberalism from its universalist social democratic position at the beginning of the 1980s, and the basis of its current policy position.

THE THIRD WAVE OF REFORM: 1997 ONWARDS

The New Labour government held basic state pension uprating to price inflation for its first year (in a clear contrast to the plans of the party in the 1992 election) and set up a fundamental review of social security under Frank Field, an MP who had built up a strong reputation for social security expertise, who was encouraged by the Prime Minister to 'think the unthinkable' in his approach to policy innovation. Attempts to ensure that a full restoration of SERPS was included on the policy agenda had been decisively rejected by the Labour leadership at the 1996 party conference, rebuffing the state-centred left-wingers. Field, as Minister for Welfare Reform, initially experimented with the idea of Stakeholder Pensions. However, there were considerable difficulties in achieving agreement by the industry and by civil servants on the details of a scheme that would have a strong mutual element, would involve regulation and would be compulsory (*Guardian* newspaper, 4 September 1997).

The 1998 Green Paper produced no specific proposals and referred to Field's idea of Stakeholder Pensions vaguely in the context of public–private partnership (DSS, 1998a, ch. 4). Field resigned. The labour government reforms, published immediately after Field's resignation (DSS, 1998b) reverted to the non-compulsory principle for the private sector, but included new state second pillar provision. The paper stated that the government's objective was to shift from the current 40 per cent of pensions provided by the private sector to 60 per cent by 2050, in line with the objectives of the previous Conservative government.

The new settlement included three elements:

- An assistance Guaranteed Minimum Pension (GMP) at a higher level than previous assistance and indexed to earnings. This would exceed the basic pension in most cases and effectively subsume it. The GMP was included in a Tax Credit negative income tax scheme from 2002.

- A new compulsory contributory State Second Pension (SSP), aimed at low to middle earners and providing blanketing in for disabled people and those with care responsibilities, subsidised from taxation. Employees can contract out of SSP into private, occupational or personal provision.
- A new private Stakeholder Pension (SHP), aimed at middle earners and regulated through an enhanced and transparent regime with mandatory indexation and low management charges.

The TUC broadly welcomed the new arrangements, but expressed some reservations about means-testing. Its consistent commitment throughout the 1990s had been to a high standard of basic NI pension, involving restoration of uprating in line with earnings, not prices, an additional well-regulated occupational second pension and a state second pension for those not in occupational schemes (see, for example, the TUC *Pensions Review*, 1998). This brought the TUC into conflict with Labour. 'The TUC cannot accept the idea that the Minimum Pension Guarantee should be means-tested, the uprating of the proposed second pension in line with prices only and the fact that employer contributions to the state second pension are not compulsory' (TUC *Annual Report*, 1999, p. 89). These features are endorsed by the CBI, which would prefer even more flexibility in occupational pensions (CBI, 1998, p. 13).

The Welfare Reform and Pensions Bill 1999 was subject to much opposition from Labour back benches, concerned particularly about provisions effectively to means-test previously insurance-based provisions for disabled and incapacitated people. The Labour majority was cut from 160 to 47, and the Bill was defeated twice in the House of Lords on these issues, but ultimately passed. The revolt has to be understood in the context of the Labour plans to eject most hereditary peers from the second chamber at the time.

Table 6.5   The UK pension system, 2000 onwards

First-tier state	PAYG basic state pension (indexed to prices only 1980–88) + means-tested GMP
Second-tier state	PAYG SERPS (from 1979; in decline from 1988) OR funded flat-rate SSP (to replace SERPS and only attractive to low earners)
Second-tier private	Funded occupational or funded portable personal (from 1988) AND/OR funded SHP (from 2002)

The new scheme effectively codifies the means-tested minimum arrangements towards which the Treasury has been working. It adds the new regulated second-tier Stakeholder Pension and substitutes a new State Second Pension for SERPS. Thus compulsion is avoided and the transfer between state and private sectors will be gradual. The pension industry has expressed concern about three aspects of the proposals, which might damage it: the fact that an individual cannot contribute to both stakeholder and occupational pensions; the possibility that some employers may move employees from occupational to the State Second Pension because it has a simpler and less onerous regulatory framework, and the complexity of regulation, which they would like further simplified (NAPF, 1999). The concerns about regulatory structure and arrangements to opt out of the State Second Pension were echoed by the DSS's 'Pensions Provision Group', consisting of industry and trade union representatives (Pensions Provision Group, 1999, sections 5–9). The government concedes the first point, so the State Second Pensions can supplement the incomes of those unable to afford adequate occupational pensions. Debates about regulation continue. While some practices (such as the right of a company to borrow from the fund of its own occupational pension scheme to finance investment) have been ended, issues such as the very limited liability of a bankrupt company to pensioners who reach retirement age after bankruptcy remain.

The chief problems with the new system as it operates in practice have been the reluctance of the pension industry to offer Stakeholder Pensions under the regulatory regime proposed, and the fact that SSP is likely to be unattractive if the GMP is adequate. Institute for Fiscal Studies projections estimate that, if the MIG is uprated by earnings, by 2025 as many as three-quarters of pensioners will fall within it (Clark and Emmerson, 2002, p. 13) so that incentives to save will be reduced.

It is difficult to combine a means-tested non-contributory pension for the poor at a decent level with contributory provision for those on lower-to-middle incomes, but it is necessary to do so if the government is not willing to tax finance provision for all those for whom the market cannot provide adequate benefits. Previously, the UK system had sought to avoid this problem with a universal basic pension at a level that took many low-income people just above the means-test. However, unwillingness to raise the hypothecated National Insurance contribution, which originally financed that benefit, meant that the basic pension fell to a level where it was unable to fulfil this role, increasing the pressure on the means-tested pension. New Labour is trapped between the desire to civilise the market by being generous to those who cannot contribute and enthusiasm for a market-based system for all who can, including those barely able to do so.

EMERGING PROBLEMS: SECURING ADEQUATE PENSIONS FROM A LIGHTLY REGULATED PRIVATE SECTOR

The issues surrounding the New Labour pension settlement will almost certainly require a further round of reforms in the near future, to ensure that the market for private pensions is protected while state pensions generate adequate incomes for the poorest pensioners. A further issue has emerged more recently concerning the downgrading of occupational pension entitlements in response to stock market uncertainty and demographic shifts.

Despite the emphasis on addressing the problem of pensioners' poverty through the adoption of tax credits (such as the pensions credits) and the MIG, there has been a shift away from the state to employers and employees in providing adequate provision for future retirees as Table 6.1 indicated. The decline in the level of Basic State Pension over 20 years and the termination of the State Earnings Related Pension Scheme mean that the burden of retirement income security now falls on private, employer-contribution schemes. This falls into three broad groups: occupational pension schemes, personal pension plans, and Stakeholder Pensions. In the past, many occupational schemes offered retirement benefits related to final salary – so-called defined benefit (DB) schemes, typically negotiated by trade unions. These applied to about three-fifths of employees. Now employers are replacing final salary schemes with defined contribution (DC) plans, transferring risks entirely to individual employees. The numbers covered by DB schemes fell from 5.6 million in 1991 to 3.8 million in 2001 (TUC, 2002).

Employers have also taken the opportunity to reduce their contributions. Typically DB schemes rested on equal employers and employees contributions. In the new DC schemes employers often pay much less 'typically . . . almost two-thirds less. The average long-term employer contribution [in DB schemes] is 15.4 per cent, in money purchases the figure is just six per cent' (TUC, 2002). This produces a saving to industry estimated at an annual £18.5 billion.

Government faces a further dilemma: any legislation that regulates or constrains these developments will be seen by employers as illegitimate interference in a market system. More broadly, policies that make provision less attractive to private providers will cause those firms to withdraw from the market. In any case the government's strong commitment to ensuring that UK business retains a good international competitive position and the labour market remains attractive to foreign investors precludes regulation that increases labour costs.

Business interests argue that pensions are becoming increasingly expensive for companies to run because of rising life expectancy and unnecessary regulations. These complaints are aimed primarily at regulations that impose minimum requirements of solvency on private occupational pension funds and require the annual reporting of assets and liabilities to company shareholders. The 'Minimum Funding Requirement' (MFR) was introduced in the 1995 Pensions Act to protect pensioners against a repeat of the Maxwell pension fund scandal and was designed to define the solvency level of pension funds, with quarterly reporting. However, it has the effect of encouraging pension funds to invest in ('safe') gilt-edged stocks, which distorts the gilts market, deters investment in venture capital products and generally results in lower returns on investments. The government agreed to review the MFR requirement. The consultation period ended in January 2001, but no major revision of MFR has yet been announced.

The new accounting standard requires firms operating occupational schemes and insurance companies to report the assets and liabilities of pension funds annually in company accounts. This move to greater transparency is opposed by the CBI and the pension industry on the grounds that it prevents the 'smoothing' of accounts between periods of profits and deficits and may influence share prices (*Guardian*, 11 May 2002).

The TUC has campaigned for a more substantial role for Basic State Pensions and restoration of SERPS. However, in pensions as in other policy areas it has had little influence on government policy. New Labour has sought to address the problem of encouraging those on lower incomes to invest in SSPs, despite the increased level of assistance by introducing Pension Credits from 2003. This benefit effectively tapers assistance entitlement at 40 per cent against contributory pension income (from SSPs and small occupational or personal pensions) rather than removing it directly the means-test threshold is reached. The new enhanced benefits are projected to have a substantial effect in reducing pensioner poverty from 11 to 6 per cent at the 60 per cent of household income standard (Emmerson, 2003, Table 1). The impact on incentives to contribute is at present unclear.

The problem of establishing satisfactory regulation of the private sector remains intransigent. Ministers have attacked private firms for using regulation as an excuse to cut labour costs (Alistair Darling, *Guardian*, 2002). Two reviews were set up in 2002, both led by senior figures from the pension industry. The Sandler review recommended compulsory employer contributions – popular with the TUC, but ignored by government. A second review, headed by Alan Pickering, former Chairman of the National Association of Pensions Funds, the industry's main lobbying body recommended relaxation of the regulation regime.

The December 2002 White Paper (DWP, 2002) was widely expected to contain the government's plans for resolving the problems with private and occupational pensions. However, it simply proposed more supervision and attempts to spread best practice but held back from intervention and specifi-cally ruled out three courses of action:

- an increase in the level of the Basic State Pension;
- a significant increase in the assistance pension;
- the introduction of a compulsory occupational pension system.

An enquiry to be headed by another industry figure, Adair Turner, will report on this in two or three years' time, introducing further delay.

The only major announcement since the White Paper is a proposal to intro-duce compulsory insurance to protect the entitlements of contributors to schemes in the event of company bankruptcy (up to 90 per cent of expected payments) on the US model. This has been criticised by professional bodies on the grounds that it may lead to further cut-backs in defined benefit schemes since the insurance will increase costs, and will tend to be an extra burden on well-run schemes that will be least likely to draw on the fund (IoA, 2003).

The government continues with its plans to rely on the private sector for the bulk of pension provision. However, it is unable to move towards a system that will provide satisfactory and secure regulation of the industry or to introduce further compulsion for employers in the provision of a uniform pension scheme on the model operated in most European countries. There is a contra-diction between commitment to the private sector and commitment to the guarantee of adequate, well-regulated provision for a range of income groups, and this appears most acutely in the area of pensions. The liberal approach to welfare runs into the problem that enthusiasm for liberal principles conflicts with the imposition of a framework for secure pensions.

THE POPULAR POLITICS OF UK PENSIONS

One puzzle in UK pension policy concerns the question of why policies that seem unlikely to serve obvious individual interests effectively, because pensions are receiving insufficient resources and are inadequately secured, just at a time when population ageing means that people will rely on them for a longer period in their life, do not arouse stronger opposition. The leading British attitude survey, British Social Attitudes, shows that pensions are seen as the top priority in social security throughout the period that the survey has run (since 1983). Increasing concern about this area of provision is indicated by the fact that the proportion of those interviewed who put pensions as first or second priority has risen from 63 to 76 per cent between 1991 and 2001 (Taylor-Gooby and Hastie, 2002, p. 79). There is serious and growing public disquiet about the adequacy of the pension system. Interestingly the level of concern is almost exactly the same among the higher and lowest income quartiles of the population despite the fact that the poor tend to rely on state pensions and the better off on private ones, as Table 6.2 shows. In fact the population appears well-informed about access to private pensions. For example, they judge accurately within 5 per cent the proportion of the population likely to be entitled to private pensions when they retire (Taylor-Gooby and Hastie, 2002, p. 88). The survey evidence appears to indicate an equal and high concern about both public and private pensions among different population groups. Professional and expert groups have expressed concern about the 'pensions funding gap' (IoA, 2002) and the 'pensions prospect' (Pensions Policy Institute, 2003) for some time. This raises the question of why the public disenchantment does not find a stronger political voice.

The answer is likely to be a combination of three factors. First the British constitutional system gives the government in office great authority. Dissenting voices can be disregarded. Secondly, the main political opposition, the Conservative Party, is also committed to a private solution, and thus unable to offer more than technical objections to government policies. The party's own pension policy, as set out in a recent speech by the opposition Work and Pensions spokesperson, is to encourage individual saving in private and occupational pension schemes, stimulated by a reduction in regulation and a cutback in the level of means-tested state support, which is to move rather further in the direction in which New Labour is already travelling (Willetts, 2003). Thirdly, while different social groups are united in discontent, they tend to favour different policy directions corresponding to their different interests and are unable to generate agreement on policy. While the TUC advocates a compulsory employers' pension scheme (TUC, 2003), the CBI representing business interests is in favour of state subsidies to encourage participation in voluntary stakeholder schemes, an approach close to, but rather more expensive than, the government's own model (CBI, 2003).

Within the framework of constituencies constructed by the divided British pension system it is difficult for a common policy front to emerge. Within the British policy-making framework, it is difficult for popular concerns to gain a purchase on policy-making. Thus, rising public disquiet about the weak prospects for pensions, reinforced by warnings from expert opinion, makes little difference to a government with an over-riding commitment to expansion of the private sector, unburdened by regulation. A number of commentators (Pierson, 1994; Rhodes, 2000, pp. 261–262) have argued that in the UK system governments may be limited in their policies by concerns about the impact of unpopular measures on future election outcomes. Policies are thus constrained by 'blame avoidance' (Weaver, 1986). So far the forces ranged against official pension policy seem to be so disunited as to be unable to bring responsibility for a particular inadequacy in pension policy home to government.

CONCLUSION

The UK government response to current demographic pressures and to the problems of funding pay-as-you-go state pensions has been dominated by a general concern to ensure that intervention in this area does not damage the operation of a relatively free and flexible economy, immediately expressed through accommodation to the interests of the powerful insurance industry. Thus Labour's 1975 SERPS pensions included provisions that encouraged middle and high earners to contract out, were shaped in order to preserve the market for private occupational pensions; the initial 1986 Conservative proposals were intended simply to privatise pension responsibilities, but the settlement was modified due to opposition from the industry (which did not want to be responsible for poor risks) into a scheme that subsidised transfer out of state pensions into weakly regulated private portable pensions. Reforms to this system by New Labour sought to provide pensions that would maintain the policy of shifting the bulk of provision onto the private sector while guaranteeing adequate incomes for the poorest pensioners. The resultant settlement produced a means-tested guarantee (which later became the Pensioner's Tax Credit), new funded pensions for lower to middle income groups (the SSP) and a new regulated private SHP regime. However, more generous assistance undermined the SSP, the industry was reluctant to provide SHP, since it feared that returns would be low and the private and occupational pensions for the better paid were cut back as the industry responded to pressures from demographic change and stock market decline. Further reforms seem likely in the near future, although it is unclear how the government can design a system that encourages people to save for their own pensions, provides decent pensions at the bottom end and does not pose a threat to the attractiveness of the private sector for some groups.

The UK experience illustrates how a government in a relatively strong centralised state with few veto points and a liberal policy-making tradition can pursue private pensions, without paying much attention to opposition from the pensioners' or trade union lobbies. It shows how the existence of a powerful private industry to which many pensioners look for incomes in old age can divide pensioner interests so that pensioners constitute a less powerful force in defence of existing state provision than in many other countries. It also shows that it is difficult to arrange regulation of a large and well-established private pension industry in a way that will protect all those investing in it and enable companies to compete in providing attractive pensions, especially at a time of financial instability. In addition it indicates the problems faced by a government that wishes to use such a system to provide adequate means-tested pensions for the poor, but to contain its tax commitments by ensuring that those on relatively low wages will choose to invest in contributory pensions.

Private provision seems likely to produce low pensions for some groups, but greater regulation will be seen to damage the pension industry and the broader labour market objectives of government. The mis-selling scandal shows the difficulty in regulating private actors when government needs those actors to advance its policies. UK governments have not so far succeeded in establishing a regime that makes private pensions work in the public interest for all its citizens, despite the fact that a centralised majoritarian polity gives an avowedly centre-left government exceptional authority. Whether New Labour can succeed in doing so in the future is an open question. If a majoritarian government cannot achieve this goal, other governments, who are more constrained by the necessity for compromise, may be wise to tread more cautiously in relying on the private sector for a major part of their future pension provision.

REFERENCES

Abel-Smith, B. and Townsend, P. (1965), *The Poor and the Poorest*, Occasional papers on social administration no.17, London: Bell.

Agulnik, P. (1999), *Pension Tax Reforms and the Green Paper*, Casepaper 24, LSE.

CBI (1984), *Evidence to the Government Special Enquiry into Pensions Provision*, April, London: CBI.

CBI (1998), *CBI News*, April, London: CBI.

CBI (2003), 'Press Release: Pensions Plan', 9 May.

Clark, T. and Emmerson, C. (2002), *The Tax-Benefit System and the Decision to Invest in a Stakeholder Pension*, London: Institute for Fiscal Studies.

Commission on Social Justice (1994), *Social Justice: Strategies for National Renewal*, London: Vintage.

Daykin, C. (1998), *Funding the Future?*, London: Politeia.

Deakin, N. and Parry, R. (1997), 'The Treasury and social policy', Social Policy Association annual conference, July.

DHSS (1985a), *Reform of Social Security*, Cmnd 9517 HMSO.

DHSS (1985b), *Reform of Social Security – Programme for Change*, Cmnd 9518 HMSO.

Disney, R. (1996), *Can We Afford to Grow Older? A Perspective on the Economics of Ageing*, Cambridge, MA: MIT Press.

DSS (1998a), *New Ambitions for Our Country: A New Contract for Welfare*, Cm 3805, HMSO.

DSS (1998b), *A New Contract For Welfare: Partnership In Pensions*, Cm 4179, HMSO.

DSS (1999), *Social Security Departmental Report 1999/2000*, Cm 4214, HMSO.

DSS (2000), *The Changing Welfare State*, Social Security Paper no. 2, HMSO.

DSS (2000), *The Changing Welfare State: Social Security Spending*, HMSO.

DWP (2002), *Security, Simplicity and Choice: Working and Saving for Retirement*, Cm 5677, HMSO.

EC (2000a), *Social Protection in Europe, 1999*.

EC (2000b), *Statistics in Focus 13/2000: Persistent Poverty and Living Standards*, Eurostat.

Emmerson, C. (2003), *Rewarding Saving and Alleviating Poverty: the Final Pension Credit Proposals*, Briefing Note no. 22, London: IFS.

Fowler, N. (1991), *Ministers Decide*, London: Chapmans.

Glennerster, H. (1997), *Paying for Welfare – Towards 2000*, Third Edition, London: Prentice Hall.

Glennerster, H. and Hills, J. (1998), *The State of Welfare*, Second Edition, Oxford: Clarendon Press.

Goode R. (1994), *Pensions Law Reform*, Cm 2342-1, HMSO.

Government Actuary (1990), *National Insurance Fund: Long-Term Financial Estimates*, London: HMSO.

Guardian, various issues.

Hansard (1993), House of Commons, Hansard Society.

House of Commons Library (1995), *Social Security Reforms*, reference sheet no 85/6.

House of Commons statement, 2 April 1984.

House of Lords (1999), *Welfare Reform and Pensions Bill: Explanatory Notes*, session 1998–99, HL Bill 62-EN.

IoA (Institute of Actuaries) (2002), Press Release, 19 December.

IoA (Institute of Actuaries) (2003), Press Release, 11 June.

Mayhew, L. (2001), *A Comparative Analysis of the UK Pension System*, mimeo, Birkbeck College.

NAPF (1999), *Green Paper: Pensions in Partnership*, NAPF Policy Document.

O'Hara M. (2002), 'Minister accuses firms over pensions', *Guardian*, 11 May.

ONS (2001), *Social Trends* (annual UK statistical report).

ONS (2002), *Social Trends* (annual UK statistical report).

Pensions Policy Institute (2003), *The Pensions Landscape*, London: PPP.

Pensions Provision Group (1999), *Response to the Pensions Green Paper*, HMSO (http://www.dss.gov.uk/hq/pubs/ppg/response/group.htm).

Pierson, P. (1994), *Dismantling the Welfare State?*, Cambridge: Cambridge University Press.

Rhodes R.A.W. (2000), 'Understanding the British Government: An anti-foundational approach', in Rhodes R.A.W. (ed.), *Transforming Government*, London: Macmillan, 256–275.

Taylor-Gooby, P. and Hastie, C. (2002), 'Support for state spending: Has New Labour got it right?', in A. Park, J. Curtice, K. Thomson, L. Jarvis and C. Bromley (eds), *British Social Attitudes*, London: Sage.

Timmins, N. (1996), *The Five Giants*, London: Fontana.

TUC (1990–99, annual), *Annual Report to Congress*, TUC.

TUC (1998), *Pensions Review*, TUC.

TUC (2002), *Pensions in Peril: The Decline of the Final Salary Pension Scheme*, A TUC assessment, available at http://www.tuc.org.uk.

TUC (2003), 'Detailed Response to the Government's Pension Statement', press release, 11 June.

Waine, B. (1995), 'A disaster foretold? The case of personal pensions', *Social Policy and Administration*, **29**(4), 317–334.

Weaver K. (1986), 'The politics of blame avoidance', *Journal of Public Policy*, **6**, 371–398.

Willetts, D. (2003), *New Conservative Fair Deal Plan for Pensions*, 23 May.

7. Switzerland: Adapting pensions within tight institutional constraints

Giuliano Bonoli

INTRODUCTION

The Swiss pension system is often praised in international comparisons, for its capacity to combine successful needs coverage with a solid financial basis. This combination of what are sometimes conflicting goals is achieved thanks to a system structured around three pillars of provision. The first one is universal and has the task of providing all retirees with a minimum income level above the poverty line; the second pillar is compulsory for most employees, is fully funded, and provides earnings-related benefits. Finally, the third pillar is a purely voluntary top up encouraged through generous tax concessions. The multipillar character of the system and the inclusion of both pay-as-you-go and funded financing are its key strengths.

Praise notwithstanding, the Swiss pension system does not escape the effects of developments like population ageing or the transformation of labour markets that are putting pressure on pension systems throughout the industrial world. Expenditure on its pay-as-you-go financed first pillar is expected to soar over the next two to three decades at a much higher rate than scheme receipts. The fund of the basic pension has been making losses in several of the last few years, and a key objective of current reform initiatives is to guarantee the solvency of the scheme in the medium to long term.

Population ageing, however, does not affect the basic pension only. Second pillar occupational pensions have to deal with the issue of higher life expectancy at the age of retirement (typically between 62 and 65). As pensioners live longer, the cost of annuities increases, or put another way, with the same amount of capital accumulated, the pensioner will have to finance a longer retirement and as a result will obtain a lower annuity. This trend makes it difficult to continue to achieve the target replacement rate of the Swiss pension system, set at 60 per cent of gross earnings, unless contributions to second pillar pensions are increased. Reform initiatives in the field of occupational pensions aim at securing the current level of benefits, but without imposing excessive burdens on pension funds: an exercise that may prove to be more difficult than expected.

137

In addition to preparing for population ageing, policy-makers have also been under pressure because of the exclusionary mechanisms that exist in the system. In fact, occupational pension coverage is compulsory only for employees with earnings above about 35 per cent of the average wage. Many part-time workers, often women, fail to reach this threshold and are as a result excluded from compulsory coverage. Over the last few years this issue has been picked up by several political actors, including the government, with a view to improving pension coverage for these disadvantaged workers. One of the reasons why this issue has acquired such political salience is undoubtedly the tremendous rise in part-time employment and other forms of atypical work over the last few years. Today Switzerland has one of the highest rates of part-time employment among Western nations, concerning about a third of the workforce. More than 50 per cent of women who are involved in the labour market work part-time. Among women with young children, the proportion exceeds 80 per cent (of those who work). Those at risk of permanent or long-term exclusion from occupational pension coverage are not a marginal minority any longer, rather they are beginning to constitute an electorally interesting social group.

In sum, the Swiss pension system is under pressure from two sides. On the one hand, expected increases in expenditure on the basic pension, and the impact of gains in life expectancy on annuity prices, call for austerity measures to guarantee the long-term sustainability of the system. On the other hand, political demands for better pension coverage for disadvantaged workers push the system in the opposite direction: better provision for those who do less well in the current system.

This combination of two simultaneous and opposite pressures on the system could be seen as a major obstacle to effective reform. The system is expected to take on new commitments at a time when it may fail to honour previous ones. In this chapter, however, I make the opposite claim: rather than an obstacle to reform, this combination of pressures represents an opportunity for effective policy change. In fact, in the context of the Swiss political system, characterised by a high density of veto points, the presence of these two contrasting pressures widens the scope for quid pro quos and compromises, an essential quality of successful policy-making in the country. In practical terms, politically robust compromises can be arranged so that responses are given to both pressures. Cuts in pension entitlements can generate savings that can in part be directed towards improving the provision of the weakest in the labour market. Past instances of welfare reform have shown that such retrenchment-cum-expansion compromises are extremely politically strong, and likely to be successfully turned into law.

The chapter starts by reviewing some key features of the Swiss political system that are crucial for substantiating the interpretation put forward. It then moves on to a chronological account of pension policy in Switzerland, starting with a description of the post-war settlement in pension policy, and ending with the reforms adopted and discussed since the early 1990s. The conclusion highlights the link between political institutions and pension policy-making.

THE SWISS POLITICAL SYSTEM, VETO POINTS AND POLICY-MAKING

The Swiss political system is structured by a set of institutions that reduce the potential for power concentration with one single actor and encourage the formation of large coalitions. The constitutional order is geared towards limiting the power of the federal government, and includes a number of points at which its authority can be challenged and its decisions overruled. The result is a political system in which the extent of agreement needed to legislate is particularly large. These institutional features, which are briefly reviewed in this section, are combined with a social structure characterised by multiple cleavages: socio-economic, religious and linguistic ones, which further reduce the likelihood of power being concentrated in the hands of one group. This combination of institutional and socio-structural features has produced a political system based on the integration of dissent and on the inclusion of conflicting interests in the policy-making process, which has been termed consensus or consociational democracy (Lehmbruch, 1993; Lijphart, 1984).

Political Institutions

There are at least three institutional features in the Swiss political system that contribute to reducing the level of power concentration available to the government: de facto separation of powers between the executive and the legislative branches of government; federalism with territorial representation in the (bicameral) federal parliament, and a referendum system.

The relationship between the Swiss government (Federal Council) and parliament have been described as a hybrid between European parliamentarism and US separation-of-powers (Lijphart, 1984). Like in parliamentary regimes, the Federal Council is elected by parliament, however, like in a separation-of-powers system, it cannot be brought down by the legislature during its four-year term. Parliamentarians are not under the same pressure to support government-sponsored legislation as is the case in parliamentary systems. Conversely the Federal Council cannot dissolve parliament. The result is a system in which the government has relatively little control over parliament. Like in the US, it has to negotiate policy with the legislature, as it cannot impose it.

The second element of power fragmentation is federalism, and the representation of the territorial units (cantons) in the upper chamber of parliament. Swiss bicameralism, designed after the US model, is symmetric, and while in the lower chamber (National Council) territorial representation is proportional to the size of the population, in the upper chamber (Council of States) each canton is entitled to two representatives. The power of the numerous, but small, rural cantons is thus magnified. Members of the Council of States vote freely and not under the instruction of their respective cantonal government. Voting patterns in this chamber suggest that partisan affiliation is a much more powerful predictor of voting than cantonal origin. Bicameralism, however, still matters, because the party composition of the upper chamber is considerably more right-wing oriented than that of the National Council. The fact that only two members per canton are elected favours alliances between the politically stronger right-of-centre parties that in many cases are able to win both cantonal seats.

Third, and perhaps most notably, Switzerland has a referendum system that allows voters to bring various issues to the polls.[1] Neidhart (1970) goes as far as arguing that referendums are the key factor behind the development of a consensus-based political system in Switzerland. In fact, the government, in order to reduce the vulnerability of its bills to the referendum challenge, has adopted an inclusive policy-making strategy. By allowing the relevant actors to co-draft legislation, policy-makers have been able to limit the threat potential of referendums. While referendums are an undeniably important factor in shaping Swiss politics, it can be argued that the development of a consociational is a result of both institutionally-based power fragmentation, of which the referendum system is only one element, and of the multicultural character of Swiss society, which to be successfully cohesive requires some measure of power-sharing between the various collectivities (Lehmbruch, 1993, p. 45).

POLICY-MAKING PRACTICES

The peculiar set of political institutions described above has resulted in a number of rather unusual political and policy-making practices. One of the most striking of these is an oversized coalition government. The federal government (Federal Council), which has had the same party composition since 1959, consists of a four-party coalition that includes the Christian Democrats, the Social Democrats, the Free Democrats and the Swiss People's Party (ex Farmers' Party). Together, these parties account for some 87 per cent of the seats in the lower chamber of parliament, and 100 per cent in the upper chamber. A government could rule with the support of any three of these four parties. The strength of the governing coalition, however, is only apparent, as its ability to resist external challenges is matched by a tendency to internal cleavages, compounded by the fact that the coalition covers nearly the whole political spectrum.

A second important consociational practice is a policy-making process in which interest groups play a substantial role in the definition of policy (Papadopoulos, 1997). Typically, legislative change is preceded by a lengthy and highly structured consultation procedure, which can be more or less encompassing depending on the potential for controversy of the relevant policy. Legislation is often drafted by 'expert commissions', which normally include representatives of all the relevant interest groups. The outcome of expert commissions is usually a compromise that is acceptable to all parties concerned, as each group has a de facto veto power that it can exert by threatening the use of the referendum challenge. During the golden age of the consensus model (1950s and 1960s) the agreements reached in this way were generally accepted by parliament with very little change (Kriesi, 1982; 1995). In more recent years, and especially in pension policy, parliament has become increasingly reluctant to ratify agreements reached by interest groups and, on various occasions, has imposed changes in a more majoritarian way.

This rather peculiar set of political institutions and practices has important implications for policy-making, particularly in the field of social and pension policy. Pension policy and reform are very much about redefining distributional equilibria. Every time change in legislation is likely to result in some groups of people being better off, and some others being worse off, relative to the pre-reform situation. Given the high density of veto points, those believed to be the losers in the reform have several opportunities to challenge it, to prevent its adoption or to try and change its content by threatening to call a referendum against it. This threat is particularly effective when it comes to pension retrenchment. The pension system is strongly appreciated by the population and popular with large sections of the electorate, not only on the left. As a result, political actors who oppose retrenchment can effectively use the referendum weapon or threaten its use. The result is that in policy in general, but even more so in pension policy, it is essential to have a relatively broad agreement on a reform initiative if this is to have any chance to be adopted.

THE POST-WAR SETTLEMENT IN PENSION POLICY (1945–85)

The development of a comprehensive and comparatively generous pension system in Switzerland was the result of a process that lasted several decades. The current system, consisting of three different pillars of provision, has been operational since 1985 only. Its origins go back to the early post-war years. In fact, before World War II the federal government was not involved in pension policy, in spite of an attempt made in the late 1920s to introduce a national basic pension. The proposal was rejected in a referendum in 1931.

A federal pension scheme was first adopted in 1948 with the establishment of the first pillar of the Swiss pension system. The scheme (AVS),[2] which in the meanwhile has been subjected to numerous reforms, covers the basic needs of retirees. It is moderately earnings-related and includes a means-tested pension supplement (PC).[3] It provides universal coverage and a fair degree of vertical redistribution, due to a compressed benefit structure: the highest pension is worth only twice as much as the lowest one. Contributions, in contrast, are proportional to earnings without a ceiling. Even though its benefits are moderately earnings-related the Swiss basic pension is a scheme of Beveridgean inspiration, geared towards poverty prevention rather than income maintenance. As a matter of fact, in international comparisons AVS is often considered together with flat-rate pension schemes (for example, Schmähl, 1991, p. 48). As far as financing is concerned, the AVS works on a pay-as-you-go basis, but has accumulated funds equal to roughly one year of outlays. It is financed through contributions (4.2 per cent of salary each for employees and employers; up to 7.8 per cent for the self-employed), and receives a subsidy equal to 19 per cent of expenditures. Coverage is universal: those who are not working (for example, students) are required to pay flat-rate contributions or, if providing informal care, are entitled to contribution credits.

The second pillar consists of occupational pensions, and according to the federal constitution has the task of providing retirees with a standard of living close to the one they experienced while in work. Occupational pensions were first granted tax concessions in 1916.[4] They developed substantially throughout the 20th century, but for many years coverage remained patchy. In 1970, some 50 per cent of employees were covered by an occupational pension. For women, the proportion was a much lower 25 per cent. Since 1985, however, occupational pension coverage is compulsory for all employees earning at least twice the amount of the minimum basic pension (CHF 25 320 per annum in 2003, or about 35 per cent of average earnings). Today, the rate of coverage approximates 100 per cent for male employees, but reaches only 80 per cent in the case of women (DFI, 1995, p. 10). Benefits vary according to the type of pension fund, though the law prescribes minimum requirements. As far as financing is concerned, occupational pensions are funded schemes. They are financed by employer/employee contributions, the former contributing at least as much as the latter. The law prescribes limits on how the funds can be invested. For example, bonds issued by the federal government can constitute up to 100 per cent of a pension fund's assets, but only up to 30 per cent of funds can be invested in stocks. In 1998 private sector pension funds had their assets invested mostly in bonds (28.9 per cent of all assets), in stocks (22.0 per cent) in investment funds (16.2 per cent), and in real estate (12.4 per cent) (OFS, 2001).

When, in 1985, occupational pension coverage was made compulsory, many employees were already covered by voluntary arrangements of this kind. Just before the coming into force of the new law in 1985, some 80 per cent of all employees already had access to occupational pension coverage, though for a quarter of them the level of provision was lower than the compulsory minimum (Conseil Fédéral, 2000b, p. 6). The situation was such that legislation needed to take into account the existence of a relatively developed system of voluntary occupational pension provision. As a result, it was decided to introduce a compulsory minimum level of provision (known as 'Obligatorium'), which is calculated on the basis of notional contributions,[5] leaving relatively wide room for manoeuvre to existing pension funds regarding how to deliver and finance that minimum level of provision. Many pension funds (especially in the public sector, or those sponsored by large employers) offer better conditions than Obligatorium (Vontobel, 2000).

Individual pension funds are thus free to adopt the rules they wish to determine the level of benefits, provided that the final benefit is at least equal to what a worker would have received if covered by Obligatorium. The latter is calculated on the basis of notional contributions. Depending on the employee's sex and age, notional accounts are credited with a percentage of insured earnings, ranging from 7 to 18 per cent (see Table 7.1). An interest rate decided by the government is then applied to the amounts credited. At the time of the introduction of the law this rate was set at 4 per cent per annum, and remained unchanged until 2003. It was then reduced to 3.25 per cent, and in 2004 further lowered to 2.25 per cent. Upon retirement the notional capital accumulated

Table 7.1   Notional contribution rates for mandatory occupational pensions (percentage of insured earnings)

Men		Women	
Age	Rate	Age	Rate
25–34	7	25–31	7
35–44	10	32–41	10
45–54	15	42–51	15
55–64	18	52–62	18

Source: Loi fédérale sur la prévoyance professionnelle, 1982.

over the years is converted into a pension, on the basis of a conversion rate set by the government (currently of 7.2 per cent). These rules determine how the minimum benefit (Obligatorium) is calculated. This is best seen as a 'test' that a pension benefit must fulfil in order to be legal. In fact, pension funds are totally free to use different rules for the calculation of benefits, though many follow the rules of Obligatorium quite closely.

Individual pension funds enjoy substantial room for manoeuvre also with regard to the financing of pension funds. The law prescribes only that the fund must have sufficient reserves to fully fund the commitments made (which is determined on the basis of actuarial calculations), and that the employer should contribute at least 50 per cent of the total amount paid into the fund. As a result, one finds big variations in the way pension funds are financed. Many have adopted age-related actual contributions that reproduce the notional contributions determined by law. Others have preferred an age neutral contribution rate. There are differences as well in the way in which contributions are shared between employers and employees.

Together, the first and the second pillar of the Swiss pension system have the objective of replacing 60 per cent of gross earnings up to a ceiling equal to three times the maximum AVS benefit. For very low paid workers, this goal is achieved by the moderately earnings-related benefits provided by AVS. For this reason, occupational pension coverage is compulsory only for earnings comprised between the lower limit (CHF 25 320) and the ceiling (CHF 75 960). Most of those who are excluded are part-time workers (most of whom are women), whose earnings do not reach the threshold that provides access to occupational pension coverage.

Finally, the third pillar of the pension system, private provision, consists of tax concessions for payments made to personal pension schemes. Employees who are already covered by an occupational pension can deduct from their taxable income contributions paid into a third pillar pension up to approximately CHF 6000 per year. Tax concessions are more substantial for people who are not covered by an occupational pension (like the self-employed). Personal pensions play a relatively small role in the Swiss pension system. The size of this industry, however, is expanding fast. Between 1996 and 1997 assets held by third pillar pension providers increased by almost CHF 10 billion, to 78 billion (or 20 per cent of GDP).

THE 1990S: ECONOMIC CRISES AND CONCERNS FOR SUSTAINABILITY

The early 1990s constituted a turning point in the recent economic history of Switzerland, as the country faced a profound economic recession and its first

Table 7.2   Receipts, outlays and balance of the AVS pension scheme, 1990–97 (millions CHF)

	1990	1991	1992	1993	1994	1995	1996	1997
Receipts	20 355	22 034	23 160	23 856	23 923	24 512	24 788	25 219
Outlays	18 328	19 688	21 206	23 046	23 363	24 503	24 817	25 803
Balance	2 027	2 345	1 954	810	561	9	−29	−583

Source: *Sécurité Sociale*, various issues.

employment crisis since 1945. The unemployment rate went up from 0.5 per cent in 1990 to 3.9 per cent in 1993; economic growth was negative for three consecutive years between 1991 and 1993. This dismal economic performance had obviously little to do with population ageing, but contributed to create a pessimistic political and social climate that proved fertile ground for cata-strophic scenarios concerning the non-sustainability of current pension arrangements. In addition, as a direct consequence of economic difficulties (lower contribution receipts) the balance of the AVS scheme deteriorated in those years (Table 7.2).

The early 1990s, perhaps because of the economic crisis, were also the years of an unprecedented political offensive of some sections of the business community, mostly the export-oriented sector, which expressed its dissatisfaction with the overall post-war political economy settlement on various occasions (Bonoli and Mach, 2000). The long-term sustainability of the pension system became one of the arguments that were put forward in an attempt aimed at redefining distributional equilibria. The critique concerned both the first pillar and occupational pensions, even though what came under attack in relation to the latter was not so much the financial commitments undertaken (these are fully funded) but the compulsory character of the programme (Pury et al., 1995).

Concerns for the long-term sustainability of the pension system entered the public debate in the early 1990s, but it is not until 1995 that the government provides some figure concerning likely developments in this respect. The first high profile forecasting exercise was included in a report published by the government on the future of the three pillar pension system (DFI, 1995). The current and projected costs of the basic pension were expressed in equivalent points of VAT, even though, as seen above, VAT is not directly used to finance pensions. Expenditure was expected to rise from the equivalent of 13.8 VAT percentage points in 1994 to 17 or even 18.2 in 2010, if the worse case scenario was to become realised (DFI, 1995, p. 59). One of the conclusions of the report was that a reform was needed to guarantee the long-term financing of the basic pension in the light of expected demographic trends. It was to be the eleventh reform of the basic pension. Concerning occupational pensions, the report did not raise issues of sustainability, but indicated that improvements in provision were needed (full indexation of pensions after retirement, extension of coverage).

Demographic projections were the key feature of two subsequent reports, which had the task of assessing the long-term sustainability of the whole social security system, including other social insurance programmes like health or invalidity insurance. The first one was published in June 1996 (IDA FiSo 1), and the second in December 1997 (IDA FiSo 2), and confirmed the views expressed in the 1995 report, but took the projection forward until 2025. The most recent projection exercise is an update of the 1997 report, and, based on assumptions made under more favourable economic conditions, it depicts a less worrying picture. According to this report, expenditure on the basic pension, if expressed in VAT percentage points equivalent, will rise from 10 in 2000 to 11.4 in 2010 and to 14.2 in 2025 (DFI, 2002).[6] These reports provided the background to much of the pension policy-making that went on in the 1990s and early 2000s.

The 1995 Pension Reform (Tenth AVS Revision)

As concern for the long-term sustainability of the Swiss pension system was mounting in the first half of the 1990s, policy-makers were busy with a reform of the basic pension scheme (tenth AVS revision) that had started over a decade earlier, and had the objective of introducing gender equality and improving pension coverage for women. Progress on this reform, however, was slow, so that a bill was first presented in parliament in 1990. It dealt with all the elements of gender discrimination that existed in the previous legislation, but maintained a differentiated age of retirement for men and women, at the time set at 65 and 62 respectively. The 1990 pension bill, however, was substantially redrafted by parliament. New elements were introduced that improved the coverage for women, such as contribution sharing between spouses and contribution credits for carers. More controversially, amidst concerns for the financial sustainability of the scheme, a coalition of right-of-centre MPs managed to put through the introduction in the bill of an increase in women's retirement age from 62 to 64.

This decision, unexpected by most actors including the government, became the most controversial element of the reform. The overall aim of the pension reform was to achieve compliance with the constitutional article on gender equality, which theoretically applied to retirement age as well as to the other areas of pension policy. However, when presenting the 1990 bill, the government had argued that given the persistence of substantial inequalities in the labour market at the expense of women (wages, access to occupational pensions, and so forth), the difference in retirement age was justified for the time being, and the issue would be dealt with in the next (the eleventh) revision of the AVS pension scheme (*Feuille Fédérale*, vol. 2, 1990, 1–231). Switzerland does not have a constitutional court, and the interpretation that the government makes of the constitution tends to be regarded as the most legitimate. From the legal point of view, thus, parliament was not under pressure to equalise the age of retirement. Nonetheless, the proponents of this measure gave two reasons for raising the age of retirement for women: to comply with the constitutional requirement of gender equality and to achieve some savings in view of the predicted worsening of the contributors/beneficiaries ratio within the state pension scheme (Bonoli, 2000, p. 107).

The trade unions considered the increase in women's retirement age unacceptable, and decided to call a referendum against the pension bill. They succeeded in collecting the 50 000 signatures needed to that effect. The vote took place in June 1995 and saw a relatively clear prevalence of those in favour of the bill (60.7 per cent). Opinion poll data, collected soon after the vote took place, suggest that an increase in retirement age for women, adopted independently from the improvements included in the bill would have been at a much higher risk of being defeated in a referendum. What made possible the only retrenchment element of the reform was its combination with a series of improvements.

As Table 7.3 shows, the main division among voters was between those who believed that the expansion aspects outweighed the retrenchment ones on the 'yes' side, and those who believed the opposite on the 'no' side. The

Table 7.3   Reasons for accepting or rejecting the 1995 pension reform in the referendum (spontaneous replies, multiple answers were possible)

Reasons for voting 'yes'	per cent	Reasons for voting 'no'	per cent
1. It is a general improvement	25	1. Higher retirement age for women	59
2. Higher retirement age for women	10	2. Unemployment	20
3. Gender equality	17	3. It is a drawback	10
4. Contribution sharing	14	4. Was not necessary	3
5. Contribution credits	15		
6. Savings	6		
7. Recommended by government	8		

Source: Vox, 1995.

reasons given by a clear majority of 'yes' voters concern the improvement side of the bill (items 1, 3, 4 and 5). According to the poll, only a minority would have supported the bill regardless of the presence of these improvements (items 2, 6 and 7). The bill would have encountered stronger opposition had it not included elements that were widely regarded as improvements. Conversely, among 'no' voters, the main reason for opposing the bill was, overwhelmingly, the increase in women's retirement age (59 per cent). Items 2 and 3 in fact refer to the same reason, as an increase in retirement age was expected to impact negatively on employment.

The analysis of the process that led to the adoption of the 1995 pension reform is important in highlighting the mechanisms that make possible retrenchment-oriented reforms in a fragmented political system like that of Switzerland. Two sets of measures, improvements and retrenchment, were included in a single piece of legislation. As a result, the left was unable to challenge the one element of retrenchment, the increase in women's retirement age, without taking the risk of undermining the parts of the bill it supported (the improvements). The combination of elements of retrenchment and expansion in a single piece of legislation was imposed by the right-wing parliamentary majority against the will of the left. This strategy, of combining different components in a single act, proved very effective in securing the adoption of the 1995 bill and was used equally successfully in other instances (see Bonoli, 1999; 2001).

ADAPTING PENSIONS TO AN AGEING SOCIETY

The declared objective of the tenth AVS revision was to deal with the gender equality problems that existed in the pre-1995 structure of the scheme. Policymakers, however, were not completely oblivious of the financial difficulties that pensions were going to face in the following years. As a matter of fact, during the final years of the 1995 pension reform process, work had already started on the eleventh revision of the AVS scheme, which had the objective of adapting pensions to population ageing.

Together with this initiative, which concerns the basic pension only, the government started work on a second reform, this time of the law on occupational pensions, known as the first revision of LPP.[7] Here too the objective was also to adapt to population ageing. In fact, even though in the public discourse on pensions it is generally claimed that funded pension provision is insensitive to demographic shifts, the increase in average life expectancy that has occurred over the last few decades, and will most likely continue into the foreseeable future, constitutes a major problem for the level of pensions that can be financed with a given amount of capital. In the Swiss case, as seen above,

DC pension schemes must apply a conversion rate set by the government. This, currently set at 7.2 per cent was calculated on the basis of the average life expectancy of the early 1980s. Today, the actuarially determined rate would be around 6.5 per cent. Against this background, the objective of the reform of the occupational pension law is to adapt the conversion rate to the new demographic structures without generating reductions in pension entitlements. This can only be achieved through higher contribution rates.

The Eleventh AVS Revision

The eleventh AVS revision was presented in parliament in early 2000. Initially, it had two main objectives: to guarantee the solvency of the scheme until 2010–15, and to introduce more flexibility in the transition from work to retirement, by means of early retirement, part-time pensions or delayed retirement, a set of measures that became known in Switzerland as *retraite à la carte*. These two objectives were to be pursued with a mix of expansion and retrenchment measures, in a way that very much reflects the final result of the tenth revision.

The bill contained a long catalogue of measures aimed at increasing revenues and at containing expenditure. The most important element was certainly the increase, in two stages, of the VAT rate to bring additional finance to the basic pension. The standard rate of VAT was to be increased by 0.5 percentage points in 2003 and by 1 point in 2006 (approximately). The extra funds thus collected would be assigned to the basic pension scheme. The rest of the bill was a list of rather minor measures that either reduce outlays or increase receipts of the scheme. These included the abolition of widows pensions except for parents who have at least one child aged less than 18 (and some other cases); the change in the timing of benefit indexation from every two to every three years; the increase from 7.8 per cent to 8.1 per cent of the maximum contribution rate for the self-employed; a further increase in women's retirement age from 64 to 65; and the abolition of an AVS contribution-free amount of income to which AVS beneficiaries still in employment are entitled.

Together with these measures, the bill presented in 2000 also included provision for a more flexible transition from work to retirement. Early retirement was to be made possible at the earliest three years before the standard age of retirement, and was to be facilitated for those on low income, by applying more favourable conditions than those determined actuarially. For example, someone on a very low income would see his or her benefit reduced by 6.6 per cent if he or she were to retire three years before retirement age. The reduction would then increase gradually for higher incomes up to the ceiling of 16.8 per cent for someone whose lifetime earnings exceeded CHF 72 360 per annum, a

Table 7.4   Current and projected receipts, outlays and balance of AVS pension scheme (million CHF)

	With current legislation			With proposed legislation		
	Receipts	Outlays	Balance	Receipts	Outlays	Balance
1998	25 321	26 715	–1 394			
2000	28 792	27 722	1 070			
2002	28 930	29 095	–191			
2005	29 127	30 791	–1 664	30 601	29 968	+403
2010	30 056	33 900	–3 844	34 768	33 900	+1 198

Source: Conseil Fédéral 2000a: Annexe 1 and 2, and *Sécurité Sociale*, various issues.

reduction that would still be lower than the actuarially determined rate (18.6 per cent). *Retraite à la carte* also included the chance to take part-time retirement starting from six years before the standard age of retirement, with more favourable conditions offered to low earners.

The reform was supposed to guarantee the solvency of the basic pension until 2010 (see Table 7.4). The task is facilitated by a previously adopted measure consisting in the increase of one percentage point of the VAT rate, entirely assigned to the AVS pension scheme. VAT-raised funds were first paid into the AVS budget in 1999 and explain the improvement in the balance between 1998 and 2000. After 2010, further measures will be needed in order to guarantee the solvency of the scheme, as the proportion of the population aged 65 and over is expected to continue to increase from the projected 17.5 per cent for 2010 to 25 per cent in 2040. This will be the task of the twelfth AVS revision, for which a bill is expected in early 2004.

The reform bill presented in February 2000 contained many of the features that are typical of Swiss compromises. In particular, it included both savings measures and expansion elements (extra financial resources and improvements in provision). In the past, reforms that comprised these two types of measures have been more successful in gaining the necessary level of approval, both in parliament and with voters when challenged by a referendum (Bonoli, 1999). However, as it happened on other occasions, this carefully crafted compromise was to be overhauled by parliament.

The bill was first debated in the National Council. First the Social Security Commission and then the Council as a whole seemed to be strongly divided on a number of issues, essentially the abolition of widows' pensions and subsidised early retirement. In the end the bill was accepted with some modifications. First the increase in the maximum contribution rate for the self-employed was abandoned. Second, widows' pensions were to be maintained for all women who have had children, regardless of their age. With regard to early retirement, the government proposal was maintained. However, most parliamentary groups expressed their dissatisfaction with it: according to the Left, subsidies for early retirement for low income workers were insufficient: these should amount to 800 million per annum while the Right was against the idea of subsidising early retirement. The increase in the VAT rate was also accepted by a majority of the council. In the final vote, the reform was adopted, but by a very narrow margin: 62 votes in favour; 60 against and 63 abstentions. The Christian Democrats were the main supporters of the bill, the majority of the Right abstained, and the Left rejected it.

The bill was then transferred to the Council of States in November 2002 and again subjected to some modifications. The decision taken in the National Council, to keep widows' pensions for all women with children, was maintained, but the level of their pensions was lowered from 80 per cent to 60 per cent of a full pension. Most importantly, the upper chamber eliminated the subsidies for early retirement for low income workers completely. Early retirement was thus to be compensated by actuarially determined benefit reductions for everyone. In addition, VAT was not to be increased in order to bring additional finance to the pension scheme. The bill was accepted by all parties represented in the Council of States except the Socialists.

The bill was then sent back and forth between the two chambers of parliament, with the objective of finding a version able to obtain a majority in both. This was achieved only in October 2003 by a conciliation committee comprising members of both chambers. In the final version of the bill, adopted on 3 October 2003 in each of the two chambers, early retirement is to be subsidised, but only for a limited period and only for women born between 1948 and 1952, with a total cost of 140 million CHF. VAT is to be increased, but only by 1 per cent instead of the initially planned 1.5 per cent. In the final vote in the lower chamber, the bill was accepted by 109 against 73 votes. The Right was behind it. The Christian Democrats were divided, but mostly supported the bill, and the Socialists opposed it. A few days after the vote the Socialists and the unions announced their intention to challenge the bill in a referendum. The popular vote took place in 2004 and resulted in the rejection of the bill.

The First LPP Revision

The original objective of the first LPP revision was to adapt the law on occupational pensions to increasing life expectancy and to improve the coverage of atypical workers, especially part-time employees. Because of the existence of an access threshold to compulsory affiliation to second pillar pensions, many part-time workers, mostly women with children, are de facto excluded from compulsory occupational pension coverage. In a consultation procedure organised prior to the preparation for the bill, the idea of lowering or abolishing the access threshold to compulsory coverage (an option favoured at the time by the unions and by the Socialists) was firmly rejected by employers. The government's assessment of the result of the consultation procedure was that the extent of support for this particular measure was insufficient and it was consequently not included in the first version of the reform bill.

The bill was presented in parliament on 1 March 2000. It dealt mostly with the issue of adapting the calculation method of the minimum compulsory occupation pension (Obligatorium) to rising life expectancy. In particular, it included the reduction of the conversion rate from the current 7.2 per cent to 6.65 per cent in 2016. In order to avoid a reduction in benefits, the notional contribution rates, which are used to determine the amount of the capital available to employees, were to be increased. The result was expected to be neutral in terms of pension benefits, but during the transition period some male employees were thought to face a slight reduction in their benefits.

The main criticism against the bill concerned the fact that it did not address the issue of pension coverage for low paid, atypical, mainly part-time workers. This choice was attacked mostly by the Socialists, but also by some Christian Democrats and Radical members of parliament. The Socialists and the trade unions had already made clear their support for the outright abolition of the lower limit for the compulsory affiliation to a pension fund. This measure was opposed by employers, on the grounds that it would engender unreasonable administrative costs, especially in relation to casual, temporary employment, and that it will inhibit job creation for low skill workers. The government decided not to take up the issue, even though it had previously acknowledged that there is a coverage problem for low paid workers in the Swiss pension system (OFAS, 1995).

The bill was discussed in the National Council in April 2002. The Social Security Commission, which had examined it before, supported a modified version of the bill, which included the halving of the access threshold to compulsory occupational pension coverage (from 24 000 to 12 000 CHF per annum approximately). The party composition of the Social Security Commission of the National Council reflects that of the Council as a whole. However, possibly because of self-selection, its members coming from centre-right parties tend to be those with a more pro-welfare orientation. For this reason, it often takes positions that are more expansionist than those defended by the government and by the National Council as a whole. It is thus not a surprise that its proposal was rejected by a majority of the Council, but a more moderate reduction of the access threshold (to CHF 18 000 per annum) obtained a fair majority (132 votes against 38). The bill was further modified by the inclusion of a distinction between the access threshold and the amount of non-insured earnings. In the current system these two parameters coincide, but in the modified version of the bill, non-insured earnings were to be defined as 40 per cent of total earnings. This solution was more favourable to part-time workers who would see as a result a bigger proportion of their earnings insured. Finally, the reduction of the conversion rate was somewhat moderated: instead of 6.65 per cent the new rate was to be set at 6.8 per cent. The effect of this reduction in the conversion rate on benefits was expected to be compensated by the reduction in non-insured earnings. As a result the increase in notional contributions became unnecessary and was thus dropped from the reform.

The bill was transferred to the upper house of parliament, and debated in November 2002. By then, the economy and the outlook for public finance had worsened, and the declared objective of the Council of States' Social Security Commission was to reverse the decision to lower the access threshold to compulsory occupational pension coverage and the amount of non-insured earnings. The Council accepted the commission proposals and the bill was back in its original shape, also with regard to the conversion rate and increased notional contribution rates. This time, centre-right MPs voted consistently against the idea of improving provision for low income and part-time workers.

Like for the eleventh AVS revision, the LPP bill went back and forth a few times between the two councils, and majorities in both chambers were found only in October 2003 on a proposal that included lower income workers in occupational pensions but in a somewhat less generous way than in the proposal accepted by the National Council in spring 2002. Basically, the access threshold was lowered to 19 000 CHF per annum, and the amount of non-insured earnings to about 22 000 per annum. The conversion rate was lowered to 6.8 per cent and notional contributions will not be increased. Given the more moderate increase in insured earnings than in the previous proposals, the reduction in the contribution rate will result in pension losses, especially for the transition generation for whom the new conversion rate will be applied, but who will not have a sufficient number of contribution years with the higher insured earnings to compensate for the reduction. This carefully crafted compromise was strongly supported in both chambers. In the Council of States it was accepted by unanimous vote, and in the National Council it received the approval of all political groups except some right-wing MPs.

CONCLUSION

In spite of the multipillar structure of its pension system, the politics of pensions in Switzerland is not so different from what one can observe in the rest of Western Europe. On the one hand, concerns for the long-term financing of current commitments have prompted employers and right-of-centre parties to advocate retrenchment in this field of social policy. On the other hand, the trade unions and the Socialist Party not only resist such moves, but claim that improvements in the provision for selected groups are needed. Pensions, at least in Switzerland, are a field that seems to provide relatively little scope for cross-class agreement. On most crucial issues the predominant cleavage line is between employers and the trade unions and their representatives in parliament.

This political confrontation, however, takes place against the background of a political system that requires very large majorities if a policy option needs to be turned into a law. In this context the overall popularity of current pension arrangements constitutes a major asset in the hands of the expansionist coalition. They can trade their support for moderate retrenchment against the inclusion of improvements for selected groups of workers (low paid workers, women). From their point of view, this strategy has the advantage of making possible the adoption of expansion measures that would otherwise be unable to attract sufficient support. The attachment of Swiss voters to their pension system works as an amplifier of the power of the expansionist coalition, which is otherwise unable to impose its views against the will of the relatively strong right-of-centre majority that one finds both in parliament and in the electorate.

Retrenchment combined with selective expansion seems to be the most likely development in the Swiss context of a popular pension arrangement and a fragmented political system. However, this approach may be favoured in other countries as well. If the degree of power fragmentation of Swiss political institutions is found nowhere else in the world, popular attachment to pensions is in contrast a feature of most high income societies. In this respect, it is possible that the kind of quid pro quos that seem to make pension policy happen in the current context may be applied in other countries as well. For this to happen, it is essential, however, that those who are hit by labour market insecurity and sub-optimal pension coverage and those who benefit from the pension arrangements we have inherited from the post-war years are represented by the same political actor (a trade unions confederation, a Social Democratic Party). Actors who mostly represent older male workers (the trade unions in many continental European countries) are unlikely to be satisfied with a compromise that worsens the position of their constituents while improving that of younger employees or female workers.

NOTES

1. The Swiss constitution makes provision for various types of referendums. Constitutional change as well as accession to a supranational organisation is automatically subjected to a referendum. Constitutional change can also be put forward by voters by means of a 'popular initiative', if they are able to back their proposal with 100 000 signatures. For these

referendums to succeed, the double majority of voters and cantons is required. Voters can also challenge at the polls any act passed by parliament, if they are able to produce 50 000 signatures to that effect. In this case, a simple majority of voters is sufficient for the referendum to succeed (see Kobach, 1993 for a comprehensive account).

2. Assurance Vieillesse et Survivants (Old Age and Survivors pension).
3. Prestations Complémentaires (Pension Supplement).
4. On Swiss occupational pensions (LPPs), see Helbling (2000) or Hepp (1990). For a comparative analysis including Switzerland, see Lusenti (1990).
5. Typically, the concept of notional contribution is used with reference to PAYG pension schemes (for example, in Italy or Sweden). In the Swiss case, pensions are fully funded, but the calculation method for the compulsory minimum is based on contributions determined by law that do not necessarily reflect actual payments. The use of the term 'notional contributions/accounts' here is consistent with other English language publications on Swiss second pillar pensions (see for example, Queisser and Vittas, 2000).
6. The difference between this projection and the one carried out in 1995 is largely a result of an increase in the yield of VAT between the two exercises. Differences in expenditure are thus not that big if expressed in absolute terms.
7. Loi sur la prévoyance professionnelle (Law on occupational pensions).

REFERENCES

Bonoli, G. (1999), 'La réforme de l'Etat social en Suisse. Contraintes institutionnelles et opportunités de changement', *Swiss Political Science Review*, **5**(3) 57–78.

Bonoli, G. (2000), *The Politics of Pension Reform. Institutions and Policy Change in Western Europe*, Cambridge, UK: Cambridge University Press.

Bonoli, G. (2001), *Political Institutions, Veto Points and the Process of Welfare State Adaptation*, in P. Pierson (ed.), *The New Politics of the Welfare State*, Oxford: Oxford University Press.

Bonoli, G. and Mach, A. (2000), 'Switzerland: Adjustment politics within institutional constraints', in F.W. Scharpf and V. Schmidt (eds), *Welfare and Work in the Open Economy*, vol. 2, Oxford: Oxford University Press, 131–174.

Conseil Fédéral (2000a), *Message Relatif à la Révision de la Loi Fédérale sur l'Assurance Vieillesse et Survivants (LAVS)*, Bern.

Conseil Fédéral (2000b), *Message Relatif à la Révision de la Loi Fédérale sur la Prévoyance Professionnelle (LPP)*, Bern.

DFI (1995), *Rapport du Département Fédéral de l'Intérieur Concernant la Structure Actuelle et le Développement Futur de la Conception Helvétique des Trois Piliers de la Prévoyance Vieillesse, Survivants et Invalidité*, Bern: OFAS.

DFI (2002), *Rapport Concernant un Aperçu Général Actualisé des Besoins Financiers Supplémentaires des Assurances Sociales Jusqu'en 2025*, Bern, 17 May.

Feuille Fédérale, various issues.

Groupe de travail interdépartemental (1996), *Perspectives de Financement des Assurances Sociales (IDA FiSo 1). Rapport sur les Perspectives de Financement des Assurances Sociales (eu Égard en Particulier à l'Évolution Démographique)*, Bern: OFCIM.

Groupe de travail interdépartemental (1997), *Perspectives de Financement des Assurances Sociales (IDA FiSo 2). Analyse des Prestations des Assurances Sociales. Concrétisation de Modifications Possibles en Fonction de Trois Scénarios Financiers*, Bern: OFCIM.

Helbling, C. (2000), *Personalvorsorge und BVG*, Bern: Haupt.

Hepp, S. (1990), *The Swiss Pension Funds, An Emerging New Investment Force*, Bern: Haupt.

Kobach, K. (1993), *The Referendum. Direct Democracy in Switzerland*, Aldershot: Dartmouth.

Kriesi, H. (1982), 'The structure of the Swiss political system', in G. Lehmbruch and P. Schmitter (eds), *Patterns of Corporatist Policy Making*, London: Sage, 133–162.

Kriesi, H. (1995), *Le Système Politique Suisse*, Paris: Economica.

Lehmbruch, G. (1993), 'Consociational democracy and corporatism in Switzerland', *Publius: The Journal of Federalism*, **23**, 43–60.

Lijphart, A. (1984), *Democracies. Pattern of majoritarian and consensus government in twenty-one countries*, New Haven and London: Yale University Press.

Lusenti, G. (1990), *Les Institutions de Prévoyance en Suisse, au Royaume Uni et en Allemagne Fédérale*, Geneva: Georg.

Neidhart, L. (1970), *Plebiszit und pluralitäre Demokratie. Eine Analyse der Funktionen des schweizerischen Gesetzesreferendum*, Bern: Frank.

OFAS (1995), *Rapport du Département Fédéral de l'Intérieur Concernant la Structure Actuelle et le Développement Futur de la Conception Helvétique des Trois Piliers de la Prévoyance Vieillesse, Survivants et Invalidité*, Bern, OFAS.

OFS (Office Fédéral de la Statistique) (2001), *La Prévoyance Professionnelle en Suisse. Aperçu des Principales Données de la Statistique des Caisses de Pensions*, Neuchâtel.

Papadopoulos, Y. (1997), *Les Processus de Décision Fédéraux en Suisse*, Paris: L'Harmattan.

Pury, D. de, Heinz, H. and Schmid, B. (1995), *Mut zum Aufbruch. Eine wirtschaftspolitische Agenda für die Schweiz*, Zürich: Orell Füssli.

Queisser, M. and Vittas, D. (2000), *The Swiss Multipillar Pension System. Triumph of Common Sense?*, Washington: The World Bank, Development Research Group.

Schmähl, W. (ed.) (1991), *The Future of Basic and Supplementary Pensions Schemes in the European Community – 1992 and Beyond*, Baden-Baden: Nomos.

Sécurité Sociale, various issues.

Vontobel, W. (2000), 'Die Säulen- Scheinheiligen – Pech hat, wer in einem Kleinbetrieb arbeitet: Die Versicherung behält die Zinsen zurück,' in *CASH*, 1 December 2000, 44.

Vox (1995), *Analyse des Votations Fédérales du 25 Juin 1996*, No. 57, Bern.

831.40 *Loi Fédérale du 25 Juin 1982 sur la Prévoyance Professionnelle Vieillesse, Survivants et Invalidité (LPP)*.

8. The politics of pension reform in Japan: Institutional legacies, credit-claiming and blame avoidance

Toshimitsu Shinkawa

INTRODUCTION

As suggested in the introductory chapter, Japan can be classified as a member of the Bismarckian Lite category of pension systems, together with Canada and the United States. Contrary to these two countries, however, Japan faces a serious challenge to pension sustainability. What is responsible for such a contrast between Japan and the other two countries?

The generosity of Japan's public pensions as compared with the other two countries contributes partially to its fiscal tightness, but cannot explain the degree and extent of its crisis, since the earnings replacement ratio of public pension in Japan is substantially lower than in social insurance countries.[1] It is true that Japan is ageing much more rapidly and will be one of the most aged societies in the world within the next two decades, but it should be remembered that pension retrenchment started in Japan as early as the 1980s, when its ageing ratio (the ratio of aged 65 and over to the whole population) was relatively low (9.1 per cent in 1980 and 12 per cent 1990).

Pension reform is brought to the political agenda in Japan almost every five years in mandatory actuarial revaluation. Before 1985, pension reform meant the expansion of pensions, or raising the benefit level with minimum increases in contributions. In the 1985 reform, however, the government reversed the trend by tightening the relationship between benefits and contributions. Most noteworthy is that reducing the benefit level was authorized for the first time in Japanese pension history.[2] From that time on, benefit cuts and contribution increases are repeated in every actuarial revaluation. Moreover, the age of retirement was raised in the early 1990s. Thus, the keynote of pension reform in Japan has been shifted toward retrenchment since the 1985 reform.

This chapter argues that the early take-off of pension retrenchment in Japan was due to institutional vulnerability embedded in its pension system. In Japan, as elsewhere, institution matters in pension retrenchment, but not in a conventional way. Institutional settings promote, rather than prevent, changes in Japan. The fragmentation embedded in its pension system had caused fiscal tightness in specific pension schemes already in the early 1980s before serious population ageing took place, which precipitated the overhaul of the pension system.

The retrenchment process in Japan can be analysed remarkably well with reference to the concept of 'blame avoidance'. Masterful skills of blame avoidance unfolded by policy-makers successfully brought about gradual and steady changes in Japan's pension system. Their accumulated effects are quite substantial, but not good enough to absorb impacts of rapid population ageing over pension finance. As a result, the politics of blame avoidance undermines legitimacy and credibility of the pension system.

The rest of this chapter goes as follows. I first outline the structure and development of the Japanese pension system, making reference to the concepts of path dependency and credit claiming and, then, analyse pension retrenchment mainly by focusing on strategies of blame avoidance and institutional constraints.

PENSION MIX IN JAPAN

Basic Pension Plan

Figure 8.1 is a rough sketch of the pension structure in Japan. Public pension is composed of two tiers. The first-tier is the Basic Pension (BP), which covers all citizens aged 20 and over. A minimum contribution record of 25 years is required to obtain an entitlement to the BP. Forty years of paid contributions guarantee a full benefit of 67 000 yen per month. The average monthly benefit is currently 49 000 yen. It is pay-as-you-go, and subsidized substantially by tax revenues. All of its administrative costs and a third of benefits are paid out of tax revenues.

The BP includes three different types of insurants. First-type insurants are members of the National Pension Insurance (NPI), which covers farmers, the self-employed, students and the unemployed. The second-type is composed of employees in the public and in the private sector, except those working for companies with fewer than five employees. The third-type includes spouses of second-type insurants, whose yearly earnings are lower than 1.3 million yen. Since the BP was created in 1985 by absorbing the first flat-rate tiers of employees' pension schemes into the NPI, the BP and the NPI are usually used as exchangeable terms, but such usage is misleading, as indicated below.

Each type of contributor is treated differently, especially in terms of contribution payment. Even though the BP is mandatory, approximately 0.6 million

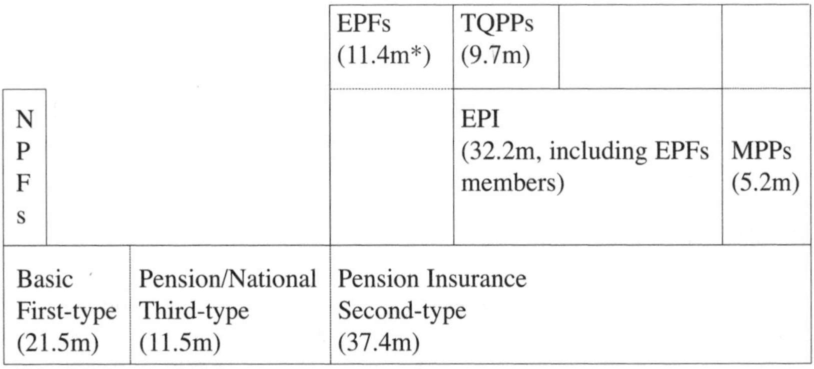

		EPFs (11.4m*)	TQPPs (9.7m)		
N P F s			EPI (32.2m, including EPFs members)		MPPs (5.2m)
Basic First-type (21.5m)	Pension/National Third-type (11.5m)	Pension Insurance Second-type (37.4m)			

Note: *Numbers are based on data of March 2001 ('Nenkin Joho' Editorial Office, 2003, p. 20).

Figure 8.1   Pension system in Japan

people, who are potentially first-type insurants, do not join the programme. In addition, more than 3 million first-type insurants are in arrears. This happens because first-type insurants are expected to register themselves and contribute the fixed amount of premiums (currently 13 300 yen per month) of their own will. Finally, over 20 per cent of first-type insurants are partially or entirely exempt from contribution due to their low incomes (SIA, 1999).

Second-type insurants cannot fail to pay contributions, because their contributions are deducted automatically from their pay cheques. They pay 13.58 per cent of monthly salaries and premiums (half paid by employers), but usually do not know how much they pay specifically to the BP, because their entire contributions go to their second-tier occupational schemes, from which a certain portion is transferred to the BP. Third-type insurants are exempt from contribution.

The difference in the type of contributions paid by first- and second-type insurants reflects the fact that the BP is an amalgam of different schemes, not a single, unified scheme. Since the major aim of establishing the BP was to rescue the NPI from fiscal deficits, no efforts were made to coordinate differences among various schemes, which might have triggered an uncontrollable resistance to the integration among employees. To make the reform acceptable, different entitlement ages were also left untouched. National Pension insurants can start drawing their basic pension at age 65, while members of employees' pension programmes are entitled to receive equivalents to their basic benefits earlier, at the age of 60 before 2001 (such a discrepancy is to disappear by raising the age of employees' basic pension entitlement gradually between 2001 and 2013).

Third-type insurants are a new category created in the 1985 reform. Before the reform, employees' spouses had no independent pension entitlements. A special benefit was added to an employee's pension for his/her spouse, but it was lost in the event of divorce. The 1985 reform abolished this special benefit and introduced the third-type entitlement. Third-type benefits are financed out of second-type contributions.

Employees' Pension Plan

The second-tier provides employees with moderately earnings-related pensions. It is composed of the Employees' Pension Insurance (EPI) provided for private sector employees, and mutual pension plans (MPPs) for public and quasi-public servants (personnel in private schools and quasi-public corporations, such as cooperatives in agriculture, forestry and fishery). The central government and local governments have their own independent schemes.

The second-tier schemes are pay-as-you-go, but their administrative costs are financed out of tax revenues as is the BP. Unlike the BP, however, no subsidies are available for the provision of benefits. Since the coverage of the EPI is much broader than the MPPs and their structures are largely identical (MPPs provide more generous benefits since public employees enjoy no third-tier pension), this chapter discusses the EPI as representative of the second-tier. Employees have no way of not paying their contributions, which are automatically deducted from their pay cheques, but employers sometimes neglect registration and contribution to avoid financial burdens. Employees are not allowed to claim exemption due to their low incomes.

The current contribution rate of the EPI is 13.58 per cent of an employee's yearly earnings[3] (half paid by his/her employer), including the contribution to the BPI. The scheme is income-related, but there is an upper limit on pensionable monthly income. Incomes surpassing the amount of 590 000 yen per month are not counted as pensionable. The average monthly benefit in the EPI as of 1999 is 176 000 yen, which is equivalent to 56 per cent of the average monthly salary of EPI subscribers.

The number of EPI members indicated in Figure 8.1 includes members of Employees' Pension Funds (EPFs). These are pension funds that can be set up by firms allowed to opt out of the EPI.[4] Although they are privately managed, EPFs are strictly regulated and supervised by the government since they include a substitute for the EPI in addition to a purely company-specific pension. An EPF is an independent juridical entity, which a sponsor company/group of companies cannot dissolve of its own accord. If investment returns are lower than the officially required interest rate, sponsor companies must make up for the difference.

Corporate Pension

The third-tier is composed of voluntary private pension schemes, most of which are employer-sponsored corporate pension plans. Corporate pensions are divided into two major types: EPFs and tax-qualified pension plans (TQPPs). While EPFs substitute for a public function as described above, TQPPs are purely corporate pension schemes. A TQPP is established on condition that an employer concludes a contract with a trust and/or life insurance companies.

The fact that the minimum number of employees to introduce a TQPP is as low as 15 makes it popular especially among medium-sized and small companies. There are 736 000 TQPPs in 2001, while the number of EPFs is only 1 737. However, the number of EPFs-covered employees reaches 10.87 million, which surpasses that of TQPPs members by 1.7 million. EPFs are predominant among large companies, while TQPPs are popular among smaller companies.

The tax-qualified pension is an upgraded version of the lump sum retirement payment, which is paid out by 90 per cent of all Japanese firms. By introducing a TQPP, employers can disperse the cost for retirement payments. TQPPs, however, usually offer a choice between lump sum payments and ten-year pension benefits. Employees take the option of lump sum payments in most cases, which are treated more generously by the tax system.

Both the EPF and the TQPP enjoy preferential tax treatment. Contributions paid by employers are deductible as social security expenses in the case of the EPF and as business expenses in the case of the TQPP. In either case, no income tax is levied on employees, until they retire and receive payments. A special corporate tax of 1 per cent is levied on a tax-qualified pension fund's accumulated assets each year as interest for arrears. The same measure is applied to an EPF, only on the portion exceeding 2.7 times the funding required to meet the benefits of the substitute component. Thus, the EPF is treated more generously than the TQPP.

In 2001 new legislation on corporate pensions was introduced, which will change the map of corporate pensions completely. Since 2002 it is not possible any longer to set up new TQPPs. All established TQPPs must be terminated by the end of March 2012. On the other hand, the 2001 legislation allows new types of defined-benefit as well as defined-contribution pension to be introduced. These new schemes are not indicated in Figure 8.1, since the new era has just begun and the new types of pension funds include few members except for defined-contribution schemes. These schemes are discussed below.

Finally, a new instrument has been introduced in 1989 in the shape of National Pension Funds (NPFs). These have the purpose of providing NPI members who are not covered by the second-tier public pension or employer-sponsored pension schemes with a supplement to the NPI. NPFs are managed by local governments or occupational organizations, but are completely voluntary and only a fraction of the NPI members join NPFs.

PENSION DEVELOPMENT: PATH DEPENDENCY AND CREDIT-CLAIMING

Historical Legacies and Path Dependency

Japan's occupationally divided pension system has its origin in public sector pensions. Naval, army and civil service pension plans were introduced at the initial stage of nation-state building between 1875 and 1894 and were unified in 1923. The National Railway Mutual Pension Plan was introduced in 1907 and subsequently similar plans were introduced in other national businesses, including tobacco, telegram and printing. On the other hand, the government was opposed to the introduction of a public pension for private sector employees, since the government shared with employers the concern that it would contribute to unionization across the firm lines and the reinforcement of labour's unity. Instead of the provision of a public pension, company-specific retirement payments spread among large firms in the 1920s, first as a means of securing skilled labour, and then as a substitute for public unemployment insurance (Shinkawa and Pempel, 1996, pp. 288–289).

Finally, after the war broke out between China and Japan, the government introduced a sailors' pension plan in 1939 to secure the manpower necessary for marine transport and, in 1942, enacted a workers' pension covering all muscle workers except for those in tiny businesses with fewer than ten employees. These acts were aimed at mobilizing financial resources into the war as well as restraining inflation. Two years later, the plan was rearranged as the Employees' Pension Insurance by extending its coverage to white-collar workers, including female clerks, in establishments with more than five employees. By the end of 1944, the EPI covered 8.32 million employees, including 2.24 million women.

During the turmoil following World War II, the concern of public welfare was limited to the protection of war victims. Under the condition that public welfare could provide little for workers and their families, employers took the lead in responding to employees' demands. Together with company housing, lump sum retirement payments came to be provided in major firms by the early 1950s and spread among smaller firms afterwards thanks to preferential tax treatment. The 1952 revision of the tax code made retirement payments non-taxable business expenses.

In the mid-1950s, as the economy got on the right track, the government embarked on the overhaul of public pension provision. Welfare bureaucrats holding the idea of universalism, influenced by the Beveridge report, wished to reactivate the EPI as an umbrella scheme providing employees in the private sector with a major source of income in retirement. The ambition of building a universal welfare state was, however, frustrated by employers, who insisted that an improved public pension in addition to retirement allowances would cost too much. As a result, EPI benefits were kept low throughout the 1950s, reaching barely a third of their counterparts in MPPs in 1960 (Tada, 1991, p. 145). The low level of EPI benefits in turn facilitated the proliferation of MPPs. Employees in quasi-public associations, such as teachers and clerks in private schools and employees in cooperatives of agriculture, forestry and fishery, successfully called for their own mutual pension plans (Tada, 1991, pp. 147–153).

Meanwhile, the Japan Employers' Association (JEA) demanded a change in the tax code in the late 1950s to spread annual expenses for retirement payments by replacing lump sum payments with proper pensions. This idea was regarded as another barrier to an improvement of the EPP and opposed by the Ministry of Health and Welfare (MHW). To gain the MHW's support, the JEA made a compromise by proposing the idea of opting out as a condition for the acceptance of EPI improvements. The JEA insisted that employers be allowed to opt out of the earnings-related component of EPI. A compromise was hammered out between the JEA and the MHW and, consequently, the tax code was revised in 1962 in such a way as to introduce TQPPs, the level of the EPI benefit was substantially raised in 1965 (and 1968), and the establishment of EPFs was allowed in 1966 in spite of labour's fierce criticism.

The system of 'pension for all' completed by imposing the NPI membership on those uncovered by employees' schemes (except housewives) only furthered institutional fragmentation. It did not mean the unification of fragmented schemes but adding a residual programme to the already fragmented system.

So far, we have demonstrated to what extent and how historical contingencies and institutional settings constrained pension development and brought about institutional fragmentation. Quite powerful as the logic of path dependency is, we need to introduce another perspective by which to complete our understanding of the fragmentation process. The politics of credit-claiming overwhelmed calls and moves among bureaucrats toward a more rational organization of the pension system. For instance, the 'pension for all' system was a direct effect of political competition for credit-claiming. Its original idea came from the Japan Socialist Party (JSP). The JSP campaigned on its promise of the NPP, anticipating a lower house election to come in the summer of 1958. The ruling Liberal Democratic Party (LDP) pre-empted the socialist idea with the statement that it would introduce a national pension scheme in the 1959 fiscal year.

A surge of social policy activity in the early 1970s was also brought about by the politics of credit-claiming. The government introduced several expansionist measures over a short period of time, including pension benefit increases (for example, a target pension benefit of the EPI was set at 60 per cent of the average monthly salary), health care improvements (for example, the coverage rate of employees' family members was raised from 50 to 70 per cent, while reimbursement for expensive medical treatments was introduced), and the introduction of child allowances.

PM Tanaka, known as a champion of state-led industrial development, surprisingly initiated pro-welfare policies. Such a turnabout, which was apparently against Tanaka's philosophy, reflected a crisis of the LDP ruling system, which was beginning to be blamed for its emphasis on the so-called production-first policy. The rapid expansion of social welfare was, therefore, understood as a policy of compensation, by which to claim credit and contain or co-opt opponents (Calder, 1988; Shinkawa, 1993).

PENSION RETRENCHMENT: NEW POLITICS AND BLAME AVOIDANCE

Strategies of Blame Avoidance

It has been popular to distinguish dynamics and logics of welfare retrenchment from those of welfare expansion since Paul Pierson asserted the resiliency of the welfare state and developed a theory of the new politics of the welfare state (Pierson, 1994; 1996; 2001). According to Pierson, the politics of welfare state retrenchment is different from that of welfare state development or expansion well explained with the old politics paradigm/social democratic model, because of their different political goals and contexts (Pierson, 1994; compare Korpi, 1983; Esping-Andersen, 1985).

Pierson's idea of new welfare state politics based on neo-institutionalist assumptions is, of course, not unanimously applauded. It faces challenges from advocates of old partisan politics or cross-class alliance. The old class politics or cross-class alliance defines the course of retrenchment where social democratic forces are predominant (compare Garrett, 1998; Clayton and Pontusson, 1998; Scarbrough, 2000; Anderson, 2001). Granted that old politics are not necessarily negated by new politics in the era of retrenchment, the new politics theme undoubtedly sheds light on aspects of retrenchment with the analysis of blame avoidance.

Kent Weaver argues that 'politicians are motivated primarily by the desire to avoid blame for unpopular actions rather than by seeking to claim credit for popular ones' (Weaver, 1986, p. 371). Voters are more likely to notice relatively concentrated costs or benefits than those widely diffused. Besides, they tend to be more sensitive to real or potential costs than to gains (Weaver, 1986, p. 373). Welfare retrenchment is an ideal case to examine the politics of blame avoidance working in reality, because it forces tangible costs upon a limited number of people, while its benefits, such as financial balance and fairness, are not tangible rewards one can easily and immediately appreciate.

Five strategies for blame avoidance are distinguished here, which are extremely useful for understanding pension retrenchment in Japan. Strategy I is limiting the agenda, or excluding blame-generating issues from the agenda. Strategy II is redefining the issue. Decision-makers attempt to prevent blame-generating by developing new policy options that diffuse or obfuscate losses. Strategy III is lowering visibility. Decision-makers can lower their visibility by passing the buck, or delaying the effect of a policy upon specific groups until some point in the future. By so doing, it is more difficult for affected groups to realize the impact of a decision as well as to trace responsibility for its effect back to given decision-makers.

Strategy IV is deflecting blame by finding scapegoats, or by playing off one group against the other. Strategy V is forming a consensus. A consensus formed across political partisanship on a blame-generating decision prevents political opponents from taking advantage of the issue, thus minimizing the risk of making a blame-generating decision (Weaver, 1986, pp. 384–390; Pierson, 1996, p. 147). When a consensus is successfully formed, a drastic change may occur. Otherwise the politics of blame avoidance would contribute to policy stability, or make a policy change marginal, incremental or gradual.

The 1985 Reform

Pension retrenchment in Japan started back in 1979. The MHW made an initial move toward a raise in the age of retirement, which had no chance to be taken seriously in the overall context of welfare expansion of the time. Entering in the 1980s, however, pension retrenchment, together with health care reform, was placed on the government's agenda as a major target of administrative reform. A grand-scale reform was finally achieved in 1985 and opened the era of pension retrenchment with the introduction of the BP and tightening up the relationship between contribution and benefit (more contributions and less generous benefits).

Moves for pension retrenchment witnessed in the early 1980s were not directly caused by population ageing. While the MHW legitimized the 1985 reform by stressing acceleration of population ageing, the aging ratio was fairly low in Japan at that time (9.3 per cent in 1980 and 10.3 per cent in 1985). In 1981, Japan spent only 10.1 per cent of national income for social security, whereas France spent 26.6 per cent, West Germany 22.5 per cent, Sweden 20.7 per cent, the UK 10.7 per cent and the US 10.2 per cent (MHW, 1984).[5]

These figures clearly show that Japan had a relatively young society and a very small government in the early 1980s, thus indicating no sign of an impending crisis in welfare state sustainability. Nevertheless, the Japanese pension system was in trouble. This was caused neither by serious population ageing nor overstretched public finances, but by financial vulnerability embedded in the fragmented pension system. Japan's occupationally divided pension system without an equalization device directly reflects the different age composition of each scheme. Such a system is manageable and sustainable, only while the population is young, a pension programme is immature, and the economy grows rapidly. Japan was losing these advantages.

Fiscal tightness became severe in specific schemes, where actively working members decreased, such as the National Railway Workers' Mutual Pension Plan (NRWMP) and the NPI. The National Railway had reduced the number of employees due to accumulated deficits since 1964. Consequently, as early as 1983, pension beneficiaries surpassed contributors in numbers. The NPI turned into the red in 1983. The decreased number of the agricultural population exerted a fiscal pressure on it. The agricultural population shrank from 8.42 million in 1970 to 5.02 million in 1983 due to transformations in the industrial structure. It accounted for 16 per cent of the workforce in 1970, but only 9 per cent in 1983. Moreover, the NPI had difficulties in collecting contributions.

To obtain financial support, the NRWMP was merged with other mutual pension plans of public corporations in 1984, while the NPI was integrated with first-tiers of employees' pension plans in 1985. Such measures worked well to loosen fiscal tightness in these programmes, but the partial correction of institutional fragmentation was not good enough to absorb impacts of coming population ageing and provide the sustainability of the whole system over the long run.

Tightening up the relationship between contributions and benefits was also called for in the 1985 reform. The 1973 pension reform guaranteed 60 per cent of the average monthly salary after 27 contribution years. Based on the scheme, it turned out that a couple were able to gain more than the average income, if a husband contributed for 40 years and his wife voluntarily contributed to the NPI for the same period of time. The 1985 reform modified the level of the future benefit in such a way as to provide a couple with 70 per cent of average monthly salary (see Shinkawa, 1993).

Institutional fragmentation and the politics of credit-claiming combined to amplify the impact of population ageing and facilitated pension retrenchment in the early 1980s. Considering the risk of retrenchment, however, political actors are not expected to go for it simply because there is a problem. For example, the LDP leadership kept a retrenchment issue off the government's agenda in the late 1970s, in spite of reinforced calls for 'reconsideration of welfare' within as well as without the government.[6] LDP leaders thus employed Strategy I to avoid blame. What changed that strategy?

Increased deficits in public finance certainly provided the most critical environmental factor to urge a shift of the strategy. PM Ohira announced a fiscal crisis, witnessing public bond dependency reach 40 per cent in the 1979 original budget. The fiscal crisis came to be perceived as an urgent issue to be handled, sooner or later, before entering in the 1980s. A policy window opened to fiscal reform, when the LDP gained a stable majority in the 1980 election. Moreover, severe competition among factions within the LDP in the late 1970s came to a halt at least temporarily because it was believed that it caused PM Ohira's death.[7] Unity and cohesion within the party practically cleared the sole veto point in a parliamentary cabinet system with a predominant party and reinforced political leadership.

The combination of the fiscal crisis and the electoral victory of the LDP provided an excellent opportunity for pension retrenchment. The strategy the Liberal Democratic government adopted to conduct it was based on a redefinition of the issue (Strategy II). Pension retrenchment was legitimized with a popular policy of administrative reform. The goal of administrative reform was shifted from the streamlining of government agencies toward fiscal reconstruction without tax increases. Pension retrenchment was couched in the rhetoric of building a welfare society with (economic) viability, or a Japanese-style welfare society (JSWS).

The idea of a JSWS can be conceived of as a Japanese version of neo-conservatism. Based on the perception that the welfare state brings about the English/European disease with symptoms of obese public finance, economic stagnancy and work disincentives, advocates of a JSWS stressed the importance of maintaining or even reviving Japanese virtues of self-help, mutual aids and strong family ties to avoid falling in a trap of the welfare state (Shinkawa, 1993). They criticized increases in social security expenditures as a harbinger of the European disease. The idea was proposed by a group of neo-liberal economists, intellectuals and business leaders in the mid-1970s, and was picked up by the LDP and the government in the late 1970s.

Strategy III was also employed effectively, together with Strategy II. To make a plan of administrative reform, the government established the Second Ad Hoc Research Committee on Administrative Reform (Daini Rincho) and delegated decisions to it. Daini Rincho not only lowered the visibility of politicians but also unexpectedly obtained zealous support among broad classes of people thanks to a charismatic chair, Toshio Doko. His presence further lowered the visibility of elected officials.

Conspicuous bureaucratic initiatives are also comprehensible in terms of

Strategy III. By contrast with pension reforms in the 1950s and 1960s, where the politics of credit-claiming overwhelmed bureaucratic calls for policy rationality and fiscal balance, welfare bureaucrats played a leading role in the process of retrenchment. As for most of the elements achieved in the 1985 reform, many point out the significant role played by Shin-ichiro Yamaguchi, chief of the Pension Bureau (see Nakano, 1992; Shinkawa, 1993). Granted his credit, it should be reminded that bureaucrats had a chance to exert a broad range of discretion only because political officials tried to keep their visibility low and let bureaucrats come to the fore. Phase-in periods introduced in the 1985 reform to increase contributions and reduce benefit standards are, needless to say, aimed at diffusing policy effects and lowering their visibility.

Strategy I was still employed partially in the 1985 reform. The issue of pension entitlements ages was cautiously excluded from governmental agenda. By so doing, the MHW successfully gained support from the mass media, which had conducted a campaign against a raise in pension entitlement ages in the previous reform.

1994 Reform

The next goal of pension reform after the 1985 achievement was to raise employees' pensionable age, which was necessary not only for cost containment reasons but also in order to correct the anomaly that different entitlement ages coexist in the BP. It was, however, far from being an easy task. In fact the MHW had failed to achieve this goal in the 1989 reform.

Retirement at the age of 60 had become a common practice in the private sector by the end of the 1980s, and a gap between effective and legal retirement age would reappear if only entitlement age was raised. The socialists and their affiliated labour unions convincingly insisted that the extension of employment of those aged over 60 be a precondition for an increase in entitlement age. The problem seemed unlikely to be solved in the short run. Unexpectedly, however, raising the age of employees' BP entitlement was accepted in the 1994 reform with no serious challenges. According to the authorized schedule, the age of male employees' BP entitlement was raised gradually up to the age of 65 between 2001 and 2013, and the same procedure would be applied to the female employees between 2006 and 2018. A delay in the female case was due to the fact that the female retirement age was being raised at that time from 55 to 60 by 1999.

What made the 1994 reform different from the 1989 attempt? Noteworthy are various measures included in the 1994 bill to extend employment provided for the aged 60 and over and introduce a smooth connection between entitlement and retirement age. First of all, the actuarial deduction applied to working pensioners was modified lest it deprived them of work incentives. Under the former system, working pensioners were unable to increase their incomes much due to steeply progressive deduction from their pension benefits. Those who earned over 250 000 yen per month could receive no pension benefits. The revision allowed working beneficiaries between the ages of 60 and 64 to increase their total incomes in proportion to their working earnings by modifying progressiveness in deduction. No deduction due to working earnings is applied to benefits of those aged over 65.

Second, the Employment Insurance Act was amended to provide employees aged between 60 and 64 with compensation allowances. When people of that age cohort continue to work and suffer a substantial loss in their incomes (more than 15 per cent of their previous salaries), the Employment Insurance Plan provides them allowances up to 25 per cent of the salary (the total monthly amounts cannot be over 361 680 yen). Third, retirement at the age of 60 or over 60 would be compulsory after April 1998. Fourth, amendments in the Labour Dispatching Law liberalized the employment of older people in the dispatching business. Finally, double payment of the unemployment and pension benefits to those aged between 60 and 64 was cancelled. That measure was criticized not only as excessively generous but also as a work disincentive. Pension entitlement is suspended, while an unemployment benefit is provided.

Impressive as they are, immediate effects of these measures are doubtful. It takes time to change labour practices and expand employment provided for the elderly, especially in the period of prolonged recession. In short, the measures adopted in the 1994 reform to delay retirement age seem not convincing enough to change the minds of the opponents. What made the 1994 breakthrough possible then? What had changed between 1989 and 1994? How can we explain the sharp contrast between the 1989 setback and the 1994 easy win?

Population ageing certainly provided a condition in favour of further retrenchment. Japan entered the stage of an aged society with the ageing ratio of 14 per cent. It is difficult, however, to explain the specific timing of a policy change by a continuous process like population ageing. Besides, as Table 8.1 shows, the ageing ratio of Japan was still one of the lowest among the selected advanced countries and its social security expenditures as a percentage of National Income was the smallest in 1993. Table 8.2 confirms that the pattern of pension expenditures does not deviate from the general pattern of social security expenditures. Japan easily ranks bottom among the selected countries. Comparatively speaking, Japan succeeded remarkably in restraining its social security expenditures.

A critical difference between 1989 and 1994 is not found in the ageing ratio or the increase in social security expenditures but in the political partisanship of government. Following the step-down of the LDP from power for the first

*Table 8.1   Social security expenditure as a percentage of National Income
and international comparison of elderly population*

Country	Social security expenditure as % of National Income Fiscal year 1983	The aged as % of the total population 1983	Social Security expenditure as % of National Income Fiscal year 1997	The aged as % of the total population 1997
Japan	15.2	13.6	17.8	15.7
USA	18.7*	12.7	–	12.7
UK	27.2	15.8	–	15.8
Germany	33.3	15.1	–	15.4
France	37.7	14.5	–	15.7
Sweden	53.4	17.6	–	17.0

Note: *   1992 figure.

Source: Table transcribed from www.ipss.go.jp.

time since 1955, all opposition parties except for the Japan Communist Party formed a coalition government in 1993. As a ruling party, the JSP not only accepted but promoted the 1994 bill. The socialists unconvincingly repeated the argument used by the MHW to persuade them to the effect that raising the age of retirement was necessary for the sustainability of the pension system, but the real reason behind their turnabout was their concession to the coalition partners on the issue to maintain the non-LDP government (Shinkawa, 1999, p. 201). The LDP in opposition had no reason to oppose the idea originally promoted by its governments.

The largest constituency of the JSP, organized labour, supported the non-LDP government and kept 'silent and compliant' in the 1994 reform (Shinkawa, 1999). The case is comprehensible with the logic of 'Nixon goes to China' (Ross, 2000). The conservatives did not raise their voice against Nixon's announcement of paying a visit to China, because they knew that Nixon was anti-communist and trusted him as their leader. By the same token, organized labour accepted the 1994 bill, because its friends were in the government.

In this way, the success of the 1994 reform was mainly due to consensus-building across political partisanship. With the success of consensus-forming, the decision-makers were able to diffuse blame, or circle the wagons. 'No one has to stick their neck out: everyone provides political cover for everyone else, making it difficult for a future political opponent to raise the issue' (Weaver, 1986, p. 389). Strategy V of blame avoidance worked so effectively to pass the bill that seemed impassable in the past.

Table 8.2 International comparison of social security expenditure by category as a percentage of National Income

Country	Total Comparison with National Income	Unit % Medical care	Pensions	Welfare & others	Total benefits Currency unit by country: million	Benefits per head Currency unit by country
Japan FY1997 FY1993	17.8	6.5	9.3	2.0	69 418 725	550 217 yen
Japan	15.2	5.9	7.8	1.6	56 797 461	455 239 yen
USA (FY1992)	18.7	6.8	8.4	3.5	906 195	3 494 dollars
UK	27.2	7.3	10.8	9.1	132 646	2 279 pounds
Germany	33.3	8.7	14.3	10.3	799 688	9 901 marks
France	37.7	9.2	18.4	10.2	1 973 922	34 313 francs
Sweden	53.4	10.0	20.1	23.3	557 135	63 708 krone

Notes: Calculations for each fiscal year for each country are based on the average for each country's yearly exchange market, such that the USA figure is 442 461 yen, the UK figure is 378 326 yen, the German figure is 667 246 yen, the French figure is 674 140 yen and the Swedish figure is 910 585 yen. The above figures for each country are based on the ILO's Social Security Survey, and the National Institute of Population and Social Security Research has taken the estimates made by each country; therefore there may be discrepancies with the figures published by the ILO.

Source: Table transcribed from www.ipss.go.jp.

CORPORATE PENSION REFORM

The view of Japanese-style welfare society (JSWS) advocates small government by expecting the expansion of welfare provision in the private sphere,
especially the increased role of corporate welfare. Correspondingly, Japanese
major firms made in collaboration with labour unions plans of lifetime
comprehensive welfare (LCW), one after another from the late 1970s to the
early 1980s. A commonly seen idea in these plans is that the firm should
provide regular employees with comprehensive physical and mental benefits
not only during employment but also after retirement. A plan of LCW was
aimed at the improvement of productivity through efficient labour management. Whether or not it was employee-friendly or patriarchal, it promised an
enrichment of corporate welfare (Shinkawa and Pempel, 1996, pp. 309–312).

The development of the LCWP became out of the question after Japan
entered a recession in 1993. A relevant issue was not the expansion but curtailment of corporate welfare. Many firms attempted to alleviate financial burdens
incurred by corporate pension schemes. The number of TQPPs went down to
73 600 in March 2002, after reaching the peak of 92 500 in 1993. The EPFs,
whose dissolution was prohibited in principle except for special cases such as
the bankruptcy of sponsor companies, did not start a decrease in number
immediately the recession started as did TQPPs. The number of EPFs reached
a peak in 1996 and turned into a decline. Since the first dissolution of an EPF
was permitted in 1994, the number of dissolved EPFs has increased almost
every year. Between 1996 and 2001, approximately 150 funds were dissolved
and the total number of EPFs decreased to 1737 in 2002. Consequently, the
total number of employees covered by corporate pension schemes (including
both TQPPs and EPFs) went down from 22.89 million in 1996 to 20.04 million
in March 2002.

The government did more than let them go. To help firms alleviate financial burdens, the government loosened its regulation of EPFs by lowering the
officially required rate of return on invested funds from 5.5 per cent to 4.5 per
cent, by reducing the amount of fund reserves that an EPF was required to
hold, by allowing an employer to directly contribute stock and other securities
to his funds to make up shortfalls in the EPF, and so on. However, effects of
these measures were too modest to ameliorate the finance of EPFs so that the
government was forced to take a more radical action.

TQPPs also needed an overhaul. The TQPP has a weakness in the protection of pension entitlement in that the employer can fail to maintain a minimum level of funding with no legal sanctions. The weak protection of the
TQPP entitlement becomes a serious problem, as the number of dissolved
TQPPs goes up. Furthermore, since it is assumed on traditional labour
management practices such as lifelong employment and seniority-based

wages, few TQPPs provided portability of pension entitlement. The lack of portability makes the TQPP outdated in the era of increased labour mobility and the restructuring of company wages (a shift from seniority-based wages to merit-based wages).

The government introduced two new laws in 2001 to overhaul the whole structure of corporate pensions: the Defined-Benefit Corporate Pension Law (the DB Law) and the Defined-Contribution Pension Law (the DC Law). The DB Law permits the establishment of two new types of pension plans: a 'contract type' plan and a 'fund type' plan. The contract type plan is similar to the TQPP and is expected to replace it. To protect pension entitlement and promote portability, it stipulates a clear obligation on the employer to maintain plan assets at specific levels and allows the transfer of pension assets more easily to other pension plans.

EPFs were allowed to dissolve even under the old regulation when their host companies went bankrupt. They are now allowed more freely to dissolve and to return the substitute component to the EPI. The fund-type plan is similar to the EPF and is expected to provide an appropriate alternative to it, when an employer decides to relinquish the EPI substitute component. To introduce a fund-type plan, an employer must have more than 300 employees. The DB Law does not require a minimum number of employees to make a contract-type plan. The new types are still DB plans, but offer a possibility to reduce the risk and responsibility of pension management by introducing the so-called hybrid/cash-balance model, under which the benefits employees will receive in the future will vary according to the performance of the investment, but the employer must guarantee a minimum standard of benefits.

The DC Law allows the introduction of the DC plan modelled after the US 401(k) plan. There are two types of DC plans: a corporate plan and an individual plan. Contributions under a corporate plan are paid by the employer, while, in the case of individual plans, contributions are borne by individuals. When an individual is employed, however, his/her contribution is deducted by the employer from his/her pay cheque. The DC plan is expected to transfer the risk and responsibility of pension management most effectively from the employer to the employee and provides full portability of pension assets.

It is too soon to identify which type will become predominant in the future, but the DC plan seems to gain popularity. The DC Law was criticized at its inception on various points, such as the low upper-limit on the amount of contribution, no permission of cash withdrawal in the middle of one's career, or no eligibility for third-type insurants for the individual type, but the number of DC plans steadily increases. As of April 2003, firms introducing DC plans reached over 400. Smaller firms are more likely to be fond of the DC plan, which limits the financial obligation of the employer.

One hundred and thirty-seven EPFs relinquished the substitute part of the

EPP in the first six months after the DB Law came into effect. Unless the economy rises up, the number will increase further. By contrast, few companies have adopted contract-type plans, which impose more risk and responsibility than the TQPP. The employer, who wants to avoid heavy obligations imposed by the contract plan, may shift their TQPPs to DC plans before the day of the TQPP termination. The worst case scenario will materialize if employers simply dissolve TQPP plans and provide no alternatives to them.

The 2001 reform responded to requirements in the new era of industrial relations. Employers in Japan have looked for the replacement of the traditional Japanese-style labour management with flexible management. Shifting the risk and responsibility for pension management to the employee and achieving pension portability certainly will contribute to the further increase in labour mobility and thus the destruction of the familial type of industrial relations. Such a drastic change, together with accumulated effects of continuous public pension reforms, will urge employees to redesign their after-retirement life. In spite of the degree and extent of its potential impacts, the 2001 reform was not much scrutinized in public debates. Corporate pension is considered to belong strictly to the private sector and therefore have nothing to do with political responsibility.

PENSION DEBATES GO ON

Increased Incredibility

Following the course set by the 1994 reform, the 1999 reform introduced an increase in the age of employees' entitlement to the second-tier. The Democratic Party, the largest party in opposition, officially opposed the plan, but actually made no serious attempts to prevent the passage of the bill. Quite a few Democrats were in favour of pension retrenchment. The Social Democratic Party (formerly Japan Socialist Party) showed a more straightforward anti-government stance, but had little influence over policy-making since it became a tiny party in the 1996 election.

Some other substantial changes are included in the 1999 reform, such as the suspension of indexing benefits to wage increases, applying actuarial deduction to benefits of those aged between 65 and 69 according to their earnings, and the curtailment of new pensioners' benefits by 5 per cent. The 1999 reform, however, is considered to have left more problems unsolved than those it solved. It is because, first of all, population ageing goes beyond the expectation. Based on the population projection released in 1992 that Japan would enter the stage of 'super-aged society', or that a quarter of the Japanese population would be those aged 65 and over in 2025, the 1994 reform set a schedule to raise the EPP contribution rate up to the upper limit of 29.8 per cent of the monthly salary in 2025. That scenario was blown away by the 1997 population projection, according to which Japan would become a 'super-aged society' a decade earlier, in 2015. Accelerated population ageing would push the EPP contribution rate up to 34.3 per cent in 2025.

The 1999 reform based on the 1997 population projection was expected to restrain the contribution rate at 27.5 per cent of the monthly salary (21.60 per cent of the total income) with the increase in subsidies to the BP from a third to a half of benefits. The latest projection released in December 2002 provides a more pessimistic view about the recovery of the fertility rate, thus urging another round of pension reform. While the 1997 projection assumed that the fertility rate would recover to the level of 1.61 in 2025, the 2002 projection lowered the expectation down to 1.38, considering the robust downward tendency in the fertility rate.[8] Consequently, at the peak of population ageing (in 2050), those aged 65 and over will represent 35.7 per cent instead of 32.3 per cent of the population.

Secondly, the 1999 reform clearly showed the limits of blame-avoidance politics, which simply cannot deal with rapid population ageing in Japan. A drastic and once for all change, rather than continuously repeated piecemeal changes, is necessary. The most negative effect of endlessly repeated reforms brought about by the blame-avoidance politics is witnessed in the undermining of pension credibility, which is explicitly reflected in the NPI in a straightforward fashion where the number of members in arrears continuously increases. The ratio of the unpaid months to the total months in which contributions are expected to be paid reached 37.2 per cent in 2002, or 8 per cent higher than the previous year.

Sixty-five per cent of those in arrears answered that they failed to pay contributions due to their low incomes, while 20 per cent said that they did not trust the NPI. Twenty per cent may seem not such a large number, but the actual rate of distrust is considered to be much higher. Among those who answered that their incomes were too low to pay contributions, more than 50 per cent joined private life insurance schemes, while 10 per cent joined both private life insurance and annuity schemes and pay 41 000 yen per month (three times more than the amount of the first-type contribution) (SIA, 1999). They apparently chose private schemes instead of the NPI.

Table 8.3 shows variations in the credit of public pensions along generational lines. It clearly indicates the correlation between the age and the degree of trust. The younger a generation is, the less it trusts public pensions.

A widely circulated discourse since the late 1990s is that future generations can receive less than the total amounts of their payments whereas the balance is quite favourable to current beneficiaries. According to an intergenerational calculation, a model couple of 1940 (composed of a male breadwinner born in

Table 8.3   Trust in public pensions (%)

Generation	Trust	Distrust
20+	32	67
30+	27	72
40+	46	54
50+	58	41
60+	68	30
70+	71	22
Average	51	47

Source: *Asahi* Newspaper, 21 June 2003.

1940, working between the ages of 20 and 60, and living the average span of life, and a two-year younger spouse) gain 2.68 times the total amount of payments, while the model couple of 1980 gain 0.73 times, and the couple of 2000 gain 0.61 times (Nishizawa, 2003, p. 33). In short, for younger generations, it is not worth contributing to the public pension.

Welfare bureaucrats attempt to remind people that the public pension is a pay-as-you-go system based on intergenerational solidarity. This argument is not convincing, however, because they had argued until recently that the public pension is a partially funded system and indicated little about intergenerational transfers. A partially funded system is lapsing into a pay-as-you-go system due to financially unsound improvements of benefits and accelerated population ageing. Therefore, no intergenerational agreement or contract exists in Japan. While a pay-as-you-go system is vulnerable to population ageing, it may be able to generate resiliency in the system due to a firm contract between the generations as well as between the state and the citizen, as seen in social insurance countries in continental Europe. Japan's pay-as-you-go-system, however, has neither resiliency nor legitimacy.[9]

2004 Reform

The 2004 reform is expected to be the final and comprehensive one, by which to accomplish fiscal sustainability as well as intergenerational equity, thereby restoring trust in public pensions. To this end, a review of the financing method is widely considered unavoidable. The most radical option so far proposed is a complete shift from pay-as-you-go to full funding. Advocates of a fully funded system argue that the problem of double payment would not be so serious if its burdens are dispersed across different generations. Privatization of public pensions and the shift to a complete-pay-as-you-go system are also advocated by some economists and pension experts (see Hatta and Yashiro, 1998; Koshio, 1998; Hatta and Oguchi, 1999; Nishizawa, 2003).

These discussions make sense, to some extent, in the case of employees' pension schemes, but cannot be applied to the NPI, in which the first and most serious problem is how to collect contributions. Because of this, quite a few support the complete tax-financing of the BP. It can resolve not only a difficulty in collecting the first-type contributions but also a controversy over the third-type status.[10]

Welfare bureaucrats are, however, quite negative towards a shift from social insurance to tax-financing on grounds that it blurs the relationship between benefits and payments or between entitlement and obligation. Besides, considering the difficulty in finding the financial resources needed to increase subsidies from a third to a half of BP payments, following the 1999 decision to accomplish it by 2004, welfare bureaucrats argue that further increases in subsidies from tax revenues are politically unfeasible[11] (interview with the chief of the Pension Bureau of the Ministry of Health, Labour and Welfare, Nippon Keizai Shinbun, 28 February 2001).

The Ministry of Health, Labour and Welfare (MHLW)[12] publicized in December 2002 a preliminary draft of the 2004 reform. The main argument in it is that the contribution rate of employees would be raised gradually from the current 13.58 per cent of annual income to 20 per cent by 2025 and kept at that level ever afterwards. Benefit levels would vary according to changes in demographic and economic factors, including life expectancy, the fertility rate, interest rates, prices and not on the basis of political decisions. In short, a shift from DB to DC is proposed here.

Curiously enough, however, such a fundamental change has not been a central issue discussed in the process of making a government plan. What has attracted public attention, instead, is exclusively the issue of how to lower the future contribution rate. The 20 per cent upper-limit was regarded as too high and eventually lowered to 18.35 per cent in the government basic plan prepared in December 2003 as a compromise between the MHLW and the employer. Welfare bureaucrats insisted that the level of 18.35 per cent be maintained to provide the benefit guaranteeing 50 per cent of the average earnings to the retiree, which the Prime Minister explicitly promised to the people.[13] The contribution rate is to go up to 18.35 per cent by 2017, while the benefit level is lowered to the 50 per cent level by 2020.

The 50 per cent level in 2020, however, is not firmly guaranteed. The argument that the 18.35 per cent contribution guarantees the 50 per cent benefit is based on demographic and macro-economic projections, which are very likely to turn out incorrect. For example, every time a new projection of the future population is released, the old figures are adapted. If the assumptions are wrong, it will become difficult to maintain the 50 per cent level, unless an institutional guarantee is embedded in the system.

With this scheme, the MHLW insists that endless increases in contributions will stop and widespread anxiety about pension sustainability in the future be done away with. However, uncertainties as regards levels of benefits may intensify rather than calm anxiety over income maintenance after retirement. A certain thing in the government plan is the preservation of the current social insurance approach.

Quickly taking a look at other issues, few progresses are witnessed in the government plan. The MHLW proposed modifying the requirement of weekly working hours from 30 hours to 20 hours to extend the EPI coverage to part-time workers, but the idea was not included in the plan of December 2003. Further negotiations with employers are necessary to settle the issue. Rejecting tax-financing of the BP, the MHLW has found no alternative to the third-type insurant status. The 2004 reform is thus predetermined to require further reviews. It will be far from the final reform as originally expected.

A major reason for the downsizing of the 2004 reform lies in the MHWL's insistence on the social insurance approach. A shift to tax-financing is the last thing MHWL wants to do, because it means a loss of its controlled huge pension assets. The MHWL successfully defined the course of the reform and excluded any possibilities of changing the social insurance principle with the support of Komeito (the Clean Government Party), the LDP's coalition partner. By holding a pivotal position in the Diet and occupying the ministership of Health, Law and Welfare, Komeito currently constitutes a veto point within the government.

Most noteworthy in analytical terms is the fact that in the preparation of the 2004 reform the existence of an intergenerational cleavage has finally come to the surface. Perceived intergenerational unfairness provides a strong momentum towards a comprehensive reform. An 'intergenerational war' is therefore understood to a certain extent as an effect of Strategy IV or the playing-off strategy. The government stressed in the 1990s the necessity of balancing intergenerational burdens. Beyond the expectation of the government, however, the perception of intergenerational unfairness has not only convinced a necessity of pension reform but undermined the credibility of public pension.[14]

CONCLUDING REMARKS

This chapter has demonstrated that the neo-institutionalist model contributes considerably to understanding the development and retrenchment of the pension system in post-war Japan. Historical legacies, path dependency and the politics of credit-claiming explain most of evolution in pension policy and why Japan came to have an institutionally fragmented pension system.

Pension retrenchment started in the early 1980s is comprehensible in terms of institutional constraints and the politics of blame avoidance. One thing unique about Japan's case is that institutions influenced pension retrenchment, but they worked in an unconventional way, at least in the 1980s. That is, institutional fragmentation caused fiscal tightness in specific pension schemes and in turn facilitated, rather than prevented, the process of pension retrenchment.

The politics of pension retrenchment in Japan also suggests the importance of veto points. When the LDP formed a stable majority in the Diet, veto points could emerge only within the LDP under the Japanese parliamentary cabinet system. Therefore, when factions within the LDP temporarily stopped competing with each other and achieved unity and harmony after the 1980 election, no veto points existed, which provided a critical condition in favour of the 1985 reform. Nor did veto points exist in the 1994 reform, as a consensus across political parties was formed. The LDP currently forms a coalition with Komeito, which provides a veto point within the government. The course of the 2004 reform is therefore likely to be defined substantially by the preference and move of Komeito.

Masterful handling of blame avoidance strategies has been illustrated. The analytical relevance of Japan's case to the model of blame avoidance is, however, not the kind of skills displayed in the process, but the increase in bureaucratic power. Bureaucracy may obtain a decent chance to pursue its own goals and interests in the process of retrenchment. Bureaucratic initiatives may be either positive or negative in terms of problem-solving, but in any case bureaucracy is likely to obtain more discretion where blame avoidance constrains political leadership. The number of veto points may affect the role and power of bureaucracy. Where there are no veto points, bureaucrats may be able to pursue their goals and interests most effectively. In the 1985 and 1994 reforms, the MHW accomplished what they had held in mind for long. Even if there are veto points, however, bureaucrats may find a way of realizing what they want. At the initial stage of the 2004 reform, the MHLW has gained support from Komeito and succeeded in protecting the ongoing social insurance principle.

The politics of blame avoidance in Japan indicates another critical implication. In spite of its success, Japan has failed to realize the sustainability of its pension system. What is worse, endlessly repeated reforms have eroded the credibility and legitimacy of the system. Japan's experience suggests that the politics of blame avoidance may be inappropriate for a rapidly ageing society like Japan. Effects of policies produced by the politics of blame avoidance operate only gradually, since they are diffused over the long run through various measures. Granted that accumulated effects can be enormous, they may come too slow for a country experiencing rapid population ageing. The politics of blame avoidance, after all, may fit countries whose population ageing proceeds gradually over a long period of time, such as those in continental Europe.

NOTES

1. The ratio of employees' pension benefits to average earnings is currently about 59 per cent in Japan.
2. Equally or more important in the 1985 reform was the establishment of the basic pension that realized equal treatment across different pension schemes, as will be discussed later.
3. Before April 2003, employees contributed 17.35 per cent of their monthly salaries (half paid by their employers) and 1 per cent of their premiums (usually equivalent to 4–5 monthly salaries). The new method is designed to keep the total amount of payments identical, except for those whose incomes are based heavily on bonuses and premiums.
4. A company with more than 500 employees can establish an EPF with the consent of more than half of the employees (and unions representing at least a third of the employees, if any). A business-affiliated group of companies can establish a fund with more than 800 employees. A group of companies with no specific ties is required to have at least 3000 employees in total to institute a fund.
5. In 1982, Japan's ageing ratio was 9.6 per cent, while its counterparts in Sweden, Britain, France and the US are 16.6 per cent, 15.3 per cent, 13.5 per cent and 11.6 per cent, respectively (MHW, 1984).
6. Witnessing fiscal deterioration and increased public bond dependency, the Ministry of Finance (MOF) started a campaign against 'fiscal rigidity' in the late 1970s and criticized generous social welfare provisions as a major cause of it. At the same time the MHW started the discussion on the restructuring of the ongoing social security schemes.
7. PM Ohira died of a heart attack in the middle of the election campaign.
8. When the fertility rate fell down to 1.57 in 1989, it was called the '1.57 shock'. Retrospectively, the figure of 1.57 was only a mid-point of the fall. The fertility rate reached only 1.33 in 2001. Compare fertility rates as of 2000, Japan's figure of 1.36 is the same as that of Germany, but much lower than its counterparts in Sweden (1.55), France (1.89) and the United. States (2.13) (*Asahi* Newspaper 10 and 11 September 2002).
9. The EPI still holds huge assets unlike a typical pay-as-you-go system, which easily cover 5–6 year liabilities.
10. Along with intergenerational equity, equity between working women and housewives is a major issue to be tackled in the 2004 reform. The third-type status given to housekeepers is criticized as unfair to working women who also do housekeeping work.
11. According to the recent government plan, the half tax-financing of the BP will be realized by 2007.
12. The MHLW was created in January 2001 by merging the MHW with the Ministry of Labour.
13. If the currently discussed idea of applying actuarial deduction to the benefit of the working elderly aged 70 and over is adopted, the upper-limit can be lowered to 18.1 per cent, according to calculation by the MHLW.
14. Another cleavage between working women and housewives over the issue of the third-type status also stands out, but it is certainly not an effect of Strategy V. Welfare bureaucrats were reluctant to review the third-type insurant status. They were forced by rising public concerns to discuss the issue.

REFERENCES

Anderson, K. (2001), 'The politics of retrenchment in a social democratic welfare state', *Comparative Political Studies*, **34**(9), 1063–1091.
Asahi Newspaper, 21 June 2003.
Calder, K.E. (1988), *Crisis and Compensation*, Princeton: Princeton University Press.
Clayton, R. and J. Pontusson (1998), 'Welfare-state retrenchment revisited: Entitlement cuts, public sector restructuring, and inegalitarian trends in advanced capitalist societies', *World Politics*, **51**(October 1998), 67–98.

Esping-Andersen G. (1985), *Politics against Markets*, Princeton, NJ: Princeton University Press.

Garrett, G. (1998), *Partisan Politics in the Global Economy*, Cambridge, UK: Cambridge University Press.

Hatta, T. and N. Oguchi (1999), *Nenkin Kaikakuron (Pension Reform)*, Tokyo: Nihon Keizai Shinbunsha.

Hatta, T. and N. Yashiro (1998), *Shakai Hoken Kaikaku (Social Security Reform)*, Tokyo: Nihon Keizai Shinbunsha.

Korpi, W. (1983), *The Democratic Class Struggle*, London: Routledge and Kegan Paul.

Koshio, T. (1998), *Nenkin Mineika eno Koso (A View towards Privatization of Pension)*, Tokyo: Nihon Keizai Shinbunsha.

MHW (Ministry of Health and Welfare, Koseisho) (various years), *Kosei Hakusho (White Paper on Health and Welfare)*.

Nakano, M. (1992), *Gendai Nihon no Seisaku Katei (The Policy Process in Contemporary Japan)*, Tokyo: University of Tokyo Press.

'Nenkin Joho' Editorial Office (2003), *Kigyo Nenkin no Shinjitsu (The Truth of Corporate Pension)*, Tokyo: Nihon Keizai Shinbunsha.

Nihon Keizai Shinbun, 28 February 2001.

Nishizawa, K. (2003), *Nenkin Daikaikaku (Great Pension Reform)*, Tokyo: Nihon Keizai Shinbunsha.

Pierson, P. (1994), *Dismantling the Welfare State?*, Cambridge, UK: Cambridge University Press.

Pierson, P. (1996), 'The new politics of the welfare state', *World Politics*, **48**(January), 143–179.

Pierson, P. (ed.) (2001), *The New Politics of the Welfare State*, Oxford: Oxford University Press.

Ross, F. (2000),' "Beyond Left and Right": The new partisan politics of welfare', *Governance*, **13**(2), 155–183.

Scarbrough, E. (2000), 'West European welfare states: The old politics of retrenchment', *European Journal of Political Research*, **38**, 225–259.

Shinkawa, T. (1993), *Nihon-gata Fukushi no Seiji Keizaigaku (The Political Economy of Japanese-style Welfare)*, Tokyo: San-ichi Shobo.

Shinkawa, T. (1999), *Sengo Nihon Seiji to Shakai Minshu-shugi (Social Democracy in Postwar Japan)*, Kyoto: Horitsu Bunka-sha.

Shinkawa, T. and T.J. Pempel (1996), 'Occupational welfare and the Japanese experience', in M. Shalev (ed.), *The Privatization of Social Policy?*, London: Macmillan, 280–326.

SIA (Social Insurance Agency, Shakai Hokencho) (1999), *99-nendo Kokumin Nenkin Hokenja Jittai Chosa (The 1999 Research on NPP Insurants)*.

Tada, H. (1991), 'Bunritsu-gata kai-nenkin seido no kakuritsu (The emergence of the divided pension system)', in K. Yokoyayama and H. Tada (eds), *Nihon Shakai Hosho no Rekishi (The History of Social Security in Japan)*, Tokyo: Gakubunsha; 140–162, www.ipss.go.jp.

Weaver, R. Kent (1986), 'The politics of blame avoidance', *Journal of Public Policy*, **6**(4), 371–398.

9. Pension reform in Taiwan: The old and the new politics of welfare

Chen-Wei Lin

INTRODUCTION

Taiwan's achievement in economic development began to draw scholarly attention in the 1980s. For many observers, the so-called 'Taiwan Miracle' (or the East Asian Miracle) was remarkable not only because of its record-breaking rapid economic development but also the concomitant democratization and equitable growth achieved by the island-nation (World Bank, 1992; Gold, 1986; Fei et al., 1979). The success story was lauded again in the 1990s. This time, however, the praise came from a different camp. Rather than industrialization and economic growth, some began to pay attention to the fast-changing welfare institutions of Taiwan (White and Goodman, 1998). There scholars also found great hopes. Beginning in the early 1980s, Taiwan launched a series of welfare reforms. Laws concerning social assistance, old age welfare, labour standards, youth welfare and many other welfare measures were revamped (Lin, Wan-I, 2002). The Kuomintang (Nationalist Party, hereafter KMT) government also expanded the enrolment and coverage of the Labour Insurance, and launched a new health insurance scheme for all farmers.[1] These efforts of improving various welfare programmes and institutions culminated in the inauguration of the National Health Insurance (NHI). The NHI not only brought Taiwan a universal health insurance, it also unified the previously fragmented medical insurance systems, and resolved the serious financial crisis some of these schemes were facing. The NHI was a tremendous success. Polls after 1995 consistently showed that more than 70 per cent of enrolees, hence 70 per cent of citizens, were 'satisfied with the NHI' (CBNHI, 2000). Some scholars began to see the 1990s as the 'golden era of welfare reforms' in Taiwan (Peng, 2001). Indeed, considering the fact that merely ten years ago, even the phrase 'welfare laggard' would have been praise for Taiwan, the achievement of the past ten years is worthy of optimism; optimism that a new kind of welfare state could emerge: one that combines low cost and efficiency with equity (White and Goodman, 1998).

However, a closer scrutiny of Taiwan's current old age pension programmes would provide an entirely different perspective. Despite the existence of a highly integrated and equitable universal health insurance system with an extensive role (both financially and administratively) by the central government, pension programmes in Taiwan remain extremely underdeveloped. At the moment this chapter is being written, aside from commercial private pensions, public pension programmes are only available for government employees and military personnel. This constitutes less than 10 per cent of the work force. Some wage earners (those other than government employees and military personnel) receive a lump sum retirement allowance that has a ceiling of 45 months' salary. The extremely underdeveloped and unfair situation becomes more peculiar when one takes into the consideration that Taiwan's population is ageing rapidly. Although the Taiwanese state has taken extensive measures to deal with the ensuing health issues, few real policies were affected concerning old age income security.

This chapter is a preliminary attempt to explain this situation. Since Taiwan is a newcomer to the literature of the welfare state, the chapter begins with a very brief discussion of Taiwan's welfare programmes and explanation for their emergence offered by recent research to set the context of our discussion of ageing and pension in Taiwan. This is then followed by a quick sketch of the ageing situation and the outlines of the current pension policies in Taiwan. The discussion will make clear that despite continuous reforms in various aspects of social security, and the substantial increase in social security expenditure, old age pension programmes in Taiwan remain mostly privileges of government employees and military personnel. Section 3 provides a more detailed sketch of the process of and reasons for the failed attempt to introduce the National Pension Programme (hereafter, NPP) in 2000. The author contends that the failure to introduce NPP was brought about by a programme design that would place heavy fiscal pressure on the government. This was, in turn, created by the institutional legacies of social insurance schemes implemented by the KMT regime in post-war Taiwan.

WELFARE STATE IN TAIWAN

Facts

Post-war welfare in Taiwan is dominated by state-initiated social insurance schemes with a heavy emphasis on health coverage. Beginning with Labour Insurance, implemented in March 1950, the authoritarian KMT government launched 16 different social insurance schemes by 1995. Most were health insurance programmes but the three largest ones, Labour Insurance, the Government Employees Insurance and the Military Insurance, included benefits such as protection against work hazard and old age allowances. Other kinds of welfare programmes remained minimal at best. Family allowances practically did not exist and income security was provided to low-income households as poor relief (Lin, Wan-I, 1990). Unemployment insurance was not introduced until 1999. In short, welfare in Taiwan was residual at best.

Still, most changes did not take place until after the 1980s. By relaxing the enrolment standards of Labour Insurance, the urban middle-class wage earners were allowed to join the scheme. This resulted in a 130 per cent increase of enrolees in the 1980s. By 1990, the ratio of insurants enroled in the three major insurance schemes accounted for more than 46 per cent of the population.[2] These reforms resulted in the increase of social security-related expenditures. By the end of 1990s, social expenditure, although still extremely small in terms of GDP share compared with that of most OECD members, became the largest item of the central government's budget.

The rapid expansion of these government-managed social insurance schemes not only altered the size but also the nature of these programmes. Social insurance in Taiwan moved from low-contribution low-coverage to low-contribution with relatively extensive coverage. Since most programmes at the outset were intended to provide minimum health coverage only and other cash benefits, enrolees were required to pay small contributions. The gradual expansion of benefits was not matched by similar increases in contributions. Hence, what was intended to be a piecemeal symbol actually became the lion's share of what the government spent.

Explanation

Until the recent few years, scholars undertaking the task of analysing Taiwan's welfare state fell into two categories. One is typified by various studies that analyse both the origin of the welfare state in Taiwan and its characteristics. The other deals more with the relationship between the political regime and the unfolding of welfare state development in Taiwan. Scholarly works of the first category usually focus on the macro-historical background and on cultural factors. The shared common conclusion is that Taiwan is considered a 'residual welfare state'. This was brought about because Taiwan lacked a coherent thinking or ideology on the social security system. Or, they argue, the priority placed on economic development and the adversarial relationship with mainland China led to the haphazard and inadequate development of the social security system. In the end, however, most analyses focused on the aspect of Taiwan being a 'welfare laggard' but failed to provide a convincing explanation as to why welfare programmes on Taiwan expanded rapidly after the 1980s.[3]

The second category focuses mostly on why expansion was possible even within the context of a conservative developmental state, an expression often used to define Taiwan (Kwon, 1998; Lin, Chen-Wei, 1999). This logic is that KMT had to provide a certain level of social protection in order to generate legitimacy for its authoritarian rule. Such logic does not provide a convincing argument for the continual welfare expansion even after Taiwan completed its transition to democracy, in which legitimacy can be fostered through regular and fair elections. Nor does it offer a plausible account of why some expansionary reforms, such as the NPP, dealt with in this chapter, ended in failure, Needless to say, neither school offer causal links on the design of welfare programmes. For example, the reason why Taiwan adopted a unified health insurance system was never properly addressed; not to mention the idea of introducing an NPP with a mixture of social insurance and individual savings and a heavy emphasis on provision to citizens who are currently over the age of 65.

In recent years, some efforts have been made to analyse the micro-politics of crucial policy change such as the introduction of the Farmers' Health Insurance, health insurance reforms, or the emergence of old age pensions as a prominent issue. These analyses have uncovered interesting aspects of welfare reforms in Taiwan. For example, the electoral system was a likely cause of welfare expansion during the post-democratic transition of Taiwan (Wong, 2001; Lee, 1996). According to these studies, Taiwan's electoral system (single non-transferable vote multi-member electoral system [SNTV-MM]) prompted candidate-centred competition, which in turn led to increasing campaign promises for social policy reforms despite the fact that popular understandings and elite ideology of welfare in Taiwan are usually branded as 'liberalist' with an Oriental tint: one that emphasizes individual and family responsibilities in securing protection from market forces. This chapter makes similar efforts in understanding welfare policy changes through micropolitical analysis but takes on a new and recent case: the failed attempt to introduce the NPP in 2000.

Old age income security became a salient political issue in Taiwan in the early 1990s. The debate surrounding old age income security heated up before every election and usually ended with the ruling KMT promising a comprehensive reform and local country magistrates doling out non-contributory old age allowance that rarely lasted more than a year. The KMT spent six years planning a National Pension Programme but never brought it into existence. Why did the issue emerge in the 1990s? What kind of pension system was being talked about? Why did the KMT and the Democratic Progressive Party (hereafter DPP) fail to implement the NPP?[4] These are the questions this chapter tries to answer. Before embarking on discussion on the NPP, we turn first to the issue of ageing in Taiwan to understand what effects, if any, it had on the heated debate of pension reforms.

AGEING AND OLD AGE INCOME SECURITY PROGRAMMES IN THE 1990S

Population Ageing in Taiwan

First we begin with the demographic situation in Taiwan (see Table 9.1). The current ratio of those over 65 in Taiwan is relatively low compared with that of industrialized countries. In 2000, the number of those over 65 represented only 8.6 per cent of the population. But one can also notice that this is the result of rapid ageing. The ratio doubled in the past 20 years and will continue to increase rapidly. By 2035, population ageing in Taiwan will have reached a stage comparable with that of other industrialized countries. In other words, although not facing serious pressure like other developed countries, Taiwan's population is ageing very rapidly.

Simple assumptions can be made that a rapidly ageing population generated pressure on the government to take up reforms on public pension programmes. In fact, South Korea already realized universal pension coverage by introducing its National Pension Programme in 1988 when its population ageing was much less obvious (those over 65 years of age represented less than 5 per cent of the population, see Kim and Kim, this volume). Japan also completed its universal, although somewhat complex, pension system by the 1960s when the ratio of over 65 was round 5 per cent of the population (Shinkawa, this volume). Taiwan remained an exception. If Taiwan had remained completely indifferent to welfare in general, this might have been easier to understand. But as we have seen from the discussion so far, there exists in Taiwan a universal health insurance and welfare expenditures have risen steadily.[5] Adding a rapidly ageing population, there should be enough reasons for Taiwan to have a more extensive pension system. One can possibly argue that Taiwan did not develop a more comprehensive pension system for the very reasons that welfare expenditures have increased rapidly. But if Taiwan were to adopt a funding system similar to that of Singapore, there would be very little fiscal pressure on the government and Taiwanese people could still have a pension system. Discussions in the next section will show why this was not the path taken and why Taiwan failed to introduce a National Pension Programme despite repeated promises made by both KMT and the DPP. First, however, we need to take a quick glance at the old age income security programmes in Taiwan.

Old Age Income Security Programmes in the 1990s

As mentioned above, public pensions are provided mostly to government employees and military personnel. Table 9.1 summarizes currently available old age benefits and retirement schemes in Taiwan. Clearly, government employees and military personnel are provided with better old age income security schemes. With Labour Insurance and retirement benefits required by the Labour Standard Law, workers seem to enjoy similar benefits as well. However, the fact that most corporations in Taiwan are short-lived small- and medium-sized companies, very few workers can actually fulfil the requirement of staying at the same workplace for more than 15 years. Further, not all companies abide by the Labour Standard Law since there existed no real penalty for not observing it. According to a survey conducted by the Council of Labour Affairs (Ministry of Labour) in 1993, less than 1.8 million workers work in places where Labour Standard Law is observed (Council of Labour Affairs, 1993). Further, according to Fu's calculation, even if workers were to receive old age benefits both from the Labour Insurance and the lump sum payment required by the Labour Standard Law, its earnings replacement rate would be approximately 33 per cent at best whereas government employees and military personnel can gather up to 90 per cent of pre-retirement income. When the special savings interest rate for government employees and military personnel is added, the replacement rate exceeds 100 per cent (Fu, 1994; Guo, 1998).

The situation for the farmers was worse. There was no programme of any sort for the farmers until 1995. In 1995, the KMT government finally implemented a non-contributory old age allowance for the farmers. Still, the fixed amount of NTD 3000 was no more than one-eighth of the average monthly income. As for the self-employed, there is nothing at all. In other words, the pension system in Taiwan heavily favours government employees and military personnel. This 'cleavage' overlapped with an ethnic one and was made more salient by the opposition party seeking electoral victory as we will discuss in the next section.

Finally, the scale of commercial private pensions might help to emphasize how underdeveloped the whole pension system remains. Private pension plans became available in 1999 only. Between 1999 and 2001, only 1278 pension plans were signed, needless to say, an almost negligible number (Zheng and Zhao, 2002, pp. 7–8). In short, old age income in Taiwan was, for the most part, to be derived from individual savings and properties. According to surveys conducted by the government, individual transfer (30.6 per cent) and work income (46.88 per cent) were the most important income sources for the aged in 1992 (Zheng, 1999).

The next section will describe what efforts were made to alter this situation and why they failed.

Table 9.1 Public pension schemes in Taiwan (1993, 1995)

		Began	Enrolees (10 000s)	Benefits	Finance method
Military personnel	Military Insurance	1953	65.4	Lump sum payment: maximum 45 months	Contribution; deficits financed by the government
	Military Retirement Scheme	1949	(14.9)	1. Retirement payment: monthly pension maximum equivalent of 90% salary before retirement 2. Lump sum payment: maximum equivalent of 60 months of salary	Funding; deficits financed by the government
Government employees & teachers	Government Employees Insurance	1958	60.8	Lump sum payment; maximum 36 months	Insurance contribution; deficits financed by the government
	Government Employees Retirement Scheme	1948	(7.0)	1. Choice between lump sum payment and monthly payment 2. Lump sum payment: maximum of 53 months of salary 3. Monthly payment: maximum is equivalent of 70% of monthly salary before retirement	Provident fund; deficits financed by the government

Workers	Labour Insurance	1950	709.0	Lump sum payment: maximum 45 months	Insurance contribution: deficits financed by the government
	Retirement benefits based on the Labour Standard Law	1985	In 1993, approximately 1.6 million were employed by the corporations that comply with the Labour Standard Law	Lump sum payment; maximum 45 months of the average monthly salary at the time of retirement	Provident fund
Farmers	None until 1995	1995	427 000 in 1997	3 000 NTD per month	Government
Self-employed	none	–	–	–	–

Source: Lin, Chen-Wei (2003).

THE FAILED REFORM: NATIONAL PENSION PROGRAMME

Even in the 1970s, there were discussions within KMT on the implementation of a more comprehensive old age income security system. However, they remained internal discussions because the ruling KMT elites were unable to resolve issues concerning financial and administrative resources (Fu, 2000, p. 234).[6] The discussion on introducing a nationwide old age income security drew large public attention after 1992. The ruling KMT made repeated promises during election campaigns that the government intended to implement a universal basic pension scheme, the National Pension Programme, and at the same time, provide a basic pension to those who were already 65 years old. This change of course was prompted by two factors. One was the inclusion of old age allowance as an election promise by the opposition party DPP. This received nationwide attention and helped the DPP to advance in national elections. The other was the adoption by the KMT of the stance of dealing with income security for aged people by planning a more comprehensive 'national pension' programme, while branding the DPP's old age allowance as a mere political show and a reckless waste of money (Zhong, 1995, p. 135). The first development brought the issue of old age income security for the currently aged to the public's attention and the second one transferred the issue of old age income security into one that demands a universal basic pension. To understand why such an issue suddenly gripped people's minds, we need to further elaborate on the problems embedded in the old age income security programmes Taiwan had prior to 1992.

Setting the Context

As discussions from the section above show, there exists disparity between government employees, the military personnel and others, especially farmers. This situation was exacerbated by the fact that traditionally government employees and military personnel were mostly the so-called 'Mainland Chinese' and farmers were usually Taiwanese. Although there are no statistics to demonstrate the ethnic constituents of these professions, it is a common understanding shared by most Taiwanese that the government and the military are staffed by Mainland Chinese. As we shall see in the following discussion, debates surrounding the old age pension began with Taiwanese farmers' frustration that Mainland Chinese retired veterans were receiving generous preferential treatment while farmers received practically nothing. Table 9.2 shows us indirectly why such perception prevailed (and still prevails) in Taiwan. It is a summary of the results of a survey conducted by scholars to identify attributes of the aged in 1989. Relying on old age benefits, retirement pension and

Table 9.2 Attributes of the economic independence of the old aged

		Survey samples	Sources of income for those who are economically independent		Ratio of those who are economically independent (%) (3) = (1) + (2)
			Those who rely on old age benefits, retirement pension, savings (%) (1)	Those who rely on income earned through work (%) (2)	
Age groups	60–64	1542	17.2	41.3	58.6
	65+	2447	16.2	16.4	32.6
Ethnicity	Taiwanese	3099	8.6	23.7	32.3
	Mainland Chinese	891	44.2	34.5	78.8
Occupation	Farmers	1291	6.1	23.6	29.7
	Non-farmers	2037	25.1	33.1	58.2
	Others	662	11.0	9.4	20.4

Notes: Percentage of those who are economically independent: 42.7% → 1704; percentage of those who are not economically independent: 57.3% → 2286.

Source: Zhang, Ming-zheng (1996) 18–19, Table 6.

savings, 42.7 per cent of the old aged were 'economically independent'. There is, however, a distinct difference between the Mainland Chinese and Taiwanese in their ability to secure income after 60 years old. While 78.8 per cent of the Mainland Chinese were economically independent, only 32.2 per cent of Taiwanese could claim that. Professionally, only 29.7 per cent of farmers could remain economically independent whereas nearly 60 per cent of non-farmers managed to secure old age incomes. For the Mainland Chinese, more than half of those who were economically independent acquired their income through old age benefits, retirement pension and savings (column 1) whereas more than three-quarters of economically independent Taiwanese had to rely on work. Since there is no data available on the saving behaviour of the two ethnic groups, it is difficult to determine whether individual savings constitute the major part of figures indicated in column 1. However, suffice to say that the impression that government employees and military personnel enjoy better welfare is an idea commonly shared by many Taiwanese, especially the farmers. This provided a rich possibility for the candidate in a heated electoral race. Tainan, the region that made old age pension the front-page news, was an area that was heavily populated by Taiwanese farmers.[7]

The Emergence of Old Age Income Security as an Issue

This disparity of public old age income security programmes was excavated by Su Huahn-Dj, a DPP candidate in Tainan County. In the Legislative Yuan election of 1992, Su made the old age pension issue one of his major campaign themes. For Su, at that time, the matter was not so much the idea of social security but the argument that Taiwanese farmers should also be entitled to the same old age allowance (nearly NTD 5000 a month) that was provided to the mainlander veterans.[8] This campaign strategy brought Su a dramatic success. He received more than 100 000 votes, in sharp contrast to the mere 10 000 in his unsuccessful campaign in the previous year's National Assembly election.

Su's victory was carefully watched by the leaders of the DPP. Since the electoral district was multi-member, DPP naturally nominated other candidates. In fact, Su was an upcoming young politician with whom most people were unfamiliar. Other DPP candidates were senior local politicians with extensive local ties. The other two DPP candidates ended up with a total of 90 000 votes, which was the amount of support that the DPP had traditionally received. This meant that the 100 000 voters Su had managed to win over were very likely former KMT supporters (Lee, 1996). By holding the old age allowance issue as the central campaign issue, the DPP went on to capture another crucial victory in the Penghu County, a stronghold of the KMT, in the magistrate special election held in February 1993. This gave a strong impression to all parties that were competing in elections that the issue of old age income was an extremely effective instrument in electoral competition.

After winning these important races, the DPP quickly made the 'old age pension' (*lao-ren nianijin* in Chinese) a major issue in its policy in the Legislative Yuan. By then, it was no longer a local issue, but a national one. In April 1993, Su submitted the first draft of a bill for a National Pension Programme in the history of the Republic of China. Other versions of a National Pension Programme were voiced and subsequently submitted to the Legislative Yuan by other legislative members as well.

DPP also organized social movements to broaden support for a nationwide pension programme. In September 1993, a group of DPP legislative members, party officials and staff members formed the 'Respect-for-the-Elderly Pension Action Coalition', which promoted an old age pension in tie-up with the 'Coalition to Promote Elders' Welfare' formed by scholars and activists engaged in social welfare. These organizations held a series of open debates and demonstration marches in October, drawing unprecedented public attention to the issue. As a result of this social mobilization led by DPP forces, all of the DPP candidates for the local magistrate elections scheduled for December 1993 adopted the campaign promise of old age allowances in amounts ranging from NTD 3000 to NTD 10 000 (*Zhongyan Ribao*, 5 January 1994; *Zhongguo Shibao*, 28 December 1993).[9] As the original advocate of a welfare state with an old age allowance as the core of public policies, the DPP successfully raised its popularity, gaining 41 per cent of the votes. This represented a 10 per cent increase compared with the 31 per cent it had won in the Legislative Yuan election of 1992. This further strengthened the impression that old age pension reform as a campaign slogan was effective in electoral competition.

The KMT government could not ignore this rapidly increasing support for an old age allowance. In September 1993, the Minister of the Interior criticized DPP for 'neglecting the issue of family and individual, and ignoring the principle of welfare' by promising an old age allowance or pension for electoral victory (*Zhongguo Shibao*, 3 September 1993). Still, the KMT had to respond in action as well. In May 1993, the Ministry of Interior already launched the National Pension Programme Research and Planning Task Force (hereafter the MOI Pension Task Force). The MOI Pension Task Force quickly announced a preliminary plan in November that year, and presented its report to the Executive Yuan in February 1994. The MOI Pension Task Force report outlined possible methods of realizing a universal pension system in Taiwan.

Aside from old age income, in July 1993, the KMT government also amended the current scheme of 'allowance for the middle and low-income elderly' and implemented a new scheme in October. With these measures, it attempted to give the impression that it had been making efforts on income security issues in general even before the DPP's call for reform. Then, in March 1994, the Council for Economic Planning and Development, which had been entrusted with planning the pension programme, established the Pension Programme Special Task Force (hereafter the CEPD Pension Task Force). The CEPD Pension Task Force began to work on the specific programmatic design.

This was how the issue of receiving old age allowance like that of a mainlander veteran next door turned into debates and concrete plans for the introduction of the NPP. However, since the debate began with non-contributory old age allowance received by the mainlander veteran, most Taiwanese lacked clear ideas on what pension programmes are in general. To a large degree, DPP had helped to create an impression that old age pension meant non-contributory old age allowance handed out by the government. This confusion hampered the formation of a national consensus and resulted in the failure to introduce NPP, as will be discussed later.

The KMT Plan

In April 1995, the CEPD completed the phase 1 planning, and presented to the Executive Yuan a report on the 'Coordination of the National Pension Programme' (CEPD, 1995). The draft prepared by the CEPD differed from the earlier version of the Ministry of Interior mainly in the formula used for benefits calculation, the availability of government contributions, and the feasibility of integrating the existing occupationally-based social insurance system. In contrast to the MOI's proposal of monthly benefits equivalent to 60–80 per cent of the previous year's average monthly household expenditure per person, the CEPD formula was 50–70 per cent of the previous two years' monthly consumption per person. This would result in a decrease in the amount of benefits to be received by enrolees from NTD 6600–8800 to NTD 4520–6400. The CEPD also declared that, in order to decrease the government's fiscal burden, the government would not contribute to the premiums. The MOI retained the option of integrating the existing occupationally-based social insurances, whereas the CEPD was lukewarm toward integration, for fear of a possible increase in administrative costs. The CEPD proposed a two-tier system in which the new NPP would serve as the basic universal pension scheme and the existing old age benefits in the various social insurance would serve as the second tier (CEPD, 1995, pp. 74–97). In spite of this difference, the plan proposed in the CEPD report followed the general guideline envisaged by the MOI draft.

After the second phase of planning in 1998, the CEPD adopted the motto of 'separating the administration, unifying the contents'. This meant that the CEPD intended to realize NPP by maintaining the existing occupationally-based schemes and their administrative structures while ensuring the consistency of benefits. The reform was intended first to complete the process of transforming the old age benefits of existing general social insurances into a pension programme. The second objective of the reform was to launch a new NPP to cover the 4.79 million people (including 0.57 million aged 65 or over), who were not covered by the occupationally-based insurances (CEPD-NPPPTF, 1998, p. 12) Under this measure, those who were already beneficiaries of some form of public insurance with old age benefits would be given the choice of staying within the present scheme or switching to the new NPP. Those who had not joined any public insurance would be given a grace period of three years, after which those over the age of 25 would be forced to join the new NPP. The premium was set at 10 per cent of the insured salary. It is shared by the government (20 per cent in general, 40 per cent for farmers and low-income earners), employers (60 per cent) and the insured (20 per cent). The old age benefit was to be set at the 50 to 70 per cent of the monthly consumption per capita in the previous two months (CEPD-NPPPTF, 1998, pp. 26–27, 47).

What merits our attention is the fact that government contribution to the premium was reintroduced into the plan and the fact that old age benefit would be provided to the currently aged at the same time the NPP was launched. The repeated electoral promises had embedded in the Taiwanese people, impressions that old age income security should be provided by the government alone and that most Taiwanese, workers, employers and self-employed alike, have grown accustomed to the idea of sharing contributions to the premium with the government since this was also the case for the NHI and most other social insurances implemented by the KMT government. This obviously created serious fiscal burden. Table 9.3 is an estimate provided by the CEPD Task Force. It shows that the minimum cost to implement the NPP proposed by the CEPD would add at least NTD 25 billion to the government's fiscal burden. The cost can climb to NTD 44 billion if the government share of contribution were increased to 40 per cent. Considering the fact that the welfare expenditure of the central government in 1998 was approximately NTD 289 billion, this is at least a 10 per cent increase for the welfare expenditures. The greatest concern, then, became the foreseen fiscal pressure. Taiwan's continuous fiscal deficits since the latter half of the 1980s had resulted in an accumulation of government debts, reaching 13 per cent of GNP in 1994. The government, in facing these fiscal constraints, proposed to raise the consumption tax from 5 per cent to 6 per cent in order to secure the necessary financial sources to launch the NPP. This proposal stirred up rigorous opposition from the business community. Despite this, the KMT, faced with increasing pressure and the obligation to fulfil its electoral promise, finally announced that the NPP would be introduced in 2000.

Table 9.3 Possible fiscal burden by the government when the NPP was implemented (NTD 100 000 000)

	Share in contributions	Old age benefit for the currently old aged		Adm. cost	Initial cost	Total	Total
	(a)	(b)	(c)	(d)	(e)	(a) + (b) + (c) (d) + (e)	(a) + (c) + (c) (d) + (e)
20% for all enrolees	50.0	155.3	232.9	17.9	30.0	253.2	330.8
Half of the self-employed are low-income earners and the government shares 40% of contributions	132.4	155.3	232.9	17.9	30.0	335.6	413.2
Two-thirds of the self-employed are low-income earners and the government shares 40% of contributions	159.9	155.3	232.9	17.9	30.0	361.1	440.7

Notes: [a]Contributions for the NPP were assumed to be NTD 910 per person. The lowest monthly salary was set at NTD 16 315 for 1999, and the growth rate set at 3 per cent.
[b]Maximum government shared contribution is set at 40 per cent depending on the income level of the entrolees.

Source: CEPD (1998), 45.

Still, most observers remained sceptical as to whether this was really possible. The KMT, however, was temporarily saved by the earthquake that struck the island in September 1999. In order to secure financial resources for reconstruction in rural areas, the KMT government decided to shelve the plan to introduce the NPP in 2000. This justified the indefinite postponement of the NPP.

The DPP Plan

The focus on the post-earthquake reconstruction and absence of heated elections put the NPP project onto the backburner. This, however, changed again in 2000. In March 2000, DPP surprised the world by beating the KMT and an extremely popular independent candidate to capture the presidential election. It was the first time for a non-KMT government to ever take power in the postwar history of Taiwan. The DPP came into power in May 2000 and the CEPD quickly presented a new report in August. In addition to NPP Plan A (a modified KMT plan), the report added a new Plan B (a defined-benefit scheme funded by general tax revenues), where no contribution would be required from the insured. The financial sources for a basic national pension, according to Plan B, would be secured from the government's general budget and by a hike in the consumption tax. It would include benefits for the elderly, disabled and orphans. The amount of old age benefits, obviously the most important portion, was set at 20–25 per cent of the average monthly spending per person for the two preceding years and no lower than NTD 3000. According to the CEPD report, Plan B was envisioned as the basic pension programme relying on tax revenues, and at the same time meant to reduce the existing premiums of Military, Government Employees, and Labour Insurance since most of old age benefits in these schemes would be absorbed by the NPP (CEPD, 2000, pp. 15–19). Plan B not only differed from Plan A in how the proposed basic pension would affect the existing social insurances, the most important difference lay in the fact that it was completely general tax revenue-funded, an idea that did not exist even at the final stage of policy planning by the KMT administration. In other words, the general tax revenue-funded scheme only came into existence after the DPP came to power.

The debate concerning old age income security drew renewed attention during the presidential race in 2000. During the election campaign, the DPP candidate Chen Shui-bian announced the '3-3-3 policy' as important electoral promises concerning social welfare for average citizens. Once elected, Chen promised to provide a monthly non-contributory allowance of NTD 3000 to those over the age of 65, free medical treatment for children under three, and housing loans at an interest rate of 3 per cent for first-time owners. Chen Shui-bian went on to win the race and had to move quickly to realize his electoral promises. Soon after he assumed office in May, Chen's administration presented bills intended to realize the '3-3-3 policy' to the Legislative Yuan. However, during the deliberations, these bills were heavily criticized for their actual necessity and social fairness. Even within the ruling DPP, many were critical of Chen's '3-3-3 policy' package. Some cabinet members appointed by Chen himself actually expressed caution publicly on pursuing these policies (*Zhiyou Ribao*, 25 May 2000; *Zhongguo Shibao*, 12 May 2000). What worsened the situation, aside from the DPP's internal strife, was that the DPP was the minority in the Legislative Yuan. Within the 224 seats in the Legislative Yuan, the DPP only secured 70 seats in the previous legislative election in 1998. Hence, it was practically impossible for the DPP to pass any bills without the cooperation of the KMT and the People First Party (PFP).[10] However, the KMT and PFP strongly opposed Plan B on the grounds that discussions concerning financial sources, amounts of benefits, institutional equity and its relationship with the to-be-implemented NPP had been less than satisfactory.

Arguments concerning financial resources unfolded around whether it would be legal and appropriate to use the second reverse fund in implementing such a 'semi-permanent' policy as the old age allowance. The monthly allowance of NTD 3000 was also criticized as being insignificant as it amounted to only one-fifth of average per capita monthly spending. Many also argued that to provide allowance to individuals earning high income would be going against social equity. Further, the DPP government had failed to demonstrate how it would coordinate and secure consistency between the to-be-implemented NPP and the old age allowance programme. Although it was scheduled in July, heated debates in the Legislative Yuan brought about the eventual delay for the implementation of the old age allowance.

Chen's administration tried to strike a deal with the opposition by shelving the old age allowance in return for cooperation in implementing a National Pension Programme. The DPP then withdrew the old age allowance bill and was preparing to submit an NPP bill (*Zhongguo Shibao*, 2 August and 3 August 2000). This calculated move by the DPP put the NPP back on the newspaper front page. Since KMT had itself for years advocated a comprehensive pension programme, the DPP felt that the KMT had less than a few reasons to reject this proposal. The KMT went along and agreed to consider a National Pension Programme. It seemed, for a few weeks there, that the DPP came away not only fulfilling its campaign promise, it was also realizing a major reform of old age income security.

This, however, turned out to be a distant dream. The draft prepared by Chen's government included two plans and Plan B came as a surprise for many observers. The emergence of Plan B can be traced back to two reasons. First, as the DPP drew attention to the need to improve old age income security in its electoral campaigns, it advocated in its policy white paper a two-tier pension programme. The pension system envisioned by the DPP consists of a basic pension (first tier) and an additional pension (second tier). The basic pension is to be financed by the sales of public enterprises as financial sources. The additional pension can be implemented by reforming the existing occupationally-based insurance (second tier) (DPP-PRCC, 1995, pp. 57–64). Plan B of the NPP bill was in many respects the basic pension advocated by the DPP before it came into power. Chen's government did, however, modify the benefit level from 50 per cent to approximately 25 per cent of average monthly spending per person and the minimum amount at NTD 3000. That this amounts to a number similar to the president's campaign pledge of '3-3-3 policy' is, needless to say, not surprising. The DPP had found a method to cope with its party policy requirements and the presidential campaign promise, and, break the legislative deadlock.

Naturally, the opposition parties moved quickly to attack Plan B, as it seemed so similar to the old age allowance. Opposition parties responded with harsh criticism of the draft through the media even before it was presented to the Legislative Yuan on 15 September. CEPD bureaucrats also staged revolts. Yu-Lan Liu, Chief Officer of the CEPD's Manpower Planning Department, who had been in charge of NPP planning during the KMT administration, suddenly announced her resignation in tears. The media began to circulate stories of how a competent expert was forced to resign because of her unwillingness to cooperate with Chen's administration on 'doling out irresponsible beef'. Although Liu eventually withdrew her resignation, the KMT and PFP gained much momentum in blocking the DPP-proposed NPP (*Zhongguo Shibao*, 31 August, 1 September and 7 September 2000). In order to prevent the DPP from gaining the credit of at last introducing a comprehensive pension system, it became increasingly clear that the KMT and PFP had little incentive to actually deliberate over the NPP bill be it Plan A or Plan B. The DPP was facing tremendous difficulty in pushing forward the NPP bill.

Meanwhile, signs of a full-scale recession in the Taiwanese economy began to appear: the downturn of the US economy and 'hollowing out effect' taking place because many labour-intensive industries were shifting their operations to the People's Republic of China. Chen's administration saw a continuous increase in the unemployment rate since it took power. Rather than what happens after the age of 65, most Taiwanese were eager to see specific policy packages to reinvigorate the economy. In order to please the public, Chen announced on 16 September 2000 that he intended to 'give priority to economic development and delay social welfare reforms'. Chang Chung-hsiung, Vice-premier of the Executive Yuan, followed and officially acknowledged that the NPP, which had originally been scheduled to start in January 2001, would be postponed indefinitely (*Zhongguo Shibao*, 17 September and 18 September 2000). Premier Tang Fei also commented that the current NPP seemed unrealistic. Taiwan was to become a member of the WTO in 2001, and this would bring about major structural adjustments in agriculture and industries. The additional fiscal burden created by the NPP would come at a terrible time. Further, since the Legislative Yuan and local magistrate elections were scheduled in December 2001, unpopular tax hikes were simply out of the question. The introduction of the NPP by raising the consumption tax was unrealistic (*Zhongguo Shibao*, 23 September 2000).[11]

COMPRESSED PENSION POLITICS: POLITICS OF OLD AND NEW

Once again in 2000, the much heated debates on implementing a comprehensive National Pension Programme ended with little concrete results. Later, DPP did manage to introduce an old age allowance for those over 65 and below a certain income level. Nevertheless, a comprehensive reform, including revamping the currently available pension schemes, is yet to be carried out. This attests the difficulties of democratic governance, which is still in its nascent stage in Taiwan. The pension issue was brought to the fore by the intense party competition and its resolution was again brought to a halt by the reinforced party competition. Put differently, after the democratic transition, political partisanship, or 'old politics', became a crucial factor in determining pension policy-making in Taiwan. And it was the overlapping of ethnic and welfare cleavages in Taiwan's pension system that provided a suitable cause for the opposition party, the DPP, which was looking for an issue to substitute to advocacy of independence.

The origin of DPP can be traced back to the Dangwai ('outside the party' in English) movement during the authoritarian rule in the late 1960s.[12] It began mostly as an alliance of local politicians who were dissatisfied with the KMT, and dissident intellectuals (Rigger, 2001, p. 17). But aside from their common cause of opposing KMT's authoritarian rule, most were also ethnic Taiwanese.[13] Since it was not until the 1980s that KMT began to expand its absorption of ethnic Taiwanese elites into its central decision-making mechanism, the KMT was perceived as predominantly Mainland Chinese.[14] Hence, it is not surprising that after the Dangwai activists formed the DPP in 1986, it not only continued but expanded its emphasis on Taiwan-ization of political life on Taiwan. This has resulted in a clear link between ethnic origin and party preference. Those who identify with the DPP are predominantly ethnic Taiwanese (95.2 per cent). Within the DPP identifiers, only a few (3.9 per cent) are Mainland Chinese. Meanwhile, the KMT is also quite popular with the Taiwanese since 82.6 per cent of its identifiers are ethnic Taiwanese. An interesting phenomenon is that the then New Party, later split and most of its members merged with the PFP in 2000, was highly identified by the Mainland Chinese. The New Party was founded by former KMT members who were mostly Mainland Chinese and pro-unification.[15] New Party's clear identification by the Mainland Chinese (46.4 per cent) demonstrates that during the early and mid-1990s, partisan politics were increasingly ethnic-based. Finally, aside from the level of education for those who identify with the New Party, other social attributes do not have a significant impact on party identification (Lin, Chia-lung, 1998, p. 424).

While ethnicity is an important factor for party identification, independence versus unification is another crucial issue for political competition. DPP is thought of as pro-independent and the KMT pro-unification. Broadly speaking most DPP identifiers tend to favour Taiwan's independence while KMT and NP identifiers are more inclined to support unification. Although some DPP leaders have argued against formal declaration of independence, DPP has always been consistent in advocating autonomy, or effective independence. It is, in fact, a stated goal of DPP that 'in accordance with the reality of Taiwan's sovereignty, an independent country should be established and a new constitution drawn up in order to make the legal system conform to the social reality of Taiwan and in order to return to the international community'[16] (Rigger, 2001, pp. 120–122).

However, for various reasons of historical and international political nature, many people in Taiwan remain cautious on the issue of independence and prefer maintaining the status quo. Even within DPP identifiers, nearly 30 per cent prefer the status quo. The DPP learned this hard lesson in 1991 when it made independence the central issue of its electoral campaign by revising its charter and called for a plebiscite. The result was a disappointing loss. Table 9.4 shows that DPP's steadily increasing vote shares dropped in 1991 by 6 per cent, from nearly 30 per cent in 1989 to 23.2 per cent. KMT gained approximately 70 per cent of the vote shares and 78 per cent of seat shares. In other words, the overly pro-independence campaign strategy had alienated certain voters and backfired. Su Huahn-Dj, the legislator whose 1992 electoral campaign brought focus to the pension issue, was also dealt a definitive defeat in 1991.

Realizing that independence is no longer the most effective electoral mobilization issue, DPP began to look for an alternative. In 1992, DPP was able to recover its vote shares by softening its stance on independence and also, mostly, because it benefited from KMT's infightings and corruptions. DPP's real comeback took place in 1993 when it staged welfare issues, especially old age allowance, as its central electoral issue. As a result, DPP captured 10 per cent more votes than the previous year and increased its seat shares in the Legislative Yuan by more than 10 per cent from 1989 (Table 9.4, Table 9.5). For the DPP, the pension issue was a new cleavage for electoral mobilization.

Table 9.4   Vote shares of major parties in elections (1980–94)

Elections	DPP	KMT	NP	Others
1980 Legislative Yuan	13.0	71.1	–	15.3
1983 Legislative Yuan	18.9	69.4	–	11.7
1986 Legislative Yuan	24.6	66.7	–	8.7
1989 Legislative Yuan	29.9	59.2	–	10.9
1991 National Assembly	23.2	69.1	–	7.7
1992 Legislative Yuan	31.0	53.0	–	16.0
1993 Country magistrates/ city mayors	41.0	47.5	3.1	8.4
1994 Provincial Assembly and Municipal Councils	39.4	52.1	7.7	0.8

Source: Diamond 2001, p. 53; Lin, Chia-lung 1998.

Table 9.5   Seat distributions in Legislative Yuan (1989–2001)

Party	1989 (%)	1992 (%)	1995 (%)	1998 (%)	2001 (%)
DPP	21 (20.8)	50 (31.1)	54 (32.9)	70 (31.3)	87 (38.7)
KMT	72 (71.3)	96 (59.6)	85 (51.8)	123 (54.7)	68 (30.2)
NP	–	–	21 (12.8)	11 (4.9)	1 (0.4)
PFP	–	–	–	–	46 (20.4)
TSU	–	–	–	–	13 (5.8)
Others	8 (7.9)	15 (9.3)	4 (2.4)	21 (9.3)	10 (4.4)
(total seats)	101 (100)	161 (100)	164 (100)	225 (100)	225 (100)

Notes: 1989 was called 'supplementary election' with which only a part of the Legislative Yuan was elected. The 1992 Legislative Yuan election was considered the 'founding election', which was the first time for the residents of Taiwan to elect the entire Legislative Yuan. The total seats were 161 in 1992, expended to 164 in 1995, and again increased to 225 in 1998. The Legislative Yuan currently has 225 seats.

Source: Central Election Commission, ROC (http://www.cec.gov.tw); Wakabayashi (1992, p. 221).

It spoke to the DPP's identifiers, mostly ethnic Taiwanese who were potentially unhappy with the differential treatment in old age income security, and at the same time was appealing to those who favour the status quo but are interested in improving general welfare conditions. In other words, it could maintain its ardent supporters while gaining new votes from those who cared less about statehood but resented the KMT's favouritism for government employees and military personnel and hoped for an improvement in livelihood.

Still, electoral mobilization only tells us why pension came to the fore of national policy debates. The question of why certain reforms, for example, the preferences for social insurance or tax-financed schemes, emerged and failed remains to be answered. As to the failure, obviously, DPP being a minority party was crucial. In 2000, DPP controlled only 87 out of 225 seats in the Legislative Yuan (Table 9.5). This made it nearly impossible to pass the bill without extensive cooperation with the opposition parties in 2000. However, as we have seen from the discussion in section 3, KMT itself was no stranger to advocating a universal pension programme. Such discussions began in the early 1990s during the KMT administration and lasted for nearly eight years before the KMT stepped down. Hence, the KMT's efforts to prevent DPP's 'credit claiming' could not be a simple opposition to universal pension but concerned the actual content of the plans. DPP's miscalculation in including Plan B complicated debates for the NPP and created opportunities for the opposition parties to oppose reform. In short, by targeting the appearance of Plan B and the 'irresponsible nature' of the old age allowance, opposition parties were able to prevent DPP from claiming the credit of pension reforms while avoiding blame for being unwilling to support welfare reforms.

However, the DPP was not alone in drawing up plans that would suddenly increase fiscal burdens of the government. As we saw in the above discussion, the KMT plan also would have increased the government's welfare budgets by at least 10 per cent. The foreseen fiscal burdens were the result of having to contribute to the pension premium and provide immediate old age benefits to the currently aged. The conditions that brought these requirements into the debates of pension reforms in Taiwan, in turn, can be found in the policy legacies of Taiwan's post-war social insurance in which government sharing contributions to premiums were common practices and disparity between ethnic groups were obvious. In other words, policy legacies in many aspects pre-determined the contents of reform efforts, which, in turn, shaped the pension politics. This is quite similar to the 'new politics' being discussed in the advanced industrialized countries (Pierson, 1996; 2000). The concept of 'new politics' is devised to differentiate the politics of retrenchment from those of expansion and hence would seem awkward to apply it to the case of Taiwan in which 'old politics' and welfare expansion were the subjects. However, we have also seen from the discussion above that concerns for the costs were essential and reform directions were heavily path-dependent. Adding the fact that pension 'reforms' themselves were in many ways triggered by the existing policies, pension politics in Taiwan were undoubtedly consequences of institutional dynamics. Much like Taiwan's experiences of economic development as a latecomer, they are often compressed. The evolution of pension politics in Taiwan is, too, compressed into a shorter time period and we see elements of both old and new politics come into play in the process of trying to adopt a universal pension scheme. This provides for us a chance to understand the puzzle of why pension programmes in Taiwan remained underdeveloped despite its continuous reforms in welfare programmes and rapidly ageing population.

NOTES

1. Until 1995, there were three major social insurance schemes in Taiwan: the Military Insurance, the Labour Insurance and the Government Employees Insurance. All schemes were of 'general' nature. This meant that all schemes provided coverage of illness, injury, cash benefits for child-bearing, death, funeral, and old age pension. Until 1985, no social insurance was available to farmers. See Lin, Wan-I (1990) for details in English, Lin, Li-zhu (1994) in Chinese.
2. The KMT government also implemented reforms in strengthening 'poor relief' for the lower-income households, old age care, social assistance and other welfare programmes. See Lin, Wan-I (2002) for further details.
3. For a more detailed review of prior studies focusing on Taiwan, see Lin, Chen-Wei (1999). See also Lin, Wan-I (1990), Goodman and Peng (1996) and Tang (2000) for structural factors and historical background; Jones (1990; 1993) for cultural factors; Lin, Kuo-ming (1997) and Wong (2001) for details of policy-making concerning the health insurance.
4. The DPP came into power in 2000 by winning the presidential election. It was officially the ruling party but was still the minority in the Legislative Yuan (Taiwan's unicameral legislative body).
5. One can possibly argue that it is exactly because welfare expenditures have risen that a more comprehensive pension programme was avoided. But if Taiwan were to adopt a funding system similar to that of Singapore, the cost would be quite limited while enabling the government to claim that it has implemented an old age income security scheme. This did not take place either.
6. Although heavily modified, parts of this section are taken from Lin, Chen-Wei (2002).
7. Since the KMT central government was in Taipei, naturally more Mainland Chinese lived in the northern area of Taiwan. Tainan was also an area where agriculture continued to be an important sector. In 1992, nearly 40 per cent of the working population belonged to the agricultural sector.
8. During an interview with the author, Su stated that there was little thinking on the importance of old age income security. It was very much an issue of wanting to receive equal treatment like the mainlander veterans. Hence, he often asked his audience during the election campaign, 'Why aren't we given anything when the "old taro" [a euphemism for the mainlander veteran] can get 5000 dollars a month?'
9. Since the DPP was still the opposition party, hence could not put into effect a National Pension Programme, the DPP opted for the strategy of handing out non-contributory old age allowance through local governments.
10. The People First Party was founded in 2000 by a former KMT member, James Soong. Soong was a high-ranking and popular KMT politician who served as the Provincial Governor of Taiwan in the 1990s. He broke away from the KMT after failing to obtain candidacy of the presidential election of 2000.
11. The financial state of the Labour Insurance was drastically improved as the medical benefits were taken out to be included in the NHI at the same time as the premium for the Labour Insurance was raised.
12. Rigger (2001) provides the most detailed studies of DPP in English.
13. However, one should not assume that all Dangwai activists were Taiwanese. There were Mainland Chinese who not only opposed the KMT rule but also were advocates of Taiwan independence.

14. For KMT's ruling mechanism and Taiwan's ethnic relations see Wu (1987).
15. See Wakabayashi (1998) for an interesting analysis of the New Party phenomena.
16. Article 1, Clause 1 of the DPP platform. DPP's platform can be accessed at www.dpp.org.tw.

REFERENCES

Central Bureau of National Health Insurance (CBNHI) (2000), *National Health Insurance Profile*, Taipei, Taiwan: Central Bureau of National Health Insurance (in Chinese).
Council of Economic Planning and Development (EPD) (1995), *Guomin nibaoxian baoxian zhidu zhenghe guihua baogao (National Pension Programme Coordination Planning Report)*.
Council for Economic Planning and Development, National Programme Planning Task Force (CEPD-NPPPTF) (1998), *Woguo shehui baoxian zhidu xiankuang yu guihua mubiao (Current Situation and Planning Objectives of Social Insurance Systems in Taiwan)*, Taipei, Taiwan.
Council of Economic Planning and Development (EPD) (1998), *Planning of National Pension Program*, Taipei, Taiwan.
Council of Economic Planning and Development (CEPD) (2000), *Guomin nianjian baoxian zhidu zhenghe guihua baogao (National Pension Programme Coordination Planning Report)*.
Council of Labour Affairs (1993), *Research Report on Labour Conditions for not Applying to the Labour Standards Act*, Taipei, Taiwan (in Chinese).
Democratic Progressive Party, Policy Research and Coordinating Committee (DPP-PRCC) (1995), *Guomin nianjin zhidu (On the National Pension Programme)*, Policies of Democratic Progressive Party Series, Taipei, Taiwan.
Diamond, Larry (2001), 'Anatomy of an electoral earthquake: How the KMT lost and the DPP won the 2000 Presidential election', in Muthiah Alagappa (ed.), *Taiwan's Presidential Politics: Democratization and Cross-Strait Relations in the Twenty-first Century*, Armonk, NY: M.E. Sharpe.
Fei, John C.H., Gustav Ranis and Shirley Kuo (1979), *Growth with Equity: The Taiwan Case*, New York: Published for the World Bank, Oxford University Press.
Fu, Li-Yeh (1994), 'A preliminary study on the stratification effect of welfare institutions of Taiwan', in Qing-chun Yi (ed.), *Popular Opinions of Taiwanese Society – A Social Science Analysis*, Taiwan, Taipei: Academia Sinica.
Fu, Li-Yeh (2000), 'Laoren nianjin, zhengdang jingzheng yu xuanju (Old age pensions, party competition, and elections)', in Michael Hsiao and Lin Kuo-ming (eds), *Taiwande shehui fuli yundong (Social Welfare Movements in Taiwan)*, Taipei: Juliu Press.
Gold, Thomas (1986), *State and Society in the Taiwan Miracle*, Armonk and New York: M.E. Sharpe.
Goodman, R. and I. Peng (1996), 'Japanese, South Korean and Taiwanese social welfare in comparative perspective', in Gøsta Esping-Andersen (ed.), *Welfare States in Transition: National Adaptations in Global Economies*, London: Sage.
Guo, Ming-zheng (1998), 'A study of combining national basic pension, government employees and teachers pension, and labour pension', in Council of Economic Planning and Development (ed.), *Compilations of Commissioned Reports on the Institutions of National Pension*, Taipei, Taiwan (in Chinese).

Jones, Catherine (1990), 'Hong Kong, Singapore, South Korea, and Taiwan: Oikonomic welfare states', *Government and Opposition*, **25**(4), 447–462.

Jones, Catherine (1993), 'The Pacific Challenge: Confucian welfare states', in Catherine Jones (ed.), *New Perspectives on the Welfare State in Europe*, London: Routledge.

Kwon, Huck-ju (1998), 'Democracy and the politics of social welfare: A comparative analysis of welfare systems in East Asia', in Roger Goodman, Gordon White and Huck-ju Kwon (eds), *The East Asian Welfare Model – Welfare, Orientalism and the State*, New York: Routledge, 27–75.

Lee, Ming-tsung (1996), *Guojia jiqi, Zhengzhi Zhuanxing, yu shehui fuli: Yi Laoren nianjin yiti zhi fazhan (1992-1995) we li (State Machine, Political Transition, and Social Welfare: A Study of the 'Old Age Pension' Campaign in Taiwan (1992–1995)*, MA thesis, Department of Social Anthropology, National Tsinghua University.

Lin, Chei-wei (2003), *Politics of Welfare Reforms – A Comparative Analysis of Taiwan and South Korea*, PhD dissertation, Department of Advanced Social and International Studies, University of Tokyo, Tokyo, Japan (in Japanese), 165.

Lin, Chen-wei (1999), 'Mo hitotsu no "sekai"? Higashi-Ajia to Taiwan no fukushi kokka (Another "world"? The welfare state in East Asia and Taiwan)', *Nihon Taiwan Gakkaiho* (1), 108–126.

Lin, Chen-wei (2002), 'The policymaking process for the social system in Taiwan: The National Health Insurance and National Pension Programme', *The Developing Economies*, **XL**(3), Sept 2002.

Lin, Chia-lung (1998), *Paths to Democracy: Taiwan in Comparative Perspective*, PhD dissertation, Department of Political Science, Yale University.

Lin, Kuo-ming (1997), *From Authoritarianism to Statism: The Politics of National Health Insurance in Taiwan*, PhD dissertation, Department of Sociology, Yale University.

Lin, Li-zhu (1994), *Questions and Answers on Government Employees Insurance, Labour Insurance, and Farmers Insurance*, Taipei, Taiwan: Pingan Publishing (in Chinese).

Lin, Wan-I (1990), *Social Welfare Development in Taiwan: An Integrated Theoretical Explanation*, PhD dissertation, Department of Social Welfare, University of California, Berkeley.

Lin, Wan-I (2002), 'Social resistance, power resources and the development of social welfare policies', in Michael Hsiao and Lin Luo-ming (ed.), *Taiwande shehui fuli yungdong (Social Welfare Movements in Taiwan)*, Taipei: Juliu Press.

Peng, Ito (2001), 'The East Asian welfare states and the new challenge: Japan, South Korea, and Taiwan', in Shakaiseisakugakkai (ed.), *Fukushikokka no Shatei*, Kyoto: Minerva Shobo.

Pierson, Paul (1996), 'The new politics of the welfare state', *World Politics*, **48**, January, 143–179.

Pierson, Paul (2000), 'Increasing returns, path dependence, and the study of politics', *American Political Science Review*, **94**(2), 251–267.

Rigger, Shelley (2001), *From Opposition to Power: Taiwan's Democratic Progressive Party*, Boulder and London: Lynne Rienner Publishers.

Tang, Kwong-leung (2000), *Social Welfare Development in East Asia*, New York: Palgrave.

Wakabayashi, Masahiro (1992), *Taiwan: bunretsy kokka to minshuka*, Tokyo, Tokyo University Press.

Wakabayashi, Masahiro (1998), 'Taiwan ni okeru seijitaiseinohendou to esunonashonarizumu: "Shinto genshou" shiron (Ethno-nationalism and transformation of political regime on Taiwan: A preliminary analysis of the "New Party phenomenon")', in Hiroaki Kaji (ed.), *Chuugoku no shousuuminzoku to kakyou (Ethnic Minorities and Overseas Chinese of China)*, Tokyo: Asahi-shimbun.

White, Gordon and Roger Goodman (1998), 'Welfare orientalism and the search for an East Asian welfare model', in Roger Goodman, Gordon White and Huck-ju Kwon (eds), *The East Asian Welfare Model – Welfare. Orientalism and the State*, New York: Routledge, 3–24.

World Bank (1992), *The East Asian Miracle: Economic Growth and Public Policy*, New York; Tokyo: published for the World Bank by Oxford University Press.

Wong, Joseph (2001), *Equity and Democratisation*, PhD dissertation, Department of Political Science, University of Wisconsin-Madison.

Wu, Naiteh (1987), *The Politics of a Regime Patronage System: Mobilization and Control within an Authoritarian Regime*, PhD dissertation, Department of Political Science, The University of Chicago.

Zhang, Ming-zheng (1996), 'Changing old age population structure and elders' economic autonomy in Taiwan', in Wen-Shan Yang and Mei-Ling Lee (eds), *Population Changes, National Health, and Social Security*, Taipei, Taiwan: Sun Yat-Sen Institute for Social Sciences and Philosophy, Academia Sinica (in Chinese).

Zheng, Ching-xia (1999), *Wuoguo Guominmianjing yu Zhiyeinianjin zhi Laoren Geifu Suizhun yu Feilu Guiha Tantao (A Stimulated Planning of Old Age Benefits Level and Contribution for the National Pension Programme and Professional Pension Programmes)*, PhD dissertation, Department of Welfare, National Zhong-zheng University, Chiayi, Taiwan.

Zheng, Qing-xia and Zhao, Qing-yuan (2002), 'Lao nian jingji anquan guihua: Geren nianjin baoxian de tantao (Planning old age income security: Possibilities of individual pension)', Symposium on Democracy and Social Welfare, National Zhong-zheng University, Taiwan.

Zhong, Pei-zhen (1995), 'Policy process of old age pension on Taiwan – A Preliminary Study on Governmental Behaviour', Master Thesis, Department of Sociology, National Taiwan University, Taipei, Taiwan (in Chinese).

Zhongguo Shibao, various issues.

Zhongyang Ribao, various issues.

Ziyou Ribao, various issues.

10. Pension reform in Korea: Conflict between social solidarity and long-term financial sustainability

Yeon Myung Kim and Kyo-seong Kim

INTRODUCTION

There are four major public pension schemes in Korea; these are the Government Employees Pension Scheme, the Military Personnel Pension Scheme, the Private School Teachers Pension Scheme and the National Pension Scheme (hereafter NPS), of which the NPS is the largest in terms of the number of participants and accumulated funds. The history of the NPS goes back nearly 30 years to 1973 when the Park Chung-hee government (1962–79) enacted the National Welfare Pension Act (NWP). However, implementation of the NWP was delayed until 1988, mainly because of economic reasons such as the first oil shock and the ensuing worldwide recession. As the Korean economy rebounded and in the wake of the radicalization of distributional conflicts fuelled by democratic movements in the mid-1980s, the autocratic administration of President Chun Doo-hwan (1980–87) declared the implementation of the NWP in 1986. The government revised the original NWP on a more conservative basis and initiated a mandatory retirement scheme known as NPS in 1988 (National Pension Corporation, 1998a, pp. 121–123; Yang, 2000, pp. 106–115).

The Korean NPS started from the beginning as an integrated occupational model covering all major groups such as white- and blue-collar workers, farmers, fishing people and the self-employed under a single umbrella. It was because there was no social basis to build up some cooperative or voluntary pension schemes by companies, labour unions or friendly societies, as the social fabric for cooperatives and the labour union movement all but disappeared during the Korean War (1950–53). During the 1970s, when the need for the introduction of a National Pension Scheme was seriously discussed, therefore, there was no social pressure to introduce occupational schemes. Moreover, the establishment of the NPS was further justified for the purpose of domestic capital formation needs (National Pension Corporation, 1998a).

At the time, Korea had embarked on an aggressive development programme in which huge resource mobilization was essential to meet the large investment requirements. For the purpose of facilitating domestic resource mobilization, a single National Pension Scheme was a better system than multiple occupational pension schemes.

The original NPS plan covered only employees in firms with more than ten employees but it was subsequently gradually extended to cover the self-employed in rural areas in 1995 and the urban self-employed and small firms with fewer than four employees in 1999, respectively. Thus, a new era of universal pensions began in Korea, in which most workers and self-employed persons were covered by the single unified pension scheme, except for the government employees, military personnel and private school teachers who were covered by the three occupational pension schemes.

In less than ten years after its introduction, the NPS had been subjected to two rounds of serious reform challenges. The first round of reform was carried out in 1997–99; the second round started in 2002 and is ongoing at the time of writing (late 2003). The main reason for the launch of these initiatives was in both cases the problem of long-term financial sustainability. The major issues faced during the first pension reform were that there was serious concern that the NPS fund might be exhausted in the early 2030s, as well as some problems associated with the coverage extension. The issue of ageing population, however, was not raised as an important issue during the first pension reform process yet. In the course of the first pension reform process, the issues hotly debated were the problem of reducing the level of benefits and the transformation of pension system structure from a mono-pillar to a multi-pillar design. In the second reform process, the financial sustainability problem remains a central issue as funds are expected to be consumed by the late 2040s. The issue of sustainability has been compounded by worries about the sudden decline in the birth rate and the rapid increase of the old age population.

As the World bank (2000) aptly pointed out, the Korean pension system is at a crossroads. While in the past, debates and discussions on pension reform were limited to academia and government circles, they have increasingly become national concerns thanks to the ever-accumulating fund resources, increasing number of pensioners and the easy access to information arising from the emergence of the Internet generation. The purpose of this chapter is to review Korea's pension reform with special emphasis on the driving forces that dictated the first pension reform against the backdrop of political, economic and social environments of that time with a view to examining some theoretical implications of the reform process and reform results.

ELEMENTS OF THE OLD AGE INCOME SECURITY SYSTEM

Korea's old age income security system is composed of the four public pension schemes, a retirement allowance system for regular workers in the private sector and social assistance for the low income elderly, as shown in Figure 10.1.

The public pension system is composed of the three occupational pension schemes: the Military Personnel Pension Scheme (MPPS), Government Employee Pension Scheme (GEPS) and the Private School Teachers Pension Scheme (PSTPS) as well as the NPS. The GEPS was the first Korean pension scheme introduced in 1960. In 2001 it had some 913 192 participants and 160 721 pension beneficiaries. There were some 200 000 participants for the MPPS, which was initiated in 1963, while the PSTPS, started in 1975, had 216 362 participants and 14 639 pensioners. The contribution and benefits under the three occupational pension schemes are earnings-related and the contribution rate was 17 per cent in 2002.

The NPS is the single largest pension scheme in Korea, covering some 16.5 million participants. At the end of 2002, the NPS provided pension coverage to 6 million workers in workplaces (38.1 per cent), 2 million farmers, fishing people and regional participants (12.1 per cent) and some 8

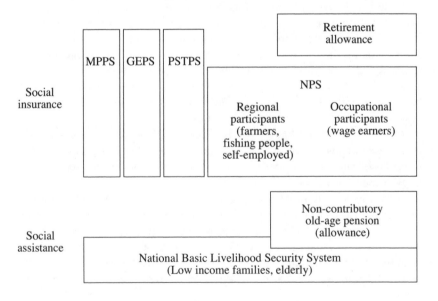

Figure 10.1   Elements of the old age income security system in Korea

million urban self-employed (48.5 per cent, National Pension Corporation, 2003). As the NPS is a relatively young pension scheme with only 15 years of history, there are only about 1 million beneficiaries.

At the time of the NPS introduction, a retirement allowance system was available for regular workers in the private sector employed by companies with more than five workers. About 6 million workers (48 per cent of wage earners) were entitled to this retirement allowance. The retirement allowance was the major source of old age income for workers before the introduction of the NPS and even during the initial years of the NPS. Under the retirement allowance system, employers pay a lump sum consisting of one month's salary for each service year (that is, 8.3 per cent of monthly salary every month). Since the NPS and retirement allowance are both serving as a major source of old age income security, this feature caused quite complicated problems in the course of pension reform as to the future roles of these two systems.

Finally, the old age income security system includes a last resort safety net for low income elderly in the shape of the National Basic Livelihood Security Act. Some 400 000 elderly (over 60 years old) are supported through this kind of means-tested provision. In addition, some 710 000 low-income elderly receive a non-contributory old age pension benefit, but this is set at a very low level (up to 50 000 won or USD 42).

MAJOR CHARACTERISTICS OF THE NPS

Institutional Characteristics of the NPS

Public pension schemes can be divided into two categories: the Bismarckian type and the Beveridgean type. Since the basic characteristics of the Bismarckian type are financing by contribution, provision of earnings-related benefits and eligibility to pension benefit through to labour market participation (Bonoli, 2000, pp. 9–13), the NPS can be considered a Bismarckian pension scheme. The major difference between the typical Bismarck-type pension and the NPS is that while many occupational pensions have been established in Europe under the Bismarck type, the NPS covers various different groups of occupations of waged workers, farmers, fishing people and self-employed under a single umbrella (integrated occupational scheme). It may reflect that the NPS contains a strong sense of social solidarity and the scope of risk diffusion is spread on the national scale. While one of the core issues in pension policy-making in Western Europe was the integration of various occupational pension schemes (Baldwin, 1990), this was never an issue in Korea.

Second, the NPS is mono-pillar scheme in which the basic pension and earnings-related pension are integrated into a single system. Unlike the two-tiered pension systems in Sweden, Japan and the UK in which there are the basic pension scheme and the earnings-related pension scheme, the NPS has one single benefit formula, which incorporates an income redistribution element and an earnings-related function all together like the pension systems of Germany and the US where there is no basic pension.[1]

A third important feature of NPS is its progressive character. It conveys a strong sense of social solidarity by incorporating income redistribution both within generations and between generations. The NPS benefit formula has been designed to guarantee an income replacement rate of 60 per cent for the average income earner who contributed to the NPS for 40 years. The NPS has been designed also to provide higher income replacement rates for lower income earners and to provide lower income replacement rates for higher income earners. Thus, NPS embodies a built-in mechanism for income redistribution.

Though the NPS is designed to favour lower income groups, this does not necessarily mean that the NPS is unfavourable to higher income individuals. In fact, the cost–benefit ratios[2] for all income groups exceeded 1 under the NPS formula. The cost–benefit ratio for a new participant in 1999 on median earnings is estimated to be 1.61 while that of someone on twice median earnings was estimated to be 1.21 (Kim, 2001a, p. 100).[3] When the cost–benefit ratio exceeds 1, this implies that the amount in excess of 1 will be a cost to be paid by future generation through increased contribution. In this regard, the NPS was designed on the assumption that the current generation will be benefiting from a subsidy from the future generation. This assumed subsidy from the future generation raised the inter-generational equity issue during the discussion of pension reform and this factor worked as a pressure to reduce pension benefit.

Characteristics in Financing and Fund Management

The main source of revenue of the NPS is the contribution paid by its members. The contribution rate is 9 per cent, which is equally shared by workers and employers, except for the self-employed, non-standard workers, and wage earners employed by workplaces employing fewer than five workers who pay the whole contribution. Since employers had been contributing to the retirement allowance before the establishment of the NPS, they complained that the additional contribution obligation for the NPS was a double burden (National Pension Corporation, 1998a, p. 128). Consequently, the NPS financing was designed to share its financial obligations equally among participants (one-third), employers (one-third) and the employer's payments to the retirement allowance (one-third). Naturally when the pension reform of 1998 was being carried out, the total contribution ratio of 9 per cent was composed of 3 per cent for workers, 3 per cent for employers (as a contribution for the NPS) and the remaining 3 per cent to be deducted from the employer's payments to the retirement allowance. Since employers were contributing 8.3 per cent of monthly wage for retirement allowance from which 3 per cent was earmarked for the NPS contribution, the actual payment for the retirement allowance became 5.3 per cent after inception of the NPS. This complex relationship between the NPS and retirement allowance has been further changed in the course of the 1998 pension reform process in a way that was rather unfavourable to employers.

With regard to financing, the NPS is partially funded. According to the financial projections announced in 1998, the accumulated fund reserves of the NPS will peak in 2020 and will be exhausted by early 2030 (National Pension Corporation, 1998b; Moon, 1995). Unless contributions are increased, the NPS will then become a pay-as-you-go funded scheme (Kwon, 1999).

The management of the fund has been the monopoly of the National Pension Corporation (NPC) for some time without outsourcing it to the specialized fund management companies. Despite many private companies specializing in fund management being created in the 1990s, a National Pension Fund Management Centre was established within the NPC and a fund management system was set up in 2000. Outsourcing of fund management did not begin until 2002 and on a pilot basis.

The accumulated fund reserves of the NPS amount to 102 trillion won (about 16 per cent of GDP) of which only a small fraction is invested in private sector bonds and securities. The largest part is invested in public bonds or the public sector.[4] In 1998, the share of public borrowing from the NPC fund stood at 71.5 per cent while the NPC's investment in the financial sector[5] stood at only 24.7 per cent. As the share of public sector borrowing reached such a high level, many NGOs voiced strong concern for the possible default by the government. Consequently, the lowering of the public borrowing was incorporated as a condition of the Structural Adjustment Loans (SAL) provided by the World Bank and IMF in 1999. As a result of this, the share of public borrowing in total portfolio of the NPC declined drastically to 33.2 per cent in 2002.

As far as the governance of the NPS is concerned, one can say that decision-making in fund management was rather undemocratic until the National Pension Act was revised in 1998. Under the old National Pension Act, the allocation of NPS funds (strategic allocation of assets) was to be made by the decision of the National Pension Fund Management Committee (NPFMC), which was composed mostly of Senior Government Officials. The role of the Fund Management Office (later reorganized as Fund Management Centre) of the NPC was minimal in the decision-making of this committee.

Moreover, committee meetings were held rarely and most decisions were based on exchanges of ideas on paper. Under such circumstances, NGOs and labour leaders demanded and obtained representation of participants in the decision-making process of pension fund management.

PROBLEMS OF NPS AND EMERGING DEMAND FOR REFORM

The NPS was facing two key challenges in the 1990s. The first problem was coverage extension to farmers and fishing people in rural areas and to some uncovered individuals in urban areas. The second problem was long-term financial sustainability of the scheme associated with the projected fund exhaustion by early 2030.

Coverage Extension for Universal Pension

Though the Korean NPS was introduced rather late in comparison with European countries, its growth rate was phenomenal. At the beginning, in 1988, it covered only wage earners in firms employing more than ten workers. Subsequently, in 1995, the NPS extended its coverage to include farmers and fishing people in rural areas and the number of its members reached 7.25 million. Considering that some 1.29 million public sector employees were covered under the three occupational pension schemes in 1995, the total number of people covered by public pensions stood at 42 per cent of the economically active population in 1995 (Ministry of Health and Welfare, 1998, p. 199). The challenge facing the NPS was to provide coverage to the remaining uncovered 58 per cent.

The coverage issue was compounded by population ageing. In fact, unlike in most of the countries covered in this volume, population ageing in Korea was not associated with concerns for rising pension expenditure. Instead, the major concern was to extend coverage of the NPS. The major emphasis of works of the Ministry of Health and Welfare (MOHW) in the mid-1990s was how fast the NPS coverage could be extended to accommodate the ageing population.

Problem of Financial Sustainability

Given the nature of the NPS, which was designed as a partially funded scheme, in the context of an ageing society, fund reserves of the NPS are bound to be exhausted sooner or later. According to the official financial projection of the government, the fund reserves of the NPS are expected to be exhausted in the early 2030s. It is further claimed that a gradual increase in contribution rates up to 25 per cent of earnings will be necessary to defer fund exhaustion of the NPS until the 2080s (National Pension Corporation, 1998b, pp. 85, 89).

As the news of the NPS fund exhaustion by the 2030s was reported by the media scepticism about the NPS grew rapidly among scholars and within the general public. This situation has been further aggravated by inaccurate media reports claiming that NPS funds mismanagement had resulted in sizeable losses. Some neo-liberal economists who believed that there were some structural flaws in NPS and even the Korea Development Institute (KDI), the most influential economic research institute in Korea, started to argue that pension reform, including the reduced benefit, was unavoidable to address the serious financial instability problem of the NPS (Moon, 1995). Thus pension reform has emerged as a core item in the political agenda.

The financial instability of the NPS has been the main driving force behind the pension reform process. However, financial problems were not directly linked to increased expenditure due to an ageing population. In fact, the over 65 group accounted for only 5.9 per cent of total population in 1995 and was projected to increase to 13.2 per cent by 2020 (Korea National Statistical Office, 1996). This share of the elderly was considered low compared with Japan and European countries so that demographic concerns did not play an important role in the first round of pension reform.

In order to achieve the two major policy goals of NPS coverage extension and improved financial sustainability, in June 1997 the government established a National Pension Reform Board (NPRB) reporting directly to the Prime Minister's office. The NPRB announced its pension reform proposal in December 1997 after heated discussions and debates, thus opening a new era of pension reform politics in Korea.

THE FIRST ROUND OF PENSION REFORM DEBATES: 1997–99

Reform Proposal of the NPRB and Partial Reform

There were two major reform alternatives in the NPRB. The supporters of the first alternative, the MOHW, the NGOs and the labour unions wanted to keep the basic structure of the NPS and emphasized the need to undertake continued pension coverage extension to rural areas. The second alternative, instead, consisted in a drastic reduction in benefits and in the adoption of a multi-pillar system as proposed by the World Bank (1994). This second alternative was favoured by the Blue House (that is, the presidency), the Ministry of Finance and Economy, business circle and neo-liberal economists. After the heated arguments and debates, the NPRB failed to reach a consensus and submitted two different views, a majority and a minority opinion.

The minority proposed a reduction of benefits by 50–60 per cent to solve the financial problems while keeping the basic framework of the NPS with its basic principles of intra-generational and inter-generational income redistribution. The majority, instead, proposed a drastic reduction of pension benefits and a two-tiered pension structure of basic pension and earnings-related pension.[6] According to the majority opinion, the financial instability problem would not arise since the NPC fund exhaustion is not expected until 2080 (National Pension Reform Board, 1997, pp. 13–28). The main contents of the majority opinion were as follows:

- Split the present mono-pillar scheme of the NPS into a two-pillar scheme composed of a basic pension and earnings-related pension.
- Reduction of the target replacement rate from the current level of 70 per cent to 40 per cent. This was to be met by the basic pension (16 per cent) and the earnings-related pension (24 per cent).
- Both the basic pension and the earnings-related pension will be operated as a partially funded scheme with the participant's contribution.
- The present contribution rate of 9 per cent will be maintained until 2025 and it will be raised to 12.6 per cent thereafter.
- Legal retirement age will be raised by one year for every five years starting from year 2013 so that it will be 65 by 2032.
- To enhance women's rights in pension provision, a system of split pension will be introduced for divorced women.
- To strengthen the powers of the National Pension Fund Management Committee and expand the representation of farmers, unions and NGOs.
- Extend the coverage of the urban self-employed in the second half of 1998.

The core issues that received utmost attention from the majority opinion of the NPRB were the reduction of benefits and the introduction of the basic pension. The majority opinion was criticized and opposed by the labour unions and NGOs because they were strongly opposed to the drastic reduction of pension benefits and they were also concerned that the earnings-related pension might be privatized if the bi-pillar pension system was adopted. The proposal was also strongly criticized in the media. The reaction of the MOHW on the majority proposal was rather negative as it would have introduced an obstacle to achieve its goal of NPS coverage extension in 1998 and it could have destroyed the solidarity dimension of the NPS altogether (Yang, 1998, pp. 62–69). The MOHW, however, accepted some proposals such as the gradual increase in the age of retirement, introduction of split pensions for divorced women and the active involvement of members' representatives in the fund management committee. Other measures, such as the cut in pension benefits and introduction of basic pension were rejected. MOHW's views are contained in the pension reform plan, which was presented in March 1998. The key elements of the plan were:

- The NPS would not be split into a bi-pillar scheme of basic pension and earnings-related pension.
- Target replacement rate (for a worker with a 40-year contribution record) will be reduced from the current 70 per cent to 55 per cent.
- The contribution rate of 9 per cent will be maintained up to 2009 and will be gradually raised thereafter.

When the MOHW announced its pension reform bill, it was expected that the measure would result in a deferral of fund exhaustion from 2031 to the mid-2050s. The MOHW further announced that the NPS fund reserves will not be exhausted before 2080 if the contribution rate could be raised to the 17 per cent level (Um, 1998). The MOHW plan drew various reactions from different institutions. Business circles criticized the MOHW for failing to adopt a lasting solution to the financial instability problem of the NPS and for increasing financial burdens for businesses by increasing the contribution rate. The labour unions and NGOs criticized the MOHW plan for being detrimental to old age income protection due to the drastic reduction of pension benefits. The increase in the age of retirement and the sharing of pensions upon divorce could have been quite controversial but were never discussed in depth because they were overshadowed by other contentious issues such as the drastic cut in pension benefits. The reorganization of the fund management system, which was strongly supported by the labour unions and the NGOs was accepted without any objection.

In parliament (National Assembly), the discussion of the pension reform bill focused on benefit reductions and the reorganization of the NPS fund management committee. On the face of strong opposition from labour and NGO, the government party (the Democratic Party) and the opposition party (the Hannara Party) agreed to limit the reduction in the replacement rate to 60 per cent of average earnings instead of 55 per cent as proposed by the government. The final pension reform bill was approved by the National Assembly in December 1998. Under this reform bill, it is projected that the NPS reserve exhaustion will be deferred from the early part of the 2030s to the latter part of the 2040s (with 9 per cent contribution rate and 60 per cent income replacement rate) and it is further projected that the NPS fund exhaustion can be deferred to the 2080s if the contribution rate will be raised to the 18 per cent level. The coverage extension programme of the NPS to cover urban self-employed was deferred until April 1999.

One of the noteworthy developments made during the deliberation on the pension reform bill was that the important change in the cost sharing structure for the NPS and retirement allowance had been incorporated in the reform bill, for which neither the MOHW nor labour union had shown support. As mentioned earlier, the reform bill proposed that the NPS contribution rate of 9 per cent is to be equally shared between workers, employers and the employer's payment to the retirement allowance. The National Assembly removed the 3 per cent share to be taken from the retirement allowance and revised the cost sharing formula by dictating 4.5 per cent equal sharing between workers and employers. While the share of workers in the NPS appears to have increased by 1.5 per cent (from 3 per cent to 4.5 per cent) the actual burden for them declined by 1.5 per cent if one considers that the employer's payment to the retirement allowance remains intact at 8.3 per cent instead of having been reduced to 5.3 per cent as in the MOHW proposal.[7]

Though this change resulted in an additional burden to employers, it will not benefit all workers. Retirement allowance, in fact, is available only to 48 per cent of the wage earners. Non-standard workers, who are not covered by this programme, will have to bear the full consequences of the reduction in the replacement rate.

NPS Extension to Urban Self-employed and Fund Separation Debate

Pension issues were again in the centre of public debates in 1999, when NPS coverage was significantly extended. Before the extension, the percentage of persons covered by public pensions was very low at 41.9 per cent of economically active population. The extension programme concerned some 9 million workers mostly living in urban areas, and included urban self-employed, waged workers employed in firms with less than five employees, non-standard workers employed by firms with more than five persons and the unemployed.

Because workers and the self-employed are integrated under a single system and also because the average income of all pension scheme members features in the benefit formula, the coverage extension of the NPS resulted in a new controversy. About 4 million new members reported their income to the NPS. Of them some 2.8 million paid their contribution. As the reported average income of urban self-employed was 840 000 won, which is barely 58 per cent of the average income of workplace employees whose reported income was 1 440 000 won, this has resulted in serious losses to older NPS members. As the substantial income under-declaration of some high-income self-employed professionals such as doctors and lawyers was highlighted in the media, some scholars argued that two separate pension schemes would be necessary to protect the existing participants from the urban self-employed.

The argument for setting up two separate pension schemes for employees and for the self-employed had strong support from the conservative sections of the labour movement, some neo-liberal NGOs and the Hannara Party (in opposition). It was opposed by more progressive trade unions, other NGOs, the government party and the MOHW. After heated debates and discussions, it has finally been decided to retain the integrated nature of the NPS.

Result and Implication of Pension Reform

To sum up, we can say that the first round of pension reform has not dealt a decisive blow to the NPS, which still maintains its principal nature of social solidarity for different occupational groups as well as different generations. Though the impending financial instability problem forced the NPS to accept reduced benefits and to undertake internal reforms, it has failed to change the basic framework of the NPS. We can say that the first round of pension reform has not brought about a paradigm shift for the NPS. In this sense, it was a partial reform.

Though the first round of pension reform failed to change the basic nature of social solidarity of the NPS, this is being challenged by the fact that some 5.46 million members of NPS (about 33 per cent of the total NPS participants of 16.45 million) are not contributing to it. Most of these non-contributing members are low-income earners employed by small firms, non-standard workers, long-term unemployed and small-scale self-employed, though there were some high-income professionals among the non-contributors. The existence of such a large number of non-paying members may be attributable to the government's inaccuracy in income assessment, insufficient administrative capabilities and contribution evasion. If these people fail to contribute for some time, they will lose their pension eligibility and lose the chance to receive subsidies from future generations. It is unfortunate that the number of non-contributing participants remains high since 1999 when coverage extension to urban areas was implemented. If the situation persists, the NPS may become a pension scheme only for the middle class and the rich, but not an income security programme for the poor.

THE SECOND WAVE OF PENSION REFORM

Pension Reform Demands by the World Bank

As soon as the first round of pension reform was over, Korea was facing the demand to undertake the second round of pension reform. This time, the demand for pension reform was initiated by the World Bank but the rapid ageing population issue that started to emerge in early 2000 through media reports and the unresolved problem of financial instability of the NPS neces- sitated the second round of reform.

In the wake of the financial crisis that devastated the Korean economy in 1997, the government received two structural adjustment loans (SALs) from the World Bank and the IMF. One of the conditions of these SALs was to undertake pension reform to provide income protection in times of crisis. Consequently, the World Bank and the IMF demanded a second round of public pension reform. In mid-1999, the Pension Reform Task Force (PRTF) was created to undertake the review of four public pension schemes. Their report was completed and submitted in June 2000 (Pension Reform Task Force, 2000). As the timing of the PRTF report coincided with the remarkable recovery of the Korean economy from the crisis, the report did not receive much attention from the public.

The World Bank (2000), on the other hand, critically reviewed the Korean public pension schemes by mobilizing its own experts. Its findings were published under the title of *The Korean Pension System at a Crossroads* in May 2000. The World Bank recommended the introduction of a multi-pillar pension system but MOHW's response was lukewarm at best. As no other government ministry showed an interest in this solution, the report has not influenced debates or policy to any significant extent.

Rapid Population Ageing and Declining Birth Rate

Though the rapid ageing population problem was raised by some scholars during the first pension reform discussions, this had no direct impact on pension reform at the time. As the Korea National Statistical Office (KNSO) announced that the birth rates were declining rapidly during 2001 and 2002 and that the pace of ageing in Korea was much more pronounced than expected, this had great influence on pension debates.

KSNO (2001) published the *Population Projection Report* (it publishes this report every five years) in which the share of the population aged over 65 is to soar from 7.2 per cent in 2000 to 15.1 per cent in 2020 and subsequently to 23.1 per cent in 2030, showing the fastest population ageing pace in the world. KNSO (2002) also announced, through its annual report on *Statistics on Birth and Death*, that the birth rate declined significantly from 1.78 in 1992 to 1.54 in 1997 and to 1.17 in 2002, the lowest figure among OECD member coun- tries. Because of a faster than expected decline in the birth rate and population ageing it is evident that NPS fund exhaustion will occur earlier than previously expected. In this regard, financial instability of the NPS became a driving force for another round of pension reform.

In this context, the MOHW instituted the Development Committee of NPS (DCNPS), which is composed of some government officials and civilian scholars with a mandate to prepare a pension reform programme. The main task of the DCNPS is to undertake actuarial assessments, which according to the National Pension Act must be performed every five years. Given the expected NPS fund exhaustion in the latter part of the 2040s and considering the rapid decline in birth rate and the fast pace of population ageing, the prevailing mood of DCNPS was further reduction of pension benefits.

In May 2003, the DCNPS (2003) presented the following three pension reform options: 1) to maintain 60 per cent income replacement rate but raise contribution rate to 19.85 per cent; 2) to reduce income replacement rate to 50 per cent and to raise contribution rate to 15.85 per cent; or 3) to reduce income replacement rate to 40 per cent and raise contribution rate to 11.85 per cent. The issue of the bi-pillar pension system, one of the core agenda items in the first pension reform, was not discussed at all. The MOHW preferred the second option on the grounds that it will defer the fund exhaustion until 2070 and this option will reduce the burden of future generations. The MOHW recently announced that it is preparing a draft pension reform bill under which the income replacement rate will be reduced to 55 per cent from 2004 and subsequently to 50 per cent after 2008. Currently, this has become a hotly debated issue. Labour unions and NGOs are opposing the draft bill while business leaders and influential conservative media support it. Like in the case of the first pension reform, the National Assembly might intervene and come up with its own version of the pension reform bill. Given the changed economic and social environments (declining birth rate, rising elderly population and deteriorating financial position of the NPS), it is unlikely that the National Assembly will do anything but support reduced pension benefits.

FINDINGS AND SOME THEORETICAL ARGUMENTS

Financial Instability as the Driving Force of Pension Reform

Behind the first pension reform discussions and the ensuing demands by the World Bank for a second pension reform lies the root cause of the financial instability ideology, symbolized by the fund exhaustion of the NPS. The reason why we define this problem as an ideology is because of the singular nature of financial instability logic. Unlike the pensions of some European countries that are facing impending fund exhaustion, the financial instability problem of NPS is not an imminent one that might happen within a few years. From the very beginning, the NPS financial sustainability was foreseen as an inherent nature of the NPS and the timing of fund exhaustion was scheduled for the 2030s. Moreover, the expected timing of the NPS fund exhaustion has been further deferred to late 2040s with the revision of the National Pension Act. And yet the concerns about fund exhaustion that might happen 50 years later have become the most powerful argument in favour of a second pension reform.

The issue of population ageing has exerted some influence during the second pension reform process, unlike the first pension reform in which it had no influence at all. However, the ageing population problem in Korea during 2002 when the second pension reform was in full swing was quite unique in that the share of elderly over 65 years in the total population was very low at 7.2 per cent, a much more favourable situation than in most European countries where the share of elderly population stood at the 15 per cent level (see Table 1.1). In this sense, population ageing was not an imminent issue so far as the NPS is concerned. According to the KNSO projection, the elderly support ratio (the ratio of elderly over 65 years to working population of 15–65 years) in Korea is projected to increase from 10.1 per cent in 2000 to 35.7 per cent in 2030 and further to 51.6 per cent in 2040. Nonetheless, the inherent financial instability problem of the NPS and population ageing became driving forces that pressed for the second pension reform.

Political System, Path Dependence and Pension Reform

One of the frequently asked questions on pension reform is why the basic framework of the NPS remains unchanged despite the strong pressure for benefit reduction and structural reform? Some neo-institutionalist scholars have tried to explain welfare policy outcomes such as pension and health insurance system reforms in connection with the political system and institutional design of the welfare state (Pierson, 1994; Bonoli, 2000, 2001; Myles and Pierson, 2001). According to their views, the pension reform bill is likely to be finalized as the original government proposal in countries with a strong centralized power system.

Traditionally, there has been strong power concentration in the policy-making process in Korea. The Executive Branch is headed by a strong president and the National Assembly is a single chamber (unicameral) parliament. There is of course a veto point between the Executive Branch and the National Assembly by law. However, since the president is generally also acting as the leader of the government party[8] and the government party has always had a majority in the National Assembly, both the president and the National Assembly have rarely vetoed bills regarding welfare policy submitted by the other.[9]

Therefore, the Office of the President and the Executive Branch in Korea exercised strong legislative initiative under this political system. The National Assembly, labour unions and welfare recipients were excluded from the process of policy-making (Kim, 2002). The executive branch of government carries almost exclusive monopoly in the whole process of welfare policy from drafting legislation to budget allocation and implementation. A bill of the executive branch that receives strong support by the government party is generally adopted, sometimes with minor amendments, in the National Assembly. The Assembly is no more than a ratification chamber of decisions taken by the executive branch.

The pension reform bill of 1998 had gone through the similar path. The National Pension Act Amendment bill, which was submitted by the executive branch, was passed to almost the original bill. The only content changed in the National Assembly was the increased income replacement rate of 60 per cent that was originally proposed at 55 per cent. The only material difference between the original bill and the final National Assembly bill was that the cost sharing formula for the NPS and retirement allowance were changed with the additional cost impacts to employers. The income replacement rate was increased by 5 percentage points because of the strong protests of labour unions and the NGOs against benefit reduction. As rightly pointed out by Weaver (1986), this can be explained as a result of a blame avoidance strategy aiming to avoid political accountability for reduced pension on the part of both government party and opposition party.

The effect of veto points could be observed not so much in relation to the National Assembly but within the executive branch of government itself. The MOHW rejected the proposal of the National Pension Reform Board (NPRB), which reflected the will of the president. This exceptional event can be explained by two factors.

First, the special political situations surrounding the presidential system in Korea enabled the MOHW to exercise veto power against the presidency. In February 1996, President Kim Young-sam (1993–97) instructed his Chief Welfare Secretary to come up with integrated policies for the elderly without providing the detailed direction of pension reform. The office of the Chief Welfare Secretary in the Blue House submitted an unofficial report (which became the majority report of the NPRB later)[10] in April 1996 and President Kim approved it (Yang, 1998, p. 138). However, the Ministry of Defence, Ministry of Education and the MOHW expressed their reservation on the Blue House draft during the inter-ministerial consultation, which they regarded as too radical. As a result of these consultations, it was agreed to exclude three occupational schemes from the scope of pension reform and that reform will be focused on the NPS.

The major concern of the MOHW, however, was the extension of pension coverage to urban areas and an ambitious programme to enter the universal pension era was being implemented. Naturally, the Blue House staff who regarded the financial instability of NPS as the most fundamental problem for pension reform and the MOHW, which was mainly concerned with coverage extension, were bound to clash in the course of pension reform. As the conflict between these two key players continued, the Blue House proposed to establish the NPRB under the auspices of the Prime Minister's Office. This is the background of the NPRB, which was officially established in June 1997 (Yang, 1998). In the course of appointing key members of the NPRB, the Blue House exerted its influence to appoint many neo-liberal economists who share the opinion that the main issue in pension reform was the financial instability of the NPS. Under such circumstances, it is quite natural that the majority report of the NPRB was very radical, as generally expected.

The fact that the MOHW vetoed the pension proposal of the NPRB, which had the president's blessing, may be explained by the special circumstances surrounding the presidential transition in Korea. Unlike in the US where the president can seek re-election after completing a four-year term, the Korean president can serve only one five-year term. The submission of the NPRB proposal coincided with the presidential election and President Kim became a lame duck president without any strong control over government ministries.[11] The MOHW, at the same time, did not care much about the outgoing president and paid more attention to the incoming presidency. As to the radical proposal of the NPRB, MOHW knew very well that there would be strong social protest on the proposal and decided to sit on it until the situation became clear. The MOHW did not express its position on the proposal in December 1997 but announced the pension reform proposal in January 1998 once the presidential election was over. When the change of government was achieved for the first time in history through peaceful elections with the victory of pro-welfare opposition candidate, President Kim Dae-jung, it was easy for MOHW to throw away the proposal prepared by the former administration.

The second aspect of the MOHW's rejection of the proposal of the NPRB may be explained by path dependence. As Bonoli (2000, p. 41) aptly pointed out, 'the institutional design of pension schemes is a powerful determinant of reform, in the sense that it limits the number and the range of possible options and it points policy-makers looking for political feasibility in some predetermined directions'. The radical reform proposal of the NPRB was out of range of the basic framework of the NPS and its political feasibility was questionable due to the following reasons.

The proposed range of income replacement reduction (from 70 per cent to 40 per cent) was too drastic and out of range for the MOHW to accept. Second, in the event of a basic pension being introduced as proposed by the NPRB, the MOHW thought that it was highly likely that the earnings-related pension would be privatized and fall into the hands of the Chaebol (Korean conglomerates). This was a likely prospect, given the business environment of Korea in which general confidence in the NPS is low and the power of conglomerates and mass media are so strong. Third, the separation of the NPS into two schemes involved fairly complex technical problems while the practical gains from undertaking this change could have been small. Fourth, if the basic pension was established as a PAYG scheme and its funding was to be based on taxation, the scheme would have been unaffordable. Considering the huge public financing requirements to implement this kind of basic pension, the MOHW had never considered this option as a feasible alternative.

According to Bonoli (2000, pp. 168–172), when the Bismarck-type pension is reformed, such a reform is usually followed by some kind of compensation to get support from labour unions and pro-welfare actors. That the MOHW gave in to the split pension system and agreed to reorganize the NPS fund management committee to accommodate the representation of private sector actors, as requested by labour unions and the NGOs, are the clear examples of compensation. However, there is no evidence that the National Assembly amended the cost sharing formula for NPS and retirement allowance benefiting regular workers was a form of compensation to regular workers.

Pro-welfare Coalition and the Pension Reform

In the course of reforming the NPS, two groups of organizations with distinctly different ideas on the direction of reform emerged. The pro-NPRB group included the Blue House, the Ministry of Finance and Economy, business leaders and neo-liberal economists while the other group opposing the NPRB proposal included the MOHW, labour unions, progressive NGOs and social welfare scholars. Some kind of alliance was formed among the MOHW, labour unions and the NGOs in supporting the basic framework of the NPS. Labour unions and progressive NGOs have become strong political supporters of the MOHW in maintaining the basic structure of the NPS (Kim, 2002). Without the explicit political support of labour unions and the NGOs, the NPS coverage extension to urban self-employed undertaken in 1999 was not possible and the MOHW's efforts to maintain the basic character of the NPS might have failed.

The pension reform in most Western European countries has been backed by either the active or passive consent of organized labour (Myles and Pierson, 2001, p. 332). In the case of Korea, labour unions were also involved in reform processes but their influence was not considerable. Labour unions were more concerned with the problem of unemployment rather than pension reform since massive lay-off and high unemployment were their key concerns during the financial crisis of 1998. Moreover, pensions were a very unfamiliar topic for labour leaders who had no expert knowledge in them. Considering that very few people were receiving pensions at the time and that little knowledge had been accumulated within the leadership, the pension reform was not considered a major issue by the unions.

The opposition to the proposal of the NPRB and later of the MOHW was initiated by some NGOs that gained strong political influence during the Kim Dae-jung administration (1997–2002) and came to be considered as public interest groups. While labour unions tend to speak only for the interests of labourers in reform process, the NGOs represent the general interests of the general public and were able to exercise a strong influence. The NGOs put forward compelling reasons to keep the basic framework of the NPS and their demands for democratic fund management and participation of pensioners were fully accepted and implemented.[12]

Globalization and the Pension Reform

The logic of globalization, in general, implies pressures for welfare retrenchment (Teeple, 1995; Mishra, 1999). In the process of globalization, some international organizations such as the IMF and the World Bank have exerted considerable influence in the direction of a neo-liberal reorganization of welfare programmes by intervening in the social reform process of individual countries (Deacon, 1997). The Bismarck-type pension is especially vulnerable to the pressure of cost containment to improve the competitiveness of firms in times of globalization due to the institutional characteristics of its financing mode.

In the process of pension reform, the World Bank presented a reform plan based on this globalization logic. Likewise, the NPRB proposal contained some concerns on the long-term effect of rapidly rising pension contribution on the competitiveness of domestic firms. The World Bank, which was instrumental in promoting neo-liberal pension reforms in Eastern Europe and Latin American countries has not been successful in influencing the pension reform in Korea. In the case of the Korean pension reform process, it was the voices of the NGOs, labour unions and the MOHW that have saved the principle of solidarity of the NPS, though at the price of reduced benefits.

The pension reform in Korea was implemented during 1997–2000 when the country was undergoing serious structural reforms in the wake of the financial crisis and when the pressures from globalization were strongest. During this period of hardship, a strange social phenomenon was happening in that the welfare state was increasing rapidly rather than declining (Kim, 2001b). The partial reduction of the income replacement rate of NPS was not influenced by the World Bank, nor affected by globalization. As rightly observed by Yang (2000), domestic political dynamics rather than pressure of globalization or international organizations played the most important role in pension reform.

NOTES

1. The current benefit formula is: Pension benefit = $1.8 (A + B) (1 + 0.05n)$, where B refers to the average life-time income of the participant concerned, A denotes the average income of all NPS participants during the last three years before the date of retirement, n refers to the years of contribution exceeding 20 years. Therefore, B is the earnings-related component while A is the basic pension component that also features income redistribution character. For reference, the previous benefit formula before the revision of the NPS in 1998 was: Pension benefit = $2.4 (A + 0.75B) (1 + 0.05n)$.
2. The cost–benefit ratio refers to the expected total amount of benefit over total contributions. When the cost–benefit ratio is 1, benefits equal the payments made whereas when it exceeds 1, this means that benefits exceeded contributions.
3. This cost–benefit ratio was calculated by assuming that the participant started to contribute 9 per cent from 1999 for 20 years and retire at age 60 and die at age 76. The cost–benefit ratios for those who joined the pension scheme in the 1980s and early 1990s were higher as the NPS offered more favourable terms in its earlier years to attract more participants.
4. The NPS fund invested largely into three sectors; public, financial and welfare sectors. Public sector refers to the funds borrowed by the government to meet the public finance requirements. In the old days, the Ministry of Finance and Economy could borrow from the NPS funds without the consent of NPS participants.
5. Financial sector refers to the investments to securities, commercial papers (CP) and other private financial products as well as the government bonds.
6. Since the economists who favoured the World Bank-supported multi-pillar pension system constituted the majority in the NPRB, their proposal was submitted as the majority opinion.
7. The revision of the cost sharing formula between workers and employers with respect to the NPS and retirement allowance remains a mystery in the 1998 pension reform bill. This change was not proposed by the MOHW proposal, nor by any other interest group of labour union, employers, NGOs and media. Nobody asked for the change. Even the labour unions who are benefiting from this change realized this change after it became effective. Employers protested against this change for imposing additional burdens on them but it was too late.
8. President Roh Moo-hyun elected in 2003 is the first president who is not head of the government party.
9. The only exception was when President Noh Tae-woo did veto the medical insurance reform bill adopted with cross-party agreement in the National Assembly in 1989.
10. The pension reform proposal of the Blue House was composed of the following elements: reduction of income replacement ratio from 70 per cent to 40 per cent; conversion of the NPS into bi-pillar scheme with basic pension and earnings-related pension; and introduction of basic pension to three occupational pension schemes. The Blue House office concerned with welfare policy was staffed with neo-liberal economists and naturally clashed with the MOHW, which was mainly concerned with the extension of welfare.
11. In the wake of the IMF/World Bank emergency loans, President Kim Young-sam lost all influence and control over his own government.
12. The role of interest groups (pensioners) is very important in pension reform (Pierson, 1994). However, the role of pensioners during the NPS reform process was almost negligible due to the small number of pensioners (barely 300 000 in 1998), who were not politically organized.

REFERENCES

Baldwin, P. (1990), *The Politics of Social Solidarity: Class Bases of the European Welfare State 1875–1975*, New York: Cambridge University Press.

Bonoli, G. (2000), *The Politics of Pension Reform: Institutions and Policy Change in Western Europe*, New York: Cambridge University Press.

Bonoli, G. (2001), 'Political institutions and veto points and the process of welfare state adaptation', in P. Pierson (ed.) (2001), *The New Politics of the Welfare State*, Oxford: Oxford University Press.

Deacon, B. et al. (1997), *Global Social Policy: International Organization and the Future of Welfare*, London: Sage.

Development Committee of National Pension Scheme (DCNPS) (2003), 'Kuk min yeon kum Jae jung dae an mit Gae sun bang an (NPS financial stabilization proposal)', paper for public hearing on Development Committee of National Pension Scheme.

Kim, Y. (2001a), 'Kuk min yeon kum jeong chack-e Sung kwa wa Dilemma (Achievements and dilemma of national pension policy)', *Democratic Society and Policy Studies*, **1**(1), 97–123.

Kim, Y. (2001b), 'Welfare state or social safety net?: Development of the social welfare policy of the Kim Dae-jung administration', *Korea Journal*, **41**(2).

Kim, Y. (2002), 'Sa hai bok ji gae hyuck kwa Sa hai jeck Kal deung-e Ku cho (Social welfare reform and structure of social conflicts)', Social Development Institute, Seoul National University, Seminar Documents (for Democratization and Social Conflict), unpublished paper.

Korea National Statistical Office (KNSO) (1996), *Population Projections for Korea: 1995–2025*.

Korea National Statistical Office (KNSO) (2001), *Population Projections for Korea: 2000–2050*.

Korea National Statistical Office (KNSO) (2002), *Statistics on Birth and Death: 2001*.

Kwon, H. (1999), 'Inadequate policy or operational failure?: The potential crisis of the Korean National Pension Program', *Social Policy and Administration*, **33**(1).

Ministry of Health and Welfare (1998), *1997 yeon Bo gun bok ji tong gae yeon bo (Annual Statistical Yearbook on Health & Welfare, 1997)*.

Mishra, R. (1999), *Globalization and the Welfare State*, Cheltenham, UK and Northampton, MA, US: Edward Elgar.

Moon, H. (1995), *Kuk min yeon kum je do-e Jae jeong kun sil wha el Wi han Ku jo gae sun bang an (Structure Improvement Measures for Financial Stabilization of National Pension)*, Korea Development Institute.

Myles, J. and P. Pierson (2001), *The Comparative Political Economy of Pension Reform*, in P. Pierson (ed.) (2001), *The New Politics of the Welfare State*, Oxford: Oxford University Press.

National Pension Corporation (1998a), *Kuk min yeou kum 10 yeon sa (National Pension; 10 Year History)*.

National Pension Corporation (1998b), *Kuk min yeon kum jae jung chu gae (National Pension Financial Projection)*.

National Pension Corporation (2003), *2002 yeon Kuk min yeon kum tong gae yeon bo (National Pension Statistical Yearbook, 2002)*.

National Pension Reform Board (1997), *Chun kuk min Yeon kum Hwank dae jeck youn-e Dae bi han Kuk min yeon kum je do gae sun (Improvement in National Pension for Universal Coverage Preparation)*.

Pension Reform Task Force (2000), *Kong sa youn kum jae do-e Ki bon ku sang (Basic Proposal to Improve Public and Private Pensions Reform)*.

Pierson, P. (1994), *Dismantling the Welfare State?: Reagan, Thatcher and the Politics of Retrenchment*, New York: Cambridge University Press.

Teeple, G. (1995), *Globalization and the Decline of Social Reform*, New Jersey: Humanities Press.

Um, Y. (1998), *Kuk min yeon kum jae do Gae sun bang an (Improvement of National Pension System)*, Materials for Public Hearing on National Pension System.

Weaver, R.K. (1986), 'The politics of blame avoidance', *Journal of Public Policy*, **6**(4), 371–398.

World Bank (1994), *Averting the Old Age Crisis: Policies to Protect the Old and Promote Growth*, A World Bank Policy Research Report, Oxford: Oxford University Press.

World Bank (2000), *The Korean Pension Systems at a Crossroads*, Report No. 20404–Ko.

Yang, S. (1998), 'Kuk min yeon kum jae do gae sun-e Jeong check geul jung kwa jung-e Kwan han Yeon ku (Studies on policy decision process in improving National Pension)', dissertation paper for MPA, Seoul National University, Graduate School of Public Administration.

Yang, J. (2000), *The 1999 Pension Reform and A New Social Contract in South Korea*, PhD dissertation, Rutgers, The State University of New Jersey.

11. Public pension reform in the United States

R. Kent Weaver[1]

INTRODUCTION

Public pension programs in the United States, like most other advanced industrial countries, have been under severe pressures from an aging population, slower revenue growth and competitive pressures to limit payroll taxes. Policymakers throughout the industrialized world have drawn on a common repertoire of options to respond to these pressures. A first option is cutback on the generosity of specific benefit and/or eligibility provisions of their pension programs. These *retrenchment* options include increases in the retirement age, cuts in indexation of benefits for inflation and targeted reductions in benefits to upper-income recipients. A second set of options involve *refinancing* pension programs by, for example, increasing contribution rates, broadening the contribution base (for example, by requiring contributions above earnings ceilings for which no pension rights are accrued), adding more general revenues to finance the pension system, or devoting other dedicated taxes to the financing of pensions. Third, governments may attempt to *restructure* their pension programs in fundamental ways. For example, governments may scale back a 'defined benefit' pension tier, in which benefits are based on workers' earnings history (usually for a specified number of years in which they have the highest earnings), and partially supplant those benefits with a new 'defined contribution' pension, in which workers each have their own individual pension account, and final benefits depend on contributions made to that account over the entire course of their working lives as well as the return on investments accrued in that account over time.

Pension policymaking responses in the United States to austerity pressures have been distinctive in several ways, however. In considering the US experience, it is useful to distinguish between countries' *policy agendas* and their *policy changes*. John Kingdon (1995, pp. 3–4) has further distinguished between what he calls the 'governmental agenda' – issues that are under consideration by actors somewhere in government – and the 'decision agenda' – the 'list of subjects within the governmental agenda that are up for active decision'. In comparison with many other advanced industrial countries, the governmental pension agenda in the United States has been surprisingly broad in recent years. For example, the United States has considered both proposals for collective investment of Social Security funds in equity markets (under the Clinton administration) and individual 'defined contribution' pension accounts. But in other respects – notably the virtual absence of consideration of higher payroll taxes from the policy debate – the 'governmental' agenda in the United States has been quite truncated. And despite substantial attention given to the issue by Presidents Bill Clinton and George W. Bush, substantial reform of public pensions has hardly ever reached Congress's 'decision agenda' over the past 20 years, whereas most other countries in the OECD have undergone several rounds of pension policy debate and reform.

The United States is also an outlier among the rich industrial countries in its patterns of policy change (for cross-national overviews of pension reforms adopted, see Weaver, 1998; Hinrichs, 2000; Gern, 2002). Like virtually all of the advanced industrial countries, the US has built on its current pension system when making changes rather than scrapping its old pension systems and starting fresh with a new program for younger workers. But the United States is distinctive in that it has enacted virtually no major changes in the Social Security program since passage of a major Social Security reform package in 1983. Indeed, the story of pension reform presents two intriguing puzzles. The first one is why a country with a pension problem that is relatively modest in comparison with most other advanced industrial societies spends so much energy debating it; the second one is why so little policy change has taken place despite numerous initiatives aimed at securing both incremental and more fundamental reforms.

This chapter attempts to make sense of these patterns of pension policy-making in the United States – its broad but somewhat skewed agenda, episodic policymaking activity and minimal policy change over the past 20 years – in terms of both the general demographic and economic forces confronting the advanced industrial countries and characteristics unique to the United States.

THE DEVELOPMENT OF PENSION POLICY IN THE UNITED STATES

The United States was a relative latecomer in providing old age pensions for its general citizenry. Except for civil service retirees and veterans pensions, providing income support for the elderly was purely a state and local responsibility until the 1930s, and few of those governments made more than minimal efforts. (On this early period, see Skocpol, 1992. For contrasting views of the role of 'big bangs' in American social policy, see Leman, 1977 and

Pierson, 1995.) The Great Depression of the 1930s created the impetus for a major expansion of social policy in the United States, however, as the economic crisis overwhelmed existing state and local programs of poor relief and stimulated social movements that agitated for more generous social benefits. The administration of President Franklin Roosevelt responded with the Social Security Act of 1935, which included two programs for the elderly: Old Age Insurance (OAI) and Old Age Assistance (OAA), a program of grants to the states for means-tested assistance for the elderly poor.

In its initial form, Old Age Insurance provided only a meager income to recipients. The Old Age Assistance program was initially much larger and more popular than OAI, because it had no prior contributions test, and thus began paying out benefits almost immediately. Efforts to expand the contributory system began almost immediately after it was enacted, however (Derthick, 1979; see also Quadagno, 1988). Benefits were added for dependents of retired workers and for the surviving dependents of deceased workers in 1939. Eligibility was also gradually expanded to the vast majority of workers, including the self-employed. Benefits were also increased through a series of ad hoc measures. The most important changes came in the 1972 presidential election year, when a bidding war between the Nixon administration and a Democratic Congress (which included several presidential aspirants) resulted in a 20 percent benefit increase and indexation of benefits against inflation (see Derthick, 1979, Chapter 17; Weaver, 1988, Chapter 4). In the same year, Congress replaced the Old Age Assistance program with Supplemental Security Income, which provided a national benefit and eligibility standard for the needy aged and disabled that is also indexed for inflation. Some interstate SSI benefit disparities remain, however, as the states are permitted to supplement SSI benefits.

The two-tiered system of public old age pensions created by Roosevelt remains in place today. Old Age and Survivors Insurance (OASI), more commonly known as Social Security, is by far the larger of the two tiers. Social Security depends entirely on payroll tax contributions (paid equally by employers and employees) and interest earned on trust fund surpluses to finance benefits: with a few exceptions, general government revenues are not used to pay benefits, and cannot be injected into the system to pay for any spending shortfalls without changing the basic Social Security legislation. Any excess of revenue over contributions are held in a 'Trust Fund' that invests only in US government securities. Benefits are loosely linked to a worker's earnings (and therefore contributions) history, with low-wage workers receiving a higher return on their contributions than high-wage workers. By Western European standards, both contribution rates and replacement rates remain relatively modest. Indeed, the US pension system fits easily into neither Esping-Andersen's 'Bismarckian' (social insurance) nor 'residual' welfare state categories – it is perhaps best seen, along with Canada, as an example of a distinctive 'Bismarckian Lite' pension system, which is likely to be financially and politically sustainable longer than its West European counterparts precisely because its cost and payroll tax are lower.

Social Security has historically operated on a 'pay-as-you-go' basis (that is, current workers' contributions are used to pay the benefits of current benefi-ciaries) rather than building up, as most private-sector pension plans do, adequate reserves to pay the expected pension liabilities of current workers. This funding mechanism has meant that Social Security is vulnerable to inter-mittent funding crises when current expenditures outpace current revenues and empty out trust fund reserves. A funding crisis can serve as an 'action-forcing mechanism' that puts expenditure reductions or tax increases (or both) on the government's agenda and gives proponents of expenditure reductions critical leverage to force spending cutbacks.

In 2001, almost $291 billion was paid to retired workers and their depen-dents (and another $81 billion to the survivors of insured contributors) under the Social Security Old Age and Survivors Insurance program, compared with only $4.96 billion paid to the aged under the SSI program.[2] Unlike Social Security, Supplemental Security Income (SSI) is financed from general government revenues. Because SSI earnings and asset tests are quite severe and benefits are quite low, the number of retired workers and their spouses receiving OASI benefits is almost 25 times the number of aged SSI recipients (Social Security Administration, 2002, pp. 190, 271).

The United States also provides a complex set of tax incentives to encour-age both employer-sponsored pension plans and individual tax-advantaged savings for retirement (on tax incentives for retirement savings in the United States, see Hacker, 2002; Howard, 1999). Employer-sponsored plans are quite unevenly distributed, however; they are more common among government employees and unionized workers than other workers. Individual tax-advantaged savings benefit primarily higher-income workers, who have a greater ability to defer consumption. Federal government tax expenditures for employer-provided pension plans, employer-facilitated retirement savings plans (known as 401(k) plans) and individual retirement savings totaled almost $161 billion in fiscal year 2002; tax benefits for retirement income totaled almost another $25 billion.[3]

EMERGENCE OF A PROBLEM

Thinking about the politics of pension policymaking in the United States can be facilitated by putting it in the context of a more general model of what Paul Pierson has called the politics of austerity (Pierson, 2001a and c). In this model, there are a number of general forces that might increase the likelihood of retrenchment, refinancing and restructuring initiatives. These include demographic pressures, budgetary pressures, competitive pressures to keep payroll taxes down and ideological critiques of public pay-as-you-go pensions. These pressures in turn are mediated by a series of political and institutional forces: most generally, politicians' desire to avoid blame for imposing losses on their citizens, but also more country-specific features of programmatic policy inheritances, political institutions and interest group alliances. Specific austerity pressures and mediating factors vary widely across countries, however. Understanding the specific attributes of the United States on each of these dimensions can go a long way toward understanding its policy agenda and policy choices over the past quarter century.

A common set of demographic-economic pressures have, as noted above, buffeted public pension systems in recent years. Perhaps the most important source of pressure for change in pension schemes in the advanced industrial countries is an aging population. Demographic challenges vary significantly across the industrialized countries, however. The United States is in better shape than most of its peer group countries, in large part because immigration rates (bringing in mostly younger workers) and fertility rates remain higher than in most other industrialized countries. In 2000, for example, only 12.6 percent of the US population was aged 65 or higher – higher than Australia (12.4 percent), and slightly lower than Canada (12.6 percent), but significantly lower than all the Western European democracies, including the United Kingdom (15.7 percent), Germany (16.2 percent) and Italy (18.1 percent). While the elderly are expected to increase to 20 percent of the US population by 2030, even greater increases are expected in most other advanced industrial countries: for example, 23.5 percent elderly by that year in the United Kingdom, 25.8 percent in Germany, 28.1 percent in Italy, and 28.3 percent in Japan (US Department of Health and Human Services, 2001, pp. 126–127).

A second source of pressure for austerity in public pension systems is increased *budgetary concerns* (Pierson, 2001b). Once again, however, the United States is in better shape than many other advanced industrial countries. OASI expenditures have increased significantly as a share of the federal budget and of GDP in recent decades, but in the near-term, Social Security is running massive surpluses of revenue intake over expenditures, because the baby boom generation is in its peak earning and contributing years; OASI had a surplus of cash income over outflow of 140 billion dollars in the 2002 fiscal year (Office of Management and Budget, 2003b, pp. 22–24, 204, 215, 282). Social Security surpluses both lower overall budget deficits and make it extremely difficult for politicians to propose and 'sell' retrenchment in benefits and eligibility.

These favorable circumstances will not last forever, however. The Old Age and Survivors Insurance (OASI) trust fund is estimated to have a cash imbalance (outflow greater than inflow from payroll taxes) by the year 2017, and to exhaust its current assets (government securities) by the year 2041, using the 'intermediate' set of assumptions developed by the Social Security Administration for its actuarial projections. Two other government trust funds, for Disability Insurance (DI) and Medicare Hospitalization Insurance (HI), are in even worse shape. And at the end of the 75-year period on which current projections are based, combined OASI and DI payroll tax revenues are 'guesstimated' to be equal to only about two-thirds of what is needed to pay benefits. The combined OASDI actuarial deficit over the 75-year projection period is currently estimated at 1.87 percent of payroll using the Social Security Administration's intermediate projections.

Governments could respond to budgetary pressures by raising taxes as well as cutting expenditures. That most advanced industrial countries have been reluctant to do so is due in part to a third, and related, source of pressure for austerity: *concerns about economic competitiveness.* Many business leaders and conservative politicians argue that the high payroll taxes associated with generous pension and other welfare state programs make firms in the countries providing those benefits unable to compete with firms in lower cost countries. These concerns have been much greater in Europe, where payroll taxes are generally much higher than the current OASDI combined tax rate of 12.4 percent of taxable payroll. And competitiveness concerns about foreign payroll tax rates have not been an important part of the US debate (although concerns about inadequate US savings fostered by a pay-as-you-go system have been part of the debate). But as we will see below, opponents of higher Social Security taxes have been strategically placed within the US political system to keep the issue off the agenda.

CONSTRAINTS ON CHANGE

Pressures for pension austerity are mediated by a complex set of political and social influences. Most generally, austerity pressures pose a common challenge for politicians in all countries: a political imperative to avoid or diffuse blame as unpopular decisions are made, at the same time that opportunities for claiming credit are limited. Politicians who are interested in seeking re-election must be particularly sensitive to avoiding blame, because voters are generally more sensitive to losses that are imposed on them (for example, cuts in pension benefits) than to equivalent gains that they have made (for example, increases in pension benefits or cuts in taxes). When politicians do engage in pension retrenchment or refinancing, they will be strongly tempted to manipulate them in a way that avoids or minimizes blame. For example, highly technical changes may be made in benefit formulae that make them hard to comprehend, the elderly and near-elderly may be 'grandfathered' under old rules to protect them from the full effects of retrenchment, and tax increases may be delayed until after the next election.

Blame avoiding pressures interact with several other political variables in mediating pressures for pension austerity. Three factors are especially important: feedbacks from current pension policies, the structure of political institutions and partisan coalitions and the constellation of political forces surrounding pension policies. As noted earlier, public pensions in the United States can be best characterized as 'Bismarckian Lite' – earnings-related and payroll-tax financed, but with substantially lower replacement rates for most workers than is the norm in continental Europe. Both the immediate budgetary burden and the liability for future payouts are much lower than in most Western European countries. Thus, the near-term pressures for pension austerity are much weaker than is the case in most other wealthy countries because the system is actually enjoying a surplus currently. Long-term pressures are also significantly weaker given low US replacement rates. This overall policy dynamic can be quite different, however, when the trust fund is nearing exhaustion.

In addition to the legacy of past policy structures, the political limitations on pension reform in the United States over the past quarter century have also been heavily constrained by political institutions and specific political configurations. The separation of powers system in the United States creates multiple veto points where controversial policy changes can be blocked. The institutional tendency toward stalemate has been exacerbated by the fact that divided government (majorities in at least one chamber of Congress by a political party different from that of the president) was in effect for all but a little over six years (1997–80 under Carter; 1993–94 under Clinton; three months under G.W. Bush) of the period from 1975 to 2002. Thus at least some degree of bipartisanship is needed to enact any major pension reform proposal. But pension reform is an issue on which the gulf between the parties has generally been quite wide. Equally important, it is an issue that has enormous potential for generating blame against any politicians who are seen as favoring benefit cuts. The blame avoiding challenge is especially strong in the United States because relatively weak party discipline in Congress weakens legislators' ability to claim that they had no choice in voting for unpopular measures, while candidate-centered elections and negative campaigning further put politicians on the spot for their records. Short electoral cycles (all of the House of Representatives and one-third of all senators are elected every two years) further increase sensitivity to loss-imposition. Thus not only does loss-imposing pension legislation face many difficult hurdles in winning adoption in this system of multiple veto points, presidents and legislative leaders may be reluctant even to propose legislation that will cost them electorally without achieving their policy objectives. Ideological polarization and intense conflict between the parties in the United States have also made it more difficult to develop and sustain cross-party 'policy cartels' that have developed over pension policy in some other countries, in which the major parties agree to negotiate painful choices behind closed doors or to delegate them to 'experts' and abide by their decisions.

Finally, the shape that national responses to austerity pressures take is likely to be influenced by the nature of interest organizations in a country. Two sets of organizations are likely to be especially critical: trade unions and organizations of seniors themselves. In many countries, trade unions and union confederations quite consciously view public pensions as a form of deferred wage and themselves as the major defenders of the public pension system. However, trade unions have more complicated agendas than seniors organizations; faced with a fiscal crisis in which they are faced to choose between cuts between pensions and cuts in health care or unemployment insurance, seniors groups are probably less likely to choose the former than trade unions. Thus powerful seniors organizations are probably a stronger bulwark against pension retrenchment and restructuring that harms seniors' interests than powerful trade unions, and countries where seniors organizations 1) are relatively autonomous from more encompassing political organizations like political parties and trade unions, 2) are relatively large in comparison to trade unions, and 3) compete among each other for members, and thus are reluctant to be seen as relatively weak in defending member interests, are probably more likely than those in other countries to be intransigent in opposing such initiatives.

The United States clearly fits all of these criteria. Unions in the US have experienced a long period of decline in the post-World War II era, while the US is unusual in the degree to which seniors groups are a large, independently-organized political force (on seniors groups, see Campbell, 2003; Pratt, 1997). By far the largest of the seniors organizations in AARP (formerly the American Association of Retired Persons), which claims a membership of more than 35 million Americans age 50 and above – nearly three times the membership of the AFL-CIO, the largest trade union confederation in the United States. AARP's membership is a broad one that includes a broad age and ideological spectrum: only half of its members are retired and approximately one-third are under age 60. The large size and ideological diversity of its membership make it difficult for AARP to take a positive stance in favor of any particular direction for policy change, but AARP is very well-placed to resist policy initiatives that attempt to impose losses on all or part of its constituency. Thus the constellation of interest pressures, like other mediating forces in the United States, militate strongly against major changes in Social Security and SSI.

Partially counterbalancing these pressures, however, are the strong resources enjoyed by advocates of Social Security privatization in the US. Calls for an increased role for pension privatization have been heard almost everywhere, but whether they have advanced to serious consideration, let alone adoption, depends heavily on 1) a fertile ideological climate in the host country, 2) a policy 'window of opportunity', usually furnished by the combination of having sympathetic politicians in office and the apparent exhaustion of incremental retrenchment and refinancing options. Here the picture in the United States is a mixed one. The political culture in the United States places an unusually strong emphasis on self-reliance. The United States has also stood out in the growth of market-oriented think tanks, several of which have pressed very strongly for privatization of Social Security (Rich and Weaver, 1998; Derthick, 2001, pp. 201–203). And the strong role and market orientation of the Republican Party have meant that privatization ideas had a strong carrier in the political arena. But while these factors kept such proposals on the broad 'discussion agenda' in the United States, other factors – most notably current Social Security surpluses – have mostly kept them off the government's 'decision agenda' for most of the past two decades.

INITIAL RETRENCHMENT AND REFINANCING

The interplay of this diverse set of pressures for pension austerity and multiple mediating forces can be seen in the history of US policy toward Social Security and Supplemental Security Income over the past quarter century. Like most other advanced industrial countries, austerity pressures led initially to incremental retrenchment and refinancing initiatives, and then to consideration of more fundamental reforms. But unlike most other advanced industrial countries, there has been very modest policy change over the past 20 years.

Incremental Change under Carter and Reagan

Repeated crises in the Social Security trust fund and overall budgetary pressures led to numerous attempts to introduce Social Security cutbacks beginning in the late 1970s. An impending Social Security trust fund crisis prompted the Carter administration's initial Social Security retrenchment initiative, in the fall of 1977. This crisis resulted from a combination of stagflation that lowered revenue inflow to the fund and a faulty indexation mechanism that gave newly retiring workers unexpected windfalls. There was little disagreement that change was needed, but neither the administration nor the Congress was willing to impose substantial short-term losses on persons already receiving benefits. Instead of immediate benefit and eligibility cuts, however, policymakers relied almost exclusively on injecting new revenues into the system to produce short-term improvements in the program's financial status. These came in the form of both increases in payroll taxes and the wage base (the amount of wages subject to the Social Security tax). These tax increases were phased in after the next (1978) congressional election to reduce political blame. Long-term savings were produced largely by reducing the initial benefit of most future beneficiaries. But policymakers did not attempt to retroactively lower the real purchasing power of workers who had already retired or those who were about to become eligible to retire. Instead, policymakers attempted to lower the visibility of the benefit cuts by phasing in the new benefit formula for initial benefits in over five years for future retirees.

Social Security cuts were considered several times during the administration of Ronald Reagan (1981–89). President Reagan had promised in the 1980 presidential campaign that Social Security would be exempt from cuts, and the new administration initially proposed only minor changes in Social Security. But in the spring of 1981, spiraling deficit forecasts led David Stockman, Director of the Office of Management and Budget within the White House, to press for a Social Security reform package that contained a large dose of immediate political pain. Proposed cuts included a three month delay in cost-of-living adjustments, a change in calculating future retirees' initial benefits that would eventually lower the percentage of a retiree's prior earnings replaced by Social Security benefits significantly, and a severe and almost immediate cut in benefits for future early retirees. The president initially backed the package, but after it generated widespread criticism, the White House quickly backed away, and a relatively modest package of cuts was enacted in 1981.

While the political dangers of proposing Social Security benefit cuts were evident, awareness of another looming Social Security trust fund crisis led the president and congressional Democrats to entrust Social Security's financial problems to a bipartisan commission that was to report after the 1982 elections. Although the commission almost came to an impasse, the threat that there soon would not be money in the trust funds to send out Social Security checks stimulated compromise. The commission provided a political cover allowing negotiators for the president and congressional Democrats to come to an agreement that was eventually approved, with some additions, by Congress (for a detailed discussion see Light, 1995). Because both parties shared responsibility for reaching the agreement, the potential for blame was minimized and the ability of the various participants to stick to the agreement was maximized.

The 1983 legislation made major changes in Social Security on both the tax and benefit sides. In the immediate term, the most important change was a six-month 'delay' in inflation adjustments for benefits that really amounted to a permanent benefit cut for current (but not future) recipients. In the longer term, the legislation imposed a gradual increase in the standard retirement age (the age at which full Social Security retirement benefits are received) from 65 to 67. This increase was phased in gradually, beginning in the year 2000 and ending in the year 2021. Workers can continue to retire at age 62, with a greater actuarial reduction in their benefits. However, the long delay between 1983 passage of the Social Security rescue package and the initial retirement age increase, along with its gradual phase-in, lessened near-term blame associated with the cuts. Although Republicans accepted an acceleration of previously scheduled payroll taxes as part of the rescue package, they adamantly (and successfully) opposed further increases in payroll tax rates. They also accepted taxation of half of the value of Social Security benefits for middle- and upper-income recipients – a measure that will expand its 'bite' over time since the income limits at which taxation begins are not indexed.

The 1983 Social Security rescue package dramatically altered the short- and medium-term financial condition of OASI. As noted earlier, the trust funds are currently generating surpluses, which have made it politically very difficult to either raise Social Security taxes or cut benefits. Continued concern over the budget deficit and the recognition that large expenditure reductions were unlikely without a contribution from Social Security led Republican politicians to propose pension cutbacks on several occasions in the final years of the Reagan and George H.W. Bush administrations, but in the absence of a trust fund crisis, each attempt fizzled (for a description of these episodes, see Pierson and Weaver, 1993). Indeed, these retrenchment initiatives suggest that efforts to use cuts in Social Security benefits and eligibility in the battle to shrink the overall federal deficit in the absence of a looming trust fund crisis are almost certain to fail. Increasingly, as Martha Derthick (2001) has noted, 'central to deficit politics was a ritual of declaring Social Security to be off the table'.

Retrenchment Initiatives in the Clinton Years

The absence of a short-term funding crisis in the Social Security program continued to act as a fundamental brake on retrenchment initiatives after Bill Clinton assumed the presidency in 1993 (for a comprehensive overview of Social Security policymaking during the Clinton administration and its relationship to the budget, see Elmendorf, Leibman and Wilcox, 2002). The only significant exception was a provision adopted as part of President Clinton's 1993 budget package that made 85 percent of benefits taxable for beneficiaries at the upper end of the income scale. But this provision affected relatively few Social Security recipients.

The story was initially the same after Republicans gained control of

Congress in 1994. House Republicans, having learned from the Reagan experience with Social Security retrenchment initiatives, and seeking to avoid proposals that did not enjoy popular support, explicitly excluded Social Security cutbacks from their 'Contract with America' campaign pledge in the 1994 congressional election (Balz and Brownstein, 1996). Even when congressional Republicans endorsed very unpopular (and ultimately unsuccessful) Medicare and Medicaid cuts in the fall of 1995 in an effort to make their deficit and tax reduction promises 'add up', they resisted Social Security cuts. The Clinton-Republican budget agreement of 1997 also excluded Social Security cuts.

The major Republican initiative on retirement benefits during the 1995–96 'Gingrich Revolution' concerned benefits received by non-citizens under the relatively small and heretofore largely uncontroversial SSI program. There is little dispute that non-citizens who are legal permanent residents and contribute to social insurance programs such as Social Security, Medicare and Unemployment Insurance should be eligible for benefits on the same basis as citizens. Controversy over the means-tested SSI program increased in the early 1990s, however, as solid quantitative evidence began to emerge in government studies that non-citizens, especially refugees and elderly persons admitted to the United States as part of family reunification policies, were heavy users of means-tested benefits. In the Supplemental Security Income program, non-citizens increased from 7 percent of aged recipients in 1983 to 30.2 percent of recipients in 1994 (House Ways and Means Committee, 1996, p. 1305). The new Republican majority that took over control of Congress in 1995 passed legislation that barred most non-citizens from receiving Supplemental Security Income and Food Stamps until they became citizens. Moreover, the bill's SSI retrenchment provisions took effect almost immediately, and did not exempt current recipients. These provisions proved to be highly controversial, however. The Balanced Budget Act of 1997 restored SSI benefits to those who had been receiving them at the time that the 1996 welfare law was passed: a limited backtracking on SSI consistent with the blame avoiding principle that taking benefits away from those who already have them is most likely to spark retribution (for a review of legislative changes in SSI made between 1993 and 1997, see House Ways and Means Committee, 1998, pp. 318–325).

Clearly politicians in the United States remain extremely reluctant to do anything that might leave their individual or party fingerprints on a bill that could later be portrayed by political opponents as a cut in Social Security. There are at least two potential ways around this problem. First, policymakers could delegate decision-making to non-elected bodies and limit their own discretion to overturn the decisions of those bodies, as they have done in setting up special commissions to oversee closing of military bases. Second, politicians could legislate automatic triggers that would take place in the future: for example, across the board cuts in all entitlement programs that would be triggered by deficits above specified targets in future years (Weaver, 1989b).

In practice, neither has been viable. Congress generally delegates real power to commissions – for example, saying that their recommendations go into effect automatically unless Congress can muster a majority against them – only on issues like military base closings and congressional pay where all the major actors in the legislative and executive branches are agreed on the broad outlines of a solution but need a political cover to work out the details and take the political heat (Weaver, 1989a). But on Social Security, there is no such agreement on the basic dimensions of a solution, and thus not even a hint of willingness to submit its future to a commission with binding decision-making power. President Clinton did appoint a commission to study Social Security and other entitlement issues in 1993 (a price extracted by Senator Bob Kerrey for his vote in favor of Clinton's budget package), but the commission had only the power to make recommendations, and it ended up being so divided that it was unable even to agree on a package of recommendations.

Use of automatic triggers to produce program cuts has been even more of a political non-starter. Far from agreeing to put in place mechanisms that might lead to Social Security cuts at some future point, American politicians have done just the opposite: they have either explicitly excluded Social Security from such mechanisms, or they have refused to adopt those mechanisms when there was even a hint that they might lead to Social Security cuts. The former can be seen in the case of the Gramm–Rudman–Hollings deficit reduction mechanism adopted in 1985: Social Security (and several other entitlement programs) was specifically exempted from any automatic cuts. And fear that a proposed Balanced Budget Amendment to the US constitution might lead to cutbacks in Social Security in the future was used by President Clinton and by wavering senators as political cover to justify votes against the Balanced Budget Amendment – killing it by the narrowest of margins in the Senate – in both 1995 and 1997 (Chandler, 1997; Rosenbaum, 1997).

Another option consistent with the automatic trigger strategy is to put in place a less generous indexation formula for future inflation adjustments. Early in the second Clinton administration there was a nascent discussion of adjusting the Social Security benefit indexation formula. This reflected a widely shared perception among economists that the Consumer Price Index (CPI), which is used to make annual adjustments in Social Security benefits, overstates inflation. The reasons are fairly technical, involving the difficulty in measuring price increases that reflect improvements in quality (faster computers and cars with more safety equipment, for example) and substitution by consumers of less expensive substitutes (apples for bananas, for example) when the price of goods rise. In principle, a lowering of the value of the CPI provides an opportunity to lower outlays without direct intervention by politicians, and with the eminently reasonable justification that it is not in fact a benefit cut at all, but simply a more accurate calculation that will keep the real value of benefits intact rather than falsely inflate them. If there were a methodology for reforming the Consumer Price Index that all experts and interests agreed upon, and that experts in the Bureau of Labour Statistics could simply implement as a technical improvement in the index, then reform of the CPI (and cutbacks in Social Security benefits) might be politically attainable. But there is no agreement on a methodology, or even on how much the CPI overstates inflation. That means that if the CPI is to be changed in the short term, politicians must get involved, legislating a 'best guess' adjustment in the CPI. The politics of Social Security cutbacks are so extraordinarily sensitive that a downward adjustment of benefits requires the political equivalent of a virgin birth: no politician wants to claim, or to be labeled by his or her political enemies, as the father of this baby. In the negotiations in the spring of 1997 between the president and congressional leaders over a potential budget deal, both parties sent signals that they would consider agreeing to a downward adjustment in the CPI, but only if the other side would agree simultaneously, so that they could not be assigned paternity for the idea during a later election campaign (on the president's calculus in refusing to agree to an independent commission to settle CPI revisions, see Chandler and Pianin, 1997; Hagar, 1997). As budget negotiations neared completion in the spring of 1997, Senate Majority Leader Trent Lott seems to have decided that Republicans would ultimately take the blame for cutting inflation adjustments if they were included in a budget agreement, so he took them off the table (Pianin, 1997; Stevenson, 1997). The achievement of a federal budget surplus beginning with the 1998 federal fiscal year at least temporarily put cuts to the CPI used to index Social Security benefits on the back burner once again: the political risks associated with such cuts in a period in which Social Security contributions were fueling budget surpluses were too great.

TOWARD FUNDAMENTAL RESTRUCTURING?

The United States has not adopted any fundamental restructuring reforms in its public pension system over the past 30 years (the last major innovation was the federalization of Supplemental Security Income in 1972). And like most other wealthy countries, the United States has not created a mandatory individual accounts tier. The United States has, however, substantially expanded the role for defined contribution pensions in two ways – by increasing the scope of employer-sponsored retirement plans that allow workers to defer taxes on earnings put in special retirement savings accounts (known as 401(k) pension plans), and by not intervening to prevent 'policy drift' among occupational pensions away from defined benefit toward defined contribution plans (Hacker, 2002).

In addition, there has been a growing discussion in the US of a more fundamental restructuring of the Social Security program. Debates on Social Security restructuring have largely focused on two broad sets of alternatives: 1) broadening the range of investment options for the Social Security trust fund, including investing in equities, to increase trust fund returns, and 2) varying degrees of 'privatization' of Social Security through mandatory or optional contributions to personal pensions (for an outline of major alternatives, see 1994–96 Advisory Council on Social Security, 1997). Democrats are generally more sympathetic to the first option, while Republicans have favored the second.

Calls for incorporating individual investment accounts into Social Security have been spurred by critiques from conservative policy intellectuals like Martin Feldstein and from think tanks like the Heritage Foundation and Cato Institute as well as by declining public confidence in the long-term ability of the current system to make good on its promises. The fact that the federal government was borrowing Social Security surpluses contributed to perceptions by many younger workers that the system will not pay them a rate of return on their contributions equal to what they could earn through private sector investments. A general perception on the part of political elites (especially Republican elites) that controlling entitlement spending was essential to controlling deficits and limiting government more generally also helped to generate more interest in Social Security reform (Derthick, 2001; Teles, 1998).

Conflict over Social Security privatization has centered in part on the distributional consequences of those reforms for particular groups. Privatizers have in particular focused on the lower returns to contributions by younger workers, arguing that Social Security is a bad deal for this group. Critics of individual accounts, on the other hand, have argued that because of stock market volatility, individuals who retire a few years apart after contributing over their working lives to a broad stock index fund could end up with dramatically different earnings replacement rates – and those who pulled out their funds in a stock market trough would end up with very inadequate benefits (Burtless, 2000). Proponents of private accounts have also argued that African-Americans and Hispanic Americans would fare better under a system of individual accounts because they tend to die younger (and thus draw benefits for a shorter period), while their opponents argue that when the program's progressive benefit formula plus disability and survivor benefits are taken into consideration, these groups get a higher return from Social Security than others (Hendley and Bilimoria, 1999; Kijakazi, 1998).

The Social Security Advisory Council's 1997 report also gave increased credence both to investing Social Security funds in equities and setting up individualized accounts over which workers would have some investment control. But nothing close to a consensus on a direction for reform emerged from the Advisory Council's 1997 report. The report contained three distinct proposals, none of which could command a majority of Council members (1994–96 Advisory Council on Social Security, 1997).

The course of the debates in the late 1990s over equities investment and creation of personal accounts for Social Security was heavily influenced by the political maneuverings of Bill Clinton. In his January 1999 State of the Union, Clinton proposed to reserve 62 percent of the Social Security surplus anticipated over the next 15 years to bolstering the Social Security (Old Age Survivors Insurance) trust fund. Approximately one-fifth of this amount would be devoted to investment in equities – collectively rather than individually – through a mechanism insulated from government influence. Thus returns on trust fund revenues would be raised at least modestly, but the size of the investment would also be modest enough to lessen fears about government control of the economy. In addition, another 11 percent of the anticipated surplus was to be reserved for government subsidies to new 'Universal Savings (USA) Accounts' – new retirement savings accounts through which the federal government would match individual retirement savings accounts, with extra benefits for low-income workers. These accounts would help individuals prepare for retirement based on personal choice and individual accounts, as privatizers prefer. They have one fundamental difference from privatizers' plans, however: they would not take money out of existing payroll taxes or be part of the basic OASI system. Thus they would not require cutting the existing 'defined benefits' of the OASI system, and government commitments could be scaled back when government budget surpluses shrink.

Also influencing the course of the debate were changing projections about when the OASI funding crisis would hit. For most of the last quarter of the twentieth century, the Social Security Administration's projections of when the OASI trust fund would run out of money had proven too optimistic. After each legislative change, the date when the OASI trust fund was expected to be empty would quickly begin moving forward. But in 1997, this began to reverse: with a better than expected economy, the anticipated trust fund crisis moved further way (from 2029 in 1997 to 2034 in 1999 and 2041 in 2002), lessening the already weak sense of system crisis. Although President Clinton sought to maintain sufficient flexibility that he could sign almost any piece of legislation, the positions of congressional Republicans and Democrats remained far apart, leading Republicans to fear that any Social Security initiative on their part could lead them to a political trap.

The option of investment of Social Security trust funds in the stock market has been blocked by strong opposition from congressional Republicans. Alan Greenspan, the powerful and widely-respected chairperson of the Federal Reserve Board, has also been a highly vocal critic of government investment in equities markets. Greenspan argues that no mechanisms to insulate investment managers from political pressures would be adequate (Stevenson, 1999). Critics of privatization have challenged this position, citing the experience of the Thrift Savings Plan (for federal employees) and state employee pension plans (see Munnell and Sunden, 1999).

How and how much to restructure Social Security was an important issue in the 2000 presidential election campaign in the United States. Republican candidate George W. Bush proposed allowing workers to divert part of their Social Security payroll taxes to individual accounts, while his Democratic opponent, Al Gore, argued that doing so would further weaken the viability of the current Social Security system (Sack, 2000). After the election, the new president decided to wait on Social Security until after his top priority, a tax cut, had made it through Congress. Instead, President Bush decided to appoint a commission on how best to implement an opt-out plan.

Unlike the 1981–83 Social Security reform commission, however, President Bush appointed all of the members of the Commission, although members were drawn from both political parties. All appointees had to agree in advance to support a set of principles established by the White House, including no increase in Social Security payroll taxes, voluntary individual accounts, and no erosion of benefits for current retirees and near retirees. The commission eventually decided to present a menu of policy options rather than a single plan, in part to shield the administration from criticism over the benefit cuts that would be required to fund a Social Security opt-out (President's Commission to Strengthen Social Security, 2001). Stock market declines in 2001 and 2002 also appear to have dampened, at least temporarily, support for partial privatization of Social Security. Perhaps most important, the quick post-11 September disappearance of federal budget surpluses made financing a transition to opt-out advance-funded individual accounts more difficult (Morin and Deane, 2001). Indeed, Republican candidates in the 2002 congressional election were encouraged by the party to distance themselves from the notion of 'privatization' because of its perceived political risks (Vanderhei and Eilperin, 2002; Goldstein, 2002).

The overall pattern in the United States, in short, is that while Social Security privatization is clearly now on the public agenda, it is likely far from enactment, even with George W. Bush as an advocate and Republican control of both chambers of Congress. Indeed President Bush's 2003 State of the Union address gave Social Security reform a scant two sentences mention – a strong indicator that the administration did not intend to make the issue a legislative priority in the new Congress (Dinan, 2003).

CONCLUSIONS

Public pension policy in the United States over the past 20 years has been characterized by a fairly broad 'governmental' agenda (with some important exceptions, notably with respect to refinancing), a very limited 'decision agenda', and almost complete absence of substantial policy change.

To explain these patterns, this chapter has argued that it is necessary to look both at common pressures for austerity confronting the advanced industrial countries over the past 30 years and political factors mediating those pressures. The relatively weak demographic pressures facing US policymakers in the short-term have clearly inhibited policy change, especially since they are reinforced by 'policy feedbacks' from the initial US choice of a relatively modest 'Bismarckian Lite' pension system and the more recent Social Security 'fix' put in place in 1983. The latter has resulted in Social Security surpluses in the short and medium term, meaning that pressures for immediate reductions in Social Security spending have been relatively weak. In the absence of an immediate funding crisis, further retrenchment or refinancing, let alone restructuring, is not something that politicians have been compelled to act on. Thus while the past five years have seen numerous presidential pronouncements on Social Security, serious congressional action has been limited. The combination of current Social Security surpluses and vehement Republican opposition to putting any additional revenues into the current defined benefit system are the main factors explaining why payroll tax increases have not been on the agenda in the United States.

Awareness of a looming long-term Social Security funding problem, highlighted in annual reports of the Social Security trustees, helps to explain why Social Security reform remains on the broader governmental agenda in the United States, despite the absence of an immediate funding crisis. Pressure from ideologically conservative think tanks and other policy intellectuals have also contributed to the durability of the privatization agenda.

American political institutions have also contributed to each of these outcomes. The porousness of the US political system allows many proposals to get a hearing, but relatively few of those proposals get serious consideration, let alone 'winning enactment'. In countries where a governing party or coalition have tight control over the legislative agenda, the range and number of proposals that get serious attention is likely to be much lower, but their success rate much higher. Thus in pensions as in other policy sectors, the governmental agenda in the United States is relatively broad. Alternation of the Democrats and Republicans in the White House and almost perpetual divided government help to explain why the agenda for fundamental reforms has been broad: both parties have been able to put ideas broadly consistent with their political philosophies onto the discussion agenda. But Republican hegemony in the federal government since 2000 has ensured that broadening investment of the Social Security trust fund is off the agenda for the near term.

American political institutions have also contributed to the truncated decision agenda and absence of substantial Social Security reform in recent years. Short electoral cycles and candidate-centered elections give American politicians very little leeway for taking loss-imposing actions. In addition, multiple veto points and almost continuous divided government has also made US presidents reluctant to give a high priority to Social Security reform agendas that would likely fail to make it through Congress. One can certainly imagine the elements of a reform package that would bridge the Social Security impasse in the United States, notably a trade-off involving an increase in the payroll tax, with devotion of all of that tax to a system of individual accounts, in exchange for a gradual lowering of current guaranteed replacement rates and an improved income floor for those with the lowest incomes. In the short run, however, such a compromise seems very unlikely. Positions of the two parties' political bases are very polarized, and both parties see Social Security as an issue that may work to their electoral advantage. Thus the outlook for Social Security reform in the United States remains one in which continued blame-generating and continued stalemate are likely to dominate over the next decade.

NOTES

1. The research reported herein was partially funded pursuant to a grant from the US Social Security Administration (SSA) funded as part of the Retirement Research Consortium at Boston College. The opinions and conclusions are solely those of the author and should not be construed as representing the opinions or policy of SSA or any agency of the Federal Government.
2. The SSI figure includes state supplementation. Social Security Administration 2002, pp. 151, 278.
3. These figures are outlay equivalents. See Office of Management and Budget, 2003a, p. 114.

REFERENCES

1994–96 Advisory Council on Social Security (1997), *Report*, vol. 1: *Findings and Recommendations*, Washington, DC: The Council.

Balz, Dan and Ronald Brownstein (1996), *Storming the Gates: Protest Politics and the Republican Revival*, Boston: Little Brown.

Burtless, Gary (2000), *How Would Financial Risk Affect Retirement Income Under Individual Accounts?*, Center for Retirement Research at Boston College, Issue Brief No. 5, October.

Campbell, Andrea Louise (2003), *How Policies Make Citizens: Senior Political Activism and the American Welfare State*, Princeton: Princeton University Press.

Chandler, Clay (1997), 'Playing the Social Security Card', *Washington Post*, 24 February, A8.

Chandler, Clay and Eric Pianin (1997), 'President won't back CPI panel', *Washington Post*, 13 March, A1.

Derthick, Martha (1979), *Policymaking for Social Security*, Washington, DC: The Brookings Institution.

Derthick, Martha (2001), 'The evolving old politics of Social Security', in Martin A. Levin, Marc K. Landy and Martin Shapiro (eds), *Seeking the Center: Politics and Policymaking at the New Century*, Washington, DC: Georgetown University Press, 193–214.

Dinan, Stephen (2003), 'Social Security accounts off agenda', *Washington Times*, 3 February, A9.

Elmendorf, Douglas W., Jeffrey B. Leibman and David W. Wilcox (2002), 'Fiscal policy and Social Security policy during the 1990s', in Jeffrey A. Frankel and Peter R. Orszag (eds), *American Economic Policy in the 1990s*, Cambridge, MA: MIT Press, 63–119.

Gern, Klaus-Jürgen (2002), 'Recent developments in old age pension systems: An international overview', in Martin Feldstein and Horst Siebert (eds), *Social Security Pension Reform in Europe*, Chicago: University of Chicago Press, 439–478.

Goldstein, Amy (2002), 'Action on Social Security debated', *Washington Post*, 15 November, A16.

Hacker, Jacob (2002), *The Divided Welfare State: The Battle Over Public and Private Social Benefits in the United States*, Princeton: Princeton University Press.

Hagar, George (1997), 'GOP demands new Clinton budget as CPI magic bullet misfires', *Congressional Quarterly Weekly Report*, 15 March, 619–620.

Hendley, Alexa A. and Natasha F. Bilimoria (1999), 'Minorities and Social Security: An analysis of racial and ethnic differences in the current Program', *Social Security Bulletin*, **62**(2), 59–64.

Hinrichs, Karl (2000), 'Elephants on the move. Patterns of public pension reform in OECD Countries', *European Review*, **8**(3), 353–378.

House Ways and Means Committee (1996), *1996 Green Book*, Washington, DC: Government Printing Office.

House Ways and Means Committee (1998), *1998 Green Book*, Washington, DC: Government Printing Office.

Howard, Christopher (1999), *The Hidden Welfare State Tax Expenditures and Social Policy in the United States*, Princeton: Princeton University Press.

Kijakazi, Kilolo (1998), *African Americans, Hispanic Americans, and Social Security: The Shortcomings of the Heritage Foundation Reports*, Washington, DC: Center on Budget and Policy Priorities, October 8.

Kingdon, John (1995), *Agendas, Alternatives, and Public Policies*, 2nd edn, Reading, MA: Addison-Wesley.

Leman, Christopher (1977), 'Patterns of policy development: Social security in the United States and Canada', *Public Policy*, **25**(2), 261–291.

Light, Paul (1995), *Still Artful Work: The Continuing Politics of Social Security Reform*, New York, McGraw-Hill.

Morin, Richard and Claudia Deane (2001), 'Poll shows new doubts on economy; President's tax cut, policy are questioned', *Washington Post*, 27 March, A1.

Munnell, Alicia H. and Annika Sunden (1999), 'Investment practices of state and local pension funds: Implications for Social Security reform', paper presented at the first annual conference of the Retirement Research Consortium, May 20–21, Washington, DC.

Office of Management and Budget (2003a), *Budget of the United States Government, Fiscal Year 2004, Analytical Perspectives*, Washington, DC: Government Printing Office.

Office of Management and Budget (2003b), *Budget of the United States Government, Fiscal Year 2004, Historical Tables*, Washington, DC: Government Printing Office.

Pianin, Eric (1997), 'Lott rejects lower Social Security adjustment as part of budget deal', *Washington Post*, April 29.

Pierson, Paul D. (1995), 'The creeping nationalization of income transfers in the United States, 1935–94', in Stephan Leibfried and Paul Pierson (eds), *European Social Policy: Between Fragmentation and Integration*, Washington, DC: The Brookings Institution, 301–328.

Pierson, Paul (2001a), 'Coping with permanent austerity: Welfare state restructuring in affluent democracies', in Paul Pierson (ed.), *The New Politics of the Welfare State*, Oxford: Oxford University Press, 410–456.

Pierson, Paul (2001b), 'From expansion to austerity: The new politics of taxing and spending', in Martin A. Levin, Marc K. Landy and Martin Shapiro (eds), *Seeking the Center: Politics and Policymaking at the New Century*, Washington, DC: Georgetown University Press, 54–80.

Pierson, Paul (2000c), 'Post-industrial pressures on the mature welfare states', in Paul Pierson (ed.), *The New Politics of the Welfare State*, Oxford: Oxford University Press, 2001, 80–114.

Pierson, Paul D. and R. Kent Weaver (1993), 'Imposing losses in pension policy', in R. Kent Weaver and Bert A. Rockman (eds), *Do Institutions Matter?: Government Capabilities in the US and Abroad*, Washington, DC: The Brookings Institution, 110–150.

Pratt, Henry J. (1997), *Gray Agendas: Interest Groups and Public Pensions in Canada, Britain, and the United States*, Ann Arbor: University of Michigan Press.

President's Commission to Strengthen Social Security (2001), *Strengthening Social Security and Creating Wealth for All Americans*, Washington, DC: The Commission, December.

Quadagno, Jill (1988), 'From Old Age Assistance to Supplemental Security Income: The political economy of relief in the South, 1935–1972', in Margaret Weir, Ann Shola Orloff and Theda Skocpol (eds), *The Politics of Social Policy in the United States*, Princeton: Princeton University Press.

Rich, Andrew and R. Kent Weaver (1998), 'Advocates and analysts: Think tanks and the politicization of expertise in Washington', in Allan Cigler and Burdett Loomis (eds), *Interest Group Politics* 5th edn, Washington, DC: Congressional Quarterly Press, 235–253.

Rosenbaum, David E. (1997), 'Dancing the Balanced-Budget waltz', *New York Times*, 28 February, A24.

Sack, Kevin (2000), 'Gore and Bush trade jabs on pensions and spending; Vice President sees threat to future of Social Security', *New York Times*, 2 November, A1.

Skocpol, Theda (1992), *Protecting Soldiers and Mothers: The Political Origins of Social Policy in the United States*, Cambridge, MA, Harvard University Press.

Social Security Administration (2002), *Social Security Bulletin Annual Statistical Supplement 2002*, Washington, DC, SSA.

Stevenson, Richard W. (1997), 'Lott now opposes change in inflation adjuster', *New York Times*, 29 April, A16.

Stevenson, Richard W. (1999), 'Fed chief warns of painful choices on Social Security', *New York Times*, 29 January, A1.

Teles, Steven (1998), 'The dialectics of trust: Ideas, finance and pension privatization in the US and the UK', paper presented at the Annual Research Conference on the Association for Public Policy Analysis and Management, 29–31 October.

US Department of Health and Human Services, National Institute on Aging (2001), *An Aging World, 2001.*

Vanderhei, Jim and Juliet Eilperin (2002), 'Bush's plan for Social Security loses favor', *Washington Post*, 13 August, A1.

Weaver, R. Kent (1988), *Automatic Government: The Politics of Indexation*, Washington, DC: The Brookings Institution.

Weaver, R. Kent (1989a), 'Is Congress delegating too much power to commissions?', *Roll Call.*

Weaver, R. Kent (1989b), 'Setting and firing policy triggers', *Journal of Public Policy*, **9**(3), 307–336.

Weaver, R. Kent (1998), 'The politics of pension reform: Lessons from abroad', in R. Douglas Arnold, Michael Graetz and Alicia Munnell (eds), *Framing the Social Security Debate: Values, Politics and Economics*, Washington, DC: Brookings Institution Press, 183–229.

12. Stasis amidst change: Canadian pension reform in an age of retrenchment

Daniel Béland and John Myles*

INTRODUCTION

The ongoing debate on pension reform among policy-makers in East Asian, North American and Western European countries has been framed by a conventional discourse depicting a developing demographic time bomb as the elderly population grows in relation to the overall population (Béland and Waddan, 2000). Since the 1980s, these demographic fears as well as macro-economic constraints related to economic globalization and regional integration have favoured the enactment of various pension reforms in East Asia, North America and Western Europe.

As in most countries, Canada's national pension system is largely a product of the age of welfare state expansion that extended from the 1950s to the 1970s (see Section I). The result was a public system that might be characterized as a small-scale version of the traditional Swedish design: a universal flat benefit for all seniors (Old Age Security), supplemented by a guaranteed minimum (income-tested) pension (the Guaranteed Income Supplement), and a modest second tier of earnings-related pensions (the Canada and Quebec Pension Plans). Middle- and upper-income families supplement these benefits with employment-based pensions (Registered Pension Plans or RPPs) and personal retirement accounts (Registered Retirement Savings Plans or RRSPs). All of these elements were in place by the end of the 1960s.

Since then, pension reform has emerged as a 'hot point' on the legislative agenda in three distinct periods. The period from the mid-1970s to the early 1980s brought the so-called Great Pension Debate, a high-profile but ultimately doomed attempt to expand the modest second-tier earnings-related plan to European-like levels. The appropriate points of contrast here are the set of other 'latecomer' countries (Myles and Pierson, 2001), nations that by 1980 had no (Australia, the Netherlands, New Zealand) or, like Canada, only modest (Denmark, Switzerland) second-tier earnings-related plans by 1980.

For all but New Zealand, the 1980s were a period of pension expansion, typically led by organized labour. In these cases, however, expansion took the form of mandatory, typically funded, employer plans. In Canada, mandatory employer pensions were viewed by the reformers as a second-best, inferior, solution and were never aggressively pursued. The result was no change.

Talk of expansion was quickly succeeded by the politics of retrenchment and can be divided into two periods: the first under the Conservative government of Brian Mulroney (1984–93) and the second under Liberal Prime Minister Jean Chrétien (1993–2003). In both periods, the universal flat benefit (Old Age Security) was targeted for reform with limited success. Here the appropriate points of contrast are Sweden and Finland. In both countries formerly universal flat rate pension benefits provided to all elderly citizens were 'clawed back' (to use the Canadian term) from high-income earners by means of a 'pension test' (Myles and Quadagno, 1997). The Mulroney government succeeded in introducing an 'income test' for flat rate pensions in 1989 but as we show below its effects have been decidedly modest. A much more ambitious effort to scale back Old Age Security benefits from middle-income seniors in the 1990s (see Battle, 1997), in contrast, did not get beyond the proposal stage.

Finally, amidst the usual rhetoric of 'unsustainability', the second-tier earnings-related scheme (the Canada Pension Plan) was put on the reform agenda in the mid-1990s. The results were equally modest and served mostly to maintain the status quo. Contribution rates were raised to create a surplus to be invested in the equity markets with future revenues used to finance future benefits. This increase in 'advance funding' was aimed at maintaining benefit levels while smoothing out the effects of demographic change on contribution rates across successive cohorts of workers. The appropriate points of contrast here are the rather more draconian changes to second-tier earnings-related plans characteristic of many European countries since the early 1990s.

In sum, against the comparative backdrop of the other affluent democracies, our main conclusion is that, on the benefit side, relatively little has changed to the basic pension design constructed in the 1950s and 1960s. Answering the question 'why not?', we contend, holds instructive lessons not only for understanding the Canadian case but also for making sense of larger-scale reforms elsewhere. An obvious part of the answer is that 'size matters'. Like the other Anglo-Saxon countries, Canadian public sector pension expenditures are comparatively modest by international standards (about 5.5 per cent of GDP in the 1990s) and Canadian retirees receive a larger fraction (about 50 per cent) of their incomes from private occupational pensions, personal retirement accounts and other forms of savings. The upshot is that the potential contribution of pension cuts to other policy objectives such as deficit reduction was comparatively modest and, as we highlight in the discussion, governments found more tempting targets in other parts of the social policy matrix.

Less obvious, perhaps, is our claim that the financing mechanism – the composition of the tax budget used to finance public benefits – probably matters more. Unlike most countries that rely mainly on payroll taxes to finance old age pensions, Canada's pension budget is divided more or less evenly between payroll taxes and general revenue financing. High and rising payroll taxes, we argue, create strong incentives (and unusual coalitions) for reform that are comparatively weak in the Canadian context.

More tentatively, we make a claim about the 'moral economy' of reform. At the end of the day, all would-be reformers face the challenge of legitimating reforms with their publics by demonstrating that they correspond to some form of popularly held notions of justice or fairness. Many European reforms involved changes to benefit formulas that could readily be defended on the grounds that they involved elimination of inter-personal transfers (for example, from private to public sector workers) that were indefensible. Large savings could be made by 'rationalizing redistribution' in public sector schemes (Myles and Pierson, 2001). In the US, the rhetoric of 'intergenerational equity' was deployed in (still largely unsuccessful) efforts to cut Social Security. The claim was that scarce transfer dollars that could go to poor families with children were being allocated to relatively affluent, high-income, retirees. The Canadian system disproportionately allocates the public sector share to the bottom end of the income distribution (Myles, 2000), providing precious little room for such a rhetoric to take hold (Cook et al., 1994).

Finally, and perhaps more importantly, successive Canadian governments found other targets for reform in their pursuit of deficit and debt reduction. During the golden age of expansion, political parties were eager to claim credit for new programs. Retrenchment, in contrast, is generally an exercise in blame avoidance rather than credit claiming (Weaver, 1986). Health care, post-secondary education and social assistance provided targets amenable to cost cutting without the associated political backlash likely to follow from significant reductions in pension expenditures.

THE EMERGENCE OF THE CANADIAN PENSION SYSTEM

During the 1950s and 1960s, Canada constructed a retirement income system around three tiers: 1) Old Age Security (OAS), a universal, flat rate pension supplemented by Guaranteed Income Supplement (GIS) that provides a guaranteed income for seniors without additional sources of income, both financed from general revenue;[1] 2) the Canada Pension Plan (CPP) and the Quebec Pension Plan (QPP), that provide a second tier of earnings-related public pensions financed from payroll contributions;[2] and 3) private, through tax-subsidized, employer-sponsored Registered Retirement Plans (RPPs) and individual retirement savings accounts called Registered Retirement Savings Plans (RRSPs).

Canada's first national pension legislation, the Old Age Pensions Act (OAP), was enacted in 1927 and provided $20 per month to persons over 70 on a means-tested basis (Bryden, 1974). In 1951, the Old Age Security Act (OAS) eliminated the means-test and extended the then current benefit of $40 per month to all persons aged 70 and over meeting residency requirements. The Old Age Assistance Act (OAA) extended means-tested benefits to those aged 65–69 and remained in place until 1970 by which time the age of eligibility for the universal pension (OAS) had been reduced to 65.

The Guaranteed Income Supplement (GIS) was established in 1967 as the second component of the pension system's first tier (Bryden, 1974, pp. 130–137; Guest, 1997, pp. 144–145). Though initially intended as a temporary measure until the C/QPP matured, it has remained as a permanent and critical element for providing an income floor for the elderly. Benefits are subject to an income test – benefits are reduced $0.50 for each additional dollar in other income – rather than a means-test (that is, assets are excluded from the test) so that the program functions as a guaranteed income (or negative income tax) program.[3] By the mid-1980s the combination of OAS/GIS provided an income floor equal to 50 per cent of average earnings for an elderly couple and 31 per cent for a single individual.

A second tier of earnings-related pensions – the Canada/Quebec Pension Plan – was adopted in 1965, two years before the GIS. This legislation was the outcome of a long bargaining process between the federal government and the ten provinces. As a result of Quebec's campaign for greater provincial autonomy, two separate but highly coordinated earnings-related schemes were created.[4] Financed through contributions from employees, employers and self-employed persons, the C/QPP integrates nearly all employed persons aged between 18 and 70 who make more than a minimum level of earnings during each year. These two social insurance schemes protect the contributors and their families against the loss of income due to retirement, disability and death. The replacement rate of the C/QPP monthly retirement pension represents 25 per cent of a beneficiary's average monthly earnings during his/her contributory life. Together, OAS and the maximum C/QPP benefit replace approximately 40 per cent of earnings for the average wage earner, a modest amount by European and even US standards. Between 1966 and 1970, the eligible age for C/QPP benefits dropped from 68 to 65 and since 1987 actuarially reduced benefits can be accessed at age 60.[5]

From the outset both the CPP and QPP relied on partial funding as a result of the surplus of contributions built up in the early years of the plans. Importantly, however, assets from the QPP trust fund were invested in equities and real estate to support provincial economic growth and French Canadian entrepreneurship (Thomson, 1984), while CPP surpluses were lent to the provinces at preferred rates to subsidize provincial debt. This difference was a direct outcome of the 1960s Quiet Revolution, an attempt to modernize Quebec society and to improve the socio-economic status of the province's French-speaking majority.

The third tier of the Canadian pension system was actually the first to emerge. Since the end of the 19th century, Canadian firms and insurance companies have created a variety of private pension plans and personal savings schemes. It is estimated that in 1936, enterprise-based pension plans covered less than 10 or 15 per cent of the Canadian paid workforce. Thirty-four years later in 1970, private pensions covered 39.2 per cent of the paid workforce (Bryden, 1974, pp. 40–41) a figure that was essentially unchanged by the end of the 1990s (Statistics Canada, 2001, p. 16). Since the enactment of the Pension Benefits Act in 1965, both the federal and the ten provincial governments have regulated private pension plans through the registration process and the Income Tax Act. In order to qualify for tax shelter, private pension plans must comply with specific governmental rules concerning coverage and financing.[6] It is worth mentioning that the term Registered Pension Plans (RPPs) refers to employment-based schemes for public as well as private sector workers.

The federal government also plays a decisive regulatory role in the field of personal retirement accounts, which are widespread in Canada. Registered Retirement Savings Plans (RRSPs) were created in 1957 to allow self-employed workers to save for retirement. Actually, all employees can contribute to RRSPs, even if they also participate in employment-based schemes. Employers can also contribute on a group basis to RRSPs for their staff. Upon maturity the assets are commonly used to purchase a life annuity, but two other options are possible. A guaranteed annuity may be purchased, or assets may be placed in a Registered Retirement Income Fund (RRIF), which allow more flexible timing of the withdrawals (Coward, 1995, p. 11). In 1999, almost 60 per cent of Canadian families had RRSPs or RRIFs (Registered Retirement Income Funds),[7] with a median value of about $20 000 (Maser and Dufour, 2001, p. 14). While coverage by these personal retirement accounts is exceptionally high by international standards (Pearse, 2001), the bulk of RRSP assets are held by middle- and upper-income workers.

FROM THE 'GREAT PENSION DEBATE' TO THE POLITICS OF RETRENCHMENT

The earliest stage of the current Canadian politics of pension reform can be found in the so-called 'Great Pension Debate' of the late 1970s and early 1980s. The debate was launched in 1975 when the Canadian Labour Congress (CLC) advanced a proposal to double C/QPP benefits and contributions. At the time, there was a general consensus concerning the need to increase benefits targeted at low-income elderly (especially elderly women). But the main issue at stake was over the use of the public pension system to ameliorate income security in light of tepid growth in private sector coverage. While labour unions, women's rights groups and social reform lobbies clearly supported a widespread expansion of the C/QPP to meet the needs of Canadian workers, voices within the Canadian business community opposed an increase in payroll contribution rates. From their perspective, the solution to income security problems lay in the growth of private pensions. Moreover, provincial leaders, especially those from Ontario and Quebec, could not agree on the suitable course of reform (Banting, 1987). Because the C/QPP had many qualities lacking in private pension plans (indexing, portability, low administrative costs, universal coverage of the labour force), a federal report published in 1980 favoured the public sector option supported by left-wing groups and Quebec's political leaders (Task Force on Retirement Income Policy, 1980). The inability of the business sector to reach consensus on a private sector solution also contributed to the ideological success of the public solution. While large firms were willing to accept mandatory private pensions to put an end to the coverage problem, small businesses opposed this option (Myles, 1988, p. 46).

In addition to business opposition, proponents of the public sector solution faced the de facto 'veto power' of Ontario, Canada's largest province. Because the federal and provincial governments share constitutional responsibility for this program, Ottawa must reach an agreement with at least two-thirds of the provinces representing two-thirds of the Canadian population before enacting a reform (Battle, 1997, p. 538). During the late 1970s and the early 1980s, the pro-business Conservative government of Ontario, by far the most populous Canadian province, opposed any attempt to significantly expand the C/QPP.[8] The institutional structure of Canadian federalism at the origin of provincial 'veto power' – combined with the opposition of the business sector – was instrumental in the defeat of left-wing forces supporting a public solution to the 'pension problem' (Banting, 1987, pp. 62–69). As we shall see, however, the same constitutional obstacle was a key element restraining serious consideration of cutbacks in the following decade. Despite the many and voluminous reports on the topic, the reform movement began to wither with the onset of recession in 1982.

It is instructive to compare Canada's experience in the 1980s with that of the 'latecomer' countries (Myles and Pierson, 2001), nations that had no (Australia, the Netherlands, New Zealand) or, like Canada, only modest (Denmark, Switzerland) second-tier earnings-related plans by 1980. For all but New Zealand, the 1980s were a period of pension expansion, typically led by organized labour leading to the establishment of mandatory (or quasi-mandatory) employer plans. From the outset, however, Canadian labour and its allies in the reform project rejected this strategy and the result was no change.

THE FAILED ASSAULT ON 'UNIVERSALITY'

The economic recession of 1982 dissipated these reform forces while contributing to a gradual transformation of the Canadian policy agenda. Rising unemployment and a decline in economic activity increased social spending and expanded the federal deficit. The Great Pension Debate ended as fiscal austerity and economic liberalism came to dominate the Canadian political arena. The Conservative Party's widespread victory during the 1984 federal elections concretized this ideological and political shift.[9] During the electoral campaign, soon-to-be Prime Minister Brian Mulroney publicly questioned OAS 'universal coverage', arguing that 'wealthy bankers' wives should not be receiving OAS benefits. Social movements, old age organizations and labour unions opposed the idea of targeting OAS benefits, forcing Mulroney to back away.[10] But his promise to fight the federal deficit meant that social programs financed through general revenues such as the OAS had become potential targets for retrenchment (Myles, 1988, p. 49).

In May 1985, approximately nine months after the election, the Conservatives launched the first serious retrenchment attempt in the field of pension reform. Rather than abolish universal flat rate benefits, the first Budget proposed the 'partial de-indexation' of family allowances and OAS.[11] These indirect cutbacks were aimed at saving the federal treasury approximately $4 billion dollars or so over the next five years as a result of the gradual erosion of benefits. Unfortunately for Brian Mulroney and Finance Minister Michael Wilson, the 'partial de-indexation' issue created a true 'political tempest' across the country. In addition to labour unions and anti-poverty groups, old age organizations participated actively in the two-month-long campaign that would finally force the Conservative government to discard the 'partial de-indexation' proposal. The mass media also played a decisive role in that campaign. A famous televised encounter between the tall Prime Minister and a petite but vocal French Canadian woman named Solange Denis became a national symbol of the conflict between 'greedy politicians' and the 'deprived elderly', and in this instance the politicians backed down. While this episode was then perceived as proof of the emerging power of a strong 'grey lobby' in Canada, the 1985 debate appears more as an exception than as a new 'iron rule' of Canadian politics (Battle, 1997, p. 530). Far less vocal and well organized than its US counterpart, the Canadian 'grey lobby' has never played a truly central role in pension politics since that time.[12]

The defeat of 'partial de-indexation' probably convinced Conservative politicians that 'visible' cutbacks in established social programs was a source of excessive 'political risks'.[13] During the second half of the 1980s, the Conservative government did in fact turn to a blame avoidance strategy aimed at reducing 'political risks' related to retrenchment while ending universality 'through the back door'.[14] In 1989, the Conservatives success-fully implemented a 'clawback' of OAS benefits from very high-income seniors that was largely ignored by the media. Benefits for individuals with incomes greater than $51 765 were reduced by 15 per cent for every dollar of income above the threshold with all benefits disappearing at approximately $89 000 per year. However, the cut-off point ($51 765) where the clawback would come into effect was only indexed to inflation in excess of 3 per cent so that in real terms a growing share of seniors could be affected with the passage of time. Since the huge majority of the elderly were unaffected and few politicians or journalists understood the longer-term implications of the reform, the clawback came to be identified as 'social policy by stealth' (Battle, 1990).

Low inflation and slow income growth during the 1990s, however, meant that by 2001, less than 5 per cent of all seniors were affected by the income test introduced in 1989. In 2000, full indexation was restored with the result that future savings from the clawback will only occur as a result of a signifi-cant increase in the numbers of very high-income retirees.

THE RISE AND FALL OF SENIORS BENEFITS

After some reluctance, the Liberals moved forward on pension reform in 1995. With the 'war on deficit' and demographic fears as a background, the 1995 budget formulated five principles for the reform of public pensions (1995 budget cited in Battle, 1997, p. 539):

1. undiminished protection for less well-off seniors;
2. continued full indexation to protect seniors from inflation;
3. provision of OAS benefits on the basis of family income;
4. greater progressivity of benefits by income level; and
5. control of program costs.

Far from departing from the Conservative agenda, these design criteria reinforced the logic of pension reform that emerged during the second half of the 1980s, the effective abolition of universal flat rate pensions.

Targeting was still highly controversial in 1995, but the Liberals made sure to avoid the mistake of the first Mulroney government, which was to call into question full indexation of benefits. The spectre of Solange Denis' colourful encounter with Brian Mulroney was a source of 'political learning' for elected politicians interested in reducing political risks related to pension reform (Caragata, 1995).

In 1996, the Liberals unveiled a new reform project far more explicit than the OAS 'reform by stealth' enacted in 1989. The government proposed to replace both OAS and GIS programs with a new Seniors Benefit that would integrate the two in a single income-tested scheme. Generally speaking, low- and even middle-income families would benefit from the new scheme and high-income retirees would bear the brunt of reform. For example, a family receiving $20 000 per year on top of the Seniors Benefit would gain $500 per year under the new system. But families with $50 000 per year of other retirement income would lose more than $4000 per year as a result of the new legislation (Geddes, 1998, p. 13). Unlike the 1989 clawback that was calculated on the basis of individual income, the clawback implicit in the new Seniors Benefit was to be based on family income, thus impacting a much larger pool of retirees.

To minimize the risk of political backlash among the wealthiest segment of the elderly population, Finance Minister Paul Martin stressed that *current* OAS/GIS beneficiaries would not be affected by the reform. Later, this commitment was expanded to 'apply to everyone age 60 and over as of 31 December 1995, as well as their spouses, regardless of their age' (Government of Canada, 1996a).[15]

Despite these efforts at blame avoidance, organized groups representing not only the elderly but also professional associations and investment firms slowly united against the proposal. At the beginning of 1997, the Retirement Income Coalition sealed an alliance between 21 of these groups, including the Canadian Teachers' Federation, the Investment Dealers Association and the Canadian Association of Retired Persons. This new coalition generated considerable media attention on the potentially negative impact of the reform on savings behaviour (Geddes, 1998). As Reform Party MP Keith Martin (1997) argued:

> This new Seniors' Benefit is obviously not much of a benefit at all, but a seniors tax. It penalizes those who have sacrificed and saved for their retirements. Ultimately, it will make more people dependent on taxpayer-funded, low return, government controlled pensions instead of enabling people to earn a more lucrative pension through their investments, such as RRSP's.

From this perspective, the Seniors Benefit would discourage personal savings and encourage 'welfare dependency'.

At the other end of the political spectrum, women's organizations and NDP officials also criticized the Seniors Benefits. The NDP leader, Alexa McDonough, summarized widespread feminist concerns about the proposed scheme: 'Senior women currently receive the OAS directly, but the Seniors Benefit Program will be calculated on a couple's combined income. Older women may lose their Seniors Benefit based on the income of their spouse, threatening their financial independence' (McDonough, 1997). Considering that the Bloc Québécois and most social reform organizations also rejected the Seniors Benefit, political support for this measure appeared weak.

Facing considerable pressure from social movements, the Retirement Income Coalition and opposition parties, the Liberal government finally withdrew the controversial reform proposal, more than two years before it was to take effect. Referring to renewed economic prosperity and a shrinking federal deficit, Finance Minister Paul Martin found an elegant way to justify his retreat:

> The reform of the OAS/GIS was launched at a time when our choices were restricted by the overwhelming constraint of a $38 billion deficit and, as importantly, a debt-to-GDP ratio that had risen virtually uninterrupted since the mid-1970s. Because of these two very real fiscal factors, the proposal made in 1995 represented the best choice available at the time. That being said, any choice that depended on taking money out of the retirement income system was far from ideal. Three years later, our prospects have changed for the better and a much wider set of choices is now available. (Martin, 1998)

Now that the federal government was expecting long-term fiscal surpluses, the idea that future retirees had to make significant economic sacrifices in the name of fiscal austerity was difficult to justify.

The fall of the Seniors Benefit proposal is related to a strategic mistake of the Liberal government. Instead of relying on hidden fiscal changes that silently affect wealthier beneficiaries, Paul Martin launched a highly visible reform project that attracted too much attention to neutralize the political risks associated with the politics of retrenchment. Despite their decision to postpone the implementation of the Seniors Benefit and their commitment to indexation and social redistribution, the proposal attracted widespread media attention to a reform project that upset key interest groups and a significant fraction of the population. Moreover, unpopular budget cuts enacted between 1995 and 1997 in other policy areas such as unemployment insurance and fiscal transfers to provincial governments reduced the political 'security margin' of the government in the field of pension retrenchment.[16] Hence, while OAS became a target for reform under two political regimes, at the end of the day little was changed.

THE POLITICS OF CONSULTATION: REFORMING THE CANADA PENSION PLAN

In 1995, the publication of the Fiftieth Actuarial Report of the CPP suddenly pushed this program to the centre of the Canadian policy agenda. Due to a significant increase in disability benefits and the impact of the economic recession, this report projected a higher schedule for future contributions than anticipated by the previous actuarial report. Without a significant change in the current schedule of contribution rates, by the year 2015, the CPP would no longer collect enough revenues to pay all the benefits (Battle, 1997, p. 537).[17]

While the Reform Party and Conservative think tanks such as the CD Howe Institute responded with proposals to replace the public pay-as-you-go system with private sector alternatives, the governing Liberals launched a consultative process aimed at reforming the program in an incremental manner. This consultative turn in pension reform is related to a key institutional feature of the CPP noted earlier: since the federal and provincial governments share constitutional responsibility for this program, Ottawa must reach an agreement with at least two-thirds of the provinces with two-thirds of the population before enacting a reform (Battle, 1997, p. 538).

After a first round of consultation, the Department of Finance drafted a joint report that evaluated the long-term financial situation of the CPP while setting the agenda for a consensual reform. Published in February 1996, this *Information Paper for Consultations on the Canada Pension Plan* (Federal/Provincial/Territorial CPP Consultations Secretariat 1996) formed the basis of public consultations on the CPP that were held across Canada in 1996. The consultations were part of the statutory review of the CPP carried out by the federal and provincial governments. Meanwhile, Quebec conducted its own public consultations within the province concerning the QPP (Government of Canada, 1996b). In November of the same year, the federal and provincial governments published a joint statement to frame the principles that would guide the elaboration of the next CPP reform. Among the nine principles outlined in the statement, two were especially significant:

4. The CPP must be affordable and sustainable for future generations. This requires fuller funding and a contribution rate no higher than the already legislated future rate of 10.1 per cent. In deciding how quickly to move to this rate, governments must take economic and fiscal impacts into account.
8. CPP funds must be invested in the best interests of plan members, and maintain a proper balance between returns and investment risk. Governance structures must be created to ensure sound fund management. (Government of Canada, 1996c)

While the first of these principles reflects a strong emphasis on 'economic competitiveness', the second one is the product of a policy learning process related to the existence of the Caisse de dépôt et placement du Québec, a provincial investment board that has invested QPP's money in equity since the 1960s. The relative financial 'success' of this provincial scheme paved the way to the investment of CPP surplus funds in equities by providing the federal and other provincial governments with a positive precedent.[18]

Finance Minister Paul Martin finally presented the draft of the new CPP legislation in February 1997. Following the principles formulated a year before in the *Information Paper for Consultations on the Canada Pension Plan*, it was decided to increase combined employer and employee contributions to the CPP from 5.6 to 9.9 per cent by 2003 in order to build up a larger reserve fund.[19] The fund was then equivalent in value to about two years of benefits and was projected to decline. As a result of reform, it is now scheduled to grow to five years of benefits with the surplus invested in a diversified portfolio of securities 'to earn higher returns and help pay the benefits as Canada's population ages' (Paul Martin, 1997). In order to invest the reserve fund, a CPP Investment Board was created. This new organization is governed by a board of directors and is managed by investment professionals from the private sector. By 31 March 2001, the CPP Investment Board 'had 7.2 billion dollars invested in Canadian and foreign equities and by 2011' the board 'expects to be managing at least $130 billion in a diversified investment portfolio' (CPP Investment Board, 2001).

Finally enacted in January 1998, Bill C-2 included other minor modifications aimed at improving the long-term financial situation of the CPP. For example, the annual basic exemption was frozen at $3500 so that the portion of income subject to contributions will increase faster than inflation (Government of Canada, 1997). Moreover, 'retirement pensions will be calculated on the 5-year average of the Year's Maximum Pensionable Earnings at the time, instead of the 3-year average' (Paul Martin, 1997). Disability pensions were also subject to some cost-control measures. To boost public confidence in the program, contributors will receive annual reports on their CPP accounts and the federal-provincial reviews will be conducted every three years, rather than five years. Far from radically breaking from the historical path of the program, the 1997 reform reaffirmed the contributory nature of the C/QPP. Moreover, significant (and unpopular) reforms such as an increase in retirement age were excluded from the reformers' agenda.

It is worth mentioning that the privatization of the CPP has never been considered as a serious option by Canadian policy-makers. Despite the rhetoric emanating from the Conservative Canadian Alliance Party and Alberta's Conservative Party, pressures to move from social insurance to individual savings accounts are far more diffuse in Canada than in the United States. Despite that fact that neo-liberal economists and politicians have exploited the demographic fears associated with population ageing, public support for the CPP remains strong (Townson, 2001, p. 195). The 1998 CPP reform reduced these fears by improving the system's financial balance and recent stock market instability (especially in the aftermath of the 2001 terrorist attacks) has been detrimental to the emergence of a large movement favouring pension privatization (Chevreau, 2002).

Beyond this relative lack of support for privatization, federal policies enacted during the 1980s favoured greater reliance on personal savings and private pension schemes. Conservative, as well as Liberal governments, significantly increased the level of tax assistance during the 1980s and 1990s to provide greater incentives for Canadians to save money for their retirement (Battle, 1997, p. 525). These reforms concerned both RRSPs and RPPs. Moreover, 'tax assistance limits were made fairer and more flexible' (Pearse, 2001, p. 214).

In spite of these reforms, only 39.1 per cent of the paid workforce participated in an enterprise-based pension plan in 1998 (Statistics Canada, 2001, p. 16). Poorly covered by RPPs, low-income families save little for retirement: 'The large majority of family units with no private pension assets had lower employment incomes. Considering only those economic family units with a major income recipient between 25 and 64, just over 70 per cent of families of two or more with no pension savings had earnings of less than $30,000' (Maser and Dufour, 2001, p. 5). In this context, the public pension system represents the main source of economic support for low-income elderly and has brought old age poverty to now very low levels (Myles, 2000). While some scholars have argued that even minor erosion of universality would affect the political support for state-financed pensions, it seems that the OAS and GIS programs have a strong political basis in Canadian society.

DISCUSSION

Although the window of retrenchment was opened on several occasions in the past two decades, the design put in place in the 1950s and 1960s has thus far survived relatively intact. The famous 'clawback' of OAS benefits introduced in 1989 might have resulted in serious long-term erosion of benefits for middle-income seniors since the threshold for the income test was partially de-indexed. But that door was effectively shut with the return to full indexing under the Liberals in 2000. The main result of the 1997 reform of the Canada Pension Plan was to raise contribution rates to stabilize the system. None of this was because benign spirits were directing social policy reform. Under pressure from rising deficits, both the Conservatives under Brian Mulroney and the Liberals under Jean Chrétien spent a great deal of energy, and not a little political capital, in efforts to reduce social spending. The Chrétien government was particularly successful in this venture. Though both governments flirted with large-scale pension reform, old age benefits emerged relatively unscathed. Why so?

Canadian Federalism and the Politics of Blame Avoidance[20]

The designers of the original Canadian union envisioned a strong central government and under the British North America Act of 1867 assigned all major powers to the central government, leaving what were then considered 'residual' powers related to health, education and welfare (social assistance for the poor) to the provinces. Nevertheless, in the post-war decades Ottawa took the lead in reforming all three areas. The Canada Assistance Plan (CAP) established in 1966 created a cost-sharing agreement by which Ottawa assumed half the cost of provincial welfare and social services that met specified conditions. The central governments' role in health and post-secondary education was consolidated in 1977 under Established Program Financing (EPF) that provided a federal block grant to the provinces to finance these programs. Although Ottawa established basic ground rules for their delivery, the final mix of services and benefits in all three areas remained under provincial jurisdiction (Rice and Prince, 2000).

Divided jurisdiction with regard to both the CAP (social assistance) and EPF (health and post-secondary education) proved to be a mixed blessing for Ottawa. As these programs were expanding, Ottawa received little political credit since the services and benefits they provided were delivered under provincial brand names. In a period of retrenchment, however, Ottawa was able to retreat from all three areas by cutting transfers to the provinces, leaving provincial governments to take the blame for subsequent reductions in services and benefits. In 1995, the Liberals dismantled both the CAP and EPF, replacing them with the Canada Health and Social Transfer (CHST) leading to 'savings' of 8.5 and 15.2 per cent (or about $7 billion) in the first two years of its existence (Battle, 1998, p. 330).

In contrast, OAS and GIS are purely federal programs and, in the case of the CPP, divided jurisdiction created a decisive check against any serious consideration of large-scale cutbacks. Reform of the CPP requires the consent of two-thirds of the provinces containing two-thirds of the population. The Province of Quebec made it clear that it would oppose any significant benefit cuts as would Saskatchewan and British Columbia, then ruled by the social democratic New Democratic Party, effectively removing that option from the political agenda.

The Politics of the 'New Economy'

As elsewhere, Canadian social politics in the 1990s were influenced by policy models associated with the 'Third Way', a new buzzword that captures the common elements of a still inchoate paradigm assigning welfare functions to families, markets and states. The 'old' welfare state, constructed between the 1930s and the 1970s, emphasized protecting people *from the market*. Third Way solutions, by contrast, emphasize programs that both provide incentives for and help people to succeed *in the market*. In addition to, and sometimes instead of, the welfare state's traditional mandate of 'civilizing capitalism', Third Wayism assigns responsibility for 'nurturing capitalism' (Battle, 2001) to welfare states. During the 1990s, the major targets for Canadian Third Way reforms were unemployment insurance and child benefits. In the case of the former, changes in eligibility rules greatly reduced coverage rates among the unemployed. In contrast, income-tested child benefits for the 'working poor' were greatly expanded to enhance work incentives, a path also followed in the UK and the US.

Pension policy and population ageing get on the radar screen of Third Way advocates when they are widely perceived to be reducing employment levels either by encouraging early retirement or by driving up payroll taxes. Neither feature has figured prominently in Canadian policy debates.

Because of its modest scale, changes to the age of eligibility for CPP pensions are unlikely to have large effects on retirement behaviour except among lower-income earners, creating obvious equity problems. Such a result would be perverse for macroeconomic as well as for distributive reasons. The largest gains to the economy are to be had if the most productive workers (the healthy, well educated and presumably better paid) remain in employment longer. Reform can have a potentially perverse effect if changes to retirement incentives in public sector plans mainly produce higher retirement ages among low wage, low productivity workers.

To induce large changes in retirement ages among middle- and upper-income wage earners in the Canadian context would require extensive regulation of the age at which workers can access private sources of retirement wealth (RPPs, RSSPs), on the one hand, and, on the other, reforms that eliminate incentives that now *bias* retirement decisions in favour of more retirement and less employment. Early retirement incentives and defined benefit formulae that discourage continued employment are examples. But until now, there has been precious little pressure on Canadian policy-makers to pursue such an agenda and little likelihood of reaching the political consensus required for reform if they did. Current and projected ratios of retirees to workers while higher in Canada than in the US are well below typical European levels (Pearse, 2001, p. 79).

The major pressure for pension reform in OECD countries is a product of high and rising payroll taxes to meet current and future pension expenditures. The payroll tax is a flat tax, often with a wage ceiling that makes it regressive. Unlike income taxes, there are no exemptions and no allowances for family size. Low-wage workers and especially younger families with children typically bear a disproportionate share of the cost as a result. These effects are compounded to the extent that high payroll taxes discourage employment, especially at the lower end of the labour market where the social safety net, minimum wages, or industrial relations systems make it difficult for employers to pass such costs on to employees.

Because of their impact on wage costs (for employers) and the real take-home pay of less skilled and younger workers, the threat of high and rising payroll taxes has provided a potent incentive for the formation of somewhat unexpected coalitions of business and labour favouring pension reform in many countries (Myles and Pierson, 2001). Since low-wage workers and especially younger families with children typically bear a disproportionate share of the cost, union leaders really do face a trade-off between their retired and working-age constituents if, as projected in Germany for example, payroll taxes were to rise from 22 to 38 per cent of payroll in the coming decades.

By European and even US standards, however, current and future payroll tax levels for pensions in Canada are quite modest, reflecting the modest scale of the C/QPP, on the one hand, and on the other greater reliance on general revenue financing (for OAS/GIS). In the mid-1990s, prior to reform, the payroll contribution rate for CPP was 5.6 per cent (compared with 12.4 per cent in the US) and was projected to peak at 14.2 per cent in the next century, a level already exceeded by most European countries. The 1997 CPP reform accelerated contribution rates early on to create a capital pool, the revenues from which will be used to finance future benefits. The aim was to reduce future increases. After reform, the maximum projected rate for future wage earners is a modest 9.8 per cent.

The Moral Economy of Pension Reform

During the 1980s and 1990s, a remarkable shift in policy debate occurred in a number of countries. Whereas in the 1960s the common assumption in old age policy debates was that the elderly were 'too poor', by the 1980s the claim that the elderly were 'too rich' was heard with growing frequency. In the United States, the rapid fall of poverty rates among the elderly relative to children brought themes of 'intergenerational equity' to the fore (Preston, 1984) together with charges against the elderly of being 'greedy geezers'. Although 'population ageing' is often perceived through the pessimistic lens

*Table 12.1   The distribution of the population 65+ by income quintile,
              1980–95*

Quintile	1980	1990	1995	Change, 1980–95
Bottom	39.7	25.2	17.5	–22.2
Second	22.1	29.7	32.5	10.5
Third	12.2	16.2	20.0	7.8
Fourth	13.3	14.9	16.0	2.7
Top	12.8	13.9	14.0	1.2
Total: all quintiles	100.0	100.0	100.0	

Source: Myles (2000) calculated from Statistics Canada, Survey of Consumer Finances.

of 'apocalyptic demography' (Prince, 2000), the issue of 'intergenerational
equity' has been far less prominent in Canada than in the United States
(Marmor et al., 1994). This difference, we think, has a real material base.

As elsewhere, average incomes among Canadian seniors did rise sharply
from the 1970s to the 1990s, and low-income rates among Canadian seniors
measured by the usual international standard (persons with adjusted incomes
less than 50 per cent of the median) declined (Hauser, 1997; Smeeding and
Sullivan, 1998).[21] But it was difficult to make the claim that the elderly were
becoming 'too rich' (Table 12.1). In 1980, about 40 per cent of all elderly
persons were in the bottom quintile, twice the rate for the population as a
whole. By 1995, just over 17 per cent of the elderly were in the bottom quintile, somewhat below the level of 20 per cent for the entire population.
However, approximately 80 per cent of the shift out of the bottom quintile
reflected movement into the second and third quintiles and little increase in the
proportion of seniors in the top two quintiles. While the risk of poverty fell
dramatically over the period, it was difficult to sustain the case that retirees
were becoming too rich.

The reason for this outcome is that in combination OAS/GIS, the C/QPP
and related transfers function much like an enriched flat benefit system on a
pre-tax basis, and post-tax, the overall impact is highly redistributive. This
result is highlighted in Table 12.2 where we show average (equivalence
adjusted) income transfers from all public plans by source and age-specific
income quintiles for the population 65+ in 1995.[22] Total pre-tax transfers
(column 5) of between $11 000 and $12 000 or approximately 50 per cent of
the average equivalence adjusted disposable income ($23 000) of all persons
65+ is more or less identical across all income levels.

Table 12.2   Distribution of adjusted transfers and taxes by income quintile

Quintile	(1) C/QPP	(2) OAS/GIS	(3) Other transfers	(4) Taxes	(5) Total transfers (pre-tax)	(6) Net transfers (post-tax)
Bottom	2 482	7 886	928	–181	11 296	11 115
Second	4 610	7 158	800	–406	12 568	12 162
Third	4 990	5 875	1 154	–1 546	12 019	10 473
Fourth	5 187	5 494	1 268	–3 701	11 949	8 248
Top	5 358	5 248	1 350	–12 249	11 956	–293

Source: Myles (2000) calculated from Statistics Canada, Survey of Consumer Finances.

CONCLUSION

Since the early 1980s, the universal flat benefit (Old Age Security) system was targeted for reform on two occasions but with limited success while the 1997 CPP reform served primarily to maintain the status quo. In order to understand why Canadian policy-makers enacted reforms that seem so modest from a comparative perspective, we showed that an essential part of the answer is that 'size matters'. Because of the modest level of pension-related public expenditures in Canada, the potential contribution of pension cuts to deficit reduction was comparatively limited. In this context, both Liberal and Conservative governments found more attractive targets in other areas of state intervention, especially those areas in which the federal government could transfer political risks to provincial leaders. As importantly, limited reliance on payroll taxes to finance the public system created few incentives for the emergence of the reform coalitions that have been characteristic of the high payroll tax countries. Finally, the actual distribution of public sector benefits left little room for a moral assault on public pensions by Conservative intellectuals and politicians. The upshot is that in Canada public pensions have been a point of relative stability in a world of welfare state change.

NOTES

*   The authors wish to thank Keith Banting and the editors of this volume for their comments.
1.   Most of the ten provinces and the three territories also offer benefits that top up the GIS. Considering their modest scale, this chapter does not discuss directly the fate of these provincial programs.
2.   The two programs will be referred to together as C/QPP (Canada and Quebec Pension Plans).

3. In 1975, a Spouse's Allowance (SPA) was added to the first tier of the federal pension system in order to provide one-pensioner couples facing economic hardship with more financial support. Like the GIS, the spousal benefit is income-tested; it covers only people aged 60 to 64 who meet residency requirements.

4. Benefits from either scheme are based on pension credits accumulated under both, as if only one scheme existed. On the federal/provincial bargaining process leading to the enactment of the C/QPP, see Simeon, 1972 and Bryden, 1974, pp. 129–182.

5. In Canada during the 1990s, there was no explicit attempt to increase the C/QPP retirement age.

6. For constitutional reasons, the regulation of private pension plans in Canada is divided among the 11 federal and provincial jurisdictions.

7. RRIFs are tax-deferred investments offered as payout options from RRSPs.

8. In that province, the Conservative Party was in power from 1943 to 1985.

9. The Conservatives won 211 of the 282 seats in September 1984.

10. Immediately after the election, his Finance Minister reopened the debate on universality, but Mulroney was forced to repudiate him publicly to neutralize public outcry.

11. According to the plan, OAS benefits would only increase by the amount that inflation surpasses 3 per cent. 'If inflation were 3% or higher a year, then OAS benefits would automatically lose 3% of their value. Even if inflation were less than 3%, benefits would decline by the amount of inflation (e.g. an inflation rate of 2% would reduce the value of OAS by 2%)' (Battle, 1997, pp. 530–531).

12. For a comparative outlook on the Canadian grey lobby, see Pratt, 1997.

13. In the Canadian parliamentary system, the strong centralization of power creates a high level of autonomy that could exacerbate political risks related to pension reform (Pierson and Weaver, 1993).

14. This strategy, which was also mobilized in other social policy areas, was labelled as 'social policy by stealth' by Ken Battle (Battle, 1990; 1997). See also Myles and Pierson, 1997.

15. The same strategy has been used in the US concerning the gradual change in retirement age enacted as part of the 1983 amendments to the Social Security Act (Light, 1995).

16. On these related retrenchment efforts, see Banting, 1997; Rice and Prince, 2000, pp. 110–129.

17. Between 1966 and 1986, a contribution rate of only 3.6 per cent prevailed. In 1993, such a rate had risen to 5 per cent (Emery and Rongve, 1999, p. 69).

18. During the first half of the 1980s, however, the Caisse de dépôt et placement faced criticism and suspicion from the business community and the federal government, which considered this investment board as a mere political tool of nationalism (Brooks and Tanguay, 1985). More recently, authors such as Pierre Arbour have criticized what they considered as the excessive 'economic power' of the Caisse (Arbour, 1993; 2002).

19. The government of Quebec enacted the same schedule of contribution increases to harmonize them with the federal one.

20. On blame avoidance, see Weaver, 1986.

21. By the usual international standard, low-income rates among Canadian seniors had fallen to about 5 per cent in 1994 compared with a US rate in excess of 20 per cent. And among the population 70+, Canada's low-income rate was below that of Sweden, the usual 'winner' in the international league tables on poverty reduction (Smeeding and Sullivan, 1998).

22. All incomes are adjusted with an equivalence scale to take account of differences in family size.

REFERENCES

Arbour, Pierre (1993), *Québec Inc. et la Tentation du Dirigisme*, Montréal: L'Etincelle.
Arbour, Pierre (2002), 'Détournement de mandat', *La Presse*, 28 March, http://www.cyberpresse.ca/reseau/editorial/0203/edi_102030081652.html.

Banting, Keith G. (1987), 'Institutional conservatism: Federalism and pension reform', in Jacqueline S. Ismael (ed.), *Canadian Social Welfare Policy: Federal and Provincial Dimensions*, Kingston: McGill/Queen's University Press, 48–74.

Banting, Keith G. (1997), 'The social policy divide: The welfare state and Canada and the United States', in Keith Banting et al. (eds), *Degrees of Freedom: Canada and the United States in a Changing World*, Kingston: McGill/Queen's University Press, 267–309.

Battle, Ken (under the pseudonym of Grattan Gray) (1990), 'Social policy by stealth', *Policy Options*, **11**(2), 17–29.

Battle, Ken (1997), 'Pension reform in Canada,' *Canadian Journal of Aging*, **16**(3), 519–552.

Battle, Ken (1998), 'Transformation: Canadian social policy since 1985', *Social Policy and Administration*, **32**(4) pp. 321–340

Battle, Ken (2001), *Relentless Incrementalism: Deconstructing and Reconstructing Canadian Income Security Policy*, Ottawa: Caledon Institute of Social Policy.

Béland, Daniel and Waddan, Alex (2000), 'From Thatcher (and Pinochet) to Clinton? Conservative think tanks, foreign models and US pensions reform', *Political Quarterly*, **71**(2), 202–210.

Brooks, Stephen and Tanguay, A. Brian (1985), 'Quebec's caisse de depot et placement: Tool of nationalism?', *Canadian Public Administration*, **28**(1), 99–119.

Bryden, Kenneth (1974), *Old Age Pensions and Policy-Making in Canada*, Toronto: University of Toronto Press.

Caragata, Warren (1995), 'The power of seniors', *Maclean's*, **108** (10 July), 1995, 16.

Chevreau, Jonathan (2002), 'Pension funds ratchet down their expectations', *National Post*, 6 September.

Cook, Fay, Victor Marshall, Joanne Gard Marshall and Julie Kaufman (1994), 'The salience of intergenerational equity in Canada and the United States', in Theodore Marmor, Timothy Smeeding and Vernon Greene (eds), *Economic Security and Intergenerational Justice*, Washington, DC: The Urban Institute, 91–129.

Coward, Laurence E. (1995), *Private Pensions in OECD Countries: Canada*, Paris: Organisation for Economic Co-operation and Development.

CPP Investment Board (2001), *2001 Annual Report*, Toronto.

Emery, J.C. Herbert and Rongve, Ian (1999), 'Much ado about nothing? Demographic bulges, the productivity puzzle, and CPP reform', *Contemporary Economic Policy*, **17**(1), 68–78.

Geddes, John (1998), 'Citizen's revolt', *Maclean's*, **111** (20 April), 12–13.

Government of Canada (1996a), *Government Proposes New Seniors Benefit*, Ottawa, 6 March.

Government of Canada (1996b), *1996 CPP Consultations*, Ottawa, 8 July.

Government of Canada (1996c), *Principles to Guide Federal-Provincial Decisions on the Canada Pension Plan*, Ottawa, 4 October, http://www.cpp-rpc.gc.ca/princips/principe.html.

Government of Canada (1997), *Securing the Canada Pension Plan: Agreement on Proposed Changes to the CPP*, Ottawa, February.

Guest, Dennis (1997), *The Emergence of Social Security in Canada* (third edition), Vancouver: University of British Columbia Press.

Hauser, Richard (1997), *Adequacy and Poverty Among the Retired*, Ageing Working Paper No. 3.2, Paris: OECD.

Light, Paul (1995), *Still Artful Work: The Continuing Politics of Social Security Reform*, New York: McGraw-Hill.

Marmor et al. (1994), *Economic Security and Intergenerational Justice: A Look at North America*, Washington, DC: Urban Institute.

Martin, Keith (1997), 'No benefits under the seniors' benefit', Ottawa, 20 July, http://www.keithmartin.org/policy/hrd/hrd_seniorsbenefit.shtml.

Martin, Paul (1997), *Tabling Draft Legislation to Amend the Canada Pension Plan: Statement by the Honourable Paul Martin PC, MP, Minister of Finance to the House of Commons*, Ottawa, 14 February.

Martin, Paul (1998), 'Finance Minister's statement on the seniors benefit', Ottawa, Government of Canada, 28 July, http://www.fin.gc.ca/news98/98–071e.html.

Maser, Karen and Dufour, Thomas (2001), 'Private Pension Savings: 1999', *Perspectives on Labour and Income*, **2**(12), 14–22.

McDonough, Alexa (1997), 'McDonough defends pensioners', *The New Ontario Democrat*, December, http://www.web.net/~ondp/nod/dec97/pensions.htm.

Myles, John (1988), 'Social policies for the elderly in Canada', in B.R.-M. Havens Rathbone (ed.), *North American Elders: US and Canadian Comparisons*, New York: Greenwood Press, 37–54.

Myles, John (2000), 'The maturation of Canada's retirement income system: Income levels, income inequality and low income among older persons', *Canadian Journal on Aging*, **19**, 287–316.

Myles, John and Pierson, Paul (1997), 'Friedman's revenge: The reform of liberal welfare states in Canada and the United States', *Politics and Society*, **25**, 443–472.

Myles, John and Pierson, Paul (2001), 'The comparative political economy of pension reform', in Paul Pierson (ed.), *The New Politics of the Welfare State*, Oxford: Oxford University Press, 305–333.

Myles, John and Quadagno, Jill (1997), 'Recent trends in public pension reform: A comparative view', in Keith G. Banting and Robin Boadway (eds), *Reform of Retirement Income Policy: International and Canadian Perspectives*, Kingston: Queen's University School of Policy Studies, 247–272.

Pearse, Jane (2001), 'Overview of the Canadian private pension system', in OECD, *Private Pensions Systems: Administrative Costs and Reforms* (Private Pension Series No 2), Geneva, OECD.

Pierson, Paul and Weaver, R. Kent (1993), 'Imposing losses in pension policy', in R. Kent Weaver and Bert A. Rockman (eds), *Do Institutions Matter?: Government Capabilities in the United States and Abroad*, Washington, DC: Brookings Institution, 110–150.

Pratt, Henry J. (1997), *Gray Agendas: Interest Groups and Public Pensions in Canada, Britain, and the United States*, Ann Arbour: University of Michigan Press.

Preston, Samuel H. (1984), 'Children and the elderly: Divergent paths for America's dependents', *Demography*, **21**, 435–457.

Prince, Michael J. (2000), 'Apocalyptic, opportunistic, and realistic discourse: Retirement income and social policy or Chicken Littles, Nest-eggies, and Humpty Dumpties', in Ellen M. Gee and Gloria M. Gutman (eds), *The Overselling of Population Aging: Apocalyptic Demography, Intergenerational Challenges and Social Policy*, Don Mills (Ont.): Oxford University Press, 100–114.

Rice, James J. and Michael J. Prince (2000), *Changing Politics of Canadian Social Policy*, Toronto: University of Toronto Press.

Simeon, Richard (1972), *Federal-Provincial Diplomacy: The Making of Recent Policy in Canada*, Toronto: University of Toronto Press.

Smeeding, Timothy M. and Dennis H. Sullivan (1998), *Generations and the Distribution of Economic Well-Being: A Cross-National View*, American Economic Association Papers and Proceedings.

Statistics Canada (2001), *Pension Plans in Canada*, Ottawa, December.

Task Force on Income Retirement Policy (1980), *The Retirement Income System in Canada: Problems and Alternative Policy Reforms*, Ottawa: Minister of Supply and Services.

Thomson, Dale C. (1984), *Jean Lesage and the Quiet Revolution*, Toronto: Macmillan.

Townson, Monica (2001), *Pensions Under Attack: What's Behind the Push to Privatize Pensions*, Toronto: Lorimer/Canadian Centre for Policy Alternatives.

Weaver, R. Kent (1986), 'The politics of blame avoidance', *Journal of Public Policy*, **6**, 371–398.

Index